Living the Questions

Be patient toward all that is unresolved in your heart and try to love the questions themselves like locked rooms and like books that are written in a very foreign tongue. Do not now seek the answers, which cannot be given you because you would not be able to live them. And the point is, to live everything. Live the questions now.

Rainer Maria Rilke

Living the Questions

A Guide for Teacher-Researchers

Ruth Shagoury Hubbard
Lewis and Clark College
   and
Brenda Miller Power
University of Maine, Orono

Stenhouse Publishers
Portland, Maine

Stenhouse Publishers
www.stenhouse.com

Credits
Page 9: Things I Learned Last Week copyright 1982 by William Stafford. Reprinted from
Glass Face in the Rain. Reprinted by permission of the Estate of William Stafford.
Page 92: Spelling Interview copyright 1992 by Sandra Wilde. Reprinted from *YOU KAN
RED THIS! Spelling and Punctuation for Whole Language Classrooms, K–6* by Sandra Wilde. Re-
printed by permission of Heinemann, a division of Reed Elsevier, Inc.
Page 105: You Reading This, Be Ready copyright 1998 by William Stafford. Reprinted from
The Way It Is: New and Selected Poems by William Stafford with the permission of Graywolf
Press, Saint Paul, Minnesota.
Page 105: When to Write: Strategies to Find Time for Notetaking copyright 1996 by Brenda
Miller Power. Adapted from *Taking Note: Improving Your Observational Notetaking* by Brenda
Miller Power. Reprinted by permission of Stenhouse Publishers.
Page 168: Got a Question? AskEric. copyright 1998 by Stan Karp. First appeared in the Sum-
mer 1998 issue of *Rethinking Schools* 12, 4:25. Reprinted by permission of *Rethinking Schools*.

Some of the writing for this book was supported by a grant from the Spencer Foundation. The
data presented, the statements made, and the views expressed are solely the responsibility of
the authors.

Articles from *Teacher Research: The Journal of Classroom Inquiry* are on page 316.

Library of Congress Cataloging-in-Publication Data
Hubbard, Ruth, 1950
    Living the questions : a guide for teacher-researchers / Ruth
  Shagoury Hubbard and Brenda Miller Power.
      p. cm.
    Includes bibliographical references (p.) and index.
    ISBN 1-57110-081-4
    1. Action research in education United States Handbooks, manuals, etc.
2. Teaching Resear ch United States Handbooks, manuals, etc. I. Power, Brenda Miller. II.
Title.
LB1028.24.H83 1999
371.102'07'2 dc21
98-50353
CIP
Cover and interior design by Catherine Hawkes, Cat and Mouse
Cover photograph by Andrew Edgar
Quilt ' Evelyn Beaulieu
Typeset by Technologies N Typography
Manufactured in the United States of America on acid-free paper
10 09 08 07 06 05   13 12 11 10 9 8

*For Heidi Mills, Amy Donnelly, and the entire community of learners at the
Center for Inquiry (Columbia, South Carolina)—*

May your garden of questions always bloom!

Contents

Acknowledgments

Evelyn Beaulieu is a teacher-researcher in Maine. Her work involves building and sustaining networks of adult learners and educators throughout the state. When Evelyn began to integrate teacher research into her work among the adult education community, she found it almost impossible to express the place of inquiry in her life through words. So she pulled out fabric, scissors, and thread, and began to cut and craft "We Are Each a Gem," the piece of fiber art about teacher research that is on the cover of this book. Each element of the artwork expresses a different aspect of becoming part of a research community. We find her metaphors are apt in describing our research community, too, so we will use them in thanking some of the people who are responsible for this book.

As you look at the art, the background fabric represents the Northern Lights. This is a symbol for how people are always changing and evolving. Our evolution as teacher-researchers came from apprenticing ourselves to near and distant teacher-researchers. Jill Ostrow, Jane Doan, Penny Chase, Nancy Winterbourne, Virginia Shorey, Mary Bagley, and Kerri Doyle have been the teachers recently who welcome us into their classrooms most often. Allowing us to see their many "colors" as inquirers has stretched our own thinking about research immeasurably.

The center of the artwork is the "fire of knowledge," representing the fire of inspiration researchers receive from their closest colleagues. We thank Andra Makler, Linda Christensen, and Connie Perry for being those colleagues. Whenever the daily responsibilities of our professional lives become overwhelming, they give us the humor and inspiration we need to renew our commitment to research and learning.

The gems that glitter on the ground mark how our strengths can be hidden—sometimes we have to dig a little to find them. Much of the work in this volume was first published in *Teacher Research: The Journal of Classroom Inquiry*. Without the efforts of the editorial board, especially Kimberly Campbell, Kelly Chandler, Cindy Hatt, and Cindy McCallister, most of this fine work by teacher-researchers would have remained hidden, never finding a larger audience. These editors worked with us for hundreds of hours over the past seven years to hone and craft the writing of teachers throughout the country into a journal.

Every time you look at "We Are Each a Gem," you see something new. Philippa Stratton, our editor at Stenhouse, has challenged us again and again over the years to think deeper and differently about research. Cathy Hawkes's design wizardry has created a book that allows readers multiple ways into the text, so that each reader can make it her own.

Like Evelyn, we also find words fail us in expressing thanks to all the teachers in and out of these pages, a vast community, who have shaped our vision of teacher research. Robert Finch writes, "True belonging is born of relationships not only to one another but to a place of shared responsibilities and benefits. We love not so much what we have acquired as what we have made and whom we have made it with." This book has not been written so much as made, by a community that cares deeply about listening to and learning from students. It has been stitched together from bits and pieces of insight about research shared by generous teachers over many years. Those in this community know who you are—but you can never know how truly grateful we are for how your work has transformed ours.

Why Teacher Research?

1

Research is a high-hat word that scares a lot of people. It needn't. It's rather simple. Essentially research is nothing but a state of mind. . . . A friendly, welcoming attitude toward change . . . going out to look for change instead of waiting for it to come.

Research is an effort to do things better and not to be caught asleep at the switch. It is the problem-solving mind as contrasted with the let-well-enough-alone mind. It is the tomorrow mind instead of the yesterday mind.

Charles Kettering

Brenda's niece Julie is a born researcher. When she was four, her plans one summer morning included persuading her mother to take her and her two-year-old brother, Johnny, to the playground. All morning, as her mom worked in the kitchen, Julie kept asking, "Can we go to the playground this afternoon?" The first six lobbying efforts were met with the response, "I don't know." The seventh received the reply, "I don't know, but if you ask again, the answer is NO."

A few minutes later, Johnny toddled into the kitchen. Mom spied Julie hiding just beyond the kitchen door. "Momma, go playground?" asked Johnny. Mom replied in an exasperated tone, "I don't know—we'll see." Johnny toddled back out of the kitchen, to be met at the threshold by Julie. "What'd she say? What'd she say?!" Johnny replied slowly, enunciating as clearly as he could, "She say 'we'll see.'" Julie jumped up and down in glee. "Oh goody! 'Cause 'maybe' means 'no,' but 'we'll see' means 'yes'!"

After hearing this exchange, Julie's mom monitored her own speech for the next two weeks. She realized Julie was right. She discovered every time she said "maybe," the answer was really no. And when she said "we'll see," the children got their way.

Research is a process of discovering essential questions, gathering data, and analyzing it to answer those questions. Like Julie, we are all born looking for patterns in the world. These patterns unlock the secrets of how language works, of how affection is gained and lost, of how one piece of knowledge builds upon another. In its simplest sense, research helps us gain control of our world. When we understand the patterns underlying the language we use or the interactions we have with others, we have a better sense of how to adjust our behaviors and expectations. For four-year-olds, a critical goal of research might be to gain access to a playground. But for teachers who engage in systematic and thoughtful analyses of their teaching and students, the goals are diverse and complex.

Teacher research is research that is initiated and carried out by teachers in their classrooms and schools. Teacher-researchers use their inquiries to study everything from the best way to teach reading and the most useful methods for organizing group activities, to the different ways girls and boys respond to a science curriculum.

We began with the anecdote of Julie and her mom because it conveys the simplicity of beginning with genuine questions that are truly relevant to researchers. For many years, teachers have criticized education research as not being relevant to their needs, or written in a way that fails to connect with their classroom practice. We're not denigrating the value of traditional education research—we've completed many research studies ourselves as university professors. But there's little question that even the finest education research studies have failed to find a wide audience among K–12 teachers. It's no wonder that teacher research has emerged not only as a significant new contributor to research on teaching but also as a source of systemic reform within individual schools and districts.

We also began with Julie's story because much teacher research is rich in classroom anecdotes and personal stories. While all methodologies are used for teacher inquiry, it is dominated by qualitative inquiry. In contrast to traditional education research studies, written in a distant, third-person voice, teacher research often has an immediate, first-person tone. Findings in teacher research are usually presented as narratives from the classroom, with metaphors a common means of highlighting key findings. As Jalongo, Isenberg, and Gerbracht (1995) note, "Stories are both mirrors of our own practice and windows on the practice of others" (174). In teacher research, stories are a critical tool for illuminating the deeper theories or rules governing the way a classroom community works.

As a teacher, it is natural to see research as "maybe" work—something that can be considered *after* the pressing needs of the classroom have been met. In this scheme, teacher research will never reach a high enough spot on the roster of duties in any classroom to be developed and supported.

But there are many ways to develop inquiry skills that are relevant to almost any teacher and classroom. Developing those skills, and seeing their place in teachers' lives across the country, is what this book is about.

Little r and Big R

When we first talk with teachers about the possibilities for research in their professional lives, they often recount negative experiences with research, and stereotypical views of what researchers do. As teacher Julie Ford explains,

> When I think of research, I think of the Big R type with long hours in the library, notes that could fill a novel, and a bibliography several pages long. I think of tension and stress lurking in the shadows. Feeling as I do about Research, the thought of conducting it in my classroom didn't curl my toes. But as I read the [classroom-based] research, I felt as though a door was beginning to open. My definition of research took a turn, and that familiar twinge of anxiety didn't come rushing forward. (Hubbard and Power 1993, xiv)

Teachers are surprised and delighted to realize that research can focus on problems they are trying to solve in their own classrooms. At its best, teacher research is a natural extension of good teaching. Observing students closely, analyzing their needs, and adjusting the curriculum to fit the needs of all students have always been important skills demonstrated by fine teachers.

Teacher research involves collecting and analyzing data as well as presenting it to others in a systematic way. But this research process involves the kinds of skills and classroom activities that already are a part of the classroom environment. As Glenda Bissex writes, a teacher-researcher is not a split personality, but a *more complete teacher*. While research is labor-intensive, so is good teaching. And the labor is similar for teachers, because the end goal is the same—to create the best possible learning environment for students. As Barbara Michalove writes, there is no real boundary between teaching and research within the real world of classrooms:

> When you teach a lesson and half the class gives you a blank look, you ask yourself, "How else can I teach this concept?" That's research. You observe, and respond to what you have observed. You begin to be aware of the intricate teaching and learning dance with your students. Researching took me a step further into my students' lives. The more I tune in, the better I become at knowing when to lead, when to follow, or when to play a sedate waltz or a lively rap. (1993, 33)

Barbara's words show how simple and immediate the research agendas of most teachers are—a kind of "dance" between teachers, students, and learning. Teacher-researchers rarely seek to initiate and carry out studies that have large-scale implications for education policy. Unlike large-scale education research, teacher research has a primary purpose of helping the teacher-researcher understand her students and improve her practice in specific, concrete ways. Teacher research studies can and do lead to large-scale education change. But for most teacher-researchers, the significance of the study is in how it informs and changes her own teaching.

Just as important for teachers, research can transform their understanding of students. This transformation can happen in a heartbeat, as it did for middle school teacher Maureen Barbieri as she researched literacy in the lives of adolescent girls:

> The most exciting thing that happened with the research was the day a girl said to me, "You just don't understand," and she was ferocious when she said it. She looked at me, and I looked at her, and I felt like we really saw each other for the first time. I realized what she was saying. I did not understand their position. And there was this feeling in the classroom that I had to acknowledge that and in acknowledging it, then I was able to understand a tiny, tiny bit and then that grew. (Barbieri, quoted in Frye 1997, 52)

This notion of understanding learning from the students' perspectives is central to teacher research. Strategies for research emerge and evolve from these close, intense, shifting relationships between students and teachers. The research agendas of teachers can look nothing like "Big R" research, with objective, large-scale, and distant analyses of issues.

Comparing the value of large-scale education research and teacher research confuses the purposes of these different research agendas and devalues both types of studies. John Dewey was perhaps the first major figure in education to argue for teachers' entrée into traditional education research communities. In commenting on the large array of scientific reports on education and learning in 1929, he wrote,

> A constant flow of less formal reports on special school affairs and results is needed. Of the various possibilities here I select one for discussion. It seems to me that the contributions that might come from classroom teachers are a comparatively neglected field; or, to change the metaphor, an almost unworked mine. . . . There are undoubted obstacles in the way. It is often assumed . . . that classroom teachers have not themselves the training which will enable them to give effective intelligent cooperation. The objection proves too much, so much that it is almost fatal to the idea of a workable scientific content in education. For these teachers are the ones in direct contact with pupils and hence the ones through whom the results of scientific findings finally reach students. They are the channels through which the consequences of educational theory come into the lives of those at school. [One questions] whether some of the incapacity, real or alleged, of this part of the corps of educators, the large mass of teachers, is not attributable to lack of opportunity and stimulus, rather than to inherent disqualification. As far as schools are concerned, it is certain that the problems which require scientific treatment arise in actual relationships with students. (Wallace 1997, 27–28)

Like other proponents of teacher research, Dewey chooses to emphasize the strengths that teachers can bring to research agendas (notably "direct contact with pupils" and their significant role as the "channels" for education theory). He looks at the potential of teacher research, interestingly, from the same place many teachers now look at the potential of each of their students—building from teachers' strengths rather than criticizing "real or alleged" deficiencies.

Lawrence Stenhouse noted that the difference between the teacher-researcher and the large-scale education researcher is like the difference between a farmer with a huge agricultural business to maintain and the "careful gardener" tending a backyard plot:

> In agriculture the equation of invested input against gross yield is all: it does not matter if individual plants fail to thrive or die so long as the cost of saving them is greater than the cost of losing them. . . . This does not apply to the careful gardener whose labour is not costed, but a labour of love. He wants each of his plants to thrive, and he can treat each one individually. Indeed he can grow a hundred different plants in his garden and differentiate his treatment of each, pruning his roses, but not his sweet peas. Gardening rather than agriculture is the analogy for education. (Rudduck and Hopkins 1985, 26)

This view of the teacher-researcher as a "careful gardener" is the image we hold in our minds of the ideal teacher-researcher—not a scientist in a lab coat, staring down a "research subject" (a kid!), but a human being in the midst of teaching, carefully weighing the value of different ways of teaching and learning.

Teacher Research: A Very Brief History

While teacher research has re-emerged recently as a significant kind of research in eduction, it is important to realize that the movement has deep and enduring roots. The two principles that define the teacher research movement today have been used widely in different education contexts, at different times in history:

1. *Teacher research is based upon close observation of students at work.* Education historians (e.g., McFarland and Stansell 1993) have traced the roots of teacher research back to Comenius (1592–1670), who was a proponent of linking child psychology with observational data to develop teaching methods. Pestalozzi (1746–1827) and Rousseau (1712–1778) developed and advocated observations of children to understand learning. But it was Herbart (1776–1841) who applied these methods in a systematic way in schools to develop principles of curriculum development. At the turn of the century and beyond, the work of Montessori (1870–1952) emphasized the value of teachers' using their observations to build systematic understanding of students.

2. *Teacher-researchers depend upon a research community.* There are examples of teacher-researchers doing fine studies without support, but usually sustained inquiry in schools or districts over time involves the development of a research community. One of the earliest proponents of teacher research was Lucy Sprague Mitchell. Mitchell, a close colleague of Dewey working in New York City, is famous for founding a consortium to support teacher research and the distribution of findings in 1916. This group, the Bureau of Education Experiments, became the Bank Street School of Education in 1930.

In England, Lawrence Stenhouse is widely credited with initiating an international teacher research movement. His consortium for supporting school inquiry, started in 1967, was a sensation in the English teaching community. This initiative led many English educators to begin research projects in their schools and become part of school research communities that endure today.

More recently, Nancie Atwell's work has generated much interest and excitement in the modern teacher research movement. Her studies of literacy learning in her middle school classroom in Boothbay Harbor, Maine, elegantly combine research findings with teaching strategies. Atwell was inspired by naturalistic researchers to analyze her teaching practice, and used this work to validate the research of other teachers. Atwell (1986) always acknowledges the importance of her colleagues in her development as a researcher, noting that while "one teacher can do great things, a community of teachers can move mountains" (20).

While early teacher research communities often evolved within lab school settings, in recent years these communities have become more far-flung and diverse. Internet listservs like XTAR are designed solely to build international teacher research communities through ongoing dialogue. Many professional organizations (including the National Council of Teachers of English and the American Educational Research Association) now have teacher research special interest groups, with teacher research studies representing an increasing number of presentations at local and national research gatherings.

Teacher Research Today: Will It Endure?

Given that the value assigned to teacher research has peaked and waned at different times in this century, what evidence is there that teacher research will be a significant part of education reform in the next century? There are a number of differences between the teacher research initiatives in previous decades and the current work of teacher-researchers that point to the movement's enduring.

First, teacher research in recent years has received significant new support and validation from existing education research communities. In our own field, literacy education, teacher research studies have emerged as a dominant research methodology during award competitions. For example, five of the last ten National Council of Teachers of English annual Promising Researcher awards have gone to teacher research studies.

Nancie Atwell's book *In the Middle* (1987) was the first teacher research study to win the highest research award from the National Council of Teachers of English, the David Russell Award, in 1989. Teacher research studies continue to win top literacy research awards, most recently the James Britton Research Award given to *Sounds from the Heart* (Barbieri 1995) in 1997.

Second, major funding agencies have designated existing and new funds for teacher research projects. The Fund for the Improvement of Post-Secondary Education (FIPSE) has awarded millions to new teacher research development programs in Georgia and North Carolina since 1990. The Spencer Foundation, a leading funding agency for education research, developed a new program in 1995 to support the development of teacher research networks. In its 1996 annual report, it set a new goal of integrating teacher research awards into all of its other existing grant programs, too.

Perhaps most important for teachers, we have reached a point where it is no longer possible to tackle one classroom issue or concern at a time. We face attacks in the media and at school board meetings over the quality of our work. But we also deal in individual classrooms with a science curriculum that needs to be rebuilt, or a literature circle format that works well in three groups but dismally in a fourth, or a very needy student who is disrupting an entire third-grade class. More and more, teachers depend upon using their reflective abilities to research these problems and then to build a corps of reflective learners in their schools who can work well together around tough issues.

This community of learners must have the ability to be those "problem seekers" Kettering praises in the epigraph for this chapter. It is a complex, complicated garden we are tending, and we need a diverse array of research tools and strategies to make it thrive.

If you are waiting for a "good" time to begin doing research in your classroom, give up! There is never a good time for research—and there is never a better time than now to begin. Every time a student stares you down and challenges your knowledge, as Maureen Barbieri's student did, is an opportunity to begin. Every time a lesson falls flat, as it did in Barbara Michalove's class, is a chance to unearth a research question and start collecting data. Our days are full of opportunities for research, and all we'll be left with in the end is regret if we miss them all. In Elizabeth Berg's novel *The Pull of the Moon* (1997), the main character, Elaine, notes how much those missed chances nag at us later in life: "I am so often struck by what we do not do, all of us. And I am also, now, so acutely aware of the quick passage of time, the way that we come suddenly to our own, separate closures. It is as though a thing says, I told you. But you thought I was just kidding" (143).

So, start your research while you can, however you can. Follow Colette's admonition, "We will do foolish things, but do them with enthusiasm!" and take a few risks. Remember Diane Mariechild's advice to "trust that still small voice that says this might work and I'll try it," and believe in the many strong skills of observation and reflection you bring to your work as a novice researcher but veteran teacher.

And with those first small, tentative steps you take in becoming a researcher, you'll be joining a community of teachers throughout the world who are changing the way we think about teaching and learning—one classroom at a time.

How This Book Is Organized

Careful gardeners have their own preferences for their plot of earth. Some gardeners are crazy about tomatoes; others plant only flowers. And every gardener deals with constraints, too—the woodchuck who serves as a personal nemesis, the short growing season in some climates.

We can't anticipate your passions as a teacher or the constraints that you face in your research. But we can share the passions and constraints of teacher-researchers from throughout the world who have tackled all sorts of research projects and in the process developed creative methods for making research a vital part of their lives.

Each chapter of the book includes an essay in which we present snapshots of teachers doing research, presenting research, or musing about their research process. We distill their best advice about research methods and strategies into brief, practical essays. We then present a Research Workshop section—an opportunity for you to test out the methods and ideas of the section through some research activities of your own. Each chapter closes with a Featured Teacher-Researchers section, showing a range of strategies used by teacher-researchers in their work.

Remember the importance of developing a research community. Try to find at least one other colleague willing to read and try the Research Workshop strategies with you. Many of them work best if you have a partner to test out the concepts with you and to sustain your motivation when it lags. Annie Keep-Barnes has stated emphatically that the Alaska Teacher Research Network (ATRN) has been her lifeline to other teachers asking questions about learning and teaching. Her group's encouragement allowed her to write honestly about her classroom dilemmas (see Chapter 2).

All careful gardeners begin from the same place. They plant seeds, they wait, and they hope. We hope this book plants enough seeds to allow some possibilities for teacher research to sprout in your own classroom, school, or district. Every teacher has wonderings worth pursuing. Teacher research is one way to pursue those wonderings in a thoughtful, systematic, and collaborative way.

RESEARCH WORKSHOP

Celebrating "Things I Learned Last Week"

In the pages that follow are examples from new and veteran teacher-researchers who explain how they dig into their data and cope with the messiness of their evolving research. Some of the advice deals with the little things we learn, that, if we pay close attention to, can get us through the day and help us reconnect with the research questions that intrigue us. It takes practice to notice the small details. It may involve looking through a new lens, readjusting our focus, and celebrating what we see as we document what we have learned.

The poet William Stafford believes that it is these details in life that are the "golden threads" that lead us to what he calls "amazing riches." In his poem "Things I Learned Last Week," he celebrates the learning that comes from close observation, from reading, from reflecting on his own actions:

Things I Learned Last Week
William Stafford

Ants, when they meet each other,
usually pass on the right.

Sometimes you can open a sticky
door with your elbow.

A man in Boston has dedicated himself
to telling about injustice.
For three thousand dollars he will
come to your town and tell you about it.

Schopenhauer was a pessimist but
he played the flute.

Yeats, Pound, and Eliot saw art as
growing from other art. They studied that.

If I ever die, I'd like it to be
in the evening. That way, I'll have
all the dark to go with me, and no one
will see how I begin to hobble along.

In the Pentagon one person's job is to
take pins out of towns, hills, and fields,
and then save the pins for later.

When we take up William Stafford's challenge to look closely at "what we learned last week," what might we collect? After reading this poem, a group of teachers in Portland, Oregon, changed their lenses and looked closely for a week, discovering:

Things I Learned This Week

Pigeons bob their heads because
they use one eye to stay focused on the ground
and the other to look for food. The combination
creates the bobbing movement.

Vegetables from your own garden
taste the best.

A string of eucalyptus seeds will
keep mosquitoes away.

You can't catch a kitten in a bad mood.

Toni Morrison hears stories
being whispered to her
by her characters.

Another group of experienced teachers, this time from Maine, did the same exercise together, focusing on their work with students:

Things I Learned This Week About Teaching

There's a connection between watering the plant
on my office windowsill and paying
attention to the needs of my students.

Getting new braces is much more important
to talk about than acute and obtuse
angles.

When registering children for
kindergarten, you can't keep just the
well-behaved children and kind parents.

As much as I think I know about students,
they still surprise me with new insights,
and, this week, excuses.

Sometimes teachers who are innovative,
nurturing, and kind in their classrooms
do not treat colleagues the same way.

Teachers have to learn what to ignore.

A short piece of writing can unlock a big hurt.

Sometimes you have to hold chuckles inside, like when a second grader writes about how he "knocked up" an alligator instead of how he knocked it out.

Children know more than we give them credit for. They let me know who the great authors are and they're not the ones I would have chosen.

Setting these details down—recording and keeping track of them even for a week—helps us process the daily small moments that inform our lives. And hearing what others have learned motivates us to look closely at the small details that are the building blocks of our lives as researchers as well. The Oregon group of teachers decided to extend their close examination and ask what they learned "last week" about their processes as teacher-researchers. This group poem summarizes those details they are learning about research:

Things I Learned About Research

The more I write or reflect,
the more questions I ask.

Some projects are like icebergs—
they look small on the top
and turn into monsters in the end.

Topics are subject to change and
events can enliven or
dampen my enthusiasm.

The computer is my friend.

I feel better about what I'm doing
and why I'm doing it
because I feel I can substantiate everything
with some kind of evidence and my own
personal thoughts.

I find I am researching when I'm not researching.

I'm starting writing more like a real writer,
mimicking writing I've read before.

Knowing there is an audience
helps me "toe the line."

I learn what I know by trying
to explain it to others.

Everyone's research informs my question.

What will you learn this week? Try your hand at crafting your own "things I learned this week" poem about teaching or research, either alone or with your inquiry group. You may find yourself surprised at how varied the learning is.

featured TEACHER RESEARCHER

Teaching and Researching Riffs

Jane A. Kearns

"Are you *still* teaching?"
   I looked at my questioner.
   "Are you *still* teaching?"
   The tone of this question suggested that the speaker would have been pleased if I had moved into another field rather than *still* teaching. Do other professionals get asked that question: Are you still doctoring? still lawyering? Are you still an architect?

No. They don't get asked those questions. So why do people ask teachers?

I think people ask us are we still teaching for one reason: they realize that teaching is an intense, complex, and stressful profession. They assume that teachers will burn out and change careers more than other professionals. And they imagine no adult wants to spend all day with thirty children or preteens, and certainly not with teenagers.

Perhaps the questioners are in the vast majority of people who admit they just could not take the anxiety, the tension, the challenge of dealing with thirty young minds in every class. Teachers are catalysts—doing so that someone else will learn. Our goal is to have ideas spring forth, like the mythological dragon-teeth warriors, to be conquered by the students' desire to know. The best days for teachers are those when knowledge filters in a new word or world or wonder.

Some days we knapsack thoughts in quiet, controlled classes; other times we choreograph spinning swoops and headlong leaps toward discovery. Eyes flicker, pencils roll, minds percolate.

It is difficult to explain to adults who ask questions like "Are you still teaching?" why we *are* still teaching. Their easy answer is we must do it for the summer vacation. People who believe this will never understand teaching or teachers. Teachers love the exhilaration of the challenge, to get students to be curious. Most jobs lean on predictability; teaching leans on the improvised, based on knowledge and experience. And that is why many teachers are becoming researchers, to further hone their improvisational skills.

In this way, teaching and research are a lot like playing jazz, being in three places at once; many rhythms happening at the same time, playing together, going solo. Fluid blends of all the performers.

In both teacher research and jazz, you have a certain arrangement, a theme, a goal, but it is in the getting there that teacher research and jazz happen. The multiplicity of energies in the class and in the band balance and then sway, pitch, roll. From improvisation, the soul of jazz and of teacher research, comes the best—instinctive, being in the zone. Start with the basic guides and then go with the flow, react, extend, reach, and stretch.

Quiet one moment, then all out strummin' goin' to town, sweet clarinet together with funky keyboards. Listen and talk, talk and listen, and play.

A good class is like The Jam, a free-wheeling interplay of improvisational riffs. Surprise. Point. Counterpoint. Point counterpoint. Spontaneous and effortless, with each participant growing and scaling new heights.

I love the passion of jazz. I love the passion of teacher research. Triple-time thrummin' and drummin', smoky and mellow, mellow and wry and wild.

Jazz has a sense of humor; you need one in teacher research, too. Both speak to me of the hope in our world. Upbeat. Heartbeat. Your own beat thumping, pounding high energy, entering unexplored space.

I love the pulse of each note alone or in raucous/smooth harmony. Jazz is straight from the heart. No two performances alike; each one full of surprises—funky and fun. Jazz struts and dances, careens. Just like a good class. Just like a good research project.

I bought my first jazz album when I was a teenager. Captivated by the cover of a Dave Brubeck record—*Red, Hot and Cool!* I played it all the time—when I was alone. With friends, it was the new rock 'n' roll. I never shared my jazz because I didn't know how to explain the music or my soaring feelings.

Then I heard Sarah Vaughan in person. *The Divine One.* Her voice traveled places I didn't know any instrument could go. Into a different world, a different dimension of excellence. And freedom. And power and heightened awareness.

Preservation Hall Jazz, Dixieland, Creole, and Chicago. Scott Joplin. Bessie Smith. Billy Eckstine.

"Charlie Parker played bebop. Charlie Parker played saxophone. Never leave your cat alone" (Raschka 1992).

The Count, the Duke, and Jelly Roll Morton. Joe Williams every day; stompin' at the Savoy, striding, taking the A train.

The mellow tones of Mel Torme and Bobby Short, George Benson and Ella.

Errol Garner swinging on piano, BB King wailing on guitar; Kenny G sweet toning on clarinet.

Louis.

The new jazz of Pat Kelly, Gary Burton, and David Benoit, Pat Metheny and Harry Connick. Andy Narell making warm-weather jazz with steel pans and drums. In the zone.

I still can't find the words to explain why I like jazz—though Leonard Bernstein's *What Is Jazz?* (1981) helps me understand what it is but not how it reaches me. Why does it reach me?

I can't explain the nuances of a good research project either, "at once spontaneous and deliberate, passionate and controlled, controlled in ways that make its passion all the more convincing" (Williams 1993).

Jon Pareles (1993) wrote in the *New York Times* that jazz advances right through "a bewildering world." So does teacher research. Improvised jazz sits like a good research project—it can't be replayed in exactly the same way. Teacher research, like jazz, is a solo art even when completed in a group. Teacher research gets us involved to the point that we seem to be all working together, with the sum of the parts as great as the whole. Whether in isolation in our own classroom, or teaming with others, a teaching moment, like a gig, brings out the best in each of us. Good teacher-researchers involve students in working things out together, like a jam session, individuals all, but building strength and risk taking from each other. Harmony.

A good research project is the result of knowledge and intuition. Our improvs are based on sound knowledge of the students and of our own craft. We assess what is going on as it is going on and build on that moment, in that moment. As teacher-researchers we know that the truth is often in the unexpected, not the planned. We wish for and wait for and relish those sidebars into new energies. In teacher research and in jazz, mistakes are not mistakes, they are calibrations for the mind.

Martin Williams in *The Jazz Tradition* (1993) wrote of Louis Armstrong:

> And his genius is such that he can apparently take any piece, add a note here, leave out a note there, condense or displace this melodic phrase a bit, rush this cadence, delay that one; alter another one slightly, and transform it into sublime melody, into pure gold. He can turn something merely pretty into something truly beautiful and something deeply delightful. Conscious taste has little to do with such transformations; they are products of an intuitive genius, and of the kind of choice where reason cannot intrude. (15)

This defines every great teacher-researcher I have learned from, or observed, or worked with, or listened to, or read about. Good teacher research cannot be explained away in neat packages or labels. Good teacher research swings.

Jazz—and teacher research—affirm who we are, where we have been, and where we are going. This is why we teach. Why we research. And why, yes, I am *still* a teacher! I would not have it any other way.

We Have Met the Audience and She Is Us: The Evolution of Teacher as Audience for Research

Judith Bradshaw Brown

When I first began to teach in the late 1960s, I worked with eighteen-year-olds who had managed to get to senior year in high school without being able to read. That fact caused me to ask some important questions. How could that have happened? What might I do about it at this point? I had not learned the answers in my excellent teacher preparation program, but I was aware of the research sources I might go to for some support.

The research available to me was of the experimental variety. It was not helpful. What gave me the information and support I needed were books like Ashton-Warner's *Teacher* (1963), Holt's *How Children Learn* (1967), Kohl's *36 Children* (1967), and Holbrook's *English for the Rejected* (1964). Teachers' stories. Children's stories. None just like my own, most quite different. Yet I found what I needed in Ashton-Warner's documentation of her Maori readers on the other side of the world and in Holt's observations and thoughts about his inner-city elementary students. I was able to generalize to my own situation in spite of the warnings of education researchers about the dangers of generalizing from isolated particulars.

I found that I agreed with novelist Kinnan Rawlings (1942), who said, "A man may learn a deal of the general from the specific, but it is impossible to know the specific by studying the general" (359). It is the generalizing nature of traditional research, in which large numbers of people are studied in order to wash out the effects of particular individual differences (Bissex 1987), which made it so difficult to transport it into my classroom.

No one was assigning the books that I found helpful in my education courses. It seemed to me that my preferred resources were considered spurious and lightweight, and that consequently I was unprofessional to prefer them. If I were truly a professional, I'd be eschewing practices "unproven" by rigorous research and choosing those borne out by such research. In my master's program, I read and wrote papers on the "real" research and dutifully studied my text, *Research in Education* (Best 1977), which mentioned something called "action research" in passing. I designed a study according to experimental guidelines and continued to read what really spoke to me and my teaching "in the closet."

What informed my teaching were the case studies, the "sloppy" first-person accounts of teachers teaching, the observations of what classrooms looked and felt like. The general feeling I sensed in the academic community was that reading them was like reading *People* magazine, interesting but not serious.

Returning to school full time to seek a doctorate after twenty-five years of teaching, I discovered that it's safe to come out of the closet now. If it weren't, I would not have made the decision to seek an advanced degree.

The kinds of studies that always fed me now abound and are taking their place alongside the counting and testing studies. Why was it, I wondered, that I had never before seen myself as the audience for these experimental studies? Who were they written for? It seems that, far from being the exception, I was the rule.

I'm Not Alone

Bolster (1983) sees education, compared to other professions, as the least affected by the findings of professional research. Speaking from the perspective of a teacher working simultaneously in a public school and a prestigious university, he examines the reasons for that and finds that "the minimal effect that university-sponsored research has had on classroom practice is itself a forceful argument that our traditional modes of inquiry are inappropriate to the production of knowledge that teachers will believe in and use" (308).

Florio-Ruane and Dohanich (1984) observe that teachers often find themselves recipients of research findings written in technical jargon and offering esoteric, theoretical constructs that do not address teachers' needs or experiences (725). They note that "in their everyday work lives, teachers and researchers occupy different speech communities" (726). "Even when researchers have completed rigorous studies and reported them responsibly to the research community, they are likely to miss entirely the community of teachers for whom their research is thought to be useful" (727).

Bolster (1983) suggests that the "merits of a researcher's conclusions are not formally determined by practitioners of the profession under inquiry, but by colleagues in the investigator's discipline" (301). What is wrong with this picture?

Eisner (1993) recounts his own experience in graduate school in the 1950s, when, to become a researcher in education, it was necessary to study educational psychology and that entailed work with statistical methods on either correlational or experimental studies:

> The particulars of the world—individual students, specific teachers, individual schools—were essentially fodder for the creation of mathematical abstractions. The more mathematically abstracted, the better. As a result of this aspiration, attention to the uniqueness of the individual was neglected. Idiosyncrasy was regarded as noise within a distribution. What one wanted was pattern and regularity, not specificity and particularity . . . the timeless rather than the timely, the universal rather than the individual, the general rather than the particular. (51)

Allen's (1995) work offers an example of research written by a teacher for an audience of teachers, signaling a shift not only in her work but in the field: "For years when I heard *research* I pictured scientific experiments, laboratories, and university research staffs. My readings of research coming out of places like the University of New Hampshire helped me develop a new definition of *research*" (51). Why had the traditional definition been the only one? Where has this new definition come from? How have we gotten from there to here?

The Research Road Diverges

During the late nineteenth century, German social theorists such as Dilthy made a distinction between natural science and human science, positing that humans differ from other animals and inanimate entities in their capacity to make meaning. But when education research began to develop as a discipline in the early twentieth century and flourished after World War I, researchers chose to adopt the methodology of experimental psychology, which had in turn chosen the paradigm of the natural sciences. It is at this point that the firm grip of positivist thinking on education took hold, and it lasted until the late 1970s. Smith (1936) sees the publication of the Thorndike scale in 1910 as the beginning of the contemporary movement for measuring education products scientifically. Education researchers rejected the methodology of anthropology, which was developing simultaneously, considering such data to be "soft." The two types of research are often called positivist/behaviorist and interpretive. The prevailing scene for most of my years of teaching from the late 1960s to the late 1980s had been the positivist tradition. What has been appearing more often and gaining credibility since the late 1970s is interpretive research. To understand the current situation, it is helpful to trace the development of this interpretive tradition, seeing it as a change not only in defining research and its audience but in how we think about learning and teaching.

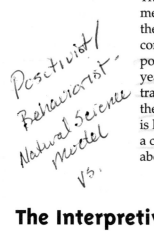

Positivist/Behaviorist - Natural Science Model vs.

The Interpretive Tradition

Erickson (1986) sees interpretive research and its guiding theory as developing out of an emerging interest in the lives and perspectives of people in society who had little or no voice in the late eighteenth century. Erickson traces a shift in the view of the poor in works such as Beaumarchais's *Barber of Seville,* which presented one of the first sympathetic characterizations of a servant figure. He notes this shift in view and accompanying concerns for social reform and innovations in pedagogy in Rousseau and in Pestalozzi, who established schools for children previously considered to be unteachable.

Olson (1990) sees the origins of the current "teacher as researcher" movement in Pestalozzi and Herbart. Later in the nineteenth century, attention to reforms shifted to working-class populations of growing towns. In England, Boothe documented everyday lives of factory adults and children. In turn-of-the-century America, muckrakers like the journalists Jacob Riis and Lincoln Steffens and the novelist Upton Sinclair brought the lives and wrongs of this segment of the population to public notice. In the late nineteenth century there was also an interest in unlettered people who lacked power and about whom little was known. Detailed accounts of nonliterate people in European-controlled colonial territories received attention from the emerging field of anthropology. The term *ethnography* (from the Greek *ethnos,* "race," "people") was coined.

Contributions of Anthropology

Erickson (1986) recounts the contributions of Bronislaw Malinowski, who was sent to the Trobriand Archipelago in 1914 and who published a study in 1922 that revolutionized the field of social anthropology with the specificity of its descriptive reporting and "by the sensitivity of the insights presented about the beliefs and perspectives of the Trobrianders" (123). Malinowski presented insights about explicit cultural knowledge and implicit cultural knowledge (i.e., beliefs and perspectives) so customary for Trobrianders that they were held outside of conscious awareness and could not be readily articulated by informants. Some attacked Malinowski's work as too subjective and unscientific.

In 1928, Margaret Mead published the first monograph-length education ethnography, *Coming of Age in Samoa.* Mead-influenced ethnographies turned directly to issues of education after World War II under the leadership of Spindler at Stanford in the 1950s and Kimball at Teachers College, Columbia University in the 1970s. In the 1960s, Lawrence Stenhouse and his associates in Great Britain carried on this tradition. The year 1968 marked the formation of the Council on Anthropology, and the 1970s saw the creation of the National Institute of Education.

Moving to the Classroom

Francis Parker and John Dewey were among the first to evaluate pedagogical theories in practical settings in their experimental schools in the 1930s (Olson 1990). Eisner and Peshkin (1990) see the emergence of a growing interest in teaching and in the lives of classrooms in America in the mid-1960s. These books agree on the importance of B. O. Smith's 1962 study of teaching practices as they actually occurred in classrooms. Eisner and Peshkin (1990) cite Bellack's 1966 work on the language of the classroom and Jackson's *Life in the Classroom* (1968) for interpretation and narrative of long-term observation and analysis of life in the classroom. In an article in *School Review* in 1969, Schwab made a "compelling case that curricularists in particular and educationists in general had become so infatuated with intellectual respectability that they failed to recognize that the practice of education was not a theoretical undertaking but a practical one" and that "the kind of knowledge that people in practical enterprises needed was personal, practical knowledge" (4).

A movement called action research, which involved teachers as researchers and consumers of research, surfaced in the 1940s with its early proponent Stephen Corey of the Horace Mann-Lincoln Institute of School Experimentation at Columbia University (Olson 1990). Corey voiced concerns about the gap between research and practice and "chastised research professionals because they considered research their territory and the research efforts by teachers as substandard" (9). Corey's work

> sparked much interest from educators—not all positive. . . . Interest in action research faded in the late fifties. University-level researchers severely criticized teacher-conducted studies for their lack of research precision and the inability to generalize from a limited population sample in specific situations to a larger population. The criticism finally caused the movement's downfall as teachers lost interest in conducting research. Research efforts in the sixties and early seventies became firmly focused on basic research rather than applied studies and university-level researchers and educators conducted those studies. (10)

During the past twenty years, it has become increasingly legitimate to use qualitative methods to study teachers, classrooms, schools, and educational materials. Eisner (1993) contends that "the grip of positivist assumptions on the educational community has been loosened" (53). He feels, further, that this movement represents a fundamental reconceptualization not only of what we regard as acceptable forms of education research but of the way we think about knowledge, validity, generalization, and education itself.

Case Study Research

The alternative research tradition in psychology is exemplified in the case studies of Freud, Piaget, Cazden, and Bettelheim. Publication of Emig's *The Composing Processes of Twelfth Graders* (1971), in which she presents case studies of high school students' writing, marks an early milestone. Emig cites Holbrook's *English for the Rejected* (1964) and Kohl's *36 Children* (1967) as the only precursors to her work. Bissex published her dissertation study of her son, *GNYS AT WRK: A Child Learns to Write and Read* in 1980. Trends related to qualitative programmatic research surface in the 1980s in the work of Donald Graves and his colleagues at the University of New

Hampshire, Lucy Calkins in New York City, and Nancie Atwell in Maine. Early (1991) sees their work as illustrating "the transition from product- to process-centered research in language arts. This transition . . . was accompanied by changes in methodology from empirically based analyses to descriptive, anecdotal, and example-filled documentation, more like reportage than research and, consequently, more readable. And *they exemplify the profession's mounting concern for the role that teachers play in the learning process*" [italics added] (149).

Early also mentions the work that came out of large-scale writing projects such as the federally funded Iowa Writing Project and the Bay Area Writing Project and its offshoot, the National Writing Project, which she sees as influencing the changing concept of research, i.e., the emergence of teachers and classrooms as sources of research ideas, not simply as subjects of others' investigations or as vehicles for verifying or demonstrating the results of others' research. Early notes that "if a single trend stands out in the recent history of educational research, it is the increasing value assigned to the role of the teacher in research, not only as the subject of investigation or a source of problems and data to be analyzed by others, but as a key participant in defining classroom variables and identifying appropriate directions for change" (157). And, I would add, as the audience for education research.

Involvement of Teachers

Harste (1994) frames the evolving conception of education research in terms of conversation, with teachers as instigators of and participants in the conversation. Harste suggests that "inquiry used to be something that was handled in departments of educational psychology and something studied by advanced graduate students in education. Undergraduates and master's level teachers didn't need it. In contrast to this skills view of inquiry, today inquiry is seen as philosophical science in education, as a perspective from which to view the whole of what education is about" (1230). The only real difference he sees between learning and inquiry is that inquiry has some additional requirements that have to do with making public what you learn and leaving "a trail so that others can examine the conclusions reached and decide whether or not they agree" (1230).

Another noteworthy difference in emerging concepts of research is the idea of the self as primary audience. Krall (1988) suggests that "as a result of our research, we should become more consciously intentional of our actions and more thoughtful and reflective of their consequences" (474). Krall has graduate students do autobiography as research, using personal history as a way of comprehending broader education issues, not unlike my use of my own experience in this article. Bissex (1987) offers powerful arguments for oneself as audience, suggesting that the research makes one aware of what one does as a teacher.

Out of the Closet

So now I read stories of teachers and students, and they change the way I think and teach. I no longer hide that fact from my colleagues in academe. I observe my students and my teaching and share my observations with colleagues and with those students. I observe colleagues teaching and share my observations with them. I write case studies of my observations and share them at conferences. Birnbaum and Emig (1991) suggest that "since case study documents dense and specific human history, the mode may flourish especially under those psychological and political arrangements that honor uniqueness—under, that is, mature democracies and political systems. The status of case study in a culture may well prove then as an index not only of investigative but also of societal sophistication" (195). Grumet (1990) says, "Teaching, which has, in our time, come to be the work of women with children, has lacked the status of art or science and has borrowed their stances and methods to know itself. But teaching . . . is both art and science. And we must study teaching as teachers. For us, teaching *is* research and research *is* teaching" (119).

I haven't found definitive answers to the questions I have about my teaching. What I've found are stories of others engaged in this challenging job, and their stories move my thinking about my own situation. I learn about the general from studying the specific, moving closer to the answers I seek and to new questions. I am a researcher as well as a consumer of research. I participate in the conversation.

Questions Evolving

2

What room can there be in that cramped skull for thoughts, imaginations, questions, wonders, for all that makes us human?

Peter Dickinson

Where do our questions come from? It's a natural part of being human to look at the world around us and wonder. Peter Dickinson, in his novel *A Bone from a Dry Sea*, re-creates the world of our ancestors, who live between the land and the sea. Li, the main character, is a child. She is the "thinker" of her people, and it is her intelligence and imagination—her questioning stance—that holds the key to human evolution. One morning, wandering off from her tribe, she catches a flicker of movement out of the corner of her eye:

> Inquisitive, she climbed down and crept across to see. The spider was crouched over its prey, bouncing gently on its springy legs. She wanted to see what the spider would do. She crouched and watched while the spider dragged the bug clear of the insect-sized track along which it had been scuttling. It climbed into the twigs above the track and rapidly wove a coarse, loose web, then returned to the earth and stretched a couple of threads across the path. It moved into the shadows and waited. So did Li.
>
> Every insect click, every faint rustle, might be a danger sound. She must go back. But first, she needed to know what the spider was up to. It was the mere knowledge that mattered. The excitement of her thoughts kept her awake. . . . There were pictures in her mind: the spider, the web dropping from the twigs. "What?" she wondered. "How . . . ?" (1992, 20)

Li's questions evolve from her interest in making sense of all that she is hearing, seeing, and noticing. She moves into the shadows, waits, watches, and asks "how." Her questions initially surprise her. From her continued observations and reflections, and ultimately the weaving of the first nets to catch fish, her questions work to change her whole tribe's way of life.

Teachers with a research frame of mind are open, too, to exploring the surprises that pop up in our teaching lives. We don't always start out with a specific, clearly formulated question. As observers of classrooms daily, we can unearth our questions by reflecting on what we see. As Glenda Bissex writes about her research process, "What attracts my attention as I observe and what I find myself recording is information to help me answer questions that I may not yet have consciously asked" (quoted in Gillespie 1993, 75–76).

Teaching is filled with researchable moments—those instants when a question suddenly snaps into consciousness. Questions may come from a teaching journal or a snatch of conversation with a colleague. For teaching intern Kelli Clark, a pile of student work was the catalyst for a research question. She recounts the experience in her essay "Harvesting Potatoes":

> My 70-year-old father astonished a young Girl Scout on a garden project by countering her assertion that potatoes come from Safeway. Her confident claim was met with a swift turn of the spading fork, unearthing a mound of potatoes at her feet. She was dumbstruck.
>
> The effect of my first encounter with teacher research was no less remarkable. Of course, I was impressed with the efforts of others and fully intended to implement a "system" for research in my own classroom. Like potatoes coming clean, sorted, and unblemished from the store, "good" teacher research questions came from well-organized Über Teachers who pulled neat packages of insights from their classrooms. As a student teacher, I didn't know if I could evolve into one of these beings, but I harbored my fantasies. Someday I would get organized and begin my research.
>
> Imagine my shock to see eyes of potatoes staring at me from a pile of rough drafts on my first major teaching project. As part of the teaching team at Mount Tabor Middle School, we were investigating Ancient Rome, under the larger theme of Demise of Cultures. My class was composed of a mix of sixth, seventh, and eighth graders. Our goal was to examine why cultures failed and whether we could use that information usefully in the future.
>
> To assess their learning, I asked students to assume the role of an emperor toward the end of the empire. Using their understanding of the reasons underlying the fall of Rome, they were to write a decree that issued orders that would effectively save the empire. I did a mini-lesson on the differences between a decree, a declaration, and a proclamation. We talked about establishing authority and the class role-played using authoritative language.
>
> Teacher research was the farthest thing from my mind when I read the rough drafts of the decrees. Several students engaged in lengthy, grandiose descriptions of their personal authority and what might happen to their subjects if they did not comply with the decree. I read as the self-described "Supreme and Undaunted Ruler of the Universe," "Leader of the Assassins," and "John the Decapitator" blew up, savagely beat, and otherwise abused the unfortunate imaginary plebeians and patricians. These students engaged in this to the extent that they often neglected to discuss Rome, or

issue any decree for which they'd described such detailed, severe penalties for noncompliance!

As I began to wonder if I'd overemphasized the authority issue, I started seeing papers that passively requested something be done. The "Most Superior Being on Earth" suggested that the people "do" something. "The Ruler Most High" said, "I think you should. . . . "

Here it was: potatoes. No neat system or detailed notes caught the clear example of gender issues in student writing. Here were aggression and inappropriate levels of violence from my sixth- and seventh-grade boys. Here was Ophelia pleading for the salvation of Rome, even as she had been given complete authority and power to toss the populace a lifeline.

Overall, 35 percent of the boys and 30 percent of the girls showed these gender patterns in their writing. Not one boy wrote in the passive voice. Not one girl blew up a plebeian.

I responded to each of these papers. Their reactions to my comments, as seen in their final copies, gave me further reason to reflect. I reiterated the assignment to the boys and asked them to eliminate gratuitous violence and solve the problems of Rome. I reminded the girls of the lesson on authoritative language and urged them to use their power to command, order, and compel. Unlike the boys, however, not one girl corrected the problem. Though half of them altered the language, the change was to another form of passive voice.

Seeing these issues so starkly in such a short span of time has given me reason to reflect again on the challenges that each gender faces during the middle school years. Ophelia is no longer out there somewhere; she is clearly in my classroom (1997, 182–183).

Like other teacher-researchers, Kelli noticed behaviors—leading to questions about gender-binding in early adolescence and what she could do to address it in her class. Her research question didn't emerge fully formed—she continued her observations and allowed her question to evolve.

Questions are often born of frustration. Andie Cunningham was bothered by what was happening with her sixth-grade physical education students. She decided to ask them about it. Her observations caused her to dig deeper, unearthing a research question. She writes,

During individual sixth-grade conferences in January, many students answered my question of how to make this class work better by informing me that I talked too much. Did I really talk too much? Was that problem universal throughout all of the grades? Was there something more I should be focusing on with my language? What would make so many of the students during individual conferences say that one way to make the class better was for me to talk less? Why was it that only the sixth-grade classes said that? My well-intentioned protecting brain said, "No way. It's just them," but my quieter, more calm side rang forth with, "What are they really saying?" (1997, 137)

This led to Andie's taping her classes to calculate the amount of time spent talking by her and by her students. But the taping didn't answer her question; instead it helped direct her to other inquiry:

> Besides helping me address the nagging question that had kept me tossing and turning at night, new questions were raised for me. I noticed that male voices were speaking loudest during class meetings, female voices sang quietly only during the activities. I also realized there were some voices that didn't seem to be speaking at all. I've discovered a deeper layer in the classroom dynamics. More specific questions now loom. Have I been speaking for the absent female voices? What platforms must be present for the girls to risk speaking out to the whole class? What will their voices sound like when they do speak up? (1997, 138)

These and other teachers' questions are woven directly into the fabric of the daily class life. And the questions are not neat and tidy—they evolved from what Kelli and Andie observed, and became more refined as they focused their attention around a particular issue.

Mining Tensions

Tension is defined as both an act of stretching and a state of uneasy suspense. Each definition of *tension* applies to teaching and research. Often, the best research questions are located in a taut spot between two points. We sometimes walk a tightrope between who we are as teachers and learners and who we want to be. Once you find a gap that needs to be traversed—between what you think will be learned in a math lesson and what is learned, between the calm, patient mentor you were yesterday and the abrupt, demanding authoritarian you were today, between your love of a book and your students' distaste for it—you have found territory in your classroom that is ripe for questioning.

There are always gaps between our expectations and those of students, misunderstandings born of cultural differences, bureaucratic constraints, and the frantic rush of the school day. In the midst of all these demands, miscommunications, and daily stresses of the profession, there is an oasis. Many teachers have found the process of generating research questions to be a healthy way to stretch toward new understanding, and to avoid having the gaps become gulfs between students and colleagues. Turning tensions into a research question can be the best mental stress reducer at a teacher's disposal.

Maraline Ellis, a high school social studies teacher, was frustrated when a lesson she tried with her students worked really well in one class but failed to capture the interest of another class. She muses in her teaching journal,

Fifth period rained on my parade. In fact it was a downpour. They went along with it, but without the interest my first period had shown. I don't think my presentation was any different. . . . I wonder, well, I wonder about a lot. I feel a brainstorm coming on. . . . I'm going to brainstorm what I wonder about—without censoring any thoughts:

> I wonder if the noise coming through the partition wall bothers the students as much as it does me?
>
> I wonder if my ninth-grade students know they have been placed in teams?
>
> I wonder how many of my students have parents in the penitentiary?
>
> I wonder how the ninth graders feel about participating in the service project?
>
> I wonder if their choices for work sites will be made based on what they really care about or what their friends signed up to do?
>
> I wonder how Kenny sees himself as a student in my class?
>
> I wonder if he is aware that he tried very hard to keep me from getting to the point in the lesson where he may have to write or read?
>
> I wonder why he tried to get kicked out of his English class but not mine?
>
> I wonder how sophomores feel about taking American Government when voting is still a few years away?
>
> I wonder what students think is important/unimportant in what I teach?
>
> I wonder what they think *I think* is important/unimportant?

At the end of her journal entry, Maraline concluded, "I think I will ask [the kids] to write about this tomorrow—tell me what they think." With her students' input, Maraline framed a research question that helped her continue to explore curriculum issues with more of a student-centered focus: What happens when I base my government curriculum on what is of concern to the students?

We don't always need a long list, like Maraline, to get to the heart of our teaching tensions. Sometimes our research questions begin with nagging worries about one student. Seventh-grade teacher Carolyn McCrea's research question emerged from her frustration with Marcy:

> First day of seventh-grade language arts class, Marcy wouldn't stop talking—never really said anything to anybody; never really said anything that made any sense. Just annoyed me. And puzzled me, because she really was just talking to herself. She doesn't do that all the time now, but there are times when a subject comes up that she just has to talk about. And she does—nonstop—to herself. Her conversation with herself becomes so animated that she can't stay in her seat. But she can never get those conversations on paper. As time goes on, there are other things about Marcy that

make an impression. She always wears black, shirt to shoes. Black is also the color of her notebook. When standing, she leans to one side. She doesn't appear to have any friends or enemies. She also doesn't appear to ever have any fun. Marcy takes some assignments, such as mini-lessons, very seriously and works more meticulously on them. Others, no matter how many suggestions you make, she cannot get started on. If she didn't care, she wouldn't do anything. But if she really cared, she wouldn't just sit as if in a coma and pretend you should never expect anything of her, because of course, she's in a coma, can't you see? The question is, what motivates Marcy?

The Value of Subquestions

Carolyn's reflections on Marcy led her to a research question. With this main question in mind, it may help her to think about the kinds of subquestions she wants to answer as she pursues her research. It can be extremely useful to list the follow-up questions that evolve from our initial research brainstorming.

Several underlying questions emerged from veteran teacher-researcher Karen Gallas's curiosity about the value of her sharing time:

> What is the value of sharing time in the primary grades? . . . As I began to reflect carefully on the different kinds of talk in my first-grade classroom, and more particularly on my influence on classroom discourse, I had become uncomfortable with my role as the central figure in classroom talk. I was curious about what would happen if I began the school year by turning sharing directly over to the children. How would the talk develop once the model of a teacher-run, teacher-focused sharing time wore off? What would happen to a group of children when they spent time each day talking together about their lives, and what would I, in the process of documenting this event, learn about language and the children I taught? (1994, 18)

With high school writers, Bret Freyer started with his primary research question, How does modeling of the questioning stage of the peer review process affect the way students question their classmates' writing? This led to several subquestions:

> What is the level of engagement in peers' writing?
>
> What types of questions do students write on their peers' writing?
>
> What type of questions do students voice about their peers' writing?
>
> How do we modify teaching strategies to model questioning better for students?
>
> What effects do peer editing sheets and questions have? Are they restrictive or helpful?

HOW TO **Refine a Research Question**

Start with four core principles:

1. Ask only real questions. Don't do research to confirm teaching practice you already believe is good or bad. Ask questions whose answers you are not sure about.
2. Avoid asking yes/no questions.
3. Eliminate jargon.
4. Avoid value-laden words or phrases.

For example, the question might begin as follows:

Do LD/ADHD students engage in meaningful discussions during literature circles?

The final answer to this question, a yes or no, won't get at key issues of how/why/when these students are involved in talk. There is also the sense that the researcher is setting out to prove a preconception—either he supports certain students being in these groups, or he doesn't.

First, change the research question so that it is open-ended:

What happens when LD/ADHD students engage in meaningful discussions during literature circles?

Next, underline any words that are jargon and rewrite them so that any reader could understand what you mean:

What happens when LD/ADHD students engage in meaningful discussions during literature circles?

The definitions of *LD* (learning disabled) and *ADHD* (attention deficit hyperactivity disorder) are debated even among educators and would likely be unknown to a lay reader. *Literature circle* refers to a specific curricular innovation that is defined differently among teachers.

The revised research question becomes

What happens when students identified with special needs engage in meaningful discussions during reading instruction?

While *identified with special needs* and *reading instruction* are much broader, they are terms anyone can understand, and they can still be defined more specifically in the actual study.

Finally, underline and change any value-laden words that would require explanation for readers:

What happens when students identified with special needs engage in meaningful discussions during reading instruction?

Part of the goal of this research will be to get at how the teacher and her students define *meaningful*. This word needs to be cut from your research question so that the values the researcher shares with her students, and the values that might divide the classroom community, can emerge from the study.

But it is a terrific exercise for any researcher to consider the ideals lying beneath value-laden words. When refining your research question, try to brainstorm on your own how you define words like *meaningful,* and also ask students to define what makes a literature discussion meaningful. By ferreting out value-laden words in your research question and subquestions, you can begin to get at your biases and preconceptions before the study begins.

The final refined research question becomes:

What happens when students identified with special needs engage in discussions during reading instruction?

Another important aspect of these teachers' research questions is the focus of the study—their students. Often, questions in the initial raw stage center on our work as teachers. High school teacher Denise Sega warns against falling into this trap when she tells the genesis of her own research question:

> When I began the work that led to my article "Reading and Writing about Our Lives," my original research question asked how *I* could motivate a group of uninterested students to learn. What could *I* do to help them achieve? However, as my work progressed, I realized that *I* was not the center of the study—the students were. This sparked the concept of collaboration, refocusing my reflection to see how we—the students and I—could discover a new way to learn together, rather than my deciding on a way to teach. It was this idea of collaboration that led to more meaningful research and discoveries than I ever would have found alone. (1997, 174)

Like Li's questions mentioned at the beginning of this chapter, your research questions may come from a glimpse of something out of the corner of your eye that intrigues you. They might burst forth from students who keep you up at night, observations that surprise you, tensions in your class, or from individual students that just plain mystify you. Here is a list of questions that teachers we know are pursuing:

> How can parents help set student goals and assess their child's growth?
>
> What are the patterns of engagement during group work in my math classes?
>
> What happens when Title I students are incorporated into regular classroom literacy groups?

How do reading response journals serve as a tool to help students become more thoughtful readers?

What happens when students use self-reflection in science as a means of assessing growth?

How does role playing affect first-grade writing?

How will home-school communication journals influence the student-parent-teacher collaboration?

What happens when I encourage Sheila to voice her opinions and insights?

How does math literature influence the oral and written communication of math concepts?

How can a child with severe physical impairments demonstrate reading ability? (special education with a child who is wheel-chair bound and cannot speak)

How does the use of storytelling help students connect to historical information?

What happens when I parallel a movement workshop to a writing/reading workshop?

What effect do the artwork and other artifacts posted on the walls of my middle school art room have on my students' art literacy?

In my two-way bilingual class, what happens to Spanish language usage by my "English experts" when they have focused Spanish lessons for English-only speakers?

In what ways might participation in deliberately designed rites of passage provide teenagers a clearer passage into adult life?

How does incorporating writing and art into science instruction affect female attitudes toward science?

How does self-esteem affect creative expression in writing groups?

What happens when choice and collaboration become an integral part of the fifth-grade science curriculum?

What are the changing attitudes of my students toward French language and culture as they acquire French as a second language?

What questions do my first-grade students ask one another during writing time?

These questions show that any curriculum, grade, or concept is open to exploration by teacher-researchers. What matters isn't how experienced you are—it's how willing you are to ponder questions with no easy answers.

RESEARCH WORKSHOP

Strategies for Working Toward a Research Question

JoAnn Portalupi

Two years ago, my nine-year-old son came home from school with an assignment to write a book report over the spring break. The weekend passed into Monday. Tuesday and Wednesday came and went before I finally decided to ask him about his plans for completing it. I wanted to gently remind him that he wouldn't write it out clean onto the final draft paper the teacher had given him but would want to draft it first and work to bring it to its final form. He glanced at me impatiently and replied, "Mom, this isn't writing workshop!"

It is a sunny morning in a first-grade classroom and the room buzzes with the noise of busy writers. Two boys decide to share their work with each other in the corner with the big stuffed pillows. I am interested in the kinds of response first graders give to one another. They agree to let me listen. Jonathan reads first his story about a visit to New York City. When he finishes, Brent says, "Good." He picks up his paper and begins to read about his cousin sleeping over during the weekend. When he finishes, Jonathan nods approvingly, picks up his story, and says, "Okay, my turn." Once again he reads about his New York visit. I leave a little later as Brent is starting in on the second reading of his story.

These are but two incidents among many that have caused me to wonder about the nature of work in classrooms and about the nature of learning in general. When my son remarked, "This isn't writing workshop!" I wondered why the process he practiced during that particular time of the school day was not something he sought to employ during other writing experiences. It caused me to speculate about my work as a staff developer. Had I been negligent about helping teachers see writing workshop as connected to the rest of the time spent in schools?

When I was listening to Jonathan and Brent, I was struck silly over the clash between my expectations for peer conferences and those of these first graders. It was clear they were getting the kind of "help" they had hoped to receive. I left the classroom wondering exactly what it is that first graders expect to get out of conferences with their friends?

Asking questions of our classrooms is as natural as breathing. Teachers who conduct classroom-based research turn those wonderings into research questions they can systematically pursue. Those who continue to incorporate research into their teaching know two things. They understand research to be an integral and energizing aspect of teaching. They have learned how to streamline their research questions so they fit into both the dailiness of teaching and into the long-term learning goals they hold for their students.

A colleague of mine hangs a sign on her classroom door: The first real step in learning is figuring out the question. For teachers wanting to do research, this is often the first struggle encountered. Framing the question can feel like a "chase in the dark" game. The teacher-researchers I've worked with over the years have expressed a wide range of response to this frustration. Some see too many questions to ask, yet when they try to single one out they find themselves holding a tangled knot of questions. Others wonder when the process of framing a question ever really ends. Just when they think they have the elusive thing pinned down, it shifts before their very eyes. Question posing can at times present a conundrum—many teachers report their ability to frame the question only after they get a glimpse at the answer. Nonetheless, the process of articulating a question is an important one. Not only does it initiate the research but it plays an important part in the research process itself.

There are a number of strategies you can use to guide yourself through the process of "figuring out the question." I'll explore some of these with attention toward helping you integrate your research and teaching.

Tap your available resources—your daily work and the wonderings that arise from it.   Though questions are informed by the theories we bring to our work—personal theories and theories we've read from others—they are most commonly born from our day-to-day experiences with students. Glenda Bissex (1987) writes that teacher research begins not with a hypothesis to test but more with a wondering to pursue. Begin by paying attention to these wonderings. Adopt your first research tool—a journal—where you can record the queries that arise during the day. Don't worry that they are always framed as questions. Include the things that surprise, concern, or delight you. After a week or two, go back and reread your jottings. Are there themes of interest that emerge?

List questions about the area of interest you discovered.   You'll probably find it easier to generate a list of related questions before writing one inclusive one. I have a general interest in how teachers learn to teach writing. In thinking about that broad question, I wrote a series of smaller questions. How does a teacher's own writing affect his or her teaching? How does a teacher's history of learning to write affect his or her development as a teacher? What do the shifts look like in teachers' thinking as they make pedagogic changes? What supports teachers' growth as they implement a new approach? What hinders? What kind of talk do teachers trade about the teaching of writing? How does it impact their daily actions? Why do some teachers make the shift to a process approach more easily than others?

Examine your list of generated questions.   In generating this list of questions, I'm careful that each one is genuine. I don't want to ask a question that leads me to document something I already know to be true. For instance, I can pretty much answer the question, What happens when a writing process approach is mandated in a school? My experience leads me to a fairly knowledgeable hunch about the answer. There is, however, much I can pursue about the topic. I am genuinely interested in understanding what conditions support teachers' implementation of a mandated approach.

I also want to read my questions to see if they can be answered. The best research questions often begin with the words *what* or *how*. *Why* questions ask you to trace the source of a phenomenon. You can develop a hypothesis as to why something occurs, but to conclusively identify the source is virtually impossible. By contrast, *what* and *how* questions lead you toward descriptions of phenomena. These are more easily documented and identified.

You can work with a *why* question to envision the *what* and *how* questions that compose it. Consider my question, Why do some teachers make the shift to a process approach more easily than others? This requires me to look at teachers who have made the shift. What specific changes have they had to make in their practices in order to do so? What problems do they encounter? How do they work through these problems? I may also want to look at teachers who have not made the shift. What factors contribute to their rejection of the approach? What do teachers say in defense of making change? If I can begin to describe the actual process teachers take either toward or away from a direction of change, I may be able to speculate about why some teachers make the shift and others do not. Then again, I may not. Regardless, I will have some interesting descriptions to inform my future work.

Force yourself to write a succinct* what *or* how *question. I've chosen this one: What are the stories teachers tell about their own experiences learning to write? I'm not sure the question is just right yet, but it points me in the direction I want to go. I want to explore the impact of a learning history on a teaching present. So I'm beginning small. This question allows me to start at a decisive point, gathering stories from a selected group of teachers. As they tell their stories, I suspect they will reflect on the meaning they bring today and the ways in which the stories affect their teaching. Beginning with a small focused question will often lead you toward a bigger one. The data I uncover from this question will likely lead me to understand other factors that have an effect on how teachers learn to teach writing.

Practice tunneling in on your question. Don Graves (1994) uses the term *tunneling* to describe the process of anticipating the kinds of data you will need in order to answer the question. This procedure can help you fit your question to the natural structures of your classroom.

One teacher-researcher phrased the question, What is the effect on student writers when their teachers publicly demonstrate their own literacy? In order to answer that question a series of smaller questions will need to be addressed. Notice how each of these questions is written in order to point exactly to the place she will look to gather the data.

What literacy demonstrations does the teacher present in the classroom? (This involves observing and recording visible acts of literacy.) What student perceptions exist about the teacher's use of writing? (You can get at this by talking with students. Some of this talk will naturally occur during writing conferences.)

What literacy acts do students engage in? (Again, this information can be collected through observation and gathering actual products. If you have the task of taking surveys on your class job chart, students can share the responsibility of documenting the kinds of reading and writing that occur throughout the day.)

This teacher will need to define for herself exactly what constitutes an act of literacy. Since she is looking at the effects on writers, not simply writing, she will also want to understand the ways in which students define literacy. This process of tunneling is another way to test the feasibility of pursuing the question. If it is difficult to see where the data to answer a question lie, then you can be fairly certain the question will be difficult, if not impossible, to pursue.

Be aware of the impact a research question will have on your students.   I remember Nancie Atwell sharing the effects her interest in journal writing had on her students' work. She describes the scene in September when she was eagerly writing notes of interest about the thinking students recorded in their reading journals. By June students were beckoning her with reading journal in hand: "C'mere. This is really interesting!"

Students will inevitably pay attention to whatever you're choosing to attend to. If you are looking at the way in which students are affected by a teacher's own literacy, you can be certain that your question will ensure they pay attention to that literacy. My question about the stories teachers tell is bound to orient a teacher toward the histories she brings to her teaching.

Think of your question as a grow light. When shined upon your students, you should see them flourish. Here is where the potential effect of teacher research on student learning is made most visible. Capitalize on it when you decide your area of inquiry. If you want to see improvement in peer conferences, ask a question that will allow both you and the students to pay attention to this aspect of the day. If you want more successful writing in science journals, shine the grow light in that direction. One teacher-researcher I know did just that with the questions, What kinds of writing do eight- and nine-year-olds write in science learning logs? and In what ways do their entries change when they are shared in large class-size groups and small response groups? Research should not be an appendage to your teaching. When carefully thought through, it can be a teaching strategy that helps you realize the learning goals you and the students have set for the year.

One way to ensure that your research supports such learning is to spend ample time in the process of question posing. Don't rush to state a question so your research can begin. Figuring out the question is an important part of the research. Once you've arrived with a question ready to pursue you will look back and see that you are already deeply involved in the work of conducting a classroom-based inquiry, one that will guide the learning of both you and your students.

featured **TEACHER RESEARCHER**

Real Magic: Trusting the Voice of a Young Learner

Susan Harris MacKay

In this case study of Eric, a kindergartner who speaks Vietnamese at home, Susan Harris MacKay shows how research questions serve as the impetus for a study but also evolve and change as the research continues. She starts with the simple question, What are the connections between home and school learning for Eric? A home visit produces new subquestions about Eric's family and learning: How must it feel to be ultimately responsible for a child enmeshed in a system totally foreign to you? How must it feel not to be able to ask any questions? What happens to your concern for the well-being of your child? Does it consume you, or do you have to let it go a little? Working with Eric in the classroom led to further questions about his language learning and traditional ways of teaching kindergartners.

I think good research questions are found in the unexpected. Only when I look back over my notes, lists, and questions do I begin to see the interesting patterns that help me form The Research Question. I certainly couldn't have known what Eric would teach me until after I had the opportunity to work with him. In fact, every time I try to set up questions beforehand, I seem to be distracted by questions I find more compelling as time goes on. What I thought would happen is always less interesting than what actually happened. This parallels everything I've learned about teaching, too. Good teacher research is exactly like good teaching. It requires careful listening, observing, and a good idea of where you want to go—combined with a focus on what is happening right now and a knowledge of how it all connects to what happened yesterday. Most important is the determination, in the midst of all this, to remain open to possibility.

I had never made a home visit before, and I was nervous about arriving unannounced. I was going to teach a kindergarten/first-grade multiage classroom, and I wanted Eric, a kindergartner in my classroom the year before, to continue with me into first grade. I walked slowly down the passage between the two short rows of dingy one-story apartments, while the bright, late August sun beat down.

I lack any ability at all to imagine the homes from which my students come. So it is at once unsettling and relieving for me to cross over into this other world that belongs solely to them. The tension caused by simply not knowing is relieved, but at the same time, it feels strange to find someone so familiar in a place so unfamiliar. In the classroom, we are so much entangled with each other's lives.

Eric's family lived behind the last door on the right, and so I knocked. Not realizing that the sun had blinded me, I was surprised when the door opened inward on complete blackness. I smiled, knowing whoever was there could see me, and tried to introduce myself when his familiar happy voice yelled, "Hi, Teacher!" I relaxed and was invited in.

My eyes adjusted to a small, dark apartment full of smiling, friendly people. Because none of them except Eric spoke any English at all, I was pulled and pushed into a chair, and patted and grinned and nodded at. I was hoping with all my heart that my six-year-old friend would be able to translate, as they all waited for me to explain the reason for my visit. Not knowing yet how I would explain the situation to them, I made small talk with Eric. I asked him about his summer vacation while I glanced around the living room. I saw the version of "The Important Book"—an idea I borrowed from Bobbi Fisher (1991)—that our class had written the previous year. Eric's page stated clearly, "The important thing about Eric is that he is Eric." Seeing this somehow bridged the gap a little for me between home and school. I felt more sure that Eric's family would support what I was there to propose to them.

Slowly and seriously, I gave small pieces of information to Eric and asked him to translate. It was very important to me that his family understand Eric would not be repeating kindergarten—that I would be his first-grade teacher. Without any discernible enthusiasm or concern, they quickly agreed. How must it feel, I wondered, to be ultimately responsible for a child enmeshed in a system totally foreign to you? How must it feel not to be able to ask any questions? What happens to your concern for the well-being of your child? Does it consume you, or do you have to let it go a little? I left Eric's house happy that I would be able to work with him for at least another year, and frustrated that I could not tell his family so.

Eric's immediate family consists of his grandmother, grandfather, and himself. They are Mien people. Eric's school registration form states that he was born in Thailand, in November 1988. His older brother has finished high school. Eric mentions him more this year than he did last year, but I have never met him. I have been told that Eric's parents are both dead, but I do not know the whole story. I keep hoping that someday Eric will be able to tell it to me.

Eric is one of the most energetic, wide-eyed little boys I have ever had the pleasure to know. Everything seems exciting and interesting to him—most especially, dinosaurs, sharks, the X-men, and recently, swordfish and frogs. The first notes I have about him are dated September of last year: "English is very limited." I had just been hired for my first full year of teaching, and my first responsibility as the kindergarten teacher was to assess all incoming students with the Early Screening Inventory (ESI). I was unprepared, but generally unconcerned, to meet a child who couldn't speak English. My first meeting with Eric only served to reconfirm my dislike and distrust of the ESI.

I wondered what would have happened to Eric if he had landed in the hands of a teacher who relied heavily on the scores of the Early Screening Inventory and set her expectations for children accordingly. I could have decided right then that Eric was "at risk." But I didn't. The ESI told me little enough about any of the children; but for a child who did not speak English, I was sure it could tell me nothing at all. I knew that Eric would be immersed in English in his new classroom. I would try never to separate language from context—never to isolate skills or drill him on anything. He would allow me the privilege, for the first time, to observe someone in the process of acquiring English as a second language.

I haven't been disappointed. Over the past year and a half, Eric has undergone a transformation. The once shy limited speaker of English has become one of the most dominant members of our classroom. He has proven himself to be a kind person, as well as a wonderfully independent and creative learner.

For me, Eric has come to represent all the reasons for student-centered, constructivist classrooms. My perception of his experience has made me less tolerant of teachers' resisting change. The more success Eric has, the less tolerant I become. What if Eric had been subjected to "letter of the week" activities and worksheets in kindergarten? What if Eric's teacher had spent twenty minutes or more of precious time drilling him daily on letter names and sounds out of context? Twenty minutes that he could have spent finding a reason to use language, and using it.

As early as November of last year, I noted that Eric was writing and sharing stories that he had written with the class. "I can't believe the growth this child has undergone—he writes and shares stories! He participates!" (11/28/94). The next day I noted that he was "making predictions during story reading." Eric was learning English and becoming literate. One of my favorite memories of Eric comes from a time last year in January, when I was reading *Millions of Cats* (Gag 1928) to the class for the second time. Eric's big, silver-toothed grin stretched wide across his face as he bounced on his knees and chanted along with me enthusiastically, "Hundreds of cats, thousands of cats, millions and billions and trillions of cats!" I remember being struck by his attempts to recite the whole book along with me, and his obvious pleasure in having at least mastered the repetitious lines. He was oblivious to the others around him. His world was the story and the story was his world in that precious moment.

A year later, there remain few stories about which Eric is unenthusiastic. And he is absolutely irrepressible about the rest. During shared reading, it is nearly impossible to keep him in his seat. He'll cry out, "Teacher! I notice something!" and almost without fail, my impending reprimand—the one that would implore him to wait his turn—is rendered soft with a look at the excitement in his face. He is bursting with ideas and observations that simply will not be contained. This year, he has become as excited about facts as about fiction, although the line between the two remains blurred (as it is always in first grade). In January of this year, while we were studying the water cycle, I happened to ask the class if anyone knew the word that meant water was being taken back into the air. Eric's immediate reply was a self-confident and emphatic, "Abracadabra!" Proof enough of this child's magic in the surest sense.

As I marvel over this incredible child who can turn a big, flat piece of cardboard into a pretty blue tractor for his classmates and him to ride in, and who can teach a younger child to apologize to another for unkind words, I can't help but wonder what it would take to strip this little boy of his powers. What if we concentrated for a moment on what Eric can't do— or at least by some standards, doesn't do very well. If we were to return to September of his kindergarten year, we would see a child who spoke no English, couldn't write his name, knew no letter names, and couldn't count with one-to-one correspondence. He was quiet and seemed reluctant to play with the other children except for the two Mien girls. He was not read to at home. His guardians spoke no English at all.

By midyear of first grade, Eric is only beginning to grasp letter-sound associations. He is only recently able to read a simple pattern book using one-to-one correspondence. His math computation skills are below grade level. He continues to confuse the pronouns "he" and "she," even with constant correction from the other students and occasionally from the teacher. He cannot seem to remember to put up his hand before he speaks. He tends to stutter.

I am frightened and saddened by how easily Eric is reduced to this list of deficits. I am angered by how difficult it is to find room in this list for Eric's fluent and elaborate ideas. For his sharp eyes and quick memory. For his intense interests, his independence, his creativity, his love of learning. For the responsibility he takes in doing his homework every night—checking a book out from our classroom library, doing his best to read it at home with no one to help him, writing in his journal about his favorite part, and showing it proudly to me every morning. For his concern the day the book had accidentally fallen out of his bag onto the classroom floor and he didn't know what had happened. For the time he built the set for the *Frog and Toad* puppet show—claiming his form of participation in the response to a book that was too hard for him yet to read but which his friends had read to him.

As his teacher, I can choose to kindle these flames or snuff them out—depending on the lens through which I choose to see him. As Herbert Kohl (1994) has said, "Any limit on expectations will become a limit on learning" (83). It is my responsibility to expect and hope the world for Eric, and I do. My very conscious decision has been to encourage everything I see he is capable of, and to provide an environment where he has the opportunity to discover for himself everything else he can do. There simply isn't room to see the things he can't do. Eric is proving to me, without question, that he knows what he needs as a learner better than I ever will. If I allow him the opportunity to show me what he needs, and I am prepared to *see,* he will share with me the things I need to be a good teacher.

Above all, I think, Eric is teaching me the importance of time. As I have witnessed his growth, I have learned to trust all the children I teach as competent proprietors of their own learning. This year, my palms have sweated and my heart has raced as I have tried to find balance in a Negotiated Classroom (Ingram and Worrall 1993). I have tried to find out what would happen if five-, six-, and seven-year-olds were given the responsibility to plan and organize the majority of their time at school. What would they choose to do? What would my role be? How flexible could I be in valuing different methods of "performance," or representations of learning? What I have learned from Eric is indicative of the whole process. One particular aspect of Eric's writing development provides a helpful illustration.

It has been obvious for some time that Eric values reading and writing. During our extended, twice-daily workshop times, Eric chooses writing first, almost without fail. At the end of kindergarten, I interviewed Eric about his developing literacy. I asked him how he learned to read, and he simply answered, "Try." He told me that he believed himself to be a capable reader and writer. More recently, when I asked him what his favorite part of school was, he said, "Writing, and reading to you." This year, Eric has worked hard to develop his concepts about print and phonological awareness. In the past month, the school ESL teacher asked Eric to tell her the sounds associated with the letters of the alphabet she had printed on a sheet. She mentioned to me how struck she was that Eric associated whole words to each letter, and not just isolated sounds. When she pointed to O, Eric said, "Cheeri-o's!" (This is a child who knows what letters are for!)

Although Eric has not been any more or less exposed to Wright Group pattern books than any other child in the class, he has been the only child to use those patterns consistently in his own writing. He used the pattern in *The Ghost* (Cowley 1990)—"I see the _____"—for many of his books early this year. Eric's pattern in his first few books, however, was written "I C the _____ ." It was a wonderful moment when I finally asked Eric to compare the pattern in *The Ghost* to his own book. I asked him to find the word *see* in *The Ghost* and then look at it in his version. In his face, I saw that flashing moment of disequilibrium of which learning is made, and he diligently went about the task of correcting his error throughout his book. If I had corrected it for him, would the moment he discovered his mistake have been as powerful?

Similarly, I wonder if his learning would have been any more or less efficient if I had told him to use these pattern books as models for his writing, or discouraged him from doing so. These patterns seem to be very important for him. On February 15, Eric wrote a story about taking a boat ride with me and some other kids, and having to kill a shark that attacked us. He first shared the book with me in its wordless state—five or six pages of his wonderfully elaborate drawings, which showed the progression in which we boarded the boat, the detail of his own "mad" face when the shark attacked, and the problem solved as Eric harpoons the shark. After drawing a harpoon in his picture, he pointed to it and asked me what it was called. When he finished telling me the story, he returned to the writing table to add the words. I was excited because, for the first time in a long while, Eric had not used a pattern to tell me this story.

A few minutes later, Eric brought me the finished product. He read, "Eric came to the boat. Ms. MacKay came to the boat. Tyler came to the boat. The shark came to the boat." I'm afraid I wasn't terribly successful at hiding my disappointment. "Eric," I said, "that's great, but what happened to all that cool stuff about how you were mad at the shark, and how does it end?" He looked at me seriously and said, "I need to write that." And I thought, "Well, good."

After lunch, Eric brought the revised edition to me. He had crammed a string of letters on the page where the shark appears, but when he tried to read it to me, he got stuck. In frustration, he erased them and rewrote new letters until it was impossible to see what was what. He wasn't nearly as pleased with this new version, and I was sorry. I had asked Eric to give me what *I* wanted, and it didn't work. Using those patterns had been extremely important to Eric. He wasn't ready to let go of them, and he knew it. But how easily he was persuaded to do what the teacher wanted him to do.

In early March, Eric broke out of the patterns on his own, with a book entitled "Fishing." It reads, "I didn't catch a fish. I caught a fish. I went home. I cooked it to eat." Now I see why those patterns were so important to him. They were giving him a foothold—allowing him a comfort zone. He knew exactly what he was doing. When I stepped in his way, I confused and frustrated him. But because he respected me and knew I cared for him, he was willing to do as I asked. It is possible that Eric broke out of the patterns because I had made that earlier nudge. But it is equally as possible that he would have done so on his own anyway.

As the teacher, I need to remain constantly aware of my opportunities to learn from the children I teach. In the kindest way possible, Eric has shown me the importance of being in control of and responsible for one's own learning. His face beamed at me as he held his rough draft high and announced, "I want to publish *this* book, Teacher!" He knew an accomplishment when he felt one, and I only needed to be there to congratulate him. Eric and the other children have shown me that my role is much larger and much different than to direct each and every child's learning through assignments. It is to provide the tools (such as pencils, mini-lessons, tape recorders, Legos, and handwriting practice) and the environment (both physical and social), demonstrations, expectations, time, and opportunity for engagement by loving each child enough for him/her to see themselves as members of the "club" (Frank Smith 1986)—as potential doers of literate activities. And then I need to step out of the way.

In February, I had the opportunity to return to Eric's home—this time with a translator. I wanted Eric to go through the testing process for the Talented and Gifted (TAG) program, and I needed his grandparents to sign the consent form. I was very excited about the opportunity to tell them, finally, how proud I was of Eric, and how much I enjoyed him. For a second time, I was received warmly into Eric's home. In the tiny, dark apartment, Eric's work still hung prominently on one wall. As the translator presented the TAG form to Eric's grandfather, and he agreed to sign, I was reminded that

Eric will be one of the first in his family ever to read and write. Eric's ancestors did not use written language. As I watched his grandfather give his signature, I could see that learning to use a pen came very late in life. It was a painfully arduous task. Shaky lines slowly formed the letters of his name.

We talked for half an hour about Eric and school. They were mostly pleased to know that he was a "good boy" and that he was staying out of trouble. They said they regretted that they could not help him with his homework, and I told them how impressed I was that he worked so hard on it. I had brought Eric's portfolio along with me and tried to encourage Eric to share it with them. Although he happily pulled out the photographs and shared those, he seemed reluctant to share his writing.

I was confused by this until I realized that the books and the writing weren't meaningful to them, except in the sense that they were Eric's, and Eric knew that. Why would he bother to translate his stories for his grandparents, when writing was not something they valued or used? Eric's grandparents made a point to share with me the importance they placed on Eric's understanding of and feeling good about "where he came from." And I could see, in the midst of all my excitement about Eric's success in my culture, their concern that he retain *theirs*. Humbled again by the experience of this child, I reconsidered my perspective.

It is easy for me to see why, as a teacher, I am responsible for respecting the voices of the children I teach. In order to hear those voices clearly, Eric and the other children have taught me, this year particularly as we practiced the art of negotiation, the importance of choice in the daily life of school. If I had made all, or even most, of the decisions for them, I would have denied them the opportunity to learn what it means to be responsible for their own learning. By implication, I would have taught them that their voices aren't important or right. Eric would have begun to learn that there is no way to reconcile the culture he was born into—which has given him his voice—with the culture in which he lives now. Forcing him to choose between the two would cause him to reject one, to live either on the fringe of American society or on the fringe of his own family.

It is difficult, but possible, to bridge this gap, and it is the responsibility of his teachers to help him learn how. Eric's polite refusal of my idea that he share his writing with his family in his home is, I think, evidence of beginning success. Eric will need to continue to be comfortable with and increase his ability to be critical of situations that impact cultural aspects of his family life, or face the risk of ostracism. He will also need to experience continued success in a classroom where his voice is valued. He will need to feel justified and comfortable in saying, as he did yesterday both gently and sincerely, when a fellow classmate started sharing a poem that sounded too much like a story, "Hey! That's not poetry!"

And if "poetry" is what we hope for all the children we teach, we will need to listen.

featured **TEACHER RESEARCHER**

Real Teachers Don't Always Succeed

Annie Keep-Barnes

Did you ever read any of those "Teacher as Savior" books? You know, the ones where the teacher meets the troubled learner, sees what needs to be done, and then in a nine-month span (often less) she saves him? Well, I read way too many. I came out of my undergraduate program with an imaginary S emblazoned on my chest. I was not just a teacher, I was a Special Ed teacher. I was going to fix kids. I've been teaching for eleven years. I should know better by now.

When I met Robert, a virtual nonreader/writer and victim of over-programmed instruction, I assumed that, armed with my understanding of language and my strong theoretical background, I would fix him. Well, the reading is finally happening, but writing looks like a long time coming.

His mother came in today. She called yesterday just before a staff meeting and said she had just found Robert's reading journal. "Ms. Keep-Barnes," she said, "I can't read this! Angie does better than this in first grade. What's my boy doing up there?"

She blew into my room armed and dangerous. "Ms. Keep-Barnes, what has my boy been pulling on you?"

I smiled, although inside I was sick. This wasn't just any child; this was a child I have taught in special education for almost three years. Not only that, this was a child I agonized over and read books over and watched and studied. This was a child I loved. This was my glorious failure.

"He hasn't been pulling anything on me."

"Oh, Ms. Keep-Barnes," she cried. "I know my boy. He can do better than this! He's a smart boy. My boy has you exactly where he wants you. 'Oh, Ms. Keep-Barnes,' he says. 'I just love her.' You're so sweet to him. When we go shopping, he'll see some pretty flowers and say, 'Mama, I want to get those for Ms. Keep-Barnes.' He's got you exactly where he wants you."

"Do you think I'm too easy on him?"

"Yes! I do. My boy should be doing better than this. I guess I'll just have to do it myself. I'll need to make a new strategy."

"Mrs. Johnson, I'm not too easy on Robert. I know he can't spell. I've been beating myself over the head for three years. I teach him strategies. When I'm hanging right over him, he does very well. When I turn away, I can't read what he's written. I believe that writing is for communication. I give it back to him and say, 'I can't read this. Write it over.' You saw that in his journal. I'd write, 'Robert, I can't read this.' When he turns in a paper that's indecipherable, I say 'Now, rewrite it so I can read it.'"

"Well, I know my boy. He's lazy."

"I'm not going to disagree with you. I feel that sometimes he just can't be bothered, but he also has a lot of trouble understanding written language. I don't know why it's so hard for him, but he has a huge struggle. Robert has a learning disability."

"He's lazy and he's got you just where he wants you. He thinks you've got this little soft heart and he won't have to try."

I was fascinated at this portrait of me with the little soft heart. I do love my students, but I can't believe that I have ever not expected things of them because I was "soft." Which of course, is the bottom line here. If I wasn't such a soft, undemanding teacher, Robert would be fixed.

In eleven years of teaching special education, I can count on one hand the number of kids that I've taught who were truly learning disabled in reading and writing. Usually, I explain to parents that a child qualifies as learning disabled if there is a significant difference between aptitude and achievement. But generally, I see it as a developmental issue or poor instruction or something else rather than assuming the child is neurologically impaired. Most kids have been behind or confused or slow. Very seldom have I come across a child who is completely perplexed by print. Robert is one of them.

I have clung tenaciously to my understanding of the developmental nature of language. Fragmented print never crossed his path, while graphophonemic, syntactic, and semantic strategies were religiously coached, in balance and in the context of real reading events. His retellings have been supported and his responses respected. I have helped him in his writing, encouraging fluency while following his leads in ideas, celebrating meaning while suggesting strategies to use while spelling. When he failed to meet his communicative intent, he was advised to rethink and revise.

His reading has improved, although nothing miraculous has occurred. As a matter of fact, the first story I was going to tell you is one of simple patient victory. How after nearly three years, he is finally reading—tentatively, with fear, but still reading. Though wildly overpredictive, he catches himself eventually. When I read aloud, he can follow along. He takes his turn in a partner situation and can sneak into the back of the room and read into a tape recorder, finally staying engaged for the entire Silent Sustained Reading period. He's going to be okay.

I wish I could say the same for writing. In almost three years of process writing instruction, he still can't spell. He'll sit down and write madly for fifteen minutes. I'll come by and look at what he's written and, except for a very few high-frequency words, be completely unable to reread what he's written. When I ask him to read what he has written, he will confidently rattle off something, yet what he says does not match what he has written, not graphically, not even structurally. I ask him to point while he reads. He can't do it. He has no idea what those words on the page are.

A few weeks ago, we had a spelling bee in the school. It's something that must be endured. The kids like it, but I hate it, for it seems that spelling is always harder when done out loud. After all, spelling is for writing, not for speaking. Robert entered. I was sick. Here this boy, who is such a problem speller, is going to go up in front of the school and embarrass himself.

The students were getting knocked out right and left. As many as ten sat down in succession in the first round. It was Robert's turn. The word was *numeral.* He started in: "Numeral. N, u, m, e, r . . . , numeral." Good grief! He was so close! He could never come that close in writing. What could it mean? It should be easier to spell when you can see the writing on the page. That's why spelling develops along with reading, right?

So, I did an experiment. I extracted words he had spelled from his writing and I dictated to him one word at a time and had him spell them orally as I wrote them down:

First Spelling	Oral Spelling	Actual Spelling
cald	calld	called
thed	shuod	should
alled	old	old
aet	out	out
sand	soud	sound
cand	came	came
sade	sead	said
nane	name	name
salva	slave	slave
at	that	that
akict	asx	ask
sater	streg	strange
hes	his	his
hin	him	him

Over half the words he spelled correctly. The other half had much greater similarity to the actual spelling.

Somehow, his auditory channel is stronger than his visual. This confirms my suspicion that if he just slowed down and vocalized, he might be able to communicate better. Or, if he went back over every draft and labored out the spelling once he got his thoughts down, his drafts would make more sense.

I have been asking him for over a year to vocalize when he spells. I see the first graders doing this all the time. They're writing and talking continually. I feel this is important for him. He says the other kids will laugh at him, that I don't know what it's like. I say I've never seen him try.

Which brings me to this. Why hasn't he been trying? His mother says she knows her child and that he's lazy. Well, I think she's right. Special educators always see that as the first line of accusation from teachers and parents, "This kid would be doing more if he (or she) weren't so lazy." This assumes the child is to blame for failure. I have always looked elsewhere. It's too easy to say that and then not assume any responsibility. This is not my way.

And perhaps this, too, is my failing. This child has not taken responsibility for his learning. I cannot make him vocalize. I cannot put his eyes to the printed page. All I can do is provide the context where these things happen. And he really is lazy; I have to admit, sometimes kids are lazy. Instead of accusing him of laziness, I have focused very closely on making sure that every writing act was enjoyable, that he not become frustrated. My belief has been that when it does finally happen for him, he'll understand that literate acts are positive, fulfilling experiences, not a chore that needs to be endured.

But should I have pressured more? Should I have told him early on that it was his life and I was there to help, but that he needs to choose his level of commitment? I think so. It has been his responsibility all along, but I never wanted him to hate the written word by applying too much pressure.

I've been successful. He said only last Friday that he wants to be a writer when he grows up. I tried to help him celebrate the writer within, even when I couldn't see it on the page. The problem is, I still can't see it.

This isn't so much Robert's story as it is mine. Mrs. Johnson said to me, "You've got a job. You'll be here next year and next. But my boy, he's got no time. Every year matters."

I know that. I do understand her panic. Yet I want to ask her why she just noticed. Haven't I sent her updates on his progress and samples of his work? Haven't I begged her to read and write with him at home?

Yet in her eyes, his failure is my fault alone. If I were a better teacher or less "soft-hearted," he would not be such a failure. And truthfully, my self-esteem as a teacher is tied up with his success. I want him to succeed not just for him, but for me as well. And I feel like a failure.

When she left, I wanted to lay my head on my desk and cry, but I had a ten-year-old friend waiting for a ride, so I swallowed the lump in my throat and left the school. I feel like crying now as I write this, because I'm scared I did blow it for this boy who has so little time. Do kids leave school illiterate even when someone has done all she could imagine to prevent it? Should I leave my job so someone else can try with him before he goes on to junior high? If I can't teach him, shouldn't I find someone who can?

I have failed. I failed Robert not by neglecting his learning needs, but by not trying harder to connect with his family. I've known from the start that this child was one of the truly disabled. Since I inherited him having been in special education for three years, I assumed they knew. I should have looked them in the eye the first time I met them and said, "Your son has a serious problem. I cannot help him on my own. You must be committed to reading with him every night, to writing with him daily. You must be responsible for looking over his work." While I advised these things regularly, I did not really tell them straight out. Perhaps I enabled their denial and ultimately brought this down upon myself.

And I failed Robert by not making it more clear to him that it was up to him to try. I mean really try. It's important to keep learning stress-free, but it is equally important to know how to gauge and engage a child's commitment.

Since my meeting with Mrs. Johnson, it looks like Robert has shaped up somewhat. He is taking more care in writing. He's trying to make his writing resemble words more closely, if not grapho-phonemically, then at least in spacing and neatness. This actually helps a great deal in understanding what he is trying to say. He will go back over his drafts and vocalize to closer approximate spellings once he's got the ideas down. All this progress toward personal ownership.

As for Mrs. Johnson, she did not come in for conferences; I guess she'd said all she wanted. None of the notes I've sent home have been responded to in any way. We had a very important celebration last Friday for my troubled learners who have mastered the multiplication table. I planned to take the five boys dog mushing, something they'd never done. Robert was one who was scheduled to come. His mother did not bring him although she promised him she would and he wanted desperately to go. That, too, is part of his problem.

I'm muddling through this so you may help me find what it means. As I examine the idea of moving on to give him a chance with someone else, I realize that I still have ideas for him. There are visible cornerstones upon which to build. I want to keep trying.

I need to see my encounter with his mother as a blessing. It is not an easy thing to have someone think you have let another down, especially when the life of a child is at stake. I'm hurt. That's me, however, and my pain is nothing compared to hers and the knowledge that her child is at risk for failure in life if he cannot become literate. And hers is nothing to the anger and disappointment that Robert must feel now and will feel forever if the two of us do not help him.

As I said before, this is not the story I set out to tell. I was delighted with Robert's growth as a reader and wanted to share that with you; but reading in school is only part of becoming literate and I was tempted to tell you a partial truth. A more complete truth is that I have succeeded as well as failed with this child. And yet, by examining my failure, I find ideas. So, I submit this to you as a report and proposal. I am asking now:

How can I help this boy take responsibility for his learning?

What is motivation for the chronically unmotivated?

How can I work as an ally with his mother rather than as an adversary?

How will Robert learn to fit his ideas into the standard lexicon?

I'm not superteacher and he's not superstudent, and she's not supermom, but we're all this boy has. I'd like to have been the one who saved him—that was part of the fantasy. But this is the real world; real teachers keep trying.

Research Plans

3

Walk around feeling like a leaf.

Know that you could tumble any second.

Then decide what to do with your time.

Naomi Shihab Nye

It may be true that the best-laid plans often go awry. But without any plan at all, it's unlikely you'll complete your research study. Naomi Shihab Nye's thoughts about time capture our vulnerability in the classroom. Research is a fragile enterprise, easily disrupted by our needs and those of our students. The research plan is a kind of backbone for your study—a skeletal frame on which to hang all your emerging thoughts about your research question, data collection, and how you might sustain your research. When it feels like your research is falling apart, a glance back at your original design can be the glue that holds your work together. A plan, like writer Annie Dillard's schedule, is "a net for catching days."

Teacher-researchers we work with swear by the power of a research brief—a detailed outline completed before the research study begins. In designing a research brief, researchers work their way through a series of questions to develop a plan for their study. The brief often includes these topics, derived through these questions:

Research Brief Guidelines

Research purpose	Why do I want to study this?
Research question	What do I want to study? What subquestions do I have?
Data collection	How will I collect data?
Data analysis	How will I analyze my data?
Time line	When will I complete the different phases of my study?

| Support | Who will help me sustain this project? |
| Permissions | What permissions do I need to collect? Are there ethical issues to consider? |

It takes time to develop a strong research plan. Many teachers we've worked with keep a journal or notes for weeks or months, highlighting emerging questions or issues before they begin to draft a research plan. They might test out a data collection strategy or two, tape recording a few discussion groups or taking notes during a science activity to rev up for generating a research brief. We've found summer is often the best time for teachers to develop a full-scale research plan. Teachers can be too immersed in the back-to-school rush in September to think through all the logistics of gathering and analyzing data.

The following research plans by teachers at the elementary, secondary, and college levels show the range of ways you can develop a plan. You might be surprised at how unique each plan is. Even though researchers are working with common headings and steps, their interests and personalities shine through.

Drawing a Fish Tail: Patrice Turner's Research Plan

While the plan is a blueprint for your research, it's important to realize that your plan will change as you begin your research and discover what works and what doesn't. That was exactly the case for Patrice Turner, a kindergarten teacher who studied kindergartners during writing time. Figure 3.1 shows the research brief she wrote in the summer before the school year began.

In October, six weeks into the research process, Patrice took the time to reflect upon her original plan. She discovered that her plan, and her view of herself as a researcher, had changed:

> Planning to do research in my kindergarten classroom was exciting and fun, but I found myself getting really nervous as the new school year approached. I have taught for twelve years but have never been a teacher-researcher before. The label scared me at first, but the thought of actually doing research in my room was even scarier. Even though I had my research design, my notebook, and my special pen, I was shaking in my new school shoes!
>
> In the first few weeks I discovered some great surprises and some new beliefs about my research. One wonderful surprise was the excitement that Jeanne, our kindergarten aide, had when she read my research brief. She literally got goose bumps. I was thrilled to have discovered an unexpected research partner.
>
> I had planned to use tape recorders and clipboards to collect data on questions children ask each other during writing time. I didn't really know

Figure 3.1

PATRICE TURNER'S RESEARCH PLAN

Research Purpose

As a kindergarten teacher, I am intrigued by the process young children go through as they begin to write. I am curious about their needs as writers and what they want to know about beginning writing. I hope that through this research I can discover more of what they need and immediately begin to offer mini-lessons to help satisfy that need, so the children will feel more confident as we work through the process of writing together. I also hope to encourage and model the importance of asking questions to learn from one another.

Research Question

What questions do my kindergartners ask one another during writing time?

Subquestions

Do certain children ask more questions than others?

Do certain children get asked more than others?

Does gender play a part? Do girls or boys ask more questions?

Are more questions asked directly to another student or open to anyone at the table?

Do children direct certain questions at some children and other questions at other children?

Are there children who never ask questions?

Are any children ignored when asking a question?

Do children give examples when they answer a question?

Do the questions change over time?

I have a lot of subquestions (maybe far too many), but I am hoping I can manage them. If I find I can't, I will simply let a question or two go. The data should be very explicit, so I should be able to answer many of my questions by doing a lot of tallying.

Data Collection

- I will tape the children at the writing table once a week for about twenty minutes. Because of the placement of outlets in my room, I will need to keep the tape recorder at one table. I will keep track of the children I tape, and tape a wide range of children. If things go smoothly, I certainly can increase the number of times I tape the children. I plan to do this throughout the school year.
- I will try hard to keep a teacher journal and do some notetaking.

- I may even attempt a little video recording during writing.
- I will survey the children with a brief interview later in the year. I am thinking about January, because we will have had more exposure to writing by then. An example of the survey follows:

  Do you ever ask other people at your writing table questions?

  What do you ask for help with? or What kinds of questions do you ask? (I need to decide between the two, but I'm leaning toward the second one.)

  Who do you ask for help?

  Do people ask you questions?

  Do you like to ask questions?

  Do you like to answer questions?

  The last two questions are not a part of my research, but I'm curious. I could make them into yet another subquestion.
- I may try to have an adult/teacher/principal come in to take notes on any questions that the children ask one another during writing time. I wonder, though, whether or not an adult will influence their questioning. Will the children ask the adult more questions than each other?

Possible Codes for Types of Questions

Ideas

Illustrations

Letter formation

Sounds

Punctuation

Capital letters

Spaces

Left to right

Direct/Open

I will need to revisit these after two or three weeks.

Data Analysis

- I plan to listen to the tapes at home where it is quiet and I can focus on listening while relaxing. I have a small room at my house with the computer and a day bed. I have found that I do the majority of my reading and writing for my courses in this room. I feel very comfortable picturing myself listening to the tapes in the evenings. I think this can easily become a ritual without interrupting my school or family life. I plan to listen to the tapes on a weekly basis. I will transcribe the questions asked on the tapes and tally them.
- I plan to read over my teacher journal on the same night I listen to the tape.
- I plan to create a sociogram each quarter. I will focus on who asked questions of whom.

Tentative Time Line

September

- Talk to principal.
- Send permission slips home.
- Explain to kiddos what I'm doing.
- Model asking questions in mini-lessons.
- Discuss with children the importance of asking questions and learning from one another.
- Start taping the very first week (even if they're just drawing at the writing table, it will be considered writing).

Two or Three Weeks into Research

- Revisit list of potential codes.

September–May

- Continue to tape once a week or more, transcribe and analyze the tapes, and cook my teacher journal entries.

Twice a Month

- Meet with my inquiry group at Timberhouse [a local restaurant].

November

- I will share my research process with the parents during conferences.
- I may share my research process at a kindergarten meeting.

January

- I will share my midpoint findings with my inquiry group.

Reflections Before Beginning

I think this is do-able. I feel focused and ready. I'm ready for the learning that will go with this project: the unexpected, the questioning, the thrills, the letdowns (what if they don't ask questions?). I will seek help and encouragement. I am excited about the insight I will gain as I analyze my data. As I discover patterns, I can adapt my teaching to the needs I have discovered.

what to expect at all. I was standing there thinking about what was going to happen, and the kids started right in asking questions as they worked. Jeanne and I each grabbed paper from the recycle box because it was the closest paper. In my excitement I folded my paper crookedly and had no sturdy backing to write on as I recorded my first piece of data: one of my students looking up at me so seriously and asking, "Do you know how to draw a fish tail?"

Jeanne and I were like two buzzing bees. We recorded questions that the children asked one another and wrote down who was asking whom. I had planned to be so neat, serious, and very professional with my work. Well, that crooked paper worked just fine, and I didn't have time to be really professional about it. It was all in a rush, and I was almost frazzled, but in an exciting way. These emotions just weren't in my original plans.

I discovered, too, that I was not going to make my kids do things just for my research. My kindergarten program comes first, although I hope my research will help me improve my program. With that in mind, I relaxed a little about my informal collecting of data. This made the research more fun for me, and Jeanne and I could get the bigger picture by watching and scripting, instead of using the tape recorder.

Being a teacher-researcher is more enjoyable and less stressful than I thought. I also find that I am more involved in the process than I thought I was going to be. Taking pressure off myself about what I thought I should be has paved the way for a more meaningful experience.

And, by the way, Ronnie and I made an awesome fish tail together!

Patrice had to let go of the formality of her original plan in order to be comfortable in her research. But she was able to gather a surprising amount of data right from the start of the year because she had a clear focus and a research partner as eager as she was to learn from the children.

Patrice also gave herself permission to find her own style and rhythms as a researcher. She knew she was trying on the cloak of teacher-researcher at the start of the year, wondering if it would be as comfortable as those new school shoes. It was a fit because Patrice allowed the research to be a wedding of her questions, her research partner's questions, and the needs of the children. Dewey's (1938) ideas about planning research from decades ago echo in Patrice's work: "The plan, in other words, is a cooperative enterprise, not a dictation. The teacher's suggestion is not a mold for a cast-iron result, but is a starting point to be developed into a plan through contributions from the experience of all engaged in the learning process. The essential point is that the purpose grow and take shape through the process of social intelligence" (72).

Like Patrice, all teacher-researchers work through issues of how their research fits in the classroom and how they will balance their research and teaching responsibilities. Research is a mold with a shifting form—and it is the social relationships in the class that will teach you how your plans need to change.

The Bridge Between Our Strokes and Our Soul: Andie Cunningham's Research Plan

Grappling with curriculum change can be difficult and soul-searching work. Physical movement teacher Andie Cunningham found her research design (see Figure 3.2) was a format to help her examine and frame her changes in practice and to make plans to document her process as well as her students:

> For me, my work is a combination of my self and my soul, the professional and personal parts of thirty-five years and a lot of gray hair. This project is truly an extension of me into my professional world. As I worked on my research brief, struggling until I reached tears and sobs at my computer, I saw connections that I've been afraid of questioning, pushing back subconsciously for a long time. I want to be fair and hear each individual, and I want my classroom to be a safe place for everyone who enters the door. I have worked consciously for that to be true, and have probably been successful on many levels. But I keep an arm's distance from many of my middle school students. It's been a safety net. I can't do that now if I really want voice and choice in my room, because the voices will be alive in here, and I will need to see, hear, and feel what's going on if all goes right.

Working through the issues of her plan required Andie to work through problems in her teaching. Her reworking involved both changing curriculum and thinking through relationships with students.

Andie's research plan is not a dry, distant recitation like a grocery list, but a melding of mind and heart, intellect and affect. In tandem with the drafting and revising of her research brief, she wrote and revised a poem describing her process:

> I reach the island tired,
> floppy from my journey of swimming through
> hard swells,
> the old, the was.
> I lay, breathing deep gulps,
> feeling the muscle I've gained from the
> treacherous trip,
> inside
> my heart banging as it
> sings and wails.
>
> I look into the blue sky,
> the bird flies by,
> and I watch it soar.
> I stay.
> Knowing I can.
> Voices echo beside me
> leaning in to hear, leaning out to learn
> we discover the bridge between
> our strokes and our souls.

In planning to do research, Andie learned that her actions as a researcher and teacher (her "strokes") are always entwined with who she is as a person (her soul)—what she believes, values, and desires for her students and

Figure 3.2

ANDIE CUNNINGHAM'S RESEARCH PLAN

Purpose

I want to discover the living impact of student voice and choice in a movement workshop. Similar to Linda Rief and her reading/writing workshops, I want my students to make decisions about their movements in and out of my classes. I also want to discover what my students truly know, and how I can guide them to discover what movements are valuable to them. I am curious to identify pertinent assessment components that I believe we as an industry in physical movement are overlooking. I want to discover a realistic method for documenting student growth in movement other than existing skills testing and fitness testing. Peer and self-assessments coupled with teacher- as well as teacher-and-student-generated scoring guides can be excellent, useful tools, but what more can there be? Will a movement workshop invite students to develop and demonstrate their movement expertise? Will my students feel safe enough to risk beyond their current demonstrated work? Can I become an artist of assessing movement and develop a more effective way to record and interpret the knowledge of physical movement students possess and demonstrate?

Question

What happens when I parallel a movement workshop to a writing/reading workshop?

Subquestions

What will work and what won't?

How can I invite students to work at the edge of their confidence?

What impact will a movement workshop have on my assessment process and ideals?

What will happen to student learnings and the method of conveying that information?

Will the students eventually be able to ask their own questions in this process?

How can I help my students organize strategies without limiting them?

In what ways can I more effectively invite my students to play?

Current Workshop Design Ideas

- Use both classes in one week for the workshop. Students will have a variety of equipment available for their use. Discuss the one or two teacher-designed questions with students; students will respond to one in drawn or written form. A scoring guide will be used to score the assignment, and will be posted for student viewing. Students and teacher will score student work on the scoring guide.
- In the current twice-a-week forty-five-minute-or-less classes, I can guide for the first fifteen minutes, then have the students explore for the next ten in a self-directed way, and then share for the last ten minutes.

Data Collection and Note Cooking

With my current schedule of having each class twice a week, I will plan a week of movement workshops once a month, with a total of up to eight sessions per trimester. I will continue with my refined notetaking method, including what I see and what they say. Student opinions and suggestions as well as my ideas and educated guesses will continue to impact my scoring guides for written and drawn assessment. I will gather the same three to five students' work from each workshop and note my impressions of content, demonstrated student work, and creativity. I will also compare their response work with their videotaped physical demonstrations and audiotaped interviews. I will attempt to identify patterns in their written/drawn responses that indicate learning, growth, or setbacks. I will experiment with the category chart from my cooked notes to discover impacts on my assessment for classes.

Possible Student-Response Questions for Movement Workshop

When you play, what do you create?
What did you learn when you played?
What did you learn when you worked?
What did our work/play remind you of?
What problems did you discover in your play today?
What is necessary for you to be invited to play?

I will teach a lesson and then ask them for questions. Post the list in class and work/play to discover the answers. Do my kids feel like their attempts make sense and that they are all capable thinkers and movers?

Support

My writing group/teacher research group

Brynna, if I am doing this for an independent study and maybe even if I'm not

Rosemary—I will use her rarely, but would like someone to brainstorm with around the world of assessment

Laurie

Sheila—physical movement teacher in Colorado—maybe

Writing in my "cooked notes"

Audience

Me—to inform my teaching
Physical educators

Books to Explore

Teresa Benzwie. *A moving experience: Dance for lovers of children and the child within.*
Robert Cohan. *The dance workshop: A guide to the fundamentals of movement.*
Naomi Epel. *Writers dreaming.*

Anne Green Gilbert. *Creative dance for all ages.*
Martha Graham. *Blood memory.*
Ruth Hubbard. *Workshop of the possible.*
Langston Hughes. *The book of rhythms.*
Vera John-Steiner. *Notebooks of the mind.*
Stephen Nachmanovitch. *Free play.*
Linda Rief. *Seeking diversity.*
Gabrielle Roth. *Sweat your prayers.*
Jennifer Donohue Zakkai. *Dance as a way of knowing.*

English Journal
National Association of Sport and Physical Education. *Moving into the future.*
National standards for physical education: A guide to assessment and content.

herself. Her list of books to explore will help to inform her as she adapts her curriculum and the structure of her movement classes.

Not all research briefs include lists of books to read, as Andie's does. For some researchers, this additional reading is integral to the research process. But for others, the main "texts" read in their work will be observations of students and artifacts collected—field notes, audiotapes, and work samples.

Reflections on Reflection: Wally Alexander's Research Plan

Research at the college level involves different constraints and opportunities than research in elementary or secondary classrooms. Professors work with students over a shorter period of time, and there are even more concerns about ensuring that the research be a natural fit with the goals of the course. But at the same time, research at the college level can focus and energize teaching. That was the case with Wally Alexander, as he used his research to question some basic assumptions about the role of reflection in learning (see Figure 3.3).

Wally had a keen sense of the ethical issues inherent in this study. He wanted to enlist his students as co-researchers. At the same time, he realized that young adults who are "adept at playing the game" might feel coerced to participate, or give answers they thought would please him rather than being honest. Because he had a detailed plan, he was able to think through these issues in advance and consider a range of strategies for dealing with his concerns.

Figure 3.3

WALLACE ALEXANDER'S RESEARCH PLAN

Purpose

Self-reflection is critical to the learning process. It is important that we can relate our work to that of others, and that we can connect it to what we did yesterday, and see possibilities as to where it may take us in the future. All of this depends on our ability to step back from our work constantly, look at it carefully, and assess and refine it, gleaning new insights about ourselves as learners in the process. Self-reflection is fundamental to authentic assessment, yet this vital element is largely overlooked in most classrooms.

Considering the important role reflection plays in learning, it seems that development of reflective behaviors should be a goal of our work with undergraduate students aspiring to teach. Becoming more aware of what reflective practices students bring with them and determining what activities promote self-reflection are among my goals for this study.

Assumptions

- These students are reluctant to believe their thoughts will actually be valued. Why? Where did this come from? Issues of trust?
- Different events are paradigm breakers for different people. Gender may be an issue. People jump aboard at different times.

Research Questions

What happens to undergraduate education students when they engage in self-reflection activities that are valued?

Subquestions

What are their past experiences with self-reflection?

How do they define self-reflection?

Are they reluctant to believe that their reflective thoughts will be valued? If so, why?

Do they see self-reflection as important to learning?

Can we identify "ah-ha" moments when the value of reflective behaviors becomes self-realized?

What can we learn from students who value self-reflection and already have self-reflective behaviors?

Data Collection

Survey of baseline data: where are they starting from?

This survey will try to identify reflective behaviors in these students. I'd like to do this at the beginning of week 2. The survey will be completed in class. Compiled results will be shared. Possible survey questions include:

How are you more comfortable with grading? Grading self? Teacher grades? Combination?

Are there people you use as a sounding board? Who?

How do you feel about revising your writing?

Do you ask for feedback on your work?

Do you talk over your plans with others?

Do you discuss schoolwork with classmates or friends?

Do you carry on conversations with yourself about your work?

How do you get good (better) at something?

What does self-reflection mean to you?

When you complete a project, do you think about what went well with it, and/or what you would change if you had it to do over again?

Observational notes of students during "shining moments" activity
This is a very reflective activity that we'll probably do on the second day of class. Observer notes might produce more baseline data (maybe an observer in the back of the room?).

Weekly reflective responses from students
- I'll keep copies.
- Responses will be analyzed for evidence of presence/evolution/valuing of reflective behaviors.
- Responses will be analyzed for evidence of "ah-ha" moments.

Notes from reflective assessment conferences—midterm and final
- Main topics for conferences will be brainstormed with the class.
- Students will be prepared with written notes, which I'll keep or copy.

Reflective free-writes (periodic)
- I'll keep copies for analysis and coding.

My anecdotal notes from observing cooperative teams at work and other activities
- Possibly their notes too, which I'll copy.

Interviews with students who value self-reflection and already have self-reflective behaviors
- Students who appear to have effective self-reflective behaviors will be interviewed to attempt to find out how they got where they are.
- Protocol for interview will be open-ended, aimed at getting *their* story.

Data Analysis
- Compile and code survey results.
- Code anecdotal notes, weekly student reflective responses, and reflective free-writes, looking for trends, evidence of reflective behaviors, and changes in students' perspectives on the value and usefulness of self-reflection.
- Compile and code assessment conference notes (mine and students').
- Compile and code interview results.

Time Line

Week 2 of Class (mid-September)

- Survey and discussion of project with class.
- Compile survey results.
- Permission/releases.

Late September

- Code notes from "shining moments" and survey results.

October

- Begin analyzing student weekly responses, anecdotal notes, and free-writes.
- Midterm assessment conferences.

November

- Analysis of information from conferences.
- Continue coding weekly responses, anecdotal notes, and free-writes.

December

- Final assessment conference.
- Work on final analysis.

Semester Break

- Write.

Support/Collaboration

- Bimonthly meeting and frequent e-mail with Julie, Patrice, and other members of our newly established, as yet unnamed, teacher research network.
- Connect with XTAR, the teacher research e-mail discussion group.
- Semiregular meetings with Kelly [another college instructor and potential collaborator] to plan, analyze data, and write.

Issues I'm Struggling With

- How and when do I inform the students about this project? I'd like them to know what I'm doing and why, but I don't want them to artificially become self-reflective because that's what I'm looking for. Undergrads are very good at playing the game. This question really has me stumped at the moment. Maybe it isn't a big deal. They'll soon know what I value anyway. Even as I'm writing this, I'm thinking that I need to share my question with them.
- Can I enlist them in notetaking in their cooperative teams?
- When do I get permissions/releases? If I fill them in early, could I ask for blanket releases?
- More work is needed on identification of reflective behaviors.
- What will be the best format for initial survey?
- What in my data is going to show presence/evolution/valuing of reflective behaviors?

Permissions and Ethical Issues

Wally confronted the subtleties of ethical issues right in his research brief. The ethical issues inherent in your study will become apparent when you begin to plan your study and think about getting permission to do your research.

As you make your plans to do research, you will need to think about permissions and notifications. As a rule, we encourage all teachers to get signed permission forms from parents of students involved in their research, or from the students themselves if they are over eighteen years old. Even if your research doesn't involve any data collection or work on the students' part outside of normal classroom expectations, it's still helpful to let parents know what you are studying in the classroom. It also helps give parents a different perspective on what teaching is, and how much of it involves understanding and analyzing students as they work.

Even when you use pseudonyms for your students, there are ethical issues involved in writing about children's actions. Karen Gallas wrestled with this when she wrote about the themes of power and gender in her classroom:

> Well, there's always issues when I write about children who are doing things that could be hurtful to other kids. I have to think hard about, "How do I write about these children?"—children who I don't want to present as bad people, because they aren't bad people. The ethical issue for me there is accurately presenting them from a number of dimensions. Their behavior should be seen within the context of their whole way of acting in the world rather than just isolating this one thing and saying "Look at what this child did here!" and assigning it "X, Y, or Z." So, when I'm writing about unpleasant things, I feel it is my obligation to find ways to present children as part of a larger picture.
>
> I have to say, I wonder if this is going to come back at me. Especially with my "bad boy" work. You can imagine the parents who had those little boys. They know who I'm writing about. But what I tried to do was to create a broader picture of both the child and the behavior. So they could see their child in all his glory as well as his . . . struggle. So that's the trick. So far, those parents know their children and they've appreciated those descriptions. (quoted in MacKay 1999)

Karen's words show how complicated a researcher's work is—the task is to show how complex and varied students are yet still find ways to respect everyone in the classroom community. Teacher-researchers live daily with the consequences of their work, and how they represent students, colleagues, and themselves can affect relationships (positively and negatively) for years to come. Developing a permission form is the first step in sorting through these issues of representation, honesty, and respect.

Sometimes, it's clear from the beginning that the research will be focusing on aspects of children's work that doesn't require confidentiality. Teacher-researcher Jill Ostrow sent the permission form shown in Figure 3.4 home to the parents of her students. Though your research may be very different, you can adapt this format to meet your needs. For example, if children's confidentiality is important in your research, you could substitute the sentence, "In any reports of this research, a fictitious name will be used to protect your child's privacy."

Any permission form should include the following:

1. A brief explanation of the research project.
2. Request to use student samples or other artifacts in publishing.
3. Explanations of confidentiality.
4. A clear description of how students will not be hurt in any way if they do not participate.
5. A phone number or other forum for parents to discuss the project with you.

Figure 3.5 shows the model form that Stenhouse Publishers sends to its authors to adapt for their student permission forms.

What if a child or parent chooses not to participate? We like the writer Lillian Ross's advice: "Do not write about anyone who does not want to be written about" (Murray 1990b, 47). At the same time, a refusal to participate can be a red flag—it may signify other concerns the parent has about your classroom and teaching that are worth exploring before misunderstandings escalate.

We also encourage you to share your research plans with administrators in your school and district. Rarely is an administrator anything but enthusiastic about a teacher's willingness to tackle a new project. But again, concerns can point to potential future conflicts if they aren't resolved in the planning phase of your work.

The two statements of ethics shown in Figure 3.6 can be helpful guides in thinking about the ethical issues of your research. The National Writing Project will also provide readers with the *Guide to Ethical Issues in Teacher Research.*

Planning and Pleasure

The research plan can give you lots of insight and joy if you accept it for what it is—a starting point for your work, not a rigid summary of what must be done when. Research is a cyclical, not a linear, process. Throughout your research, you'll want to circle back to your original plans, revising, extending, and abandoning parts of the plan that don't represent the actual work of your research. Researchers are sometimes discouraged in their work when they don't see the plan as something that can be altered, as

Figure 3.4 Permission Form

Dear Parents,

In my math curriculum, the children are surrounded with mathematical concepts constantly. These concepts will be integrated into language, science, geography, and history through problems that I and the children create. This year, I will be looking closely at the variety of strategies the children use not only for solving problems but for explaining problems they have solved. These strategies include drawing, pictures, manipulatives, and symbols.

I especially want to look at the thinking processes of the children as they solve problems and explain in writing and orally how a problem was solved. Through these written stories of their thinking processes, I hope to be better able to understand how they internalize concepts and how they begin to transfer that knowledge to more complex thinking strategies. I'll be interviewing the children about their processes as part of my teaching, as I always do. Occasionally this year, I'll also be audiotaping these interviews and conversations. When the whole class shares their math problems and thinking strategies or gives oral presentations, these conversations may also be recorded on occasion. The purpose of these recordings will be to give me a chance to examine the children's comments more closely and repeatedly in order to catch things I might miss if I only heard them once.

I'll also be making copies of some of the writing, drawing, and problem solving the kids have done, with their permission. I know the class will benefit from the better understanding we will have of the children's mathematical understandings.

I would appreciate your permission to include copies of your child's written work and art work in the articles or chapters I may write for publication. I am planning to use your child's real name in my writing, since all examples I use will be a celebration of what children *can* do. I have spoken with the children and that is what they prefer. (However, if you would prefer that I use a fictitious name to protect your child's privacy, please write your name choice here: _____.)

If you are willing to grant permission for me to use copies of your child's work from our classroom in written reports for publication, please sign the permission form at the bottom of the page and return it to me as soon as possible.

Thank you for your consideration.

Sincerely,

Jill Ostrow

_____
Child's Name

_____
Parent or Guardian

_____
Date

Figure 3.5 Permission Form

Dear

    I am . . . (add concise but specific description of what it is you are writing, e.g., "working on my Master's thesis and also writing an associated article which I hope will form a chapter in a professional book for teachers" or "starting to write a book for other teachers on teaching first grade, based on the work we do in my classroom here at . . . school.")

    The project is in the early stages of development, and one of the things I am doing is collecting samples of children's work for possible inclusion in the (thesis/article/book). From time to time I may also be taking photographs of the children.

    At this point I don't know exactly what I will and won't be able to include, but I would very much appreciate having your permission to reproduce your child's writing, drawing, or photograph in the publication. Would you please sign both copies of this form and return one to me, keeping the other for your files.

    If you would like to discuss this further, please call me at school any morning/afternoon between _____ and _____.

Your name:

I grant permission for the use of the material as described above.

Child's name:

Parent or guardian's signature:

Name and address:

Date:

a team of teachers completing a long-term study in Georgia discovered: "Probably our most serious mistake as novice teacher-researchers was to commit ourselves to a two-year research design before we had any experience at research. We stuck doggedly to the two-year design even when it wasn't working because we thought we had to. We didn't realize that a written design is seldom the lived design of classroom research. More experienced teacher-researchers might have cautioned us to be prepared to adjust our plan, to speed it up, slow it down, change its emphasis, or abandon it midstream" (Keffer et al. 1998, 30).

    The time you spend planning your inquiry should be some of the most enjoyable time you spend as researcher, especially if you realize that your final research project may end up looking very different than you had

Figure 3.6 Ethics Statements

Statement of Ethics
The Teacher Research Special Interest Group
American Educational Research Association
Drafted by Marian M. Mohr

1. *The Teacher-Researcher Role:* Teacher-researchers are teachers first. They respect those with whom they work, openly sharing information about their research. While they seek knowledge, they also nurture the well-being of others, both students and professional colleagues.
2. *Research Plans:* Teacher-researchers consult with teaching colleagues and appropriate supervisors to review the plans for their studies. They explain their research questions and methods of data collection and update their plans as the research progresses.
3. *Data Collection:* Teacher-researchers use data from observations, discussions, interviewing, and writing that is collected during the normal process of teaching and learning. They secure the principal's permission for broader surveys or letters to solicit data. They also secure permission to use data already gathered by the school to which they would ordinarily have access as part of their teaching responsibilities (such as standardized tests) or for school information that is not related to their assigned responsibilities (such as protected student records).
4. *Research Results:* Teacher-researchers may present the results of their research to colleagues in their school districts and at other professional meetings. When they plan to share their conclusions and findings in presentations outside the school or district, they consult with the appropriate supervisors. They are honest in their conclusions and sensitive to the effects of their research findings on others.
5. *Publication:* Teacher-researchers may publish their reports. Before publishing, teacher-researchers obtain written releases from the individuals involved in the research, both teachers and students, and parental permission for students eighteen or younger. The confidentiality of the people involved in the research is protected.

Ethical Responsibilities of Researchers
Clayton Action Research Collaborative
Clayton, Missouri

Participating in a research project requires that some attention be paid to the ethical responsibilities of researchers. We have adapted the following five rules that Hitchcock and Hughes (1989) recommend:

1. Establish whom you need to get permissions from.
2. Be clear and straightforward in articulating the nature and scope of the research.
3. Anticipate potentially sensitive areas or issues the research may focus upon.
4. Be sensitive to the hierarchy of the school or district.
5. Be aware that the aims and objectives of action research are to make changes. Recommendations for practice in a particular direction may challenge colleagues.

Before you begin to collect data, think through how you intend to make use of the data. If you intend to quote sources by name, the sources should know this in advance of participating in the project, and permission to do so should be obtained in advance of any data collection. Share your plans for shielding identities and maintaining confidentiality with those you might use as sources of data collection.

Action research is aimed ultimately at helping students. You would never want to do anything as a researcher that would impede or jeopardize that process.

originally envisioned. In the busyness that is everyday life for teachers, we rarely give ourselves the gift of stepping back and creating a larger portrait of what we know and what we want to learn more about. In talking about teacher research, Deborah Meier notes the power of enjoying those moments of insight: "This is the sustainable thing: the pleasure we can take from the imperfect instrument that we've created, and the imperfect kids we have, and our imperfect selves. If we're only looking at ourselves as something that we're going to like later on, then we're not going to like who we are now, either. I think there's a lot of that happening now. We're under such pressure to produce results—outcomes—we don't allow ourselves a lot of enjoyment in the here and now" (Meier quoted in Campbell 1997a, 23).

The research plan is a snapshot of the here and now of you as a researcher—what you care enough about to study, what strategies you've developed to answer your questions, who the colleagues are that can sustain your growth as a researcher. Take time to enjoy the researcher you are now, and use your research plans to chart the researcher you hope to be one day.

RESEARCH WORKSHOP

Hanging Around

Brenda Miller Power

There are many variations on the "hanging around" activity, which is a terrific way to help novice researchers go through all the phases of research design and implementation in a short period of time. More important, it exposes researchers to the concept of understanding others through understanding their cultures. Any place people meet and interact is a potential research site, as Mary Catherine Bateson (1994) writes, "Participant observation is more than a research methodology. It is a way of being, specially suited to a world of change. A society of many traditions and cultures can be a school of life" (27).

This activity will get you started as a researcher in that "school of life." You will need:

- One or two research partners.
- A good people-watching spot at a mall, a restaurant, or a retail store.

Begin at your school or at a central meeting spot before you go to the "hanging around" site. After you've identified where you want to do your research, answer these questions individually (from Kirby and Kuykendall 1991):

- Considering what you know about this place, product, or service, what do you expect to find?
- How do you expect the place to be organized?
- What type of clients/customers would you expect? Would one age group or gender predominate? Would you expect a certain income or educational level to dominate?

You and your partners then compare notes, highlighting differences in expectations. You then go to watch people in the location of your choice. Your goal is to describe fully the scene, events, actors, and interactions.

On site, start with the basic components of understanding the site by answering more of Kirby and Kuykendall's questions:

- How many cars are in the parking lot?
- What are the "arrival behaviors" of the customers? (Do they pause to look in the window, or rush in; do they speak to other people—what greetings do they use; do they ask for information, and so on.)
- Note the number of customers arriving alone and the size of groups. Keep a running tally of customers by age group, gender, and ethnicity.
- If possible, talk to one customer who doesn't seem to be in a hurry. What brings the customer there? How often? What do they think of the place? Ask similar questions of an employee about the clientele of the place.

Set aside at least fifteen minutes to write down random observations of the site. Ask yourself these questions as you take notes:

- Who's in charge? How is power gained or lost as the actors interact?
- Who controls conversations? What are the topics of conversation?
- What are the key elements in the scene?
- What are the relationships of the actors?
- What language or actions seem culture- and scene-specific?
- What ethical concerns arise from the assignment?

You and your partners should take notes separately and then compare them. This activity should be repeated the following week, with at least a couple of hours set aside for discussion of notes. Your final collective analysis should describe the scene, events, actors, and interactions fully in any form—narrative, poem, fiction, role play. You should also include a detailed map of the scene. It's best to do this activity with groups of researchers going to different sites. You can then share your findings at a final meeting and discuss how what you've learned transfers to your classroom research planning.

We have done this activity many times with students and colleagues, and we are amazed at the range of research design issues that emerge as people work in teams to understand a place outside of school.

For example, one group decided to hang around at McDonald's. They were surprised at the differences in the behaviors of customers who seemed to be "regulars" and those who seemed to be making a quick stop for food. Their final write-up of their research was a poem, describing with spare, clean phrases the routines and rituals. They used the hanging around experience to think more about the rules and routines in their classrooms—and what role they played in establishing these routines.

Another group spent time at a large chain bookstore/coffeehouse. They catalogued all the differences in cultures present, from the youths with pierced noses to the dapper retired professors in tweeds. These researchers learned the importance of noting the most telling details to describe members of different social groups, knowledge they would use to explore the more subtle differences between students in their classrooms.

The team of researchers who observed customers at the local Department of Motor Vehicles found it was essential to include the snippets of conversations, both from the waiting line and between clerks and customers. Their observations led them to include more tape recording and transcriptions in their research studies, because they saw that research informants come to life on the page when their lives are presented in their own words.

A trio who observed at a local restaurant found that sketches of where customers sat and how space was used by customers were most helpful in understanding their site. They decided to collect more visual information in their research project, including photographs and daily charts of where children choose to sit and who they choose to work with.

As you have insights about what you're seeing, keep returning to your research plan. How does this change the way you'll want to collect data? What is most helpful to you in understanding this site with others, and how can that understanding inform the way you analyze your data? How do your teammates support you? When do they get in the way of your work? How can you use this knowledge to find the research partners who will be able to help with your classroom project?

We've had findings presented as poems, songs, want ads, original art, plays, pantomime, and narratives. The final presentations may be the most important part of the activity. Researchers see that they can take a small amount of data and still have insights about how people interact and cultures form.

RESEARCH WORKSHOP

Testing the Water with Mini-Inquiry Projects

Jerome C. Harste and Christine Leland

Engaging teachers and undergraduate interns in mini-inquiry projects is an effective way to encourage classroom-based research. Mini-inquiry projects are just that: quick investigations of issues that get raised through professional reading, conversations, or occurrences in classrooms. Some of the questions and comments that led to mini-inquiry projects and were subsequently investigated by teachers and interns at the Center for Inquiry in Indianapolis follow:

> "I think *The Witch's Broom* is too hard a book for first graders."

> "I don't think children can correct their own spelling errors; if they could, they wouldn't make them in the first place."

> "I think kids like books that are concrete (about things they have had experience with) rather than abstract (fantasy)."

> "Are manipulatives as important for older kids as they are for the younger ones?"

> "Instead of focusing on the elements of literature—characters, setting, events, main ideas—as we talk about books, will an open conversation lead to coverage of these same topics?"

> "If I get Terrance to talk about the successful strategies he uses when reading, will this make him a better and more confident reader?"

Each of these musings has been the basis for a mini-inquiry project at our school. While questions might provide the most direct route into the inquiry process, statements that are shared in collaborative settings become inquiries when speaker is asked, "How do you know that?" In our combined group of teachers and interns, for example, it was one of the interns who originally commented that *The Witch's Broom* was too hard a book for first graders. Others in the group immediately asked, "How do you know that?" and "How can we find out if that's true?"

The formulation of questions leads to hypotheses and plans for gathering classroom data that will test them. More often than not, these plans are generated through collaborative discussions. In our case, teachers and interns worked together to figure out the best ways to collect appropriate data for the various mini-inquiries that members of the collaborative were interested in pursuing. With concrete plans in mind, teachers and interns now saw their classrooms as places for doing research as they went about their teaching. They agreed to gather data for a specified period of time (a week, in this case) and to come together again to discuss, interpret, and analyze what they had found.

Sometimes the discussion with others led participants to revise their plans for data collection or to conclude that they had not collected enough data. In addition, we frequently found that new questions were generated before the original ones had been answered, causing inquiries to take sharp turns in new directions. In most cases, the final result was a one- or two-page write-up that was shared with the whole group.

Mini-inquiry projects, we believe, have done more to establish an attitude of inquiry among our community of teachers, undergraduate interns, and university faculty than anything else we have tried. While we also engaged in some larger inquiry projects like a "sense of place" study that focused on Indianapolis, we found that these required significant investment in terms of time, travel, trips to the library, finding people to interview, and so on. Although these projects were beneficial in many ways, we all felt that the mini-inquiries provided easier access to a greater variety of explorations into various aspects of teaching.

We see mini-inquiry projects as a low-stress way to start messing around with inquiry. Their inherent simplicity helps to ensure that inquiry is seen as a way of life rather than as a big deal.

Philosophically, education-as-inquiry is meant to suggest that the whole of education is inquiry—everything from building curriculum according to the personal and social interests of children to seeing teaching as inquiry and ourselves as teacher-researchers. When paired with opportunities for systematic collaboration, mini-inquiries can be powerful curricular invitations that do much to support us all in becoming more reflective practitioners.

We also think that there is something to be said for the idea of venturing slowly into unknown territory. New Englanders, for example, know that the idyllic beauty of their rocky coast needs to be juxtaposed with knowledge of the frigid ocean water that can literally take one's breath away if approached without due restraint. Visitors who wish to swim there soon learn that there is less of a shock when they test the water with their toes and wade in gradually. We think there's an analogy here to teacher research. Mini-inquiries help us test the water before plunging into something that might otherwise be pretty scary. Doing teacher research (like swimming in cold water) doesn't have to leave us breathless if we start small. We might even be surprised to find that once we're used to it, the new perspective is quite refreshing.

featured **TEACHER** RESEARCHER

Research Design

Michelle Schardt
Elementary Bilingual Teacher

Research Purpose

Bilingual education was developed after so many language minorities were found to be failing in regular education programs. By teaching subject matter and literacy in the first language while the student is acquiring English, he or she can be more successful. Two-way bilingual education programs developed when schools realized they could use the language minority population to help English-only speakers acquire a second language, too. This is the type of program I have been involved in for five years at various schools in California and Oregon, with Spanish and English being the languages. One aspect of all the programs that has bothered me is the English-only students' lack of Spanish proficiency. As we try to "sell" these programs to parents, I am feeling more and more dishonest saying that our goal is for all the children to be bilingual. It seems the focus is still on the language minority children. While we are having a lot of success in this area, we have to put more energy into the Spanish language development. My research will see if I can do just that.

Research Question

In my two-way bilingual class, what happens to Spanish language usage by my "English experts" when they have focused Spanish lessons for English-only speakers (without "Spanish experts")?

Subquestions

Will English experts play/work with Spanish speakers more frequently?

How will the English speakers use their acquired language?

Will they enjoy Spanish more?

Will they take more risks?

Will they ask Spanish experts for help?

Data Collection

- Starting at the beginning of the year, three times a week I will take running notes during "Big Workshop" (free-choice time), recording which children choose to work together. I will make record sheets with each area of the classroom and fill in names to make it easier.

- I'll code the language users with S or E. I'm sure a few students would want to take over this job soon after I begin. I will also record what subject is being discussed.

- During different group work times (patterning, free exploration, journals) in which students choose whom they work with or sit by, I will take photographs. Later I can show the students the pictures and ask them why they chose to work with that person. I think it will be interesting to have the students be a direct part of the observation.

- With a tape recorder, I will bug the playhouse, reading corner, and math center once a week to capture which languages are being used and which books are being chosen.

- I will initiate a dialogue with the parents in our interactive homework journal to see how the children's attitudes about Spanish change over the year.

- I will do surveys with all my English experts at the beginning and end of the school year. Possible questions:

How do you feel on Spanish days?

Do you understand Spanish?

Do you want to learn Spanish?

Do you like Spanish?

How much Spanish do you know? A little, a lot, or a medium amount?

Data Analysis

I will look through my notes once a month and count up the interactions lasting more than ten minutes with a Spanish expert and an English expert. I will ratio that with what language was used (for example, out of twenty-five encounters, nine were in Spanish in September).

The photographs will provide a visual record of the children and the partners or groups they are choosing to work with. They will also be good springboards for conversations among the students involved about why they are choosing to work with the people the pictures show them working with. I will record our interviews the week I do them instead of bugging the room, and then transcribe when I do the regular tapes. Once a week in my morning prep, when it's nice and quiet, I will transcribe the tapes I collect with my kindergarten partner for the next year. She will be collecting tapes, too. This will tell me what the kids are actually saying (if anything!) in the target language. I will be able to hear what they are getting out of their Spanish language instruction.

The dialogue journals will provide me with individual accounts regarding the attitudes of the students. I'll put copies of pertinent information in their files to follow the phases of their feelings toward Spanish. At the end of the year, I'll use these as well as the surveys to analyze how attitudes have been affected. I will triangulate the findings from the different forms of data and see if they are congruent. I will report the results in narrative form as an overall evaluation. I will share this information with students and parents.

When discussing language, I will use a code system to record what type of language is used. A possible system might be

D: directing, telling what to do

H: asking for help

VH: help on vocabulary

WH: help on work being done

L: labeling, naming objects, colors, numbers, etc.

S: social

Support/Collaboration

I plan to do this project with the other kindergarten teacher who will be teaching the English language development part of the program. We will be pooling our kids and planning our lessons together, so it will be natural for her to follow along with the research with her English experts. Heather will be professional and motivating, even though she is new at all this. I also plan to use a group of teachers I've met through my course work and with whom I'm in a new writing group. They will question me about my research every time we meet! I want them to expect to read the transcripts and the results of my surveys. Maybe I'll pick one to really watch me and my progress!

Bibliography

Cummins, J. 1997. "Metalinguistic Development of Children in Bilingual Education Programs." In *The Fourth Locus Forum 1997*, ed. M. Paradis. Columbia, SC: Hornbeam Press.

Diaz, R. M. 1983. "The Intellectual Power of Bilingualism." Paper presented at the New Mexico Humanities Council, Albuquerque, NM.

Edelski, C. 1996. *With Literacy and Justice for All*. Bristol, PA: Taylor and Francis.

Fergusen, C. 1978. *Talking to Children: A Search for Universals*. Vol. 1, 203–204. Stanford, CA: Stanford University Press.

Freeman and Freeman. 1996. *Between Worlds*. Portsmouth, NH: Heinemann.

Hakuta, K. 1986. *Mirror of Language: The Debate on Bilingualism*. New York: Basic Books.

Halliday, M. A. K. 1977. *Exploration in the Functions of Language*. New York: Elsevier North-Holland.

Krashen, S. 1982. *Principles and Practices in Second Language Acquisition*. Oxford, UK: Penguin.

featured **TEACHER RESEARCHER**

Research Design

Joseph Kelley
Fifth-Grade Science Teacher

Purpose

This year I am using portfolios as a means of assessment in the science program. As part of each lesson, students will reflect on what they have learned. Students will decide what papers will be included in their portfolios along with a statement as to why the papers were chosen and what this shows about them as learners. They will also set goals for the next unit. I want to see how students perceive themselves as learners.

Questions

What happens when students use self-reflection in science as a means of assessing growth?

Subquestions

How are my teaching practices affected by student growth?

Is there a change in the students' attitude when they review their growth?

What growth did students have in their knowledge base?

What new skills do students have and how are they used?

How does student writing change?

Are students setting realistic goals? How do they perceive themselves accomplishing those goals?

Method

I will be working with two groups in science three times a week. Students start each unit by webbing their knowledge and developing a list of questions they would like answered. In cooperative learning groups, students complete science experiments and lab reports that encourage them to make predictions, develop a hypothesis, analyze, observe, compare, order, and infer.

At the completion of each lab, students will reflect on what they have learned, what role they had in the experiment, and questions they may still have. At the same time, I will do notetaking on what I see individual students doing. I will compare my observations with student reflections once a week with each class.

Students will develop portfolios that will be passed in at the end of the second, third, and fourth quarters. I will analyze self-reflection in the portfolios and compare with the weekly observation notes I've made.

Data Collection

- Student responses
- Videotapes
- Photos
- Conference notes
- Artwork
- Graphs and charts

Calendar

August

- Letter to parents
- Develop survey questions
- Start teacher journal

September–January

- Notetaking
- Keep teacher journal
- Student folders
- Model self-reflection
- Survey records kept in teacher log
- Review student responses weekly
- Make and review one student videotape weekly
- Talk with co-teacher to share information
- Parent partner to make observations and meet weekly to discuss and see if there are any connections at home
- Look for patterns

February–April

- Analyze student growth in portfolios
- Continue all of the above

June

- Draw conclusions from portfolios
- Complete a final survey
- Review entry and exit survey/compare differences
- Summary statement

featured **TEACHER** RESEARCHER

Research Brief

Sharon Frye
Middle School Social Studies/Language Arts Teacher

Origins of the Question

About two months ago, I brought my three-year-old daughter to my seventh-grade class for part of the day. When I asked for volunteers to read to her during reading time, I was surprised to discover that nearly half the class wanted to read picture books to her. The students were a mix of good and struggling readers. A little while later, I brought in *The Stinky Cheese Man* (Scieszka 1992) and I asked if anyone would like to read it. Again, nearly half the class wanted to read the book. I gave it to one struggling reader, who looked at it, passed it on to another student, then picked up another picture book that had been on our bookshelf all year. No one had picked up any of the picture books before this; it was as if I had given them permission to consider picture books as valid reading material. This experience got me wondering how picture books could fit into our reading and writing program and what benefits reading picture books might have on students' self-confidence as readers and writers.

Questions

How do picture books fit into our reading and writing program?

What happens to students' reading and writing skills when they are exploring literacy through picture books?

Do students' perceptions of their skills change when they are reading and writing picture books in middle school?

What We Will Be Trying

Individually and as a whole class, we will read picture books to discuss the terms the authors used in creating their books. We will also write and illustrate our own picture books. Students will choose their topic, the audience they will target, and the mode of writing they will use. When they are finished, we will read our books to authentic audiences in the target age ranges.

Data Collection

- Journals: Students will keep journals to reflect on what they are learning. I will read and respond to these journal entries.
- Writers' surveys: Students will complete writers' surveys before the project begins and again at the end of the project. The surveys will ask students to reflect on their own skills and perceptions as writers.

- Observations/field notes: I will take field notes daily to track engagement in the project, enthusiasm level for students, and progress I may observe. I will also keep a daily journal to record my observations.
- Interviews: I may choose to interview a few students individually. I will choose students of differing ability levels to see how they respond to the project.
- Writing samples: I will compare writing samples from this project with writing samples from earlier in the year to determine growth.

Reflection/Analysis

- I will review my journal entries weekly, the students' journal entries, and my field notes to reflect and note any observations I make.
- I will read the initial writers' surveys within the first week and write a journal reflection recording insights and observations I note.
- I will meet every other week with a support group to discuss what I have noticed.
- After three weeks I will review the data I have collected to determine if I need to conduct individual interviews.
- Once the project is complete (I anticipate it will take three to four weeks) I will compare writing samples and writers' surveys to determine what changes have occurred.

Reference

Scieszka, J. 1992. *The Stinky Cheese Man and Other Fairly Stupid Tales.* New York: Viking.

featured TEACHER RESEARCHER

Research Brief

Susan Pidhurney
Reading Recovery Teacher

Purpose/Audience

Last year was my training year for Reading Recovery. A huge component of this program for students is nightly rereading of a familiar story and the reassembly of a cut-up sentence. The homework takes no more than ten or fifteen minutes. Of the six students I worked with, only one parent did the homework on a semiregular basis. Despite notes and phone calls, I had very little success improving this area. I am interested in finding out if regular contact through journals will facilitate home involvement with my students. My primary interest is to see how increased parent involvement affects these students. Hopefully this will help other Reading Recovery teachers in their interactions with families.

Research Question

What happens when I begin to use take-home journals with my Reading Recovery students?

Subquestions

How will it affect home/school connections?

Does it matter who responds? (Mom, Dad, other adult)

Is attendance related to regular journal use?

If families aren't responding, what reasons are they giving?

How are students' attitudes reflected in parents' journal entries?

How are parents' attitudes reflected in students' behavior/attitudes?

Data Collection

1. Journals
2. Field notes
   a. observations
   b. phone calls
   c. running records
   d. book graphs

Data Analysis

1. Go through the journals looking for
   a. Is there a response?
   b. Who is responding?
   c. What categories of response are emerging?
      (i)   positive comments
      (ii) negative comments
      (iii) questions
2. Check attendance records
3. Check in-class anecdotal notes for any patterns

Time Line

1. First ten lessons ("roaming in the known") for two weeks:
   a. Initiate contacts with home
   b. Open House
   c. Take photo for cover
   d. Talk with child about journal
2. Beginning with Week 3:

a. Send home familiar text and cut-up sentence with the journal in a bag each night

b. Respond as often as home person responds

c. If no response, date and put "no response," then write my entry

3. Every two weeks:

a. Look at responses and see what categories are developing

b. Analyze data and make revisions accordingly

4. At the end of the child's program, take exit survey questionnaires/parent comments and look for categories

Support

1. Other Reading Recovery teachers
2. Classroom teachers of my Reading Recovery students
3. Families

Permissions

1. Let my principal know what I intend to do. (Since parent participation has been an issue, I am sure he will be supportive of anything that will help.)

2. Send home standard Reading Recovery permission slip to selected students.

3. I will request permission to use examples from the journals in the event I write an article (with assurances of the anonymity of the writer). Any material I want to use will be given to the writer as well, and I will make clear that the intent is to share information with other parents and Reading Recovery teachers.

Ideas for Prompts to Keep Dialogue Moving

1. Tell about myself/family (to model an entry). "Tell me about your child."
2. "What do you remember about school?" (good/bad)
3. "What are your goals for school this year?"
4. "What would you like me to know that will help me be successful with your child?"
5. "What does your family like to do for fun?"

Research Brief

Sandy Brown
Secondary School Art Teacher

Origin

At the beginning of each school year when setting up my art classroom I think about what I can do to create an atmosphere that inspires creativity and artistic literacy. Besides the walls and bulletin boards, I intentionally place artwork and art-related information in obscure places around the room, for example, around the corner from the pencil sharpener, on the backside of both paper towel dispensers, and below eye level on most cupboards. All of the places just described are not in any direct line of vision from anywhere around the room. You really have to strain your neck to see them, and I have noticed more than quite a few heads turn. I want my students—no matter where they are sitting, paying attention or not—to be visually stimulated. The information posted around the room rotates, changes, and is added to depending on what quarter electives I teach and the specific artist or art technique we are studying. I also post current gallery and museum information weekly, monthly, and yearly. My intention is to create an atmosphere that inspires creativity and artistic literacy. But I have often wondered if my students view the room as I do.

Question

How does the artwork and related information posted on the classroom walls of my art room affect creativity and enhance artistic literacy in my teenage students?

Data Collection and Methods of Analyzing Data

Student Survey

I know the attached survey is quite long and asking any one student to complete in one sitting is unrealistic and a bit overwhelming. My intention is to use these survey questions throughout the quarter in many forms: journal entries, individual conferences, and all-class discussions. When I compile the results, I will look for correlations that my students are making based on their surroundings and the artwork they produce in class, and their expression of what creativity means to them. These data will also be an important tool to enhance my teaching abilities to better meet their needs.

Art Portfolios (Journals)

I see the art portfolio not only as a collection and reflection of growth in student artwork but also as a dialogue between my students and myself where we make connections regarding artwork by asking specific questions and advice of one another. "Writing encourages both visual and verbal expression and can reveal more about thinking, creating, and discovery. Writing also aids in student understanding and formation of new ideas intensified by thinking" (Ernst 1994, 50).

Student Work Samples

Student work samples may include artwork in progress and completed artwork, journals, the student room survey, and anything else I can collect that will help me in making connections concerning the advancement my students are making in artistic literacy and creativity.

Work samples to consider for added study:

- Have students leave the room and draw from their memory the room layout and wall design. What connections are they making?
- Ask students to create and display a "student-centered" class bulletin board, with the focus being the artist or art technique of study.
- Create a new book cover design by team-teaching with an English, science, or history teacher as described in *Seeking Diversity* (Rief 1992, 149–179).

Teacher Observations

Recording observations, questions, and connections regarding student work process, teaching, and learning strategies and techniques will be some of the key ingredients in my teacher observation journals.

An idealistic observation entry might look like this:

October 27, 1998: Today I noticed Valerie reading the "Tile Makers" article in the back of the classroom near the art cupboards. After reading and exploring the photographs that accompany the article, Valerie was impressed to discover that the two women who designed the tile walls in the new Longview McDonald's are local tile artists. She later asked me if they might be able to come to our classroom and share with us their experience.

Other questions I might address and experiment with are:

What happens to student learning, creativity, and artistic literacy in the room when the walls are bare and blank?

What happens when students create the environment?

Art Critiques

Critiques encourage collaboration and dialogue of art-in-process where students and teachers can both learn from one another. When discussing specific artists and art styles, critiques encourage artistic literacy by helping students discover "art vocabulary." For example, when I introduce the "Jack -in-the-Pulpit" series by Georgia O'Keeffe, I might say to the class, "Notice the white vertical line in the center of this composition. This is the focal point. You can tell because of the contrasting blue and green organic shapes that surround the vertical white line. The artist planned this, bringing you, the viewer, up close and directly into the center of the flower as an active participant." These art critiques also encourage discovery and provide a place where new ideas may emerge. I will document them in my teaching journal as well.

Student Survey Questions

Define in your own words what *creative* means.

What inspires you to be, act, think, or feel creatively?

Do you find this room to be a creative place to work?

Looking around the room, do you see anything posted that inspires or interests you as an artist?

What have you learned about art by *reading* the information on the classroom walls?

What did you learn about art by *looking* at the information on the classroom walls?

Is there any area of the room that you found to be more visually stimulating than any other area? Where? Why?

When you are working on a specific art project—let's say, clay tiles—do you find anything in the classroom to be of inspiration to you while you are creating clay tiles?

Did you at any time this quarter relate any of the information posted on the classroom walls to any art projects? Explain yes or no answers.

Did you find the teachers' demonstrations helpful?

Was your level of class participation better or worse depending on your level of interest in any given assignment?

What did you do to help another student?

What was most helpful to you in your learning about art and art-related topics (student critiques, class decisions, looking at examples of past student work, questions and responses from your art journal, etc.)?

What are your suggestions for making this room a more visually stimulating and creative place to work?

Choose an art project you learned this quarter to teach to someone else. What would it be and to whom would you teach it?

Do you see yourself taking art classes in the future?

Harvesting Data

4

Some say it is no coincidence that the question mark is an inverted plow, breaking up the hard soil of old beliefs and preparing for new growth.

Saul Alinsky

Saul Alinsky's notion of question marks as inverted plows brings us back to the metaphor of our classrooms as garden communities. Equipped with our questions and our research designs as tools of our trade, we are faced with the task of harvesting the rich crop of data that surrounds us in our classrooms.

The harvest is most fulfilling when we connect it to practices that are already a part of our teaching lives. Many teachers rely on their observations and reflections to help them make sense of their students' learning and to make their teaching plans. As teacher-researchers, we just record these observations and reflections in a more systematic way, building on existing skills.

Journals and Notes

With so much going on around us, it can be easy to overlook the little things that add up to the big things—the chance observations that might lead someday to breakthrough findings. Slowing down and being open to our impressions, living in the moment with a mindful stance—being ready to take in the world around us—is the starting place in collecting data. This is the stance that teacher-researchers like Karen Gallas (1998) describe as essential in their ability to harvest large crops of data: "It began with what appeared to be many discreet observations on my part, and an approach one might describe as alternately befuddled, amused, and outraged. I was a collector and a reactor. I collected indiscriminately and reacted quite personally to what I gathered. It was very much like an aesthetic exercise: some things pleased me, some repelled; all fascinated" (24).

Taking notes is one of the main tools in teacher-researchers' repertoire. Teachers have long relied on what Simon Ottenburg (1990) calls headnotes—our memory for details and history in our classrooms. But some of this must make its way into recorded writing, even very brief jottings. It's looking back on those written notes and elaborating on them that can provide a bridge between what you are experiencing in the classroom and how you translate the experience into larger meaning.

Educational ethnographer Harry Wolcott (1995) reminds beginning note-takers that observation is "a mysterious process": "At the least, it is something we do 'off and on' and mostly off. A realistic approach . . . is to recognize and capitalize on the fact that our observations—or, more accurately, our ability to concentrate on them—are something comparable to a pulse: short bursts of attention, followed by inattentive rests. Capitalize on the bursts. Be especially observant about capturing little vignettes or short (but complete) conversational exchanges in careful detail" (98).

One of the mysteries for many novice teacher-researchers is how teachers find time to observe and take notes in their classrooms. When you see experienced teacher-researchers at work, the process isn't too mysterious at all. Veteran teacher-researchers rely on those "short bursts" of time. They may take notes for only ten minutes during any teaching day, but they really focus their attention for that period. What matters is not how much time you spend taking notes but how consistently you make focused observation a regular part of your day.

If you look back through the research designs in Chapter 3, you'll notice the main data collection strategy teacher-researchers rely on is collecting and recording these observations:

> "I will continue with my refined notetaking method, including what I see and what they say." (Andie Cunningham)

> "Starting at the beginning of the year, three times a week I will take running notes during Big Workshop (free-choice time), recording which children choose to work together. (Michelle Schardt)

> "[I will rely on] my anecdotal notes from observing cooperative teams at work and other activities." (Wally Alexander)

> "I will take field notes daily to track engagement in the project, enthusiasm level for students, and progress I may observe. I will also keep a daily journal to record my observations." (Sharon Frye)

> "I will try hard to keep a teacher journal and do some notetaking." (Patrice Turner)

Patrice set out to record her data with some uncertainty and trepidation. Like many beginning teacher-researchers, she wondered, "What will my notes look like? How will I manage to collect them?" Susan MacKay, in her essay "Breaking in My Research Tools," shares her own uncertainty and how she found a way to build on her "kid-watching" strategies:

Since I am a beginner at teacher research, my research tools are mostly new. None of them tucks neatly behind my ear or rests comfortably in my hand. None of them feels soft and broken in.

I'm most at home with my anecdotal notes—the kid-watching tool I learned to use in my teacher education program. After playing with different kinds of notebooks, sticky papers, and grids, I've settled on a red three-ring binder with a divided section for each child in my class. I record various notes at various times on a few sheets of looseleaf paper in each section.

On the first day of school, and periodically throughout the year, I run through all the names of my students and write down the first things that come to mind. Other times, I flip through slowly and jot down the important things that bubble up in my memory as I think carefully about each child. On some days, things happen that just beg to be recorded right away. I note connections children make—between books and life, between their stories and other stories, between math and reading, between a new problem and a problem solved.

I record anything that helps make the familiar become unfamiliar. I look for that all the time. I want the unexpected to occur. It's no great surprise that these themes run central to all my questions about teaching and learning. My anecdotal notes have become a place to chart paths toward the answers to my questions—and the asking of more.

Various teaching journals go hand in hand with the anecdotal notes. The red notebook works well as an assessment and research tool, but the journals have turned me from a good kid-watcher into a beginning teacher-researcher. In the teacher journals, unlike the anecdotal notes, my plans and questions get muddled with the kids' plans and questions, and the questions become much clearer. I also have a legal pad on which I am constantly writing. I note kids' choices, plans for later, things that must be finished. I jot down pieces of conversations, questions, ideas—both mine and theirs. This pad of paper is helping me to integrate my research with my teaching and helping them become seamless.

I usually write in the other journals after school, although, I admit, without any degree of consistency. I take them with me when I work with other teachers or go to a staff meeting or development opportunity. I list questions I have and processes I observe. I quote other people. I jot down the titles of good professional books and children's literature. I sometimes also take the messy thoughts written on the legal pad and straighten them out on a clean page in another journal. More questions, thoughts, and connections always follow. (1997, 154–155)

Susan doesn't rely on one strategy to record her observations. Legal pads, three-ring binders, journals, Post-its, clipboards, and index cards are all part of her repertoire. She documents some notes "in the midst" of her teaching, and others "after the fact," depending on the nature of her task, the information she needs, and her own writing preferences. Susan adopts a strategy common to many novice teacher-researchers—she tries a range of notetaking materials, forms, and times for writing, experimenting to find what style of notes and observations best suits her needs as a teacher-researcher. Many teachers begin like Susan with a wide array of notebooks, Post-its, labels, stickers, journals—keeping the methods that work and discarding those that don't.

Like Susan, Title I teacher Carey Salisbury relies on various notetaking strategies, recording her anecdotal notes on clipboard sheets (see Figure 4.1). In her very brief jotted notes, she captures a phrase or two that she can flesh out later. She uses her teaching journal to fill in more details of encounters and to reflect on them. For example, on the day she recorded "Billy: looked up at clock once—wandering—looked for book George and he talking about" on her anecdotal note sheet, she turned to her journal that evening and used her anecdotal notes to jog her memory, writing: "Billy still has problems. I select several books he may be interested in. He says he really wants to read *The Mixed-Up Files,* but then he continues to fumble through it. I have to separate him from the group because he cannot help

Date	Student	Notes
	Billy	Looked up at clock once — Wandering — looked for book — George & he talking about
	~~Dan~~ Daniel	Conversing w/ Mrs. F.
	Dimitry	Finished early & looking for a book to read — started w/ Berin bears & changed to Jokes.
	Joke	Jokes
	Mrs. Carter's group	all very engaged.
	Justin	Chose
	Cody	The Yearling
	Billy	Wandering
	Sergi	Continued reading

Figure 4.1 Anecdotal Notes Sheet

talking. The class is somewhat noisy because of all the groups working on their vocabulary goals—look words up and find out what they mean. Could this be the destructive piece in this whole plan? Those who are easily distracted, like Billy, and need quiet to read, aren't getting it?"

At the end of her first year of taking notes, Carey reflected that recording her observations systematically "has forced me to do it better. I learned that by looking at my notes, I can tap into things I really need to be doing for the kids, like checking with Billy's teacher, who thinks he should be reading at a lower grade level than is maybe right for him." She also realized that her words and ideas flow far more easily when she sits down at the computer at home periodically, and she has found that writing time to be essential: "Without all that writing, where do the thoughts go and how can they be transformed into ways to substantiate what happens in the classroom?"

Having a teaching journal handy can also be useful for recording those moments of insight in the classroom. Lisa Merrill noted her experiences with a very challenging student in her teaching journal: "He moved about the room weaving a web of destruction. While participating in group activities, he criticized the work and ideas of his peers. 'I don't understand this!' he loudly accused during math as students around him worked on geometric quilt patterns. 'I don't want to read!' he argued during quiet reading times when I asked him to move away from our class pets and find a book. I spent today extinguishing the fires that blazed wherever Andrew went."

Quickly writing about one student can give notetaking immediate value for teacher-researchers—students like Andrew often require written notes for meetings with specialists and parents to discuss behaviors in specific ways.

Carey, Susan, and Lisa all continue to use their journals to observe and document the undercurrents in their classroom life. But while most of us recognize the importance of documenting what we notice, what we hear, and what sense we can make of it, it can be difficult to find the right vehicle for regular written reflection. We've talked to more than one teacher-researcher who resists starting yet another teaching journal because she's simply "journaled out," overdosed on journals as course requirements—journals with specific formatting whose pages were filled out of a sense of duty rather than as a tool for genuine inquiry and reflection.

Yet when we use writing for our own purposes, and in the midst of our teaching lives, we can tailor the format we choose to our work style and preferences. Donald Murray writes daily reflections at his computer in his "day book," and artist Julie Cameron considers her "morning pages," written by hand in her notebook, a pivotal tool in her creative life. It doesn't matter what time of day or what kind of recording devices you choose; what matters is finding what works for you.

In order for our tools to fit more comfortably into our hands, it's also very helpful to find ways to record events as they are happening. We can do this by fitting this into our current record-keeping strategies, as Susan MacKay did with her red binder of her "kid-watching" notes. We can also create recording sheets that meet the particular demands of the questions we wish to answer.

First-grade teacher Nancy Csak decided to take a closer look at her story-telling time, and she created just such a tool:

> Armed with my questions, I set out to gather data using a recording sheet on a clipboard [see Figure 4.2]. I discovered some interesting things. I noticed that there were some children who consistently chose to pass. Happily, there didn't seem to be a pattern of children being willing to share with a

Name	① Total oppor. to tell	② # of times shared with group	③ # of times shared with me	④ avg. # of turns	⑤ Long, med or short turns	⑥ Comments * Special attention
1. Henry	4	4	4	4.75	short/med.	Glad to see he's not just talk about Nintendo anymo
2. Art	3 (ab.)	1 ← (different days) → 1		3	short	* Often tardy/absent misses storytelling
3. Graham	4	3	4	4.5	med.	turns themselves a often long w/out prompt
4. John	4	1 ← same day → 1		4	short	* this info confirms what I have noticed - often comments I don't hav anything to write about".
5. Jimmy	4	4	4	10/4	long	Loves to talk! long turns. Sing-songy voice during storytelling
6. Jake	4	4	4	4.75	short/med.	Is more verbal in class than this data indicates
7. Juliet	3 (ab.)	3	2	7.5	long.	Each turn is long, w/out much urging. She lights u at storytelling!
8. Craig	4	3 ← same days → 3		3.3	short	* Seems unsure about sharing - encourage more
9. Lisa	4	2	3.	4.7	short	Very shy. Although she h several turns, they are short Lots of nods as responses
10. Carmen	4	4	3	8.3	long	Seems to enjoy this! Passed when busy on white board
11. Laura	3 (ab.)	2	1	4	short	* This surprises me. Laura + I have good rapport. I think?
12. Janna	4	3 ← same days → 3		4.5	long	Has lots to say, long, is often unconventional, difficult to follow
13. Kara	4	4	4	6.25	med.	Very caught up in famil size. Understandable
14. Hannah	4	4	4	7.5	med/long	Enjoys this - covers a variety of topics

Figure 4.2 First Recording Sheet

group but not with me. Although it happened a couple of times, I noted that when they chose not to share with me, they were engaged with an activity they didn't appear to want to leave. I hope this means they are comfortable with me. In fact, there were a couple of instances where children did not share in the group, but did share with me. I was also able to pinpoint a couple of students who seem to be rushing to tell everything they can. I have the feeling they are trying to say their piece before time runs out! Interesting. One of these students includes two topics each day, beginning her story with, "I have two things. . . . "

As I recorded the number of turns in each exchange, it struck me that the number of turns is not as important as the quality or length of these turns. So I adapted my recording sheet to tap more information. I began noting either "short," "medium," or "long," indicating the perceived length of the entire story when it was completed. Although this is not very scientific, I did find that as I went back and sort of averaged these in conjunction with the number of turns, it gave me a rough idea of who talks a lot and who gives a short sentence or two without much elaboration. I want to expand on this, and note which one of us talks more, and what kind of language is used in the discourse.

Also, as I listened, I realized that the topics of the questions discussed were not a part of my original set of questions but that this interested me a great deal. So I quickly added a column to my recording sheet and jotted down a brief description of the topic each child discussed each day. Looking back at the data I have so far, this is fascinating to me.

As Nancy continued to collect data, her research questions changed. And so did her recording sheet (see her revised sheet in Figure 4.3). While she continued to take notes on storytelling time each morning, she shifted the focus from the number of turns to the topic each child told about:

As I began to look at these notes, another question came to mind. What was the time of the event relative to when the story was being told? In other words, did it happen long ago, just yesterday, that same day, or was the storytelling anticipating future events? I was curious about whether these young students would mostly tell about the concrete—something that had already happened—or whether they were interested in looking ahead and perhaps speculating about what might happen in the future. I came up with a code to label the topics, based on clues the speaker gave, such as "A long time ago," "Last night my mom," "Tomorrow we're going to," or "Someday. . . . " The labels I used were LP = long past; RP = recent past (I considered "recent" to be within the last few days, for instance, telling about the weekend on a Monday); SD = same day; NF = near future; and DF = distant future. I marked the relative time while the speaker was telling her story, so that I would not forget when her words were over.

Nancy's process of revising and adapting her record-keeping forms as she continued her research is a good one. As categories and findings begin to emerge, you'll want to revisit your plans for written observations. There

Figure 4.3 Revised Recording Sheet

Name	Oral topics	relative time	Written topics	relative time	Comments
Kathy	- Visiting Dad on weekend	Recent Past	* Going to Dad's house + staying with friend.	RP	Good variety of topics
	- Grandpa is moving	Future (?)	* Grandpa got married again + is moving.	RP + future	
	- Got in trouble for not eating dinner	R.P.	- Her cat Charley is cute + sleeps with her.	Ongoing	
	- Being babysat by her sister	RP	- Tooth fell out at school.	RP	
	- Helping Mom in garden	RP	- "I wonder how you..." didn't finish	?	← This brought to mind other intriguing star left unfinished. Did she run out of ideas, or was she interrupted?
	- Baby sister	RP	- Name song	Environmental	
	- Going to the beach	Near Future	- Writing numbers	Environmental	
Emma	- Dressed up her cat!	RP	- "I like school!"...	Ongoing	She has six notebooks- Is writing a lot!
	- Has a loose tooth	Ongoing	* Shrew got into the house.	RP	Has several out a day. Seems to come back to it whenever possible.
	- Mom pulled her tooth	RP	- Sand dollar from Willie (classmate) describing it.	RP	Likes many things "really much"! :)
	- Cat is sick	Ongoing	* Lost her tooth at recess + couldn't find it.	RP	Writes a lot about her cat. May need new topic ideas.
	- Has another loose tooth	Ongoing	- Played with her cat- described her.	RP-ongoing	
	- Family argument	RP	- Likes the Spice Girls + wants their CD- looking forward to bdays.	Ongoing	
	- A shrew got into the house	RP	* Cat again	"	
	- The cat caught a rat	RP	- Cat	"	
	- Missing tooth - spot is sore	Ongoing	- Cat	"	
Lisa	- Her cat sleeps with her	Ongoing	- Capital alphabet	Environmental	Lots of connection between oral + written topics. She is not very sure of herself + I think she uses the storytelling to "try out" her topics before she is confident enough to write about it. For her, storytelling definitely supports writing.
	- Talked to Kamrie on the phone last night	RP	- "I like Stacie because..."	Ongoing	
	- Dancing with a friend	RP	- Easter egg hunt	RP	
	- Staying up late on weekend	RP	- Numbers 1-46	Environmental	
	- Past vacation - Indian village + saw a mtn. - Not Hbd.	Long Past	- "My mom got sea-sick..."	R.P.	
	- Playing with her cat + cat's habits	Ongoing	- Someone pushed her + she fell + bumped her tooth out	RP	
	- A story Garrick told her in the gym - a kid with matches	Same day / RP.	* Dancing with her friend	RP	
			* A boy with matches	Same day / RP	
			- Playing with her friends.	Ongoing	
			* Playing with her cat.	Ongoing	

may be other ways of indexing and coding your "in the midst" notes that can help you analyze your data later.

Interviews

Another important tool for the teacher-researcher is interviewing—asking questions to bring out the information we couldn't learn without getting inside our students' minds. Interviewing is not a new strategy for teachers but one that can be honed as they build on their conferencing skills, asking questions through a casual conversational approach.

High school teacher Virginia Shorey reports that she often begins her interviews with comments or questions such as, "What you were telling me the other day was really interesting" or "I didn't have a chance to ask you about this before, but can you tell me a little more about. . . . " Then she continues to ask open-ended questions that follow up on her students' responses.

One of the reasons Virginia is such a good interviewer in these open-ended situations is because of her strong creative listening abilities. The gift she brings is that "breathing respect" (Stafford 1998) that she carries for the kids she works with. She is an attentive listener, but more than that; her interest in her students' answers comes across clearly. Instead of waiting for perfectly framed, preplanned questions, she begins here and now. She's not "waiting for time to show her some better thoughts" (Stafford 1998). In reflecting on her questions, she notes, "I ask questions I don't know the answer to—that I really want to find out about. And the kids can tell that my questions are real—they're *genuine*. They tell me things that are so amazing! I never know where our conversations will go, but I follow along."

Virginia's interviewing process is similar to Studs Terkel's, which he compares to jazz improvisation:

I suppose I have been influenced by jazz since I was a disk jockey and wrote columns on it. Jazz has a beginning, a middle, and an end. The framework is skeletal; at the same time there is an arrangement. So it is with a conversation. I have an idea in the beginning. I don't just shoot blind. I have ideas, but I make adjustments. You adjust. You change the sequence of questions. Suppose a person says something I didn't think he was going to say. He leads me to something else. It's like jazz. You improvise. (Murray 1990b, 49)

Many of the best interviews with students begin with an idea and then become improvisations based upon the students' responses. Sharon Frye found it helpful to interview her students about their understanding of their self-selected vocabulary words, probing further when she needed more information for her assessment. In the process, she was able to tap information that she didn't have access to through observations alone:

I pulled each student aside for five to ten minutes and asked them about their words. As they answered, I sat with a clipboard and took notes evaluating how well they understood the words on their list and how comfortable they were with each of them. Sometimes they fumbled over words, citing a dictionary-like definition but not really making a connection between the words and their own lives. Other times, they made the word their own. When I asked Kate, a ninth grader, to describe a "tumultuous" day, she described a day that would make most adolescents run home in tears:

"Well, okay, it would be a day where you woke up late and then missed the bus and had to walk to school and got there late, but then this boy you

HOW TO **Get Started with Interviews**

Many of the best interviews start with existing protocols of questions. If you are new to interviewing students, you might want to begin by revising one of these protocols. For example, one of the most widely used interviews in literacy is the Burke Reading Inventory (Weaver 1994). Here are some of the questions in the inventory:

Who is a good reader you know?

What makes him or her a good reader?

Do you think that she or he ever comes to something she or he doesn't know when she or he reads?

If yes, what do you think she or he does?

If no, suppose that she or he does come to something that she or he does not know. Imagine what they would do.

If you knew that someone was having difficulty reading, how would you help that person?

What would a teacher do to help that person?

How did you learn to read? What did you or someone else do to help you learn?

What would you like to do better as a reader?

These questions can easily be adapted to other disciplines. For example, if your research involves looking at students' scientific processes, you might ask questions like the following:

Who is a good scientist you know?

What makes that person a good scientist?

How did you learn to do science? What did you or someone else do to help you learn in science?

What would a teacher do to help that person?

What would you like to do better as a scientist?

You can even adapt these questions to get at social behaviors. For example, if you are exploring the links between learning styles and social networks in the classroom, you might ask questions like the following:

Who do you know who is helpful in our class?

What makes that person a good helper?

If you knew someone in class was having difficulty with a task, what would you do to help that person? What might someone else do to help?

Use the questions as a starting point for getting at the processes your students go through, and you'll begin to see new patterns between social networks in the classroom, individual personalities, and learning.

really like asks you out. Then you walk into this class and find there's a pop quiz, but you haven't studied at all, and then it turns out you get an "A" on it anyway, but then you find out your best friend said something really, really horrible about you. It's just everything would be either really bad or really good and just all up and down and turned around emotionally."

From her description, I could tell Kate understood *tumultuous.* It was a word she could choose to use in writing or as she spoke. That I had never before observed Kate using the word did not mean she had not learned it.

There were many times during the interviews where students had difficulty applying a word to a different situation than what they had memorized. For instance, Kate also had the word *hither* on her list. She used it as "go to hither." Through my interview, I was able to ask follow-up questions about the word. I asked her more about where she had first seen the word and where she found the definition she studied. I learned from her about possible ways she might use the word, and we talked through her use of it with a preposition.

This kind of interviewing is a tool I will use again. I learned more about what my students know about their vocabulary words, and what they can do with these words, by spending ten minutes talking with them and taking notes on their responses than I was able to ascertain through several weeks of observations. I could tell who "owned" their words, who made the words a true part of their vocabulary, and who was still struggling to adopt their words. And I was able to help those who struggled reach a better understanding of their words. The power of talking with students is incredible. (1999).

Carla Sosanya is a middle school teacher at Sauvie Island in Oregon. She used Sandra Wilde's spelling interview (1992, 164) so she could diagnose her students' spelling attitudes as well as their spelling strategies (see Figure 4.4). Questions like Who is a good speller that you know? What makes him or her a good speller? and What do you do when you don't know how to spell a word? give her important information, which she can extend by asking students to show her their strategies from an actual sample: "How did you figure out how to spell this word?" "Pick out some words that you think are spelled wrong. Show me how you could change them to the right spelling."

It might be helpful to create a list of questions that will draw out more specific information about your research topics, as Carla did. She brainstormed questions, relied on published interview questions such as the Burke Writing and Reading Inventories as a starting point, and made adaptions to meet the needs of her particular study.

Surveys and Inventories

Sometimes we want to find out what a large group of people think about a certain teaching practice or issue, and it simply isn't feasible to interview

Figure 4.4   Spelling Interview

The following interview was conducted with a thirteen-year-old boy in seventh grade who was having trouble with spelling.

Spelling Concepts and Attitudes

1. Is spelling important? Why?
   Yes, because you need it for life—for writing.
2. How do you feel about spelling? Do you like trying to figure out how to spell words?
   It's neat. I like trying to figure out words.
3. When is it important to spell correctly?
   When you're writing a book, story, or checks.
4. Who's a good speller that you know? What makes him/her a good speller? Does she/he ever make a spelling mistake?
   Jeremy. He studies and he knows the words.
5. How do people learn to spell? How did you learn to spell? Are you still learning?
   People learn by practicing and looking up words. With a friend. I got words from my teacher and from home. I'm still learning.
6. Why do you think words are spelled the way they are?
   That's a hard question.
7. What do you do when you don't know how to spell a word?
   I look at it, close my eyes, and try to spell it.
8. What else could you do?
   Study with a friend or a parent.
9. Where in the classroom would you look if you wanted to find out how to spell a word?
   The dictionary.
10. If you were at home, where would you look?
    Ask your parents or look at a dictionary.
11. How do you know when you've spelled something right?
    It looks and sounds right.
12. What do you do when you haven't spelled something right?
    I check it off and write the correct word beside it.

Questions About Specific Spelling

13. How did you figure out how to spell this word?
    Looked it up in the spell checker.
14. Why did you change this spelling?
    To know how to spell it next time.
15. Pick out some words that you think are spelled wrong. Tell/show me how you could change them to the right spelling.

He picked out some words and underlined them. We talked about spelling patterns, and he picked out several words to correct on his own. He also selected some words which were already spelled correctly but with which he was not familiar (see Figure 1).

Figure 1

mercury
IT Tacks 88 Earth days, to compleT one
RoTashon=one year. IT was named afer The Romeds
god. speeDy mesh ger. This planiT is almosT
the mosT heveisT planiT in The A4 livey Because
of The inpaKT of meters. tenpetatheres aT
Day are 427° and aT night 170°c.

everyone one-on-one. Surveys and inventories can help tap information that would otherwise be inaccessible to us.

Jennifer Allen, a third-grade teacher, says that inventories help her to understand how students and parents see the process and purpose of her research versus what she sees. She writes, "I also find that the inventories often redirect my teaching or the actual research project. Student comments lead me to new understandings."

In her study of home-school journals, Jennifer surveyed both students and parents (see Figures 4.7 and 4.8). She asked parents questions like What do you like best about the home-school journals? and What have you learned about your child through the journals? She included a section for their additional comments. For the students' survey, she asked, What is the best thing about writing in your home-school journal each week? How has the journal helped you to reflect on your learning? and What could someone learn about you through this journal? These surveys provided Jennifer with alternative perspectives on her research question and gave her further insight into parents' and students' sense of the purpose of the home-school journals.

Susan Pidhurney, a kindergarten teacher, suggests that if you are planning to involve parents of your students in your classroom inquiry, it is helpful to think through these issues before you begin:

- Not all parents are comfortable responding in writing. Be aware of their difficulties and find another way to communicate.

- Be sure to write as simply and clearly as you can until you are sure of the literacy level of the parents. Some may not be able to read very well; some may be able to read manuscript writing but not cursive. Be sensitive.

- Keep entries as positive as possible.

- Keep writing even if the parents don't . . . they will eventually get the hint.

- Don't let the home/school journal turn into a daily report card. You will soon tire of it and won't want to continue.

- Don't get discouraged by negative entries. Parents sometimes need to vent and if they feel comfortable, they'll vent at you.

- Remember your intent . . . to increase and improve communication between home and school. If the parents are having too hard a time, find another way—maybe write on weekends only, for example.

- Keep a photocopy of the journal. A colleague had an extensive dialogue going when a journal got lost—forever.

Audiotapes and Videotapes

A tape recorder can be an invaluable tool for the classroom researcher. It allows you to fit your research project into the nooks and crannies of time outside the school day. You can play back one-on-one conferences, classroom discussions, and small-group work sessions, and listen intently and repeatedly if necessary. You also have verbatim quotes, in your students' own words.

Vivian Gussin Paley, reflecting on her thirty-seven-year-long teaching career, encourages the regular use of tape recorders:

When I transcribed [tapes], I could bring back with great immediacy the errors and misconceptions and wonderful curiosities that I heard. Then I could say the next day, "John, when I listened to the tape recorder, I realized that I didn't hear your whole statement so what I told you was only for the first part." Of course, if you keep doing this for a period of over a year, you have your curriculum in logic and language built right there. And you yourself are saying, "I wonder why I said that?" You are scrutinizing yourself, too. "That didn't come across the way I wanted it to"—which is true of so much of our conversations with each other. That's all right. You're not strangers passing in the night. You can keep correcting every day that you see each other. (quoted in Teets 1998, 14)

It's important to realize that tapes can provide valuable data for your research study without the requirement of lengthy transcription of every word. There will be times when it makes sense to transcribe an entire tape; some class discussions or individual conferences beg to be analyzed, dissected, and presented to a larger audience verbatim. But much of the value of audiotapes and videotapes is that they allow you to revisit your classroom, and your research issues, long after the actual event.

Linda Christensen regularly records small-group conferences in her high school classroom and then listens to the tapes as she commutes to and from

HOW TO **Use Audiotapes in Research**
Barbara Libby

Recording and listening to students at work in my classroom can be an invaluable tool in research. The following uses are related to the research questions I had about myself and my students. Your questions may guide you in finding many other possibilities for taping to inform.

- Tape yourself during direct instruction, group discussions, reading and writing conferences, etc. Analyze these tapes for *teacher/student talk ratios.*
- You can use the same tapes to analyze your questioning levels and become more aware of opportunities for higher *levels of questioning.*
- Are there silent voices in your class? Listening to your recordings with a student checklist will make you aware of who speaks and who doesn't. You can also analyze your checklist for *gender issues.*
- Different places in the classroom can be used to record and check for a percentage of *on-task versus off-task dialogue.* This information might support use of the center or direct you to make changes. You will also think about the purpose of student dialogue, as I did.
- Model the kinds of questions you want students to ask each other during science workshop, literature circles and writing share time, then tape these activities to *monitor the influence of your modeling.*

school. Through reviewing the tapes outside her classroom, she could listen more intently to the types of conversations around literature that the students had. Rather than transcribing all the tapes, she selects ones that are particularly good examples and shares those transcripts with her students so they have student-generated models of effective literature discussion strategies. She has the added bonus of finding categories with her students of what makes a good book discussion.

Ann Hurd chose to analyze her tapes through marking who spoke in whole-group discussions, noting only short, medium, and long comments in the group (see Figure 4.5). Without words, the patterns of talk in her classroom as well as language styles of individual students are noted in ways that help her think about group dynamics and her role in whole-class conversations.

Other teacher-researchers choose to note only topic changes when analyzing tapes. Peggy Albright noted both who spoke and when the topic changed in class discussions in her study of gender differences and preferences in her seventh-grade classroom. By noting both topic changes and who controlled the conversation, Peggy over time could tease out differences between cultural patterns of talk and the dominance of certain personalities in the group.

Figure 4.5 Tallying Observation Sheet

OBSERVATION

	N.E. POETRY	CAN I KEEP HIM?	WILLOW TREE LOON	PROBLEM SOLVING	SORTING	SETS
MARK	lsm	absent	smss	lssm	lsssm	sssss
SARA				s	s	sss
MARGE	m	mssmsmm	mssss	ss	sss	ssssss
THOMAS	ms	mmmm	mmm	ssmsmms√ss	ssmssm	ssmssm
THERESA	llll	smmssm	ssmsssmms	sssmsssss	mmss√ss	ssssss
ANGELA		s			s	s
STEVE	m√√l	mssl	mssm	ss	msss	sssss
SUSAN	l++l	ss	ssm	ss	ss	ss
JOHN	mll√√√	s√√s√m	ssss√ms	s	√s	ssssss
JASON	l√l++ss	√√s√√√√√mm√√√√ √√m	√√smsl√sssss√ss√√√√sm m√mms√	sss√sss√sss	√lsms√sss√s √√	ss√√√sss√
BECKY	mll++√√	sssmml	√s√l++√√√√√	sssm	mmss√	sssss
MATT		s		ss	s	sss
LARRY	lll	s√√mmm	slsssmms	sssms	sssssss√s√	sssms√ss
BETH	m√√√	sss√√l	sss√smms	ssss	√m	ssssss

s=short comment
m=moderate comment
l=lengthy comment
l++=extremely lengthy comment
√=interruption

When teachers do transcribe tapes, they often choose snippets of conversations to illustrate key points in their research. Bilingual teacher Michelle Schardt wanted to look at how her students learning English as a Second Language know how to use English words when they aren't *thinking* about language. She used the following transcription markers in her analysis of her conversation with Ruben as they looked at a picture book:

Transcription Key

-	False start
. . .	Pause
====	Emphatic stress
CAPS	Very emphatic stress
/?/	Unintelligible word
( )	Comment

An excerpt from Michelle's transcript follows:

    M: What is that bear doing?

    R: Watching the . . . feather (a leaf) fall down.

    M: Now what is he doing?

R: . . . Go hunting?

M: Hunting maybe? What does it look like here?

R: There's an old house. There's /?/.

M: Now what's happening?

R: Him's in the /?/.

M: What?

R: Him's inside the house.

M: What does he see?

R: Some plates (bowls). See? A big plate and a big plate and a small plate.

Depending on what emerges in the conversation you are transcribing, you might want to use some other common transcription markers, such as:

[ ]   Overlapping speech

f   Forte (spoken loudly)

p   Pianissimo (spoken softly)

Some teachers create their own markers that are tailored to the particular research they are conducting, as Anne Wallace did when she was focusing on the fluency of her preschool students' language. In this case, knowing the length of pauses would be helpful, so she noted in her transcription key the following differentiation:

. . .   Pauses in speech for a half second

. . . .   Pauses in speech for one second

Videotaping also has the potential to give teachers insights into untapped aspects of their classrooms. In research like Andie Cunningham's about her students' work during her "movement workshops," video is a natural choice for data collection. Other situations, too, can be ripe for examination of the role of body language or facial expressions, or for a closer look at several things that are happening all at once that might go unnoticed in a busy classroom.

It's important to decide the specific uses for the video you are planning to record. There is a temptation to set up a video in a corner and simply record everything. The stack of tapes piles up quickly, and it can take hours to review and make sense of the data. A complete transcription of a videotape, not only the audio portion but the many actions occurring simultaneously, can require several viewings.

We recommend that you use video for very specific purposes and with definite time limits around the activity you are recording. Here are some examples of ways teacher-researchers have used videos to good advantage:

- Second-grade teacher Leslie Funkhouser arranged to videotape a student giving a "tour of the classroom." This provided her with important data on how well this student understood the organization in her classroom as well as insights into the underlying social structure and where her students' perceptions and her own differed.

- In her English as a Second Language writing class, Virginia Shorey wanted to look closely at how her three Filipino students used Tagalog to help them write stories in English. The videotape of one twenty-minute writing conference among the three girls provided fascinating data about their reliance on each other and their use of "code-switching" that would have been impossible to capture on audio alone.

- Stacy Neary was investigating spelling strategies with early elementary students and videotaped the brief strategy lessons she conducted with small groups of students. Capturing these mini-lessons on video allowed her to look closely at her own teaching, at the effect of the lessons on students, and at the ways they discussed spelling with each other. Further, she found it valuable to share these five- to seven-minute tapes with her research group; the tapes were short and specific enough to serve as a useful focus for discussion and feedback.

You might also ask visitors to your classroom—aides or parent volunteers—to do some videotaping. After they have videotaped, ask them what they recorded and why. Having your classroom recorded by someone else, with their comments about what they saw, can provide a needed new perspective on your students and your research topic.

Documenting the Classroom with Photography

More teachers are turning to photographic documentation as a data collection tool to help them understand their classrooms. Cameras are portable and fairly unobtrusive, and can capture moments in a classroom that might otherwise go unremembered. As a tool that anyone can learn to use, photography can invite students to participate in our research with us. William Bintz found he was able to "see through different eyes" when he began to use photography as a research guide:

> I selected photography as a research guide for three reasons. First, it is a medium that is accessible to almost everyone. . . . Second, photography enables students to participate in the process of data collection and analysis. Specifically, it affords them the opportunity to assume a researcher stance by inviting them to explore what symbols at the school are personally significant, and discuss why these symbols mean so much to them. [Third] . . . I selected photography because it can be used as a "medium with a memory" . . . it has an open-ended potential where photographers can use themselves and their photographs as objects of inquiry. This potential was

recognized by Diane Arbus (1972), an internationally renowned photographer, who stated: "One thing that struck me very early is that you don't put into a photograph what's going to come out. Or, vice-versa, what comes out is not what you put in." (1997, 34–35)

One way many teachers begin to collect data using photos is as a complement to written observations. Photos can jog your memory of incidents in the classroom. Like other data-gathering tools, pictures can help you notice what's going on with fresh eyes and help you focus. This in turn helps you pinpoint more specifically where and how to gather future photos.

When Jill Ostrow began to document her classroom using slides, she discovered a different perspective on how the children were working together. She realized that when she circulated in her busy multiage classroom, she was already taking quick mental pictures before moving on. The problem with these mental images, she decided, was that she was making judgments in her teaching in that split second without having a chance to review the image and compare it to others. Jill says,

> I learned so much about how the kids were working together in writing workshop. For instance, I have a sequence of four slides of three girls writing together. In the first slide, they all have their pencils in their hands, and their eyes are on the papers in front of them. In the second slide, a couple of girls are talking to each other, and in the third, you can see them all laughing. As a teacher looking across the room, when I see a group of kids all laughing like that, my first response is, "They're fooling around. Why aren't they writing?" But in the fourth picture, taken just a minute or two later, they're seriously writing again. The pictures helped show me the flow of their work together—and that I can back off and let them have that chance to laugh and talk that keeps their writing going. (personal communication, 1998)

Jill was able to use the slides to share her discovery, first with her parent helpers so that they realized the importance of watching groups of kids over time, and also with other teachers and administrators worried about "time on task" during writing workshops.

Jill came to use photography as a more focused tool when she was investigating how children use the resources in her classroom environment to learn. The photos helped her document: Who sits where during different workshop times? How do they use their bodies? Whom do they work with? "One of my favorite slides shows three kids spread out on the platform reading. One of them has a big picture book, one has a beginning chapter book, and of course, Tessia's reading *The Lion, the Witch, and the Wardrobe*. You can see the different sizes of the print over the kids' shoulders. It really pointed out to me that whom the kids choose to work with during reading workshop has nothing to do with reading ability" (personal communication, 1998).

Photographs of kids at work in the classroom can be supplemented by

HOW TO **Use Photography in Research**
Katrina Kane

Why?

This is a critical first step and will save you time and money. You need to determine the purpose for taking pictures before you begin. The purpose will drive everything that follows. Some examples might be

- Data collection for a research brief
- Recording growth over time
- Materials for your portfolio
- Reflection tool to be used with students

Who?

Once you have determined why you want to use photography as a tool in your classroom, ask who you will need to photograph. This will depend on the purpose of the photographs and how they will be used later on. Some things to think about:

- Do you need to work with a whole class, a small group, or individuals?
- What permissions do you need from parents?

What?

What do you need pictures of? Do you need duplicate copies? Always keep your negatives! You never know when you might need them later. Think about some of the following before you start taking pictures:

- Do you need photographs of students' work in progress or after it's completed?
- Will you photograph the project at the beginning, middle, and end to record growth over time?

When?

When can you best capture on film what you are looking for? Try to seek a natural time rather than a contrived one. Some other things to consider:

- What time of day should you take the pictures?
- Will you need someone in the room to help so that you can focus your attention on your research?
- Do you have enough light or too much? I suggest shooting a twelve-exposure roll at different times of the day to check the lighting.

Where?

Where you shoot your pictures is very important. You need to think about your students and how different environments affect them. You could photograph them

- In your room
- In someone else's room
- Outside or inside

Know Your Camera

- The middle of a good project is not a good time to find out that your flash doesn't work.
- A tripod is very helpful.
- If you don't have equipment of your own, borrow instead of buying. This is a good way to save some money and see if this data collection tool is for you before making a purchase.
- Simple is always best!

Know Your Environment

- How will your learners react to the lens? Should you forewarn them?
- Check with your principal before proceeding.

Know Your Budget

- Find inexpensive film and check the date.
- Find inexpensive, prompt, and local film-developing services.
- Set a small budget and stick to it. See how much photos will cost, and decide if this method is for you before you get started.

examples of their work. Not only do slides of student work save a lot of room, they are more easily sorted and stored when you begin to organize your data. Another advantage of slides is that student work can be blown up to a larger size when projected on a screen, allowing a closer examination of details within the work—and a way to share it with a wider audience.

Student Artifacts

Examples of student work can be one of the richest sources of data for teacher-researchers. It is tangible evidence of what kids are able to do and of the range of responses kids make to different learning tasks.

Karen Gallas's study of children's uses of the arts as part of their meaning-making process required that she have many samples of students' drawings and writings. She considered them an aspect of her field notes:

> "This is the actual size of my insect," [Ronit] said as she drew a line that was about two inches long. Then she stopped, her eyes widened, and she gulped.

"Oops, that's way too big," and she grabbed the eraser once again. After drawing a line that was much smaller, she continued, "Aren't I smart? 'Cause I was thinking of him in the buttercups, so I had to make him smaller, or someone would come along and be terrified." [Karen includes here Ronit's Buttercup Bug drawing.]

For Ronit, the art experience at this time became an opportunity to find out what she did or did not understand and to rethink her ideas in a new form. Watching her work on an artistic problem, I was able to see that Ronit had not understood some basic information, but I could also observe her quickly correcting herself and thinking through the problems that are inherent in this type of activity. Then, looking back over Ronit's work from the beginning of the unit, I found other points at which her artwork had revealed basic misconceptions. (1994, 142)

Because Karen had previous artifacts of Ronit's work, she could place this particular drawing and set of observations within a larger context. This points to an important aspect of collecting artifacts: Save everything! (Or as much as possible.) Though you may have a good idea of what specific sets of student work you need to save for a short-term study, it can help to have a folder of student work from over the year so that you can trace growth and notice differences.

It's helpful to let parents know early in the fall that you'll be keeping most of the students' work for the year and returning it the next summer. This gives you a chance to decide which pieces of work you will want to look at more closely and make copies of those examples.

Other useful student artifacts include both drafts and final versions of their written work, lab reports, learning log entries, self-evaluations, and peer evaluations—essentially, any of the products that emerge from their classroom work. Most of us find, though, once we start gathering the rich harvest within our classrooms, we want to collect *all* of it. It reminds us of our memories as children gathering blueberries in August. The ripe fruit seemed to fall off into our hands. Each bush had so many delicious ripe berries, it was hard to pick them fast enough. As one branch was harvested, the one below emerged similarly laden.

Instead of slowing you down as a gatherer, this kind of plenty can simply serve to whet your appetite. It makes you eager and greedy to pick everything. At some point, you need to come up with a way to organize your student artifacts. You might store them alongside field notes, as Karen Gallas does, or in separate folders—whatever system works best to help you find your way back to them. Just as with other data you collect, stacks of student work won't inform your research if they molder in piles and you never look at them again.

Becoming Your Most Important Tool

When you become a teacher-researcher, you become your own most important tool. Your tape transcripts, surveys, questionnaires, and interviews are good tools, but as Shirley Brice Heath (quoted in Power 1995) reminds teacher-researchers, "You are the key instrument, and you must keep that instrument on all the time" (27). This requires a special kind of mindfulness, a willingness to live in the moment, which can provide us with a different presence in the classroom, one that can be a gift to us as well as to our students.

In the following excerpt from her essay, "The Clay Queen," Stacy Neary (1998) writes about the joy she takes in this new role:

> I hadn't had this much fun in years! Literally! How often is it when you're working as a classroom teacher with thirty students that you feel like you can take the time to hang out and play in the corner with a bunch of girls? Well, I can speak from experience that it rarely happens if it happens at all. Why this doesn't happen is a whole other story, but today I want to share with you what does happen when you take the time to "hang out" with those amazing little people in your classroom we call students.
>
> I sat huddled in the corner of the [multiage] classroom. There I was on the floor, crossed legs, notebook in hand, listening to a group of animated little girls play and talk about their world as they constructed creative designs in clay (pigs, Spice Girls, necklaces) and chatted about numerous topics. There were so many different topics, I could hardly contain them on my paper!
>
> Taking this time, I have to admit, felt like a luxury. It was almost like I was cheating somehow by not acting like a "teacher." I had no direction, no defined outcome, no real purpose except to listen to the language these students were using. How therapeutic to just "be" with my students. Probably just as much for them as for me.
>
> Not only was this therapeutic for me (I hadn't laughed that much in a long time), but I learned so much about these young girls through the language they chose to use, the topics that arose, who talked the loudest, the most, the least. I learned about their relationships with family members and others in class. I was given an indication of what they are taking away from this crazy culture we live in and also how they use explorative, descriptive, and imaginative language to play with language and to express themselves. I was an observer, a participant, and a guest as I sat alongside these girls and was made to wear clay necklaces, crowns, and nose rings! I was firmly named "The Clay Queen" by the end of class. All this in about twenty minutes!

Stacy's experience demonstrates the paradox at the root of data collection. You need to be ready at all times, armed with tools—notepads, tape recorders, interview questions—that can be used to match what you need to learn in your research with what your students can teach you. Data collection is serious work that will take you to a new level of professionalism in your work. But you also need a healthy sense of fun in your inquiry. Allow yourself time to play with the different ways of collecting information and enjoy the new views of yourself and your students as you begin.

William Stafford captures this sense of being attuned to the moment and finding pleasure in what can be learned through close observation and listening in his poem "You Reading This, Be Ready." We hope you take his advice to turn around in your own classroom. We suspect you'll find, as Stacy did, that collecting data is a gift you give yourself.

You Reading This, Be Ready
William Stafford

Starting here, what do you want to remember?
How sunlight creeps along a shining floor?
What scent of old wood hovers, what softened
sound from outside fills the air?

Will you ever bring a better gift for the world
than the breathing respect that you carry
wherever you go right now? Are you waiting
for time to show you some better thoughts?

When you turn around, starting here, lift this
new glimpse that you found; carry into evening
all that you want from this day. This interval you spent
reading or hearing this, keep it for life—

What can anyone give you greater than now,
starting here, right in this room, when you turn around?

RESEARCH WORKSHOP

When to Write: Strategies to Find Time for Notetaking

Brenda Miller Power

For many teachers, taking notes is the key to their data collection. By observing your classroom closely, slowly compiling information about students and your curriculum over time, you build confidence in your research ability.

When you write will determine what you write and what you remember from day-to-day life in your classrooom. As Kim Stafford (1997) writes, "Memory is made as a quilt is made. From the whole cloth of time, frayed scraps of sensation are pulled apart and pieced together in a pattern that has a name" (16).

From the "whole cloth" of everything that occurs in your classroom, you will eventually be piecing together the patterns that form your research findings—the story you will tell. Pick the time of day for notetaking when it makes the most sense to gather the pieces of what you see, hear, and feel to tell that story. Determining when to take notes means you'll have to consider many factors—your personality as a teacher, the needs of your students, and the goals for your notes.

Regardless of what the story will be, there are two kinds of observational notes that can be taken: "in the midst" and "after the fact." It's helpful to test out each of these kinds of notes as you begin to get into a rhythm and routine of observations. You need to figure out when notetaking makes the most sense in your classroom, fitting both your goals and the needs of the students.

"In the Midst" Notes

"In the midst" notes are the observations you make while your students are at work. You might write "in the midst" while walking through the room, with your notepad in hand, jotting down what you see. The writing might be on Post-its, address labels, or one side of a journal page.

If you're trying to find a time when it would make sense for you to take notes, consider those times when you want students to pay less attention to you and more attention to each other. In Pat McLure's multiage primary classroom, Pat takes notes during two components of her literacy program. She writes notes, sitting on the back of the rug, when children read their writing in the author's chair to the whole class. When children glance at the back of the room, they are apt to see Pat writing. This teaches them to focus attention on the writer in the chair, not on their teacher. Pat will still make comments and redirect the group if needed, but the notetaking serves the dual purpose of being a tool for assessing the group and a means to focus the group on the writer and writing, not on Pat.

The other time Pat takes notes is during student literature discussion groups. Pat is always present when these groups of four meet. Once again, because some of Pat's time is focused on notetaking, children attend to each other and the books more than they do to their teacher.

There is another, more subtle goal for Pat in taking these notes during whole-class and small-group discussion periods. When she meets with parents for assessment conferences, many of her notes highlight how individual children are working within the class community. These notes reflect her value of placing individuals within communities rather than focusing on individual achievement.

Many teachers choose to do their "in the midst" notes with just the opposite purpose. They wander through the class, clipboard in hand, during individual conferences with students. This has almost become the standard for notetaking during workshops, and I think it's one of the reasons teachers get frustrated with keeping anecdotal records and often stop doing it. When you're in a one-on-one conference with a student, it's distracting and time-consuming to stop and take notes about what happened in the conference. There is a rhythm you establish in moving among your students, and an intensity in those individual conferences that is rarely matched in any other part of the curriculum. You are trying to listen intensely to one student and still continually survey what is happening in the rest of the room. Adding notetaking to that delicate mix of close attention and rapid, repeated scanning of the room is just too much for most teachers. Taking notes in the midst of students working together discussing their writing or literature, with their attention focused on each other, is much more manageable.

"After the Fact" Notes

"After the fact" notes are made when students aren't present. It might be in the quiet of your classroom early in the morning before students arrive. It might be at home, in the journal you keep on your bedstand to write in just before you fall asleep. It might be on address labels you write on while eating your lunch.

The benefits to writing "after the fact" are many. You can choose a quiet time, without the endless distractions that are always present when you're working with students. What bubbles up in your mind when you are alone, away from students, is likely to be the most important events that day in your classroom. The writing has more of a narrative flow—"after the fact" notes tend to be full sentences, while "in the midst" notes are brief, choppy words and phrases most of the time.

But there are also many drawbacks to writing "after the fact." Teachers are not often successful at preserving pockets of time for work that doesn't absolutely need to be done. If you rarely find time for a bathroom break in the morning, it's hard to believe you'll be able to carve out a consistent fifteen minutes of writing while your students are in morning recess.

I find it's best for me to take "after the fact" notes, and I do manage to keep to my routine even though I face the same distractions as any teacher. I meet with students for only three hours a week in each of my college classes, and there isn't a pocket of time in any of those hours where I would be comfortable taking notes. So I write for fifteen minutes after each class. I've found the only way I could develop this habit was to set some artificial rules and limits for myself.

I make myself remain in the classroom. This is important, because just being in the same physical space where I met with students sparks memories of events that occurred. I jot my notes on looseleaf paper as I write responses to the in-class journals my students have written that day. It usually takes me no more than fifteen minutes to jot down my notes, and at most another fifteen minutes to finish responses to those in-class journals.

The good thing about staying in the classroom is that it strictly limits the time I write in my teaching log and respond to student logs. Another class always comes in within half an hour during the day, and after evening classes I'm anxious to get home. When I'm sitting in the classroom, it's a quiet time when it's easy to reflect on my teaching, but I also feel the clock ticking.

Either "in the midst" or "after the fact" can be effective times for taking notes, depending upon how you work. And as you take notes, you'll find there are fewer boundaries between the two. As you sit in the back of the classroom, jotting down notes during whole-class writing discussions, it's likely you'll make a note or two about something that was said an hour earlier as you circulated during writing conferences.

Once you decide when you're going to write, find ways to preserve that time. This is no small feat for teachers. We want to capitalize on the teachable moments in our classroom, which means it's often hard to stick to routines. And, unfortunately, others rarely see the teacher's time as her own. Administrators cavalierly schedule assemblies during writing time featuring talking moose droning on about dental hygiene; colleagues stop in for a quick cup of coffee during the time they know your students are in music class; a parent can only come in for a conference during a time outside the designated conference period.

With that in mind, the following activities can help you establish some boundaries around the time you set for taking notes and observing students.

Link when you take notes to your research.   What times of the day make the most sense for you taking notes to answer your research question? List both potential times for notetaking and how notetaking during this time is linked to your research. Try to list at least a few potential times when you might take notes in your classroom.

Research Question   **Time for Notes**

_____   _____

_____   _____

_____   _____

_____   _____

Experiment with "in the midst" and "after the fact" notes.   Before you lock into a routine of notetaking, test out the different times of day you listed for making these notes. This may take a few days or a few weeks, but you'll want to explore which times of day and which kinds of notes work best for your needs.

As you test out different times for taking notes, don't worry much about what you write. Think instead of whether you are able to take notes consistently during these times. After at least a few days of trying to observe and write about students during different times, ask yourself, What period was most comfortable for me to take notes? What might get in the way of my taking notes consistently during this time?

Initiate a ritual.   Poet Georgia Heard (1989) writes, "Where I write, and the rituals I create for myself there, are crucial for keeping the writing spirit alive in me" (126). If you want to sustain the spirit of an active, questioning observer of your students, consider developing a few rituals that create a psychic space around the time you reserve for your notetaking. It might be the habit of putting on your smock when it's time for your fifteen minutes of notes; it might be moving to your desk to pull out your treasured favorite pen reserved only for your notes (and returning it to that spot after the notes are finished); it might be sitting for a couple of minutes at the rug area in your classroom as students go about their work, thinking about what you'll write. My ritual of writing briefly after my students have left is so ingrained that I really can't leave the classroom until I've finished jotting down notes—my teaching feels incomplete without it.

Think about what rituals might work for you. Is there a hat or scarf you might put on to let students know you aren't to be disturbed as you're writing? Is there a sign that needs to be posted on your door during a planning period, to let colleagues know only emergencies warrant an interruption?

Take a moment to list one or two rituals you could institute to encourage consistency in your notetaking routine.

Let colleagues and students in on your work.   If students and colleagues know you value the time you put into your notetaking, they will help you protect that time. Enlist as allies the people who might infringe upon your notetaking time, carefully explaining the purposes of your notetaking. Once they understand why you need to protect this time, some students and colleagues will become protective of your notetaking routine. As you're beginning to establish the notetaking routine in your classroom, you'll also want to schedule at least a small number of class discussions explaining why you'll need time for notes and how these notes will be helpful to the classroom community.

Save a small amount of time each week to look at all your notes from the week.   Set aside just a half hour or so in the early weeks of your notetaking to look over what you've written and to flesh it out. You can encourage yourself to do this by using project planner paper, which provides you with that extra margin for additional jottings. At least a small part of the time you schedule for your notes needs to be this reflection and clean-up time. If possible, schedule this time with a colleague, and talk together about gaps in your notes and how they might be filled.

Focusing on Student Talk

Sherry Young

The main focus of my research has been on student talk. I am interested in learning how boys and girls use language differently. I also want to know how these differences play a role in students' ability to express their ideas and opinions. My goal has been to find new strategies to help all students find their voice by learning more about the ways they interact in whole-group and small-group situations.

I designed an interview on talk that I administered individually to all my students (see Figure 4.6). I enjoyed the personal contact with the students and appreciated the seriousness and honesty with which their answers were given. It was interesting how differently students interpreted the same question. At other times I noticed how their answers sounded like what they thought their teacher wanted to hear. I heard my voice in their replies.

In two of the interview questions, students indicated strongly they had heard teacher directions about how to participate in classroom talk. One of these questions was, What do you do when you want to share something? Two-thirds of the students said, "Raise your hand." I had a hunch this might happen, so I asked a follow-up question calling for another way to share. Girls had fewer strategies for what they would do, whereas boys had several ways to get their ideas heard. Two of the nine girls had no response at all.

The second question with responses that sounded like my voice was, How do you know when someone is listening to you? This time, sixteen students, or more than two-thirds of the class, said, "When the person is looking at you." This is a strategy I have taught them to use to check for their audience to be ready.

Another set of questions asked about their feelings about speaking or participating in class discussions. Over three-quarters of the students said that they felt good about participating in class discussions. Many students said they "liked it" or they "wanted to," but others hinged their participation on being part of the group. For example, one student said, "It's important. It's part of the community. I feel like I'm part of something important." One girl said, "I feel happy because I can help people." Several boys said participating was an important part of learning. One boy said, "It helps me out. Helps me learn!" Another boy said, "If you don't participate, you might not learn something you are supposed to." Students view talk as an important part of our class, and most of them seem to have positive feelings about it. Over half of the students considered themselves good speakers.

Another section of the interview dealt with student preferences concerning the groups in which they work. One-third of the students liked working with a partner because it is easier to talk or they trust their partner will be respectful. Seven of the nine girls preferred working with partners or in

Figure 4.6 Interview

22 students
9 G   13 B

Grade 3   Talk Interview

Name: S. Young   Date: March 97

1) When you are at school and you want to share something you've learned what do you do?   Why?
Raise hand = 14   Ask teacher 4   Other 4
   5G 9B   2G 2B   2G 2B

2) What is another way you share what you know?

⨍ 3) During a class discussion, how do you feel about participating?
   Good 17   Depends 5   No 0
     7G 10B   2G 3B

⨍ 4) How do you feel if someone disagrees with what you say?
   O.K. 9   Bad 6   Mad 2   Other 5
   5G 4B   2G 3B   2B   2G 3B

5) What would a teacher do to help a person share their ideas?

X 6) When you talk to your classmates, do you prefer a small group, talking to a partner, or a whole class discussion?
Why? Small 5   Partner 8   Whole 6   Other 3
       3G 2B   4G 4B   1G 5B   2B 1G

X 7) Do you prefer a group of all boys, (or all girls), or a mixed group of boys and girls?
   Boys   Girls   Mixed 17   Other 1
    2   2   6 G 11B

8) How do you know when someone is listening to you?
   Looking at you 16   Other 6
       7G   9B   2G 4B

9) What would you like to do better as a speaker?

10) Do you think you are a good speaker?
     Yes 12   No 4   Sometimes 6
     5G 7B   1G 3B   3G 3B

X 7.b   Classmates 9   Grownups 6   Either 7
            4 G   5B   2G 4B   3G 4B

small groups. Only one girl liked the whole-group learning better, and five of the boys preferred this grouping.

When I asked if they preferred working in a group of the same gender or a mixed group, students were overwhelming in their support for mixed groups. Only two girls and two boys thought they might like to work in groups of the same gender. Students thought it wouldn't be fair to leave out the other gender: "They would want to be part of the group." Many students thought that the mix of boys and girls brought more ideas to the group. "Different kinds of people, different ideas!" "Boys know stuff girls don't! Girls know stuff boys don't!"

Another question I asked concerning groups was whether they preferred talking to their classmates or grownups. I asked this question because in an earlier interview about students' home journals, some students had indicated that they didn't like talking about a book to their parents. During the talk interview, I had the feeling students strongly preferred to talk with their classmates rather than grownups, but the final tallies did not show this. Only nine students said they preferred talking to their classmates, and six students said they preferred talking to adults. Seven students said they liked to talk to either classmates or grownups. Students thought parents or teachers could help the most when they had a problem.

While I was interviewing my students about talk, I began a new class procedure to observe our classroom talk. During our daily morning meeting time, I appointed a student observer. The observer's job was to take notes about what he or she saw and heard during this time. I also used Post-its to record comments or observations I had during this time. Before we left the group, our observations were shared with the rest of the class.

Another way I used this role was to have students run small groups while I observed. In this role I did not participate as a talker, only as a watcher. On two occasions I was able to be an observer while another adult led the group in lessons on art and a discussion of paintings. I was able to contrast the work of the small group with that of the whole group. I recorded whether boys or girls did the talking, in addition to as much of the conversation as possible.

featured TEACHER RESEARCHER

Letting Inventories Lead the Way
Jennifer Allen

One method of data collection that has worked for me as a teacher-researcher has been the use of inventories. I first experimented with inventories when exploring student-led literature discussions. I found the feedback from students to be a real eye-opener. I had a preconceived notion that student-led literature discussions would promote multiple interpretations of the books that we were reading. However, when I started sifting through

Figure 4.7 Student Survey

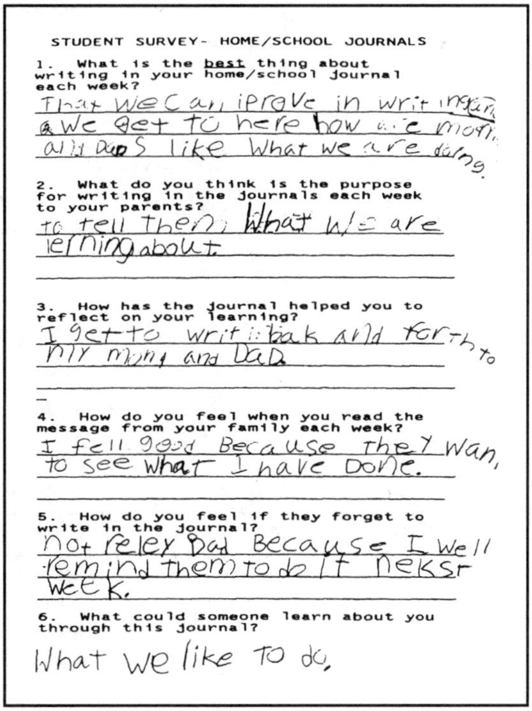
STUDENT SURVEY- HOME/SCHOOL JOURNALS

1. What is the best thing about writing in your home/school journal each week?

That we can iprove in writing and we get to here how are mom and Dads like what we are doing.

2. What do you think is the purpose for writing in the journals each week to your parents?

to tell them what we are lerning about

3. How has the journal helped you to reflect on your learning?

I get to writ bak and forth to my mom and DaD

4. How do you feel when you read the message from your family each week?

I fell good Because they want to see what I have Done.

5. How do you feel if they forget to write in the journal?

not reley Bad Because I well remind them to do it neksr week.

6. What could someone learn about you through this journal?

What we like to do,

the student inventories, I found that students perceived different purposes for literature discussions. One student thought my sole purpose for them was "to see if we were listening to the book." After reading the student inventories, I knew that my purposes did not match the purposes my students perceived.

The inventories provided me with a new lens through which to look at my research project. Because of them, I started to follow the lead of the students. Insights as a researcher led me to changes in how I approached and implemented student-led discussions. The inventories provided me with rich data and new directions for my research. They kept me in tune with students' needs and their perceptions of the project.

I have continued to use inventories during other research projects. I am currently exploring the use of home-school communication journals. Students write home to their parents every week, and parents respond to their children over the weekend. The journals return to school every Monday. I look through them but do not respond to them.

I started this project because I was hoping students, especially struggling readers, would be motivated to work through and read the journal entries made by their parents. To guide my research, I had students and parents fill out inventories on the topic of home-school journals (see Figures 4.7 and

Figure 4.8 Parent Survey

PARENT SURVEY- HOME SCHOOL JOURNALS

1. What do you like best about the home/school journals?

I like the fact that I know how my child feels about what she is learning. Also I am learning what she likes as a friend and not just a parent

2. What have you learned about your child through the journals?

How smart she really is. What her likes and dislikes are. How she feels about her family life.

3. Do you feel that the journals have kept you informed on what your child is learning at school?

Yes, I am not a person who gets involved in school events, this way I can keep up with what she is doing in school.

4. What changes would you suggest in the current format?

I leave because as it is the kids have the freedom to write what they want, and that is good because like us kids need to get their thoughts down on paper.

5. Additional Comments: _I think the journal is an awesome idea. I have my own journal and it helps so much to get the thoughts and feelings down on paper. Good and luck._

P.S. Sorry this is late! I need to check her bookbag! ☺

4.8). I wanted to see what both groups saw as the value of implementing them.

I was enlightened by both parent and student responses. It was interesting that not one student or parent saw the journals as a reading tool. Many students saw them as a way to communicate with their parents, and some of them saw the journals as a way to become better writers. Many parents felt that the journals kept them in touch with their children's learning. After sifting through the inventories, I found that the home-school journals were important to parents, students, and me—but for different reasons. My research took a new direction, one that better suited the needs of the students and parents.

featured **TEACHER** RESEARCHER

A Toolbox of Questions About Teaching

Andra Makler

When I teach, my most important question is, What's going on here? I've learned I must question my assumptions about what's happening in class, what students mean when they offer comments and questions, and how students perceive my comments, behavior, questions, and responses. This is especially important when I work with intern teachers. Every year I team-teach a three-hour seminar for a cohort of Master of Arts in Teaching (MAT) students during their semester of intense practice teaching. As my co-teacher Mary Burke-Hengen says, the seminar should help them learn "how to be a faculty for each other." The faculty we have in mind is an ideal, sometimes achieved in discussions among like-minded teachers intent on reforming their practice and the schools.

We ask the student teachers to write a comment about some aspect of their teaching or experiences in school on the blackboard when they enter class each week. Sometimes we provide prompts such as "A good surprise I had this week was . . . " paired with "Something that caught me off guard was. . . . " Statements are not signed. The class reads the comments, someone asks for clarification, and discussion begins.

I decided to write down the blackboard comments each week to see what I might learn about interns' perceptions of teaching (and my own) from systematically studying them over the semester. Would the subjects change over time? Would statements become more focused on their students' learning or their own learning as teachers? Would the nature of the expressed concerns change? Would I find patterns? stages of concern? Would it turn out that the statements were not a good tool for achieving the kind of honest conversation Mary and I desired?

The writing that students submitted for their teaching journals provided a kind of reality check on my analysis of the meaning of the blackboard comments. Their final remarks in the circle at the end of class were another source of information. In November, two months before this seminar began, I asked students to write and talk about their "teaching questions" as they prepared to teach their first class on a daily basis. That list functioned as a kind of baseline for me to compare with changes in their focus (and locus) of concern over the course of their student teaching experience.

I am always musing about what a particular student meant by a specific comment. I carry my Toolbox of Teaching Questions in my head and open it when I am making the beds, ironing, or spin-drying the lettuce. My toolbox has removable compartments and plastic bins. The biggest bin is full of worries and anxieties about whether I am really understanding what's going on in my students' minds. The anxieties come in bunches, like scallions; some are more pungent than others, like the worry over whether Tina will get organized enough to listen to kids when they ask questions during class, or whether Roy will do the necessary planning to establish an order to the ideas he wants to address in a lesson.

I also carry metaphors in my toolbox. I hate some of them, like the idea that teaching is "being in the trenches." I worry when I hear students discussing their classroom as if it were a battlefield. I am constantly trying to figure out whether the blackboard comments are manifestations of particular metaphors—and if they are, what that tells me about the students' construction of what it means to teach. Rolled up like socks, smushed into any available space, are gauzy wisps of conversations overheard as I move from group to group during class, lines remembered from journals, questions interns ask in class or in my office. I pick at these comments one after the other to see if one can help me get at the significance embedded in another.

When I was working on my dissertation research, I learned to make large charts as one step in the process of organizing emerging themes. I did this on a smaller scale with the blackboard comments. Each week I copied them onto a narrow lined yellow pad just as they were written up on the board. After class I typed them out and tried to group them into categories. Then I made overhead transparencies to share with the class the following week. I also wrote the statements in a different order on large pieces of newsprint and hung them up in the room, to hear what students would say when they saw several weeks' comments listed together.

Sometimes I think my ears are my best tool. During class I sit in the back and listen; I try to hear the little comments students make as they move around, pass papers, take a break. These are often important clues to their biggest concerns. I am always trying to connect something said this week with statements made earlier in the term. If I hear the same question, complaint, or satisfaction over and over, I mark it mentally for later retrieval to try to figure out whether it is really important or just "safe" to share. My early guesses are often wrong. Seeing *how* I was wrong is as instructive as figuring out the significance of particular blackboard statements. My mistakes show me how the students and I interpret things differently, and that is very important information for me as their teacher and teaching supervisor.

What Likes What?: Data Analysis

5

Data is a burden in that you've got so much of it. It's very much like taking twenty pounds of mashed potato and shoving it through a straw.

Dana Cox

Research projects often end in defeat when teachers try to analyze their data. Like Dana Cox, we may shake our heads in despair at that mountain of "mashed potato" and the enormous task of funneling it through a straw. Paradoxically, we quickly see many gaps in our notes, interviews, and artifacts, and regret all the information that *wasn't* collected. There is often a rush of insecurity at this point in the research process. It's one thing to write faithfully in a teaching journal for months or conduct a slew of interviews with kids; quite another to say with confidence what all the Big Truths are, culled from the information you've gathered.

The murkiness of data analysis is what scares any researcher. If it doesn't spook you at least a little, you're not opening yourself up enough to the new learning that can come during analysis. If the analysis seems very easy, you've probably only found what you already knew before the project began.

When you analyze your data thoroughly, there is a fair degree of uncertainty in the task. Human relations are complex, so any analysis of what goes on in a classroom teeming with kids will end up with some unknowns and ambiguities. Good research analyses raise more questions than they answer. If you are a neat and orderly teacher, you have to be willing to wrestle with a little more messiness in your life as you analyze your data. Susan Ohanian writes about this need for disorder:

> Only the territorialists to the right and left of us seem to know Truth. They are like Louise, a character in Josephine Humphrey's *Fireman's Fair* who finds her pleasure in the "maintenance of daily order in the real world. She kept her shoes in the original boxes." Too much of what travels under the name of research is concerned with keeping the shoes in the original boxes. For classroom research to be significant, the teacher needs to take the risk of

getting those shoes out of the boxes. She needs to ask herself a lot of hard questions and in the end learn to accept the ambiguity of the answers. (1993, 33)

While it's hard for anyone to "get the shoes out of the boxes" and tolerate unanswered questions, we'd argue that teachers are better equipped for this task than many university researchers and administrators. You need to accept change, uncertainty, and complexity to survive as a teacher for any length of time. Whether you realize it or not, you probably developed long ago the ability to see events in your classroom as far more complicated than they would appear to an outside observer.

In recounting the experience of being evaluated by a principal, Susan Ohanian challenges traditional researchers to respect the knowledge we teachers bring to our analysis of what happens in our classrooms:

The first year I was teaching . . . I had a very good university department chairman who came in once a week to my high school English class and gave me some advice. One time, I was doing one of those stand-up demonstration lessons that he had to write up, and it was on Julius Caesar. In the back of the room, one of the toughest kids in the class was reading a newspaper.

Later, when he was telling me about the evaluation, he said that he had leaned over and said to her, "Don't you think you should pay attention to what the teacher is saying?"

And she said to him, "Who the hell are you?"

And I said to him, "Well, when you think about it, who the hell are you? You come into my classroom with a briefcase; you don't know anything about that child, you don't know that it's a triumph for her to be reading a newspaper. She had been a chronic absentee. This was the first step." So I say with all due respect to the people who want to count things, "Who the hell are you?" (1992, 59)

We all need a little of Susan's chutzpah when we start to analyze our data. Hey, if not us, who? Who is better able to understand what's happening in our classrooms? Who better to determine the patterns of thinking and learning than someone who knows and cares about these students? And who else has the storehouse of knowledge about this classroom, its history, its possibilities? So we say with all due respect for both you and your research—you have the skills to analyze data. You just need to trust your ability and find an analysis process that works for you. Data analysis is daunting, but it's also fascinating work for those willing to accept a little bit of messiness and uncertainty.

Finding Patterns in Data

In the novel *Cold Mountain,* by Charles Frazier, Ada apprentices herself to another woman, Ruby, to learn everything she can about working and living in the world around her. She is amazed at how much Ruby knows—how she can answer almost any question with quiet calm. Ada finally asks her where all her knowledge comes from:

> How did you come to know such things? Ada had asked.
>
> Ruby said she had learned what little she knew in the usual way. A lot of it was grandmother knowledge, got from wandering around the settlement and talking to any old woman who would talk back, watching them work and asking questions. Some came from helping Sally Swanger, who knew, Ruby claimed, a great many quiet things such as the names of all plants down to the plainest weed. Partly, though, she claimed she had just puzzled out in her own mind how the world's logic works. It was mostly a matter of being attentive.
>
> You commence by trying to see what likes what, Ruby said. Which Ada interpreted to mean, Observe and understand the workings of affinity in nature. (1997, 107)

The categories Ruby uses to define where her knowledge comes from are all helpful in thinking about data analysis. The "grandmother knowledge" is the stuff you've always known at some intuitive level. Don't discount it as a researcher; draw upon it. As a teacher-researcher, it's all right to ignore some of the traditional research edicts like "If you didn't write it down, it didn't happen." You can draw on all of your experiences and observations of kids, throughout your history as a teacher, to analyze the data in your current project.

Some of the prior knowledge you bring to your research will provide hunches that guide you in beginning to analyze your data. It's the old concept of the hypothesis made new. One of the most powerful aspects of teacher research is that it brings those hunches, the teaching lore we carry quietly with us, to the surface of our thinking. And when we share our analysis with others, we have the chance to change policies in schools, districts, even nationally, as Erickson and Shultz (1992) write: "Adept and empathic teachers may make effective guesses about the roles of such matters as attention, trust, legitimacy in their teaching. They even may be able to make fairly accurate 'seat of the pants' judgments about the fit of particular tasks with particular students and about the varieties of student experience in their classrooms. But if this is so, their inferences are for the most part intuitive and transparent to themselves. Hence, their hunches are not available to others with a stake in their teaching—administrators, researchers, parents, and students" (471).

Once you become comfortable trusting some of your hunches in data analysis, you need your own "Sally Swanger"—someone you trust as a mentor who is willing to pore over your data and findings with you, unafraid to challenge what doesn't make sense. In Chapter 8, we show how teachers find research partners and build communities. While it's possible to collect data quietly on your own for months of a study, it's essential to have someone willing to listen to your first ideas about findings, looking

Common Analysis Terms and Methods

Audit check—A check or confirmation of your findings by someone outside the research process. This can be done at any point in the research process.

Case study—A detailed, in-depth examination of a person or people from a specific group.

Confirmability—Often used in place of the term *objectivity* by qualitative researchers; refers to the ability of others to reach similar conclusions with the same data set.

Constant comparison—A data analysis method developed by Glaser and Strauss (1967) to "enable prediction and explanation of behavior"; involves deriving categories from data over time, and then using the categories to build theory.

Semantic domain analysis—A kind of constant comparison coding and analysis.

Sociogram—A picture of a social network.

Thick description—A sufficient amount of detail in describing the research setting and techniques to allow others to make needed comparisons to research completed in other settings.

Transferability—Often used by qualitative researchers in place of the concept of "external validity"; relies on thick description of relevant research to allow outsiders to determine if findings could be transferred to other settings.

Triangulation—The use of multiple and different sources, methods, investigators, or theories (at least three) to confirm findings.

Working hypothesis—Often substituted for the concept of "generalization" in qualitative research, because hypotheses will change as data continue to be analyzed in research.

over your shoulder at the same data set, as you show the path of your thinking.

But the biggest part of data analysis involves Ruby's last piece of advice—learning to see "what likes what." These are the patterns in your work, the pieces of data that fit unexpectedly next to each other, leading to a flash of insight. It's an organic process, one of learning to be comfortable with what works for you in analyzing data and what doesn't. This was the experience of Ann Hurd, as she found herself uneasy through much of the early stage of her research: "The research has produced a variety of reactions in me. I experienced anxiety as I tried to develop a topic. More anxiety as I was advised to trust what bubbled up as I taped. More anxiety as there appeared to be nothing and deadlines loomed. Yet each time I looked at the transcripts, I began to see what I hadn't seen before. To do this, though, I had to work with handwritten words and not computer-processed words. I had to lay out my pages of type where I could see them all at once, mark them, and generally make a mess. From there I could create order."

Finding the patterns within your data, viewing each bit of information as part of a larger puzzle you must put together, is the task that will take most of your time during data analysis.

If you've been to any hobby or gift shops lately, you realize the world of puzzle making has changed. There are now far more choices than the basic 500- or 1000-piece puzzle that was the standard for years. Puzzle lovers can choose to construct 3-D structures. There are mystery puzzles that come with accompanying text—you can only put the puzzle together as you find clues in the narrative. There are even puzzles that have no picture on the box—you have to put them together without any sense at first of what the final image will be.

In the same vein, data analysis over the past decade for teacher-researchers has changed from a few limited options, defined by university researchers, to a range of creative strategies developed by teacher-researchers who find traditional analysis methods didn't make sense in their studies.

Choosing a Data Analysis Method

Narratives

In a collaborative teacher research project in Georgia conducted by Betty Bisplinghoff, JoBeth Allen, and Barbara Michalove, the group spent a year collecting data around issues of using home-school journals in Betty's first-grade classroom, and with Barbara's second-grade students. They developed codes for their data based upon the constant comparison analysis method, a respected and well-known method of data analysis for qualitative researchers:

> We studied home-school journals, written family stories, oral stories, and other artifacts. JoBeth had been studying grounded theory and suggested we use the fine-grained coding of the constant comparison method. We spent several days reading about the methodology, coding four sets of transcripts together, and generating an extensive code list. We agreed to code the other sets on our own and meet weekly to compare our analyses.
>
> We were all unhappy with the process. Betty came to the next meeting with a new plan. We agreed that we were losing the children, their families, and the real stories by reducing these rich exchanges to codes. Betty suggested, and we immediately adopted, a plan to read all the data about one child/family unit independently, write a one- to three-page narrative interpretation, and come together weekly to read and compare our analytic narratives. Studying a well-established methodology led to the creation of a

new approach, a methodology that was responsive to this particular study, its participants, and its goals. (Bisplinghoff and Allen 1998, 65)

Perhaps the most intriguing aspect of the analysis and writing process for this group was the retreats they scheduled to work together writing up their work. These were held at a beach house, without other family members or distractions. Participants would analyze their data and write in the morning, take long walks on the beach and respond to drafts in the afternoon, and read good novels in the evening. Rested and renewed, they produced the remarkable trilogy *Engaging Children* (Shockley, Michalove, and Allen 1993), *Engaging Families* (Shockley, Michalove, and Allen 1995), and *Engaging Teachers* (Bisplinghoff and Allen 1998), fine examples of the insights teacher-researchers can gain from their data if they give themselves permission to adapt and develop their own data analysis schemes.

These researchers also highlight a crucial but neglected aspect of data analysis—quiet time and space to seek out patterns and learning. As poet Rita Dove (1997) writes, "To make a prairie—or a light bulb, or the quantum theory of mechanics—you need reverie. Daydreaming. The watchful soul in the relaxed mind" (161).

Insights or new understandings often come when we find ways to free ourselves from the daily busyness of teaching lives. It's amazing how many analysis breakthroughs come during beach vacations or on quiet rainy days with no agenda. We all need space to think, and the brain can sort enormous amounts of information at an unconscious level if we aren't cluttering it with mundane responsibilities.

The Georgia research team respects different ways of analyzing data and reads widely to find different models. But in the end they don't discount their feelings of discomfort when a method isn't working for them, and they are quick to discard it.

Codes

What one teacher-researcher discards, another pulls from the trash heap, revises, and uses. Lee Anne Larsen and Sherry Young are primary teachers in Maine who were inspired by the *Engaging* teacher research series. They decided to undertake a research project similar to the one outlined in *Engaging Families*, studying the effects of home-school journals on their relationships with students. Unlike the *Engaging Families* researchers, they found developing codes early in the process essential for their analysis of data.

After reading the findings in *Engaging Families*, they decided to develop a code sheet for analyzing the responses children and parents gave in the home-school journals. Research still seems like a linear process to most of us—finding a research question, collecting data, and then analyzing what is found. Lee Anne and Sherry found they could organize and understand their data best by beginning with preliminary codes for the data, based upon what other researchers had found in a similar study. Figures 5.1–5.3

Figure 5.1 Blank Code Sheet

R TC PC I Jennifer	R TC PC I Lynn	R TC PC I Alex
P NP IV 2V BC CC	P NP IV 2V BC CC	P NP IV 2V BC C
R TC PC I Travis	R TC PC I Jennifer	R TC PC I Abigail
P NP IV 2V BC CC	P NP IV 2V BC CC	P NP IV 2V BC CC
R TC PC I Tobin	R TC PC I Shane	R TC PC I Brandon
P NP IV 2V BC CC	P NP IV 2V BC CC	P NP IV 2V BC CC
R TC PC I Mark	R TC PC I Taylor	R TC PC I Jill
P NP IV 2V BC CC	P NP IV 2V BC CC	P NP IV 2V BC CC
R TC PC I Sidney	R TC PC I Sherry	R TC PC I Dayton
P NP IV 2V BC CC	P NP IV 2V BC CC	P NP IV 2V BC CC
R TC PC I Hunter	R TC PC I Kate	R TC PC I Charles
P NP IV 2V BC CC	P NP IV 2V BC CC	P NP IV 2V BC C
R TC PC I Randy	R TC PC I Samuel	R TC PC I John
P NP IV 2V BC CC	P NP IV 2V BC CC	P NP IV 2V BC CC

Codes Explanation

Top of entry
R = Retelling Only
TC = Theme Connection
PC = Personal Connection
I = Illustration

Bottom of entry
P = Parent Participation
NP = No Parent Participation
1V = 1 Voice Response
2V = 2 Voice Response
BC = Book Connection
CC = Child Connection

Figure 5.2 Filled-in Code Sheet

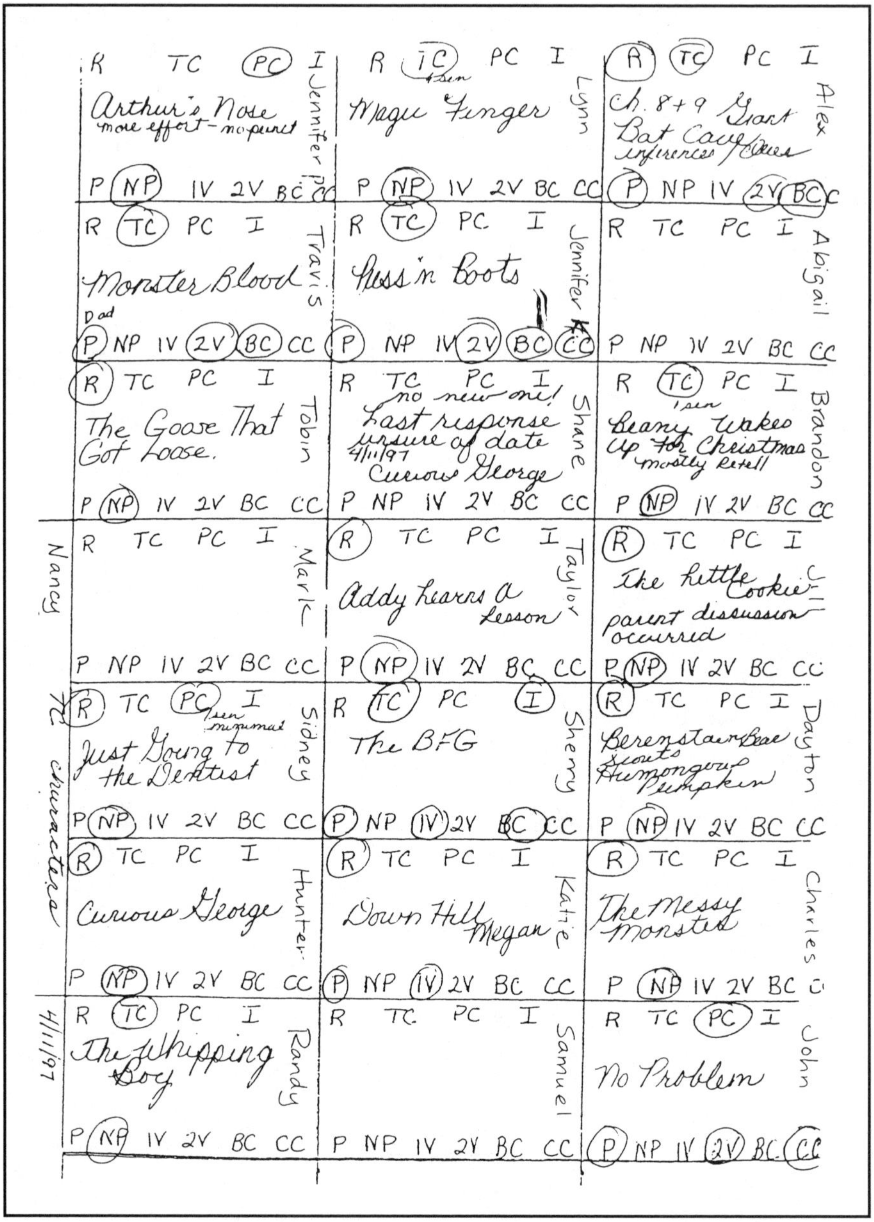

Figure 5.3 Summary of Responses

Reading Journal Response Information

Name	Week of 3/7/97	Week of 3/24/97	Week of 4/14/97	Week of 4/11/97	Week of 4/28/97	Week of 5/12/97
Retelling Only	‖‖‖‖ ‖‖‖‖	‖‖‖‖ ‖‖‖	‖‖‖‖ ‖‖‖‖	‖‖‖‖ ‖‖‖‖	‖‖‖‖ ‖‖‖	‖‖‖‖ ‖‖
Personal Connection	‖‖‖‖ ‖‖‖‖	‖‖‖‖ ‖	‖‖‖‖ ‖	‖‖	‖‖‖‖	‖‖‖
- Feelings	‖‖‖	‖‖‖	‖	‖	‖	
- Opinion	‖‖‖‖	‖‖‖ (baby book)	‖‖‖‖	‖)	‖‖‖	
- Past Exper.	‖‖			‖		‖
- Asked quest.						
Text Connection	‖‖‖‖	‖‖‖‖ ‖	‖‖‖‖ ‖‖	‖‖‖‖ ‖‖‖	‖‖‖‖	‖‖‖‖
- Character	‖‖	‖‖	‖‖‖‖	‖‖‖‖ ‖	‖	‖
- Setting			‖			
- Plot	‖‖		‖‖		‖‖‖	
- Theme						
- Moral/Lesson	‖				‖	‖
- Another Book		(genre FT) ‖				‖
- Author Style		‖		‖		
- Genre	‖‖		‖‖		‖	
- Prediction				‖		
- Asked Quest.		‖‖‖				‖ (ans. quest)
- New Learning						
Illustration		‖				
- Personal		‖				
- Text						

show their blank code sheet, a filled-in code sheet, and a summary of the response.

Coding can begin with something as simple as + and - marks on the page. This was the case for Debbie Glazier, a Title 1 reading teacher who was doing a case study of Andy. She writes,

One day, in the middle of October, I was rereading my notes from the previous few weeks. I have set up my journal to write on only the left side of the page: the right side is for comments. I picked up my pen and started making plus (+) signs next to all the times Andy was "with" us; reading a book, writing in his response journal, listening to a read-aloud, or speaking in an appropriate classroom situation (asking or responding to questions, etc.). I put a minus (-) sign next to all the times he did not appear to be "tuned in."

Reading through these new additions to my journal, I began to add words and phrases, noticing if Andy was focusing his attention on another student, an object on his desk. Next to the pluses, I noted what specifically drew Andy into an activity: a tape recorder, a student reading her story in the author's chair, a picture book read-aloud with plenty of humor.

It was a turning point for me in my classroom-based research. I wrote in my journal on September 6, "It's going to be important for us to get Andy to read and write for longer periods of time." That was the initial period when I was recording how many seconds or minutes he actually stayed with an activity. That particular day, he stayed less than two minutes with a book he had chosen to read.

I'm still using clock time to emphasize the length of time he is able to sustain an activity, but my emphasis now is on the positive happenings in Andy's responses. Because of the daily journal entries with their quick pluses and minuses right next to the description of activities, I feel I have a "fast and easy" way of retrieving the day's high points. What enables Andy to be successful today drives tomorrow's decision-making for teaching.

For Debbie, codes were a way to link her classroom research to teaching in powerful and more immediate ways.

When you choose a big research topic, coding can help you stay focused. Wanda Heath wanted to consider gender differences in discussions in her fourth-grade class. Because there are so many ways to look at boys' and girls' talk, Wanda decided to focus on only two aspects of discussions in order to make sense of the data she was collecting. She set up two different work groups of four students, one all-boy and one all-girl, and she analyzed the discussions over a month: "I was looking for different types of responses, interactions, interruptions, off-topic digressions, body language, movement, and group dynamics. I was also interested in what strengths and weaknesses were demonstrated by each group. I decided to audiotape the groups, do transcriptions to analyze, and keep a running checklist of behaviors. I chose the use of rising intonation—sharing intonation (SI)—mentioned in *Classroom Discourse* (Cazden 1988) and off-topic discussions (OT) mentioned in *Listening In* (Newkirk and McLure 1993) as the two codes to mark on my transcripts."

Wanda avoided a mistake novice researchers often make: trying to use too many codes at once. She could easily have developed codes to represent body language, group dynamics, digressions, and other topics she was interested in as she considered gender.

Wanda counted the instances of sharing intonation (SI) and off-topic discussions (OT) on each audiotape transcript. (Figure 5.4 shows an excerpt from a transcript of the all-girls group.)

She then charted the instances of each type of talk for each participant in the group, and noted striking differences in the groups (see Figure 5.5). The boys were off-topic far more than the girls, and the girls were much more likely to use sharing intonation. Looking at these findings in the context of what was said by participants led Wanda to these conclusions:

> The boys' strengths definitely lie in their group interactions camaraderie, relaxed behaviors, risk taking, play with words, digressions into great off-topic discussions, enjoyment of books, and the sharing of oral language. Weaknesses include forgetting to come back to the topic, getting too silly

---

The reading share circle consists of four seven-year-old female first graders. Their names are Mallory, Zia, Cortney, and Kayla. They have all chosen a book to read and discuss at the share circle. They are sitting around the reading table, and Mallory is the student reading leader today. I have placed the tape recorder in the center of the table.

I have used the girls' first initials during transcribing, and T denotes my comments.

SI (sharing intonation) appears where it was spoken in the dialogue. OT (off-topic discussion) appears where it happened in the transcript.

At this time C has just finished reading her book.

C: You have to clap. Questions? You guys have any questions?
M: Why [SI] did you want to read this book?
C: Because it's Kayla's book and I know how to read it. Any more questions. Nope. Oh, Mrs. Heath.
T: Who would you read this book to?
C: Anybody, you [SI], Mallory.
T: Has anyone else written a number book?
C: Nope.
Z: Nope.
M: Nope.
T: We have the author sitting right here. Let's ask her why she wrote a counting book.
K: So I could read it to a kindergarten class that didn't know how to count very high. My brother could only count to ten but I taught him by reading that book and now he can count to twenty. [OT]

Figure 5.4 Letter–Coded Interview Transcript

Figure 5.5 Summary of Results

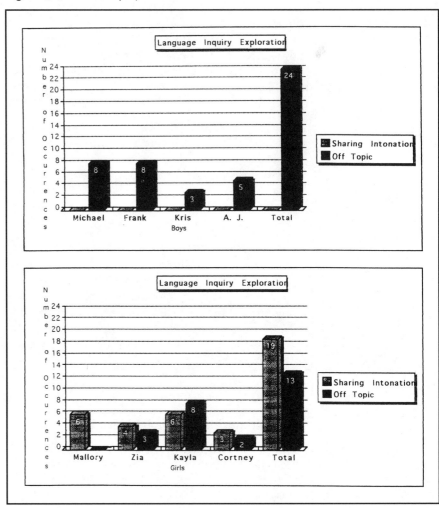

and loud, not asking more in-depth questions, extending the book, and choosing only a few types of books.

The girls seemed to have fewer strengths than the boys. Although they could stay on the topic of the book, this was both a strength and a weakness. They definitely knew the procedure for running the share group, but sometimes this also became a weakness in their ability to share. They did choose books that interested them and ones they could read, but they, like the boys, need to branch out into other genres. Because of their attention to procedure, the girls did ask more questions of each member of their group and they had a larger number of what they call "kind comments." The girls' biggest weaknesses lie in not taking risks, not being relaxed, lack of humor,

HOW TO **Cook Your Notes**

Anthropologists refer to two types of field notes—"raw" and "cooked." Raw notes are just what you've written, as quickly as possible, without any analysis. Cooked notes are the analysis of these raw materials.

One simple scheme for cooking involves codes developed originally by the famed anthropologist Levi-Strauss (adapted by Corsaro 1981). We recommend the use of three of these codes:

PN   personal notes
MN   methodological notes
TN   theoretical notes

Personal notes include any information relevant to your mood, or that of the class. Events like an argument before school with a colleague, or a child vomiting in class ten minutes before you began notetaking, will affect the notes you take, and it's good to include these to jog your memory later about why the notes might be unusual on that day.

Methodological notes include any questions or statements about *how* you're doing your work. They might be statements like "I should put a tape recorder by the science center to get those interactions" or "Maybe students should keep logs of questions asked during literature discussions."

Theoretical notes include any hunches about patterns, or *why* events are occurring as they are. A theoretical note might be as formal as "I think Tadd's behavior after time in special education supports Kohn's notions about the danger of external reward systems." But most are less formal—they are those "aha" moments that are essential to good teaching. These might include statements like "Perhaps Jason's frustration in science is due to so many absences in the past two weeks—the group seems unwilling to bring him up to date on the project."

Cooking notes can also be as simple as adding questions to them, to extend and expand your thinking about what you are seeing. The Latin root of the word *theory* means to see or behold—cooking with questions in mind extends your sight about what patterns are emerging. Questions to consider while cooking your notes might include, Why did I think this was important to write down? How does this connect with what I saw earlier in the day, week, year? Based upon what I'm seeing, what action should I take to change the curriculum or my research project?

These questions can easily be abbreviated in your notes. For example, thinking about the importance of what you're noting becomes *I?* as an inserted code. Issues of curricular change become *C?* as a code. Potential additions to assessment narratives become *A?* as a code. What you're trying to do is develop a mind-set that constantly questions as you write your notes—that is what cooking is all about for researchers.

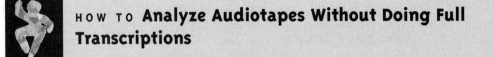

HOW TO **Analyze Audiotapes Without Doing Full Transcriptions**

- Listen to tapes, and note what strikes you. This can be done during the odd moments of the day—while you are commuting, doing yardwork, fixing supper.
- Flag only the comments of a case study informant.
- Have students listen to the tapes and analyze what is going on. If you choose this technique, you might want to frame the activity with a few guiding questions, like What went well in the conversation? What would you do differently? What do you notice about [the research topic]?
- Note only topic changes.
- Note only who controls the conversation.

All these techniques take far less time than full transcriptions, and in the end, they may give you all the information you need for your particular study.

and not enjoying the sharing of real-life experiences through the discussions.

Essentially using only two codes to analyze her data, Wanda was able to make some leaps into greater awareness of what was driving the different kinds of talk among boys and girls.

Codes for notes can be developed at almost any point in the research process. Some projects lend themselves to early coding; others require a large chunk of data to be analyzed before the codes can emerge.

When deciding upon codes for your work, start with these principles:

- As a general rule, develop no fewer than three codes, no more than six. Regardless of your research project, if you have too few codes, you are probably thinking of the categories and patterns in your data too broadly. And if you have too many codes, you will struggle to keep track of them.
- Don't be afraid to change, shift, or abandon specific codes that are no longer useful. A code that makes sense early in a project may not be useful by the end. Also, if you get too rigid about using certain codes, you might miss important new codes that would serve better.
- Try to represent the patterns emerging from your codes visually. This is a good test to see if your codes are really helping you understand your classroom. If there isn't some way to move from the codes to a visual representation of what the codes are showing you (e.g., a pie chart of different kinds of responses in math workshop; a bar graph of

who responds when during whole-group writing discussions), then you will probably struggle to move from your codes to findings later in the research.

Visual Markers

The type of data you are collecting will also affect which coding strategy works best for you. Virginia Shorey's high school English as a Second Language students had drawn quilt squares about special places in their homelands. When Virginia and her co-researcher, Ruth, read the transcripts of interviews with the students, they found categories like "the importance of pictures in their writing process" and "vivid memory details." They discovered the most helpful way to code these categories and visually find the way back to them was through colored label dots (colored flag Post-its work, too). Each color represented a category, and the dots or flags are placed in the margins to signal text that fits into that category. For example, in Figure 5.6, an excerpt from a transcribed interview, the categories are

Red	Memory detail
Green	Importance of picture to process
Yellow	Thinking in different language/learning language
Blue	Importance of talk/sharing/presentations

and in Figure 5.7, a student sample, the categories are

Green	Goes with quilt square
Red	Metaphor
Blue	Emotional ties
Orange	Sensory detail

As we search our data systematically for patterns, the process can be anything but neat. Enrichment specialist Janna Smith shares a working document of part of her process of data analysis (see Figure 5.8). She explains, "On this sheet, I began to compile and analyze data from multiple sources as it related to the subquestions underlying my major research question. I noted positive and negative patterns, and I also numbered them in order of frequency. Double lines under initials denoted a very strong or repeated expression of certain positive or negative aspects of mathematics, so I considered them significant. This charting became the basis for further categorization and writing."

Memos

It can also be a help to look at an overall picture emerging from a set of data, a kind of visual research memo on one page. Karen Hovland-Feuer initially

Figure 5.6 Color-Coded Interview Transcript

Ruth: I wanted to ask you a little bit about the place you drew. First of all, just tell me a little bit about where it is.

Cecilia: Well, it's in Acapulco, my country. It's in the beach. (Laughs)

R: Now, is this a place you went to a lot with your family? or by yourself?

C: A lot by myself. Alone, you know. I always go there . . . and sometimes with my friends and my family when we have picnics, we always go there.

R: So, this is a place that you have that's kind of a special place back home?

C: Mmm-hmm.

R: Tell me about the birds and the other things in your picture.

C: Well, the birds, they were always flying, you know. Sometimes, we see them. One time, I don't remember, when I was twelve, we saw a little turtle and he was with his mom, I don't know how long, and they were walking on the beach, and we [?] and we took pictures. So, that's we put . . .   ⟮red⟯

R: So, that's why you put that turtle in . . . oh, you didn't tell me that before. I like the way you made the sand kind of gold. What color is it?

C: It's like kind a gold, yeah.

R: So, when Mrs. Shorey asked you to draw and write about where you came from, can you tell me what happened in your head? Did you, like, see pictures, or did you think about it? Do you remember?   ⟮green⟯

C: Pictures. Pictures, you know, they have a lot of memories, of where I came from. And . . . I think about it, I saw pictures in my mind, yeah. . . .

R: Do you remember if you thought in Spanish or if you were thinking in English?

C: English. Yeah, that's my first . . . before in [?] Spanish.

R: Is that what you do most of the time? Do you mostly think in English now?

C: Uh huh.

R: Do you remember when you started thinking in English?

C: Last year.

R: Uh huh.

C: Because it's more easier to do it in . . . Russian, Spanish, too difficult. Because you have to switch the words, in English, it's not . . .

R: If you spend a lot of time talking to somebody who's speaking just Spanish, then do you starting thinking in Spanish?

C: Yeah. Yeah.

R: Do you ever feel like you're not thinking in any language? That you're just thinking?   ⟮yellow⟯

C: Yeah! Sometimes, I spend time with an American, and I'm translating, English, then I talk Spanish, then I stop for a moment . . . OK, OK, where were we? Real confusing!

Figure 5.7 Color-Coded Student Sample

Where I Came From
Tan Tran   green

Around with mountain ranges there was a little tiny village between them that
where I came from. My village seem very simple but it had a seductive. Far away,
you will see a track through a forest. The vegetation grew in a hustle beside it,
birds were throttling on old tree branches that a symbol for season. In the after-   red
noon, the roads full of animation. After a period of working everybody went
home with a smiling faces, they carried tools for farming, someone hunter shot a
lot of animals. At night my village seem dark and silent because we didn't have
any electricity, the only thing we had have oil lamp and foresight. When the echo
of Cock-crow sounded it means three o'clock in the morning. So everybody ready
to get up and going to work. Those things make ones heart rent and deeply at-   blue
tached. Right now my body is in a strange country but my soul at ones home-
land, where I was born and grew up. How can I forget those things because a
symbol that I am a Vietnamese.

---

felt overwhelmed when she looked at her case study transcripts of a four-
year-old's language patterns at play. To bring some order to her work, she
began by counting. She writes, "I counted the number of times Meredith
maintained a topic of conversation and the number of times she changed
the topic. I found the ratio was very similar in all three conversations. Before
counting, I thought that I would find significantly more topic changes with
her friend Annie than with Meredith. This was not true." From each transcript, Karen then charted the course of those topics, showing the number of
times Meredith changed and maintained the topic, and noting how the topics related to an overall theme (see Figure 5.9).

Looking at the patterns in each transcript through her visual memos led
Karen to important discoveries about Meredith's ability to use her language
to collaborate and negotiate a story together with other conversation participants. One of Karen's findings noted the ways that Meredith's talk in creative play was helping her learn to elaborate on the stories of others. She
was far more collaborative than Karen had imagined. Information like this
helped support the need for unstructured time for Meredith and the other
children in preschool to explore talk through play.

Memos needn't be visual—it can often help to look through your data
and choose one of your findings to write up in a brief narrative, a memo to
share with other teacher-researchers. This helps you focus your thoughts
and begin to write up your data along the way. (For more information on
writing up memos, see the first Research Workshop in Chapter 7, "Seeing
What Is Not Seen," suggestion 3.)

Figure 5.8 Working Document for Data Analysis

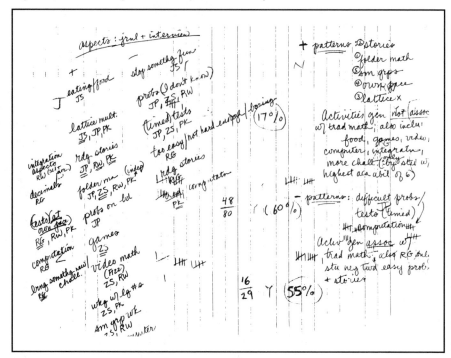

Semantic Domain Analysis

Semantic domain analysis is a useful data analysis tool for discovering different understandings of words by various cultural groups. To begin such an analysis, pick four to six words that are crucial to your research study. Define these words yourself, ask students to define them, ask colleagues to define them, and find definitions in the professional literature. Depending upon the subject of your study, one or two groups of informants may be more helpful than others. If you are looking at "folk terms" (words that emerge within the culture you are studying), you'll want to pay particular attention to the definitions from that group. For example, in Barbara Lockwood's study of social interactions among her fourth graders, she found these folk definitions among students:

Dude   Looks good, is really hip, wears neat clothes

Jerk   Junior educated radical kid

Nerd   Never-ending radical dude

As these terms show, the definitions can be sophisticated, with linguistic cues. Teachers these days are learning to ask students whether they are describing something as "fat" or "phat."

Figure 5.9 Visual Research Memo

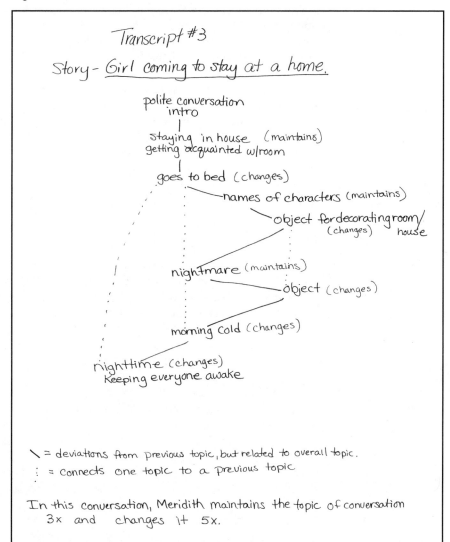

On the other hand, if you are looking at implementing a new curriculum at your school, you might want to take key words out of the curriculum, standards, or assessments provided and ferret out differences between your meanings for the critical terms and those of your colleagues or students.

When definitions vary, find out who has the different definitions and where the differences come from. In Jane Doan's K–2 multiage classroom, she asked students to describe different areas and activities in the classroom and uncovered these folk terms: "being sent to the planning chair" meant a form of punishment; "meanies" referred to a group of older girls who are mean. Jane and Penny Chase, her co-teacher, realized their "alternative" to punishment, "the planning chair," was still viewed as punitive by the students. And they hadn't realized the existence, let alone the power, of the "meanies" till they heard the word often among students and asked for a definition of it.

Reframe your study based upon your findings. Julia Crowl's study of perceptions of home-school links by seventh-grade students included home visits and activities with parents. Doing a domain analysis showed her just how defined and pervasive class consciousness was among students (many of the low-income students in her study lived in a particular neighborhood and so were defined derogatively as "scrubbers"). This information led her to do less background reading on literacy instruction and more on the effects of class distinctions on peer groups and family relations.

Sociograms

Sociograms are a useful source of information for analyzing the social networks in your classroom. What you need first is a question for individual interviews with your students that requires the students to answer with the names of their classmates. For example, If you could eat lunch with anyone, who would you sit next to? Who do you know who is a good writer in this class? If you could read a book with anyone in the class, who would you read with? Ideally, the question should have some link to your research topic, even if the link is weak.

With younger students (grades pre–K through 2), you or a colleague will need to interview each child separately, in a space removed slightly from the rest of the class. These interviews should be done very quickly—no more than a minute per student. Resist the urge to ask "why" when a student gives a surprising response—those open-ended questions are useful for other aspects of your research, but not with sociograms. With older students, you can pass out slips of paper and have the whole class silently write their responses immediately to your question—this takes less than five minutes of class time.

As you're interviewing or after you collect the slips from the students, you'll need to do a tally sheet. To do the tally sheet, list the name of the person interviewed and the names of classmates she or he lists as first, second, and third choices. For example, if you were interviewing Theresa, the tally sheet would look like this:

Theresa

1. Jennifer [her first choice]
2. Kelly [her second choice]
3. Melissa [her third choice]

This would continue for the whole class:

Harry

1. Jim
2. Joe
3. Kelly

and so on.

Once you've completed the tally sheet, make a whole-class chart with names of students on horizontal and vertical margins, giving a child three points if he is the first choice of another student, two points if he is a second choice, and one point if he is a third choice. Add the total points for each child to get a sense of who has the most social power in the class and who has least (with a positive question, students with the most points are those who have the most social power in the class, and those with the least points have the least). Many times, it's helpful to ask two questions—one from a positive social perspective, the other from a negative social perspective: Who would you want to sit with at lunch? Who would you *not* want to sit with at lunch?

When you have the negative data, you can differentiate between children who aren't noticed by classmates and those who are disliked or avoided. For example, a student who has few points for each question is for some reason not visible to classmates. But a student who has low points for the first question and high points for the second is behaving in a way that has a negative effect on their social status.

If you have the time, you might want to chart out your findings for the question (see Figure 5.18 on page 156 for an example of a completed sociogram). But many teachers save time by only adding up the tally points.

Sociograms never stand alone as a data source. The results need to be triangulated with other data sources in order to provide truly valid findings. But if you're stymied in trying to understand links between the social networks in your classroom and the learning going on, sociograms can provide terrific quick looks at complex social relationships.

Some teacher-researchers avoid sociograms because they are concerned about hurt feelings if students share choices with each other. We have not found this to be an issue with many teachers who have used sociograms, but we respect that concern.

These examples of data analysis methods are diverse, but they all show evidence of working from the same basic principles:

1. *Find something to count.* For many novice researchers, it is easier to see patterns first through numbers, then through language. Debbie Glazier moved from counting minutes on the clock to counting plus and minus

signs, to finally beginning to qualify what some of these numbers and codes might mean. Many teacher-researchers find it useful to count the number of instances in different code categories and then to chart them in some way to begin to visualize their findings. For Wanda Heath, the charting led to preliminary findings that she could then use to make changes in her teaching.

2. *Look for models from others, but feel free to adapt them.* Betty Bisplinghoff, JoBeth Allen, and Barbara Michalove were eager to try out a tried-and-true system for categorizing their data but felt free to abandon it when it didn't work for them. Wanda Heath, Lee Anne Larsen, and Sherry Young all used specific codes developed by others but tailored these codes to their own particular studies.

3. *Find and follow the story of your research.* The best lesson from these researchers may be that the codes, analysis systems, and procedures are all a means to one end—finding the narrative thread of the research. As you develop and use any analysis system, ask yourself, Is this getting me closer to the story of my students and teaching, or is it distancing me from it? If you don't find the system is revealing new truths, but instead feels cumbersome and artificial, then it probably isn't the right analysis procedure for you.

Welcome the Unexpected

Perhaps the most important advice we can give you regarding data analysis is never to allow yourself to become too comfortable with your findings. As you sort through and weigh different possibilities, there will also be some part of what you are seeing or not seeing in your research that niggles at you. It can be a sense that something is not quite true, or accurate, or honest in how you are representing what you've learned. Pay attention to those feelings of discomfort, because often they provide clues to the major breakthroughs in understanding possible through your research.

This was the case for Karen Gallas in her most recent study of gender relations in her class of first graders, *Sometimes I Can Be Anything.* She writes about an early breakdown in her data analysis:

> When I reviewed my data and tried to describe different incidents, my understanding of the purposes and motives behind the children's interactions grew muddier over time. Writing became a painful process: the children I had loved and observed so closely suddenly became symbols of every social problem that I personally found troubling. I was unable to separate what I had observed and recorded in the classroom from my own social viewpoints and events in the society at large. . . .
>
> As I examined the children's active attempts to make their world sensible and reliable, and the resulting stances they assumed to maintain that sensibility, I saw that I had to push aside my own personal labels for the

behavior I was seeing. For example, for children the concept of "sexism" or "sexist" is not a known one until that label is defined and applied by an adult. . . . Without labels I became more able to see how what I now call so-cial breaches or ruptures begin. Children's interactions do not come loaded with the political and psychosocial metaphors of the adult world. (1998, 21)

We can almost hear all those shoes falling out of their original boxes for Karen. Ker-thunk. No wonder writing became painful—without all the comfortable, adult categories for coding and analyzing her data on gender in the classroom, Karen had to see the children in a completely new light. But this new light led to some extraordinarily fresh takes on power and identity among boys and girls in her classroom.

The great Native American leader Seneca said, "It is not because things are difficult that we do not dare. It is because we do not dare that things are difficult." Data analysis is the point in research that calls for true daring. The magic in the best research studies comes from teachers who are willing to explore the unexpected places their inquiry leads. Like Karen, they explore what isn't working as they try to analyze their data. Like JoBeth, Barbara, and Betty, they are able to recognize a discomfort in their process, not as a deficiency in their skills but as a mismatch between the analysis method they have chosen and their needs as researchers. Take Don Graves's (1994) advice: "Listen to yourself and what you see in the shadows and sense just around the corner of thought" (39). A willingness to chuck old methods and categories, try new ones, and consider unorthodox possibilities can make data analysis less of a chore and more of an adventure.

RESEARCH WORKSHOP

Strategies for Analyzing Data
Ruth Shagoury Hubbard

Some truths present themselves to us when our minds are taking a break from the day-to-day problems and issues that are confronting us. On a re-cent weekend, I was taking such a break, escaping into worlds out of the classroom that give me pleasure and relaxation. One of those pleasures is music, and I indulged in really listening to lots of my favorites, tending to-ward New Orleans rhythm and blues, Chicago jazz, and Texas rock 'n' roll. But I couldn't really escape from what was on my mind—teaching, research, my students—even when I was enjoying this music. So I found myself making lots of connections between the lyrics of the songs and my work. For example, I found myself mulling over my own issues of student assess-ment and evaluation as I listened to the jazz strains of a song called "Real Compared to What?" And since I'm trying to make sense of piles of data that I've collected, I really tuned in to Irma Thomas wailing "It's not the quantity—oh, no—but it's the quality." (I think this cut could become the theme song of teacher-researchers everywhere.)

But the song that highlighted an important truth for me was an old standard with a compelling refrain: "I got a little too little . . . and a *lot* too much." This was an "ah-ha" moment for me. This phrase captured one main problem that most of us have as teacher-researchers; as we're analyzing our data, we often realize that in the categories that intrigue us, we have "a little too little." If the school year's done, and our kids are gone, there's no way we can go back and follow up on that comment, or ask about the process of this interesting piece of writing, or interview several kids to see if a particular finding has more widespread application.

And how many of us have stared with guilt at piles of untranscribed audiotapes, folders of dust-covered student work samples, even notebooks of raw field notes and teacher journals that we dutifully wrote in but haven't read and thought about for months? Indeed, *"a lot too much."*

Besides being a catchy song, those lyrics can serve to crystallize the main problems we run into when analyzing data. If we can begin to focus on how we can collect and analyze data so that we won't have "a little too little" or "a lot too much," we will have gone a long way toward making the whole process more manageable.

In the suggestions that follow, I have framed some strategies to help you tie data collection with analysis, for often it is their strict separation that is at the heart of the problem. These are just some possibilities for finding ways to protect yourself from singing the teacher-researcher blues as you analyze your data.

Build analysis into your design from the beginning.   Take a look at first-grade teacher Pat Scherler's research plan (Figure 5.10). What are some ways she might fit analysis into her mental framework of how she is approaching her research? Here are some of the strategies colleagues suggested to her.

In terms of keeping on top of her field notes, they recommended that she read through her teaching journal every couple of weeks to see what she was finding. Pat found that was a small and manageable enough chunk of time and that she could start to see patterns or nudge her memory about something she'd noticed earlier. So, she added to her design, "Every other week, read field notes/teaching journal."

Another colleague recommended that Pat also set aside a longer time, when she had about thirty to forty pages of field notes or entries in a teaching journal, to index her notes. Pat added to her design, "By the end of January, I'll index my notes and narrow my focus. I'll bring my indexed notes to my teaching partner to get some feedback."

Adding this kind of general time line to your plans can help connect data collection and analysis more closely right from the beginning. Talk through your research designs with other teacher-researchers, brainstorming how to add these checkpoints in ways that fit your own work schedule.

Index your notes to make them more manageable.   It's useful to create a kind of table of contents of what you're seeing in your data early on; this

Figure 5.10

PAT SCHERLER'S RESEARCH PLAN

Question

How do young children carry out research?

Procedures

This research will be based upon the observations, interviews, and samples from approximately sixty first-grade children at Community Elementary School. Most of these students have not had independent research activities and therefore have not had much teacher input that would interfere with discovering how children research naturally.

Time Frame

Because first-grade children grow and change rapidly in the course of a year, it is my intent to carry out this research over a six-month period, spanning the middle months of the school year. During the first two months of the school year, the children are settling into the school routine, and the last month they spend unsettling, so I will try to catch them in the middle!

Data Gathering

Data will be gathered in primarily three ways: (1) audiotaped interviews; (2) field notes; and (3) samples of data or work carried out by the children. The questions asked in the interviews will be the following:

What do you do when you want to know about something?
What do you do with the information once you have got it?
What do you think the word *research* means?

The responses may prompt my asking further questions for clarification. Field notes will be taken as I observe the children in the process of doing research. The in-class research will be carried out with a minimum of structure, the topics of study sometimes being determined by the teacher and sometimes by the individuals. The data or work samples will be any product created or found by the child in connection with his or her information gathering.

Data Analysis

Within the transcripts, field notes, and samples, I will look for patterns and categories. Out of this, I will develop a list and tally commonalities, and describe trends and curiosities that may develop from the data.

helps you see what you have already, and also helps to narrow your focus for what you need to continue to collect. In October, Blake Tomlinson read over his two months of observations and notes about his case study student, Sam. He listed the categories with the page numbers on which they appeared, and then wrote a few paragraphs reflecting on what he had learned so far (see Figure 5.11). This kind of review highlights what data are missing and gives the research more direction. Blake's reflection ties in with his role as a teacher-researcher. The data he has analyzed will clearly influence his teaching and help him continue to work with Sam in new ways.

Figure 5.11 Index of Notes

Categories and Patterns in Field Notes

Category	*Pages*
On-task engagement	1, 9, 10, 14
Boredom/distraction	1, 9, 10
Seat work	1, 9
Student-student comm./gossip	1, 3, 4, 10
Student-teacher comm.	3, 15
Sam's on-task engagement	1, 6, 7, 10
Sam's boredom/distraction	4, 5, 6, 8
Sam-teacher comm.	7, 12, 14
Sam-student comm.	6, 8, 12, 13, 14
Sam's personal behaviors	5, 6, 7, 8, 12, 13, 14
Sam's clothing	8, 13
Sam's interviews	16, 17, 18, 19, 20, 21 22, 23, 24, 25, 26, 27
Sam's writing skills	16, 17, 18, 19, 20, 21
Writing as process: understanding	17, 18, 19
Things Sam already knows in writing	17, 18 (work sample)
Sam's attitudes: school	18, 22, 23, 24, 25, 26
Sam's attitudes: life	21, 24, 26, 27 (in his writing)
Sam's attitudes: general	23, 25, 26, 27

Observations: My first thoughts when looking over my categories are that communication is a big issue in my observations of fifth period. I focused on the communication between students, students to teachers, and the communication that occurs within the context of the academic work, for example in writing. I also focused on task engagement and boredom, looking at the class as a whole and then comparing who was doing what and how often. I paid little attention to issues such as seat work, and who was working with whom.

Most of my field notes concentrate on Sam. And I feel it is through my interviews with him that vital information emerges. A question that keeps popping up in terms of my two interviews with him is, What does Sam already know? What has he revealed about his positive/negative learning behaviors and styles at Central High School? I am not sure if I should break the interview responses themselves into major categories. I already did some of that in his writing and attitude categories, but inside each particular question is a response that illustrates a unique part of Sam.

In terms of his writing, I feel Sam already knows a great deal about the writing process, and his own connection with writing. I think one of the major writing problems facing Sam is that the writing he does in school is not meaningful to him. Then again, he hasn't shown much interest in pieces that allow for student freedom; therefore I don't know if he is completely sincere in his responses.

His attitudes about Central and life in general were discovered as a result of my second interview with him. I think Central is not suitable to Sam's learning style. I really don't know at this point what Sam needs, but the institutionalized structure of Central is not helping him.

Overall, the things I need to know about Sam's learning modes come through his writing interview. I think if Sam is given the correct guidance and freedom to explore issues in his writing, then he will certainly begin to learn how to think critically. Some additional information that I will need to obtain are probably some more one-on-ones with Sam concerning specific things we can accomplish in the classroom. If we can brainstorm some possible topic areas of writing, I think Sam will rediscover the energy and enthusiasm that he lost learning at Central.

Indexing can be very useful in preparation for a teacher research meeting. Giving yourself the time to go through your notes in this way, listing your tentative categories, can reconnect you to the research question itself and to the patterns that are emerging in your classroom work. You may also find interesting connections to the categories that others are finding, sparking additional insights that you now have time to go back and explore further.

Keep on top of transcription.   I find that if my tapes are older than a month, I usually don't get to them. And again, it's often too late to go back and follow up then if you find something really intriguing. Making a commitment to keep on top of transcription also makes you more realistic and less greedy for data you won't use.

Pat Scherler had planned to interview each student. She needed to think realistically about how she could fit that into her teaching day. She decided she could interview one student per day as part of her writing workshop. Given her other commitments, she decided to limit herself to two interviews per week. On her time line, she added, "Two fifteen-minute interviews per week, to be transcribed for one hour every other Saturday morning."

For many research designs, though, you don't need to transcribe all the tapes. Suppose you are looking at patterns or at strategies that students use in whole-group sharing of math problem solving. Instead of taping and transcribing each session, you might randomly tape one per week or per month and transcribe that one right away. Or you might listen to the tapes, choose one that you consider a representative sample, and transcribe that one tape to analyze more closely. That way, you can still follow up on what you may need.

Adapt your record-keeping strategies to include data collection and analysis. The more closely you can intertwine data collection and analysis into your daily routine, the more likely you are to be able to keep on top of it. Rather than inventing something completely new, look at the record keeping you are already doing and adapt it to include collection of information that will help you answer your research question. Annie Keep-Barnes adapted the records she kept during class discussions so that she could add tallies as well as have a record of her thoughts (see Figure 5.12). Take a look at your own record-keeping procedures; how might you adapt them to help meet your research needs?

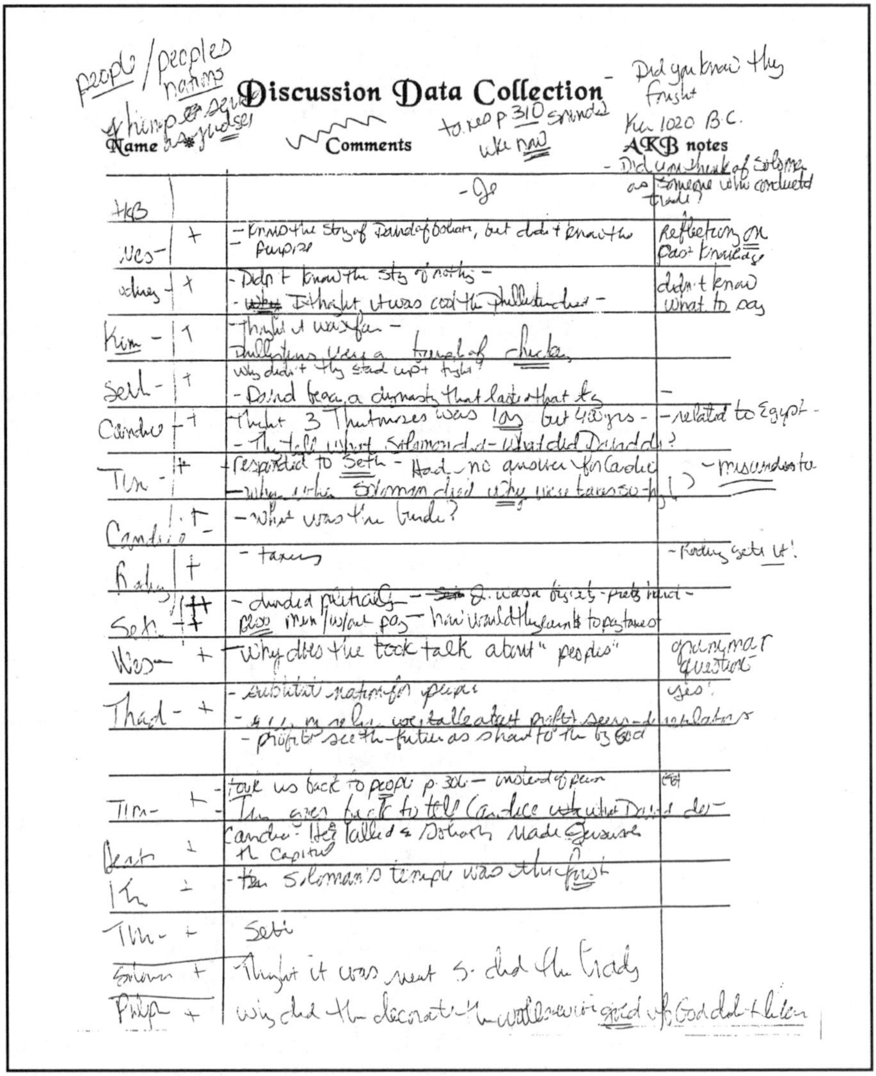

Figure 5.12 Adapted Record-Keeping Sheet

Catalogue your data in preparation for analysis. For student work, cataloguing might be as simple as having a trapper keeper or a folder for samples with the contents listed on the cover.

Initial cataloguing is also vital for videotapes, and much quicker and more useful than transcribing the whole audio track. You can make a running guide as detailed or sparse as you need. When I catalogue videotapes, I go through quickly the first time, mostly writing down phrases to serve as a memory jog. I use a cataloguing sheet with columns for the time and for describing the contents, such as "Conference with Larry." I might also put a star next to segments I'll want to review closely later (see Figure 5.13).

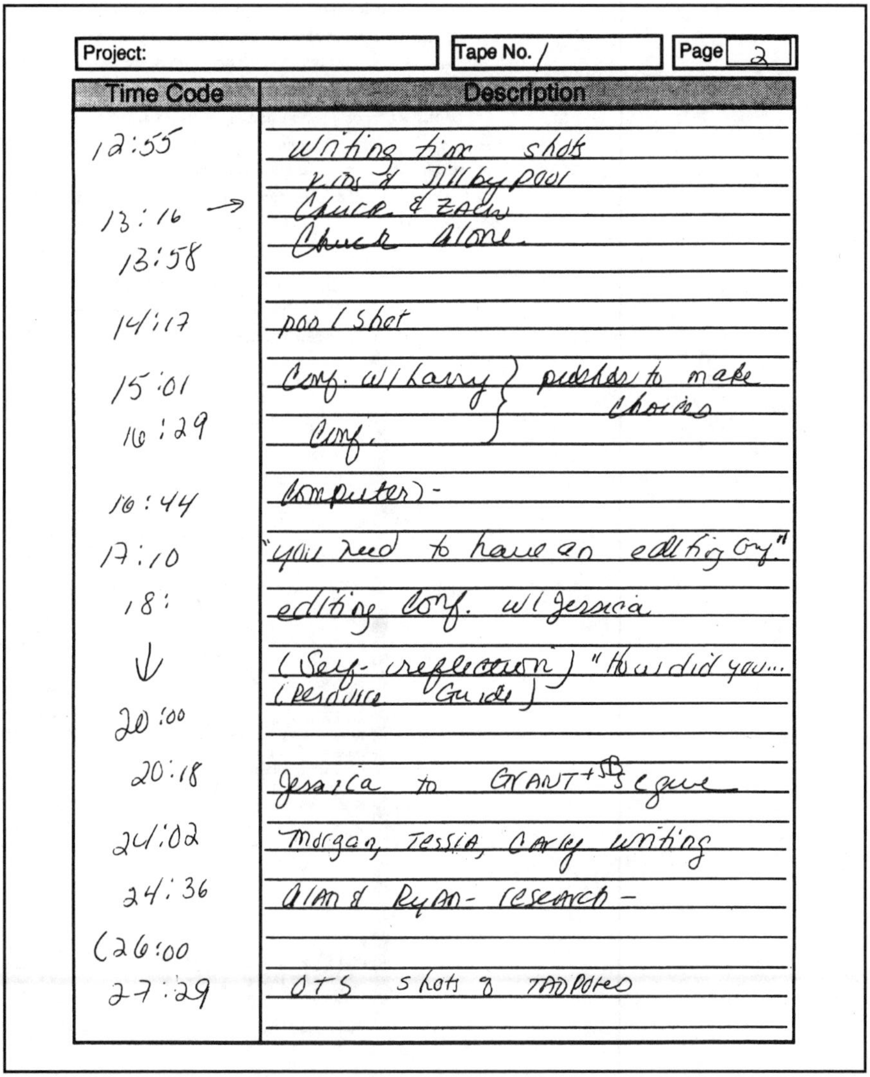

Project: | Tape No. 1 | Page 2

Time Code	Description
12:55	writing time shots
	kids & Jill by pool
13:16 →	Chuck & Zach
13:58	Chuck alone
14:17	pool shot
15:01	Conf. w/ Larry } pushes to make choices
16:29	Conf.
16:44	computer) -
17:10	"you need to have an editing conf."
18:	editing conf. w/ Jessica
↓	(Self-reflection) "How did you... (Response Guide)
20:00	
20:18	Jessica to GRANT + SB's conf
24:02	Morgan, Tessia, Carly writing
24:36	Alan & Ryan - research -
(26:00	
27:29	OTS shots of TADPOLES

Figure 5.13 Cataloguing Sheet for Videotapes

Create flowcharts or other visual aids to help you see how your data fit together.   Marilyn Hubler built analysis into her plans for data collection by creating a visual representation of how she would triangulate her data, looking for common threads among her observational records, surveys, and other resources. Having this pictorial image of her analysis helped her focus more specifically on the data she needed (see Figure 5.14).

DATA COLLECTION:

     Surveys. Surveys will be sent home with each of my 29 kindergarten students. These will provide my with a broad view of the verbalization that takes place within the home.

     Interviews.. I will invite parents to tea. My goal here would be to listen in on a conversations, tape record this session, and thereby obtain anecdotal information.

     I will visit with at least two other kindergarten teachers to discuss this project and note any relevant feedback.

     Anecdotal Records. I will listen in on classmate's conversations or any comments made to me that show evidence of communication at home regarding school experiences. I will also make records of relevant comments made to me by my parent volunteers.

     Tally sheets. I will ask for parent volunteers to keep a tally sheet on any comments within the time-frame of one week.

     I have arranged to have my data come from three primary sources in keeping with Webb's (1965) term *triangulation* and, as the chart below shows, I will be searching for the agreement of anecdotal records, parental input, and distant and/or present teachers in order to draw any conclusions.

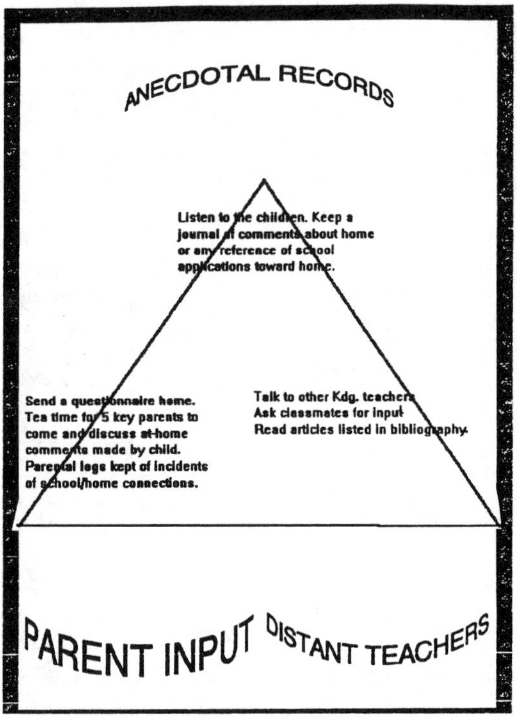

Figure 5.14 Visual Representation of Data Collection Plan

featured TEACHER RESEARCHER

Journals as a Tool of the Trade

Kimberly Hill Campbell

Last year's journal began as a survival technique. As a first-year principal in a first-year high school, I was awed by the enormousness of the job. Writing a journal in my Franklin Planner (also a new system) sustained me. I made sense of my day in the evening after dinner. I did not write every day, but I wrote at least three or four times a week.

By December, I found myself curious about the way I used my time; I felt as if I were beginning to come up for air after the whirlwind of the first few months. As I looked back through my early journal entries, I became curious about the issue of time. I had naively assumed that as an administrator I would have more control over my time; it would not be as regimented as in teaching. Instead, I felt like my time was completely beyond my control. At the end of the day, I had usually accomplished almost nothing on my "to do" list because I was too busy reacting to the crisis of the moment. If I was going to address and improve this "reactive" style, I needed to first understand it.

I turned to my teacher research tool box and reached for "indexing." I had taught several courses on teacher research and often discussed indexing but had never taken the time to use this tool in my own data analysis. Quite candidly, I was skeptical of this method; it seemed time-consuming and a little too "college professor"-like for me. But faced with pages and pages of scribbled journal entries, I thought I would give it a try. Initially, I listed categories very basically: students/parents/staff. But, as I reviewed my entries, I noticed categories within categories. I began again. Each entry was cross-referenced by date into my new categories (see Figure 5.15). As I read and categorized, I began to see patterns of time use. I saw how little of my time was spent in the role of instructional leader. Much of my time was invested in parent issues and facility issues (we were leasing space from a college of naturopathic medicine). Based on this information, I was able to present a compelling case as to why we needed to hire a counselor for the 1997–98 school year: to handle the parent questions regarding schedules and other student advocacy issues. And I had hard evidence that we needed to lease a different site.

I also made personal decisions about the way I handled my time based on the categories. I arranged for informal drop-in visits to classes and followed up with a brief conversation rather than relying only on formal observations. I learned to prioritize my time:

Staff issues

Student issues

Parent issues

District issues

Facility issues

An additional benefit of the journal was that on those days when I felt as if I had not accomplished anything on my "to do" list, I had concrete evidence of all that I had done instead. I began to redefine success: If I got more than three items on my list done during regular work hours, it was a stellar day!

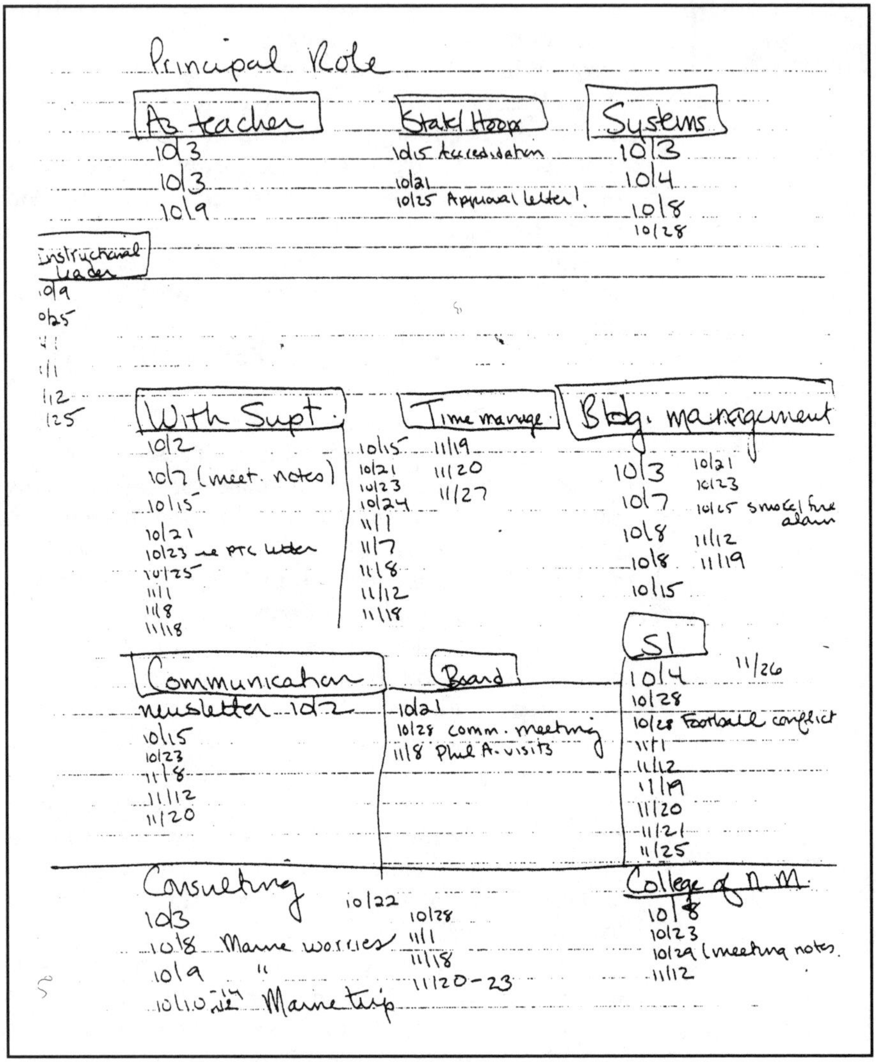

Figure 5.15 Index of Journal Data

Exploring Literature Through Student-Led Discussions

Jennifer Allen

Just the other day I asked Emily, a third-grade student, why she thought student-led discussions were beneficial when talking about books in literature groups. Her response was, "Kids connect with kids. We understand each other." I listened to Emily with a smile and knew that she held great literary wisdom.

It has been two years since I began to explore the question, What happens when students lead literature discussions? During this time I shifted back and forth between the roles of researcher and teacher. The process of implementing student-led literature discussions enabled me to grow as a teacher-researcher, improved reading comprehension among students, and fostered social growth in students.

At the onset of this research, I was interested in exploring oral language as a response to literature. I had a preconceived agenda of trying to shift students' literature responses from a literal level to a more inferential level, using students as discussion facilitators. Looking back now, I realize that I went into the process trying to design a research question to fit my anticipated data. I quickly learned that you can't always predict the paths that you will follow as you embark on your research journey.

As a teacher-researcher, I learned the tools of the trade: notetaking, listening, revision, and reflection (Hubbard and Power 1993). I carried my journals with me faithfully to every literature group and took notes for fifteen minutes during discussions. I found myself constantly shifting between the roles of researcher and teacher. Insights as a researcher always led me back to the students for their input. Moving back and forth between the roles enabled me to reflect on the process and make constant revisions during the implementation of student-led discussions.

Implementing Student-Led Literature Discussions

In the beginning, I talked to the students about my idea of having them direct their own literature discussions. My goal was for students to participate in focused discussions with their peers, based on the literature they were reading. Students showed interest in the idea, and we began to look at how student-led discussions could be incorporated into our current literature group format.

My literature group consisted of four to six students at varying developmental reading stages. Genres and groupings were temporary and changed frequently throughout the year to meet individual needs of students. At any one time students could be grouped heterogeneously, according to ability, interest, need, or gender. Although I put together the literature groups, students had choices about what books they read. I usually presented six books to the class through mini-booktalks, and had students choose three books that they would like to read. I always strove to give students one of their choices, but I wasn't always successful as I also tried to match texts to the individual needs and interests of students. If a particular book was popular with students, I assured them that I would create another literature group using the book later in the year. This selection process enabled students to voice their book choices, but still gave me the control to create literature groups that would meet their needs. Sometimes I intentionally created a group based on ability or interest. The key was that groups were never fixed for a long duration of time. I usually orchestrated four different literature groups in the classroom at the same time, with each group exploring a different book. I met with each group twice a week for thirty minutes. During literature groups, we spent the first ten minutes discussing the book. For the rest of our meeting time, we worked on a particular element of the text such as character development or a reading strategy. When I was not meeting with students, they were working independently or with peers from the same group. The literature group model was similar to that described in *Invitations* by Regie Routman (1994).

As I continued to explore the idea of student-led literature discussions, I started to involve the students more in the decision-making process. As a class we began to outline student responsibilities (see Figure 5.16). We decided that a student facilitator would be responsible for developing discussion questions for the group. The questions were expected to reflect the book and serve as the foundation for the group's discussion. The facilitator was also responsible for keeping the discussions focused and on track. We decided that our purpose for these discussions was to talk about the books we were reading, the characters we encountered, our personal connections to the books, and any questions that surfaced.

I modeled the role of discussion facilitator for a month before having students try this on their own. As the facilitator, I asked the group inferential questions and prompted literature discussions based on my personal connections with the book and characters. While we were reading the book *Morning Girl* by Michael Dorris (1992), I told the students that I could identify with Morning Girl because I, too, wake up early every morning and love the peaceful sound of dawn. I asked students questions such as the following: Based on what you know about the characters of Star Boy and Morning Girl, which one would you like for a friend, and what would you do if you spent the day together? I wanted students to explore and think about literature beyond the literal print of the text. I wanted them to personalize literature by making connections to characters and events found in books. Ultimately, I hoped to develop lifelong readers.

We also practiced strategies that would foster peer interaction. The first thing we worked on was making eye contact. I encouraged students to respond to one another by looking at the person talking, and not just at me,

Figure 5.16 Outline of Student Responsibilities

STUDENT ROLES IN STUDENT LED LITERATURE DISCUSSIONS

As defined by Jennifer Allen and Students in A-1 (1996)

REQUIRED ROLES	RESPONSIBILITIES
Facilitator	*Prepares for discussion by reading the assigned text and develops questions based on the reading
	*Initiates the discussion through prepared literature questions
	*Keeps group on task and focused
	*Encourages student participation
	*Processes the literature discussion with the group by listening to the discussion tape. Records what went well and what they want to work on as a group.

---

the teacher. I tried to participate as an equal member of their group, although I limited my responses. I wanted students to know that the role of facilitator was more than playing "teacher." It was an opportunity for them to discuss their connections to the characters and text. Student facilitators were not simply "directors" of literature discussion but were also expected to be active participants.

As students became more comfortable and involved in their literature groups, it was time for them to take more responsibility for their discussions. Since student facilitators were going to generate and present questions for the group's discussions, I decided that we needed to work on developing questions that might spark discussions.

I read the book, *The Great Gilly Hopkins* (Paterson 1978) aloud to the class. Since students were familiar with this story, we used it to generate possible discussion questions. Students then tried out their questions on the group. They quickly observed that some questions sparked great discussions and others didn't. As Emily commented, "Asking yes or no questions does not create discussions." I taught students the three levels of questioning: literal, inferential, and evaluative. I used the terms "reading the lines," "between the lines," and "beyond the lines." Students found that asking literal questions based on the text did not lead to interesting or lengthy discussions.

Finally, a month into the project, I began having students facilitate their literature discussions. Student groups met twice a week with me and twice a week without me. It is important to note that these discussions lasted only ten to fifteen minutes out of our total two-and-a-half-hour literacy block. The role of facilitator rotated among members of the group, so students were responsible for facilitating a discussion about once a week.

Like many explorers, I sometimes wandered off course as a teacher-researcher, but I never completely lost my direction. The dialogue from the following literature discussion fulfilled my vision for student-led discussions:

Title: *The Flunking of Joshua T. Bates*

Author: Susan Shreve

Student Facilitator: Taylor

Group: Taylor, Zack, Devin, Adrian

Taylor: Why do you think that Joshua said, "This is the worst day of my life"?

Zack: Because he has to repeat third grade and his teacher is a military tank.

Devin: Josh's sister is making a big deal of it, Tommy Wilheim is going into fourth grade and Josh is smarter.

Taylor: Some of his friends are making fun of him. Would you guys like to be in Joshua's place?

Adrian: No, my sister would make fun of me.

Taylor: Well, I've been through this, I had to repeat a grade.

Devin: How did it feel?

Taylor: I was mad. I wanted to go into second grade. Now that I'm in a higher grade I feel better.

It was fascinating how the four boys discussed the literature. The conversation was very natural and free-flowing as one idea led them to the next. All four boys participated reflectively, and they truly listened to one another. Their conversation shifted from a literal interpretation of the book to a more evaluative level. In the beginning, Taylor used a quotation to initiate the discussion, and Zack replied with a literal response taken directly from the text, yet by the end of the discussion they had shifted from the literal text to a more evaluative level when Devin asked Taylor what it felt like to repeat a grade. This was also the first time a student facilitator used a quotation from the book to prompt a discussion.

It must have been a safe environment for Taylor to share that he had stayed back. This is not something that he had shared before with the class. Kathy Short (1990) has written extensively about the strong sense of classroom community needed for student discussions involving text. Short suggests that classroom climate has a significant impact on students' willingness to share their ideas with their peers. Margaret Anzul's (1993) research also sheds light on Taylor's personal disclosure. Anzul found that "making connections between literature and other life situations became increasingly common for the students as they became deeply absorbed in stories" (194). This intimate and very personal example of Taylor sharing that he had stayed back showed me the importance of kids reading literature with which they could connect on a personal level. Harste, Woodward, and Burke (1984) have gone so far as to define learning as a process of making connections in order to make sense of our world. The personal connections and inferential conversations that students engaged in about literature had more to do with past personal experiences than with their developmental reading stages.

Growth as a Teacher-Researcher

As a researcher, I was constantly rereading field notes, talking to students, and making changes to our student-led literature discussions. Several themes emerged from my field notes, student reflections, and student interviews. I found that students didn't like interruptions made by their peers during discussions. They expressed that it was important to stay on track during discussions, and that everyone should have an opportunity to participate. Student facilitators tried to engage their peers with comments like, "What do you think, Kathy?" or "Have we heard from everyone in the group?"

When I started this project I knew that modeling would be integral to the success of student facilitation. However, I was not sure how to approach incorporating this type of instruction. Students told me, through interviews, that they learned to "facilitate by watching, listening, practicing, and through the teacher." Students also expressed that they would like to become better at facilitating and learn to write better questions. "Good questions make good discussions," they said.

Since students told me that they learned to facilitate by listening, I decided to incorporate the use of a tape recorder into the student-led discussions. Students began to tape-record and play back their discussions each day. Students relistened to their discussions and processed what went well and what they wanted to work on as a group. In time students created a reflection form that guided the facilitator's notes as the group processed the discussion and set new goals (see Figure 5.17).

The reflection forms indicated that students felt that they were doing a good job discussing the literature but that they needed to work on not interrupting and "talking over" each other. I talked to the whole class about this problem, and together we brainstormed solutions. Students decided to pass the tape recorder among group members. They agreed that the one who spoke would hold the tape recorder. I was amazed at the effectiveness of this strategy. Once this idea was implemented, the pace of the discussion

Figure 5.17   Reflection Form

Reflection on Literature Discussion

Facilitator:_____

Title of Book: The Hundred dresses!

Date: 3-26-96

1. What went well about the discussion?

We did not talk over!

2. What did we learn new about the book that we didn't know before?

was Peggy was the one that was mean!

3. What do we want to work on?

We nedd to stop gerbing the rerderl

4. How do you feel as the facilitator today? Why?

like's the way I tell the qustion's and then I have the answrs. I do not know? ?))

slowed down and students started responding to one another by name: "Elizabeth, I agree with you but . . . ," "Tom, I can add on . . . ," and "Yeah, Nick. . . . " As a result of this process, students stopped talking at the same time and began to listen to each other.

Students also started asking to listen to their discussion tapes during independent reading time. My initial instinct was to say no. I wanted to keep the tapes as part of my research, but eventually I stepped back and followed the students' lead. I soon set up a box of literature discussion tapes at the listening center. Once again I watched in awe as students listened again to literature tapes and talked about past discussions. The tapes provided students an opportunity to revisit stories long after we had finished with the book.

The tape recorder became an integral part of preparing students for literature discussions. I have witnessed students listening to themselves and reflecting on ways to improve their discussions. The tape recorder enabled students to process their literature discussions and helped them to grow as facilitators and participants in student-led discussions.

As I continued to observe student-led discussions, I wanted to know how students perceived themselves as facilitators in comparison to my field notes. I decided to create a sociogram, after asking students who they would like to facilitate their literature discussions (see Figure 5.18). Students identified classmates who were truly able to initiate group discussions, and not just the "popular" kids in the class. Students also filled out an inventory that asked them questions about student-led discussions (see Figure 5.19). The inventory asked students to name who they thought was a good facilitator and to explain why. Susie wrote, "Beth is a good facilitator because she asks good questions that lead to a conversation." Dan wrote, "Tom has good questions. Some of his questions make us look in the book."

I enlisted students as co-researchers as a way to collect insights directly from students. This role rotated among members in the literature groups. It was a chance for students to take field notes during actual literature discussions. Most student co-researchers tried to capture the actual class discussion. One co-researcher, Devin, wrote in the journal, "Zack thinks that Josh is having fun, Taylor said that we didn't know what Mrs. Goodwin looked like in the beginning. Adrian thinks Mrs. Goodwin is nice." Students also noted what they thought were "unacceptable behaviors." A few examples are "Dan is talking," "Devin and Cindy are arguing," and "Mrs. Allen isn't paying attention."

A student co-researcher was also used periodically to review my data. Zack wrote the following upon his review of my field notes: "A lot of interruptions. The people who were facilitating were well prepared. Members of the groups were active listeners when a member of the group was facilitating. There were a few arguments." The concepts that Zack pulled from the data were consistent with my observations.

Several months into the project, I started to notice several key words recurring in my notes. I began to code my notes according to these words and eventually grouped them together under broader themes. For example, any time a student stated a feeling such as "happy" I would code it under the theme of "self-esteem." I began with a list of twenty key words found in the raw data, then narrowed my focus down to two themes. In the end, I identified the following themes as student outcomes that were woven throughout the study: students' growth as readers, and students' social growth.

Figure 5.18 Sociogram

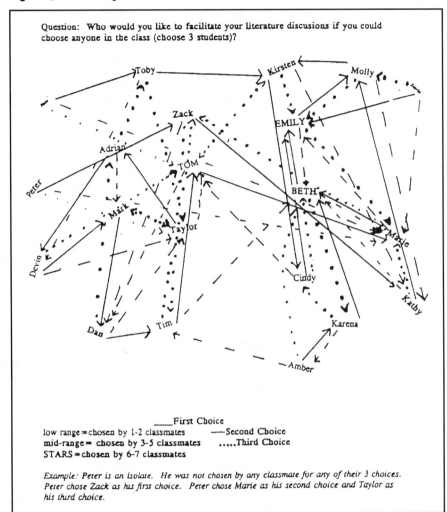

Question: Who would you like to facilitate your literature discussions if you could choose anyone in the class (choose 3 students)?

_____First Choice

low range = chosen by 1-2 classmates　　—Second Choice

mid-range = chosen by 3-5 classmates　　.....Third Choice

STARS = chosen by 6-7 classmates

Example: Peter is an isolate. He was not chosen by any classmate for any of their 3 choices. Peter chose Zack as his first choice. Peter chose Marie as his second choice and Taylor as his third choice.

Students' Growth as Readers

Students were convinced that discussions led by students helped them to understand the book better. Kirsten said, "When students facilitate, it's kids talking to each other and we can relate and understand each other." Rosenblatt addresses the issue of the "generation gap" that exists between students and the teacher in her text *Literature as Exploration* (1983). Rosenblatt states, "In many cases there is an unabridged gulf between anything that the student might actually feel about the book, and what the

Figure 5.19 Student Inventory

INVENTORY

NAME _____ AGE ___9___ DATE March 25 96

What is the purpose for literature discussions? to make sure that
you know whats going on in
the book.

Who is a good facilitator?

Why? because she has good
questions that lead to a
conversation.

What makes a good discussion? a question that
leads to a conversation that

What does a facilitator do? Ask questions that
are about the book.

How did you learn to lead literature discussions? by other peoples
questions.

How do you *feel* when you facilitate?
nervous

Do you like student led discussions? Why? Yes, exept when I
am doing question. because I don't have
a good question.

What would you like to do better as a facilitator?
have better questions.

teacher, from the point of view of accepted critical attitudes and his adult
sense of life, thinks the pupil should notice" (61).

   My field notes show that students probed on a literal level and beyond.
Students began to recognize that a literal question did not lead to a long discussion. I think students wanted lengthy discussions so that they could remain in control longer. Toward the end of the project, I heard members of
the literature group try to help the facilitator reword his or her question if

it simply required literal recall from the text. An example was during a discussion of the book *Owls in the Family* (Mowat 1961). Emily asked the group, "What is the name of the owl in the book?" She had not even finished saying the question before two students interrupted and said, "Emily, that is not a good question for discussion. Why don't you reword the question to 'Why do you think he named the Owl Wol?'" Anzul's (1993) research also supports the notion of higher levels of student thinking. She found that when student talk increased in the classroom, students spontaneously achieved and sustained higher levels of thinking.

The higher levels of thinking that students engaged in during student-led discussions was also evident in their written responses to literature. Written responses often reflected students' personal connections to the text. Students also used their responses to pose questions and make new predictions about the book. While reading the book *My Father's Dragon* (1948) by Ruth Gannett, Mark wrote, "I think that he will meet more things maybe like gorillas, monkeys, whales, and more! I also think he will get in trouble for bringing the dragon home! I wonder if he'll get to keep the dragon?" The written responses provided an opportunity for less vocal students to share their connections to the text. The quality of written responses improved for both the vocal and less vocal students as student-led discussions continued.

Students' Social Growth

Student facilitators were well prepared. Very rarely did a student forget to write a question. If that was the case, I would take over and facilitate the discussion. One student told me, "Being a student facilitator made me more responsible because I had to take extra time and prepare a question. I had to really understand the reading." Anzul's (1993) research supports this finding: "As children learned to take more responsibility for their own discussions, they also became more adept at marshalling reasons to explain their interpretations" (201). Students truly explored the text and characters when they were responsible for facilitating discussions.

All but one student wanted classmates to facilitate literature discussions. Kirsten wanted the workload to shift back to the teacher. Kirsten said, "Writing questions and preparing to facilitate is extra work. I would rather have the teacher do it." A very fluent reader, Kirsten was quite articulate during literature discussions, but she did the minimum to get by. Student-led literature discussions required her to take more responsibility for her own learning than she wanted to do.

Many students told me that facilitating made them feel happy, good, or important. Feeling important was an essential element in this project, since I am always looking for ways to help students gain self-worth. The words that touched me the most were from Peter, a developing reader who spent most of his day sketching or looking out the window into another world. He was quiet and almost invisible at times. He was an isolate, not recognized by any other classmates on the sociogram (Figure 5.18). When I asked Peter how he liked facilitating, he spoke right up without hesitation and said, "It makes me feel good because everyone pays attention and listens to me. Everyone chips in on the discussion." It was evident during my talk with Peter that the role of facilitator made him feel good about himself. I never realized how important it was to Peter to be heard by his classmates. So often he faded into the woodwork of the classroom, as if he wanted to go through the days unnoticed.

Students stated over and over again that classmates listened to one another during literature discussions. They also noted when they felt peers were not listening in group. When students facilitated literature discussions, there was almost 100 percent participation even though students were not designated a variety of roles (Daniels 1994). Students also participated in discussions by referring back to the text to support their opinions or used the text to check other student comments.

Final Reflections as a Teacher-Researcher

Working through this project was a wonderful learning experience. I learned that you can't predict the path of your research before you start collecting it. I balanced the roles of researcher and teacher as I worked to implement student-led literature discussions. I worked through the mechanics of data collection and notetaking. The inventories, field notes, and student interviews provided insights on how I could best support student-led discussions. I have answered the questions that I set out to explore but have formulated many new ones along the way. I feel that I have evolved and refined my skills as a teacher-researcher. I have learned that researching is exploring the unknown. It's like taking an afternoon drive with no destination in mind.

The most significant outcomes of the project were in terms of student growth. Students made gains in reading comprehension and in their social development. I found that student-led literature discussions made students responsible for their learning. The format provided an opportunity for children to select topics and direct their own discussions. During student-facilitated discussions, children made personal connections to the characters and events in books. Kids discussed and connected to literature beyond the literal text when they became emotionally involved in the book.

I feel like I have just returned from a great adventure where many unknowns were discovered. As I reflect on my process as a researcher, I am reminded of the following quotation from Carl Rogers (1983), which captures what I think it means to be a teacher researcher: "To free curiosity; to permit individuals to go charging off in new directions dictated by their own interests; to unleash the sense of inquiry; to open everything to questioning and exploration; to recognize that everything is in the process of change" (120).

Citing a Tea Bag: When Researchers Read

6

In her first home each book had a light around it,

The voices of distant countries

flooded in through open windows,

entering her soup and her mirror.

Naomi Shihab Nye

What we read as we do research determines in part what we see in our classrooms and who we are as researchers. Teacher-researchers are showing through our practice that we can change the old images that "a review of the literature" sometimes conjures up—paging through dry dusty tomes, squinting to decipher tiny print on microfiche, and so on. Instead, reading can be one of the joys of the research process—the stories we read of other researchers, writers, and teachers inform our inquiry, broaden our perspectives, and connect us to a wider network of writers and ideas. We are open to a world of new possibilities when we begin to "read like a researcher."

When we first began to do research, we asked a veteran researcher how to balance writing up our research narratives with citations from our readings of other researchers. She said dismissively, "Just write your own research—don't worry about citing anyone. Then when you're done, you can sprinkle a few references like croutons across the writing." We were pretty young and naive at the time, but even then we found her response a bit cynical.

After more than a decade of reading and writing research, we suspect her advice is followed by too many education researchers. Often research studies in any discipline cite the same small core of researchers in the same ways. It's the same old croutons in even the tastiest research studies.

Many teacher research studies contain few, if any, research citations. Teachers sometimes have an aversion to reading education research, and with good reason. Let's face it—the prose of most education researchers would never be mistaken for Hemingway's (or even Joyce Brothers's). No

161

wonder much teacher research is lightly referenced, citing only a few well-known and well-worn research studies.

But that's our loss as teachers and researchers. Many published research studies are compelling reads, able within a few pages to transform a researcher's sense of her own findings. And some of the most transformative reading for teacher-researchers takes place beyond the realm of traditional research writing. Teacher research challenges many traditional conceptions of the research process, and nowhere is the challenge more needed than in considering how we read other research, how we cite who influences our work, and how we connect our research to texts beyond research journals and books.

One of the reasons teacher-researchers often have few citations is because the process of learning from others during research (both in written texts and beyond) is not linear. We learn from a chance comment by a colleague down the hall, from another researcher still in the midst of his study—and we're unsure how to cite this tentative and new knowledge. It doesn't fit the traditional concept of how research knowledge builds, neatly and cleanly, from the work of others. Anne Wilson Schaef (1985) is writing about knowledge in general, but she could easily be discussing research learning: "All too frequently, our culture's prophets, philosophers and critics forget the levels of truth they have passed through and try to impose the distillation of a more advanced level on us" (159).

Teacher-researchers itch to show that undistilled, raw process of reading and learning from others, orally and in print. But because this reading, like our research, may be unorthodox, it often doesn't appear through citations in teacher research studies.

In her provocative analysis of Lucy Sprague Mitchell's influence on current teachers, Yetta Goodman exhorts teacher-researchers to think hard about who and how we cite those who influence our work (Wilde 1996). Lucy Sprague Mitchell was a teacher-researcher working early in the twentieth century. She founded the Bank Street School in New York and was a tremendous influence on John Dewey's work and on education reform at the time. But because her work was rarely cited, it is only recently that historians have begun to unearth her profound influence in fostering reflective inquiry. In contrast, Dewey is one of the most heavily cited figures from the same period, and so his value in the evolution of current theories of learning is unquestioned.

Goodman challenges us to find ways to cite other teachers who influence our work, even if those citations fall under the category of "personal communication" or "unpublished studies." Part of the emerging tradition of teacher research is the sense that knowledge in this research community is shared, cited, and distributed in different ways. We need to avoid the limits of sharing only those insights available from traditional print resources.

Once you become immersed in your research, you'll begin to see links to your studies in almost everything you read—other research studies, novels, plays, billboards. It's a process similar to what writers go through when they are working on a story, as Eudora Welty writes: "Once you're into a story everything seems to apply—what you overhear on a city bus is exactly what your character would say on the page you're writing. Wherever you go, you meet part of your story. I guess you're tuned in for it, and the right things are sort of magnetized" (Shaughnessy 1993, 189).

A researcher we were working with called us one morning with an important question about her research. After weeks of reading through dozens of studies related to her own, she'd finally found the quote she needed to summarize a section: "I was making some herb tea this morning, and the box had a series of sayings about relationships on it. One of them is perfect!" she exclaimed. "So how do you cite a tea bag, anyway?" Here was someone highly tuned to her research story, ready and eager to find her citations in unexpected places.

This willingness to link research to reading, regardless of genre, can lead to creative leaps in thinking and writing. When you read the work of veteran teacher-researchers, it's often peppered with quotes and connections from a range of literature. Sharon Frye, in her interview with the author of *Sounds from the Heart* (1995), Maureen Barbieri, noted that she always finds great books to read from what Maureen cites in her research. She went on to ask, "What books have you been reading lately?" and received a whole new batch of books she couldn't wait to get her hands on:

> *Maureen Barbieri:* I just read Ralph Fletcher's *Breathing In, Breathing Out*, about keeping a writer's notebook, and I really loved it. I have a writing notebook group at one of my schools and we read that as a text and we also read *Crafting a Life* by Don Murray, which is wonderful. I also read Randy Bomer book's *Time for Meaning*. As far as girls, there's a book of poems called *Dreams of Glory: Poems Starring Girls*. They're all different poets, but the compiler is Isabel Joshlin Glaser. It's *pretty* good, it's not as good as the title. Some nice things in here—girls doing sports, very positive girl images. Now, Carol Gilligan wrote a new book.
>
> *Sharon Frye:* I didn't know that. Tell me about it.
>
> *MB:* It's called *Between Voice and Silence: Women and Girls, Race and Relationship*. And the big question, after she wrote *Meeting at the Crossroads*, was "What about girls of color? What about girls in inner-city schools?" And so, this book looks at that. She co-wrote it with Jill McLean Taylor.
>
> *SF:* That sounds like it would be a good one to take a look at. What else have you been reading?
>
> *MB:* Well, I've read Manette Ansay's *Sister* and Mitchard's *The Deep End of the Ocean*, which I love. Last year, I read a book called *Range of Motion* by Elizabeth Berg, which is absolutely fantastic, and that led me to her other book, *Durable Goods*. *Talk Before Sleep* I had read earlier. She's just a beautiful writer. There's never enough time! I'm trying to read ESOL books, and teacher research books. There's a book called *Poemcrazy*, one

word. The writer is Susan Wooldridge, and it's fabulous. I'm very interested in poetry, so I read a lot of it.

SF: Who's your favorite poet?

MB: That's easy: Naomi Shihab Nye. My very strong favorite. I love Pablo Neruda and Mary Oliver, but Naomi's poems just really get me. (Frye 1997, 55)

Maureen's research is full of theoretical connections to others, including Ralph Fletcher, Randy Bomer, Donald Murray, and Carol Gilligan. Novelists like Elizabeth Berg, who writes with compassion and understanding about women's and girls' relationships through life, also inform Maureen's work. Poets like Naomi Shihab Nye give her ideas and images that provide poetic allusions in her eloquent and beautifully written classrooms accounts.

What a contrast Maureen is to the mythical researcher who dutifully plows through a minimal number of research studies and sprinkles a few references in her writing. Maureen merges her personal reading passions with her professional interests. In doing so, she inspires other researchers to expand their reading repertoire.

Reading Before Breakfast

Who are the writers you turn to for your morning reading? Kay Ryan (1998) writes, "The books I regularly pick up in the morning, for the few minutes or half-hour before I set about my own writing, are not casual interests. I go to these writers because they contain the original ichor. They are the potent Drink Me." Our "Drink Me" fellowship includes Marge Piercy, Karen Gallas, Saul Alinsky, William Stafford, Anne Tyler, Linda Pastan, Deborah Tannen, and Julia Alvarez. These authors' works jostled next to each other in our book bags at a recent teacher research retreat, getting us going and sustaining our thinking and writing, and not just before breakfast but throughout the day. Some to draw us closer into our work, some to help us find new ways of approaching it, and others to give our minds the needed space so that we could return to our data renewed and refreshed.

If you've been pushing your own "potent" authors aside, it's time to welcome them back, making time for reading as part of your research agenda. We think you'll find that when you're thinking about something in the back of your head all the time (like your evolving research question), you'll make connections to really different material because you don't know how it will strike you. Don't be afraid to reread old favorites with fresh eyes. We agree with Kay Ryan (1998) that reading is merely the first step to rereading:

It has just occurred to me that rereading imitates our most picturesque images of creation and transformation. We have heard it reported, for example, that a whole concerto would come to Mozart in a single flash. A composition based on melody that must move through time—pages and pages of notation—arrives stacked on top of itself, or perhaps radiates out from some middle. Or, to offer a chemical analogy, imagine a glass filled with a supersaturated solution; if you give it a tap, it could turn to crystals. Rereading is like these mysteries. Open to a paragraph, or even a line and—*tap!*—the complete composition precipitates. It is maddening, but I never can remember books, especially my favorite ones. But if I reread a line, it is all around me again, my real landscape, my real feelings, all familiar. *Where have I been?*

Which professional books or authors matter most to you? A rereading of these authors, with your own current research in the back of your mind, might prove the best starting place. What is it about these books that drew you in the past and that might continue to help you frame new connections?

As you turn to books from your reading history that have been a source of inspiration to you in the past, you might begin to notice who your reading mentors turn to. As Kay Ryan (1998) notes, "Quotes by my favorite writers offer a double joy. First, there is the attractiveness of what is quoted; and second, there is the pleasurable sensation of endless doors opening, author through author, all the way back to the first word. It is much bigger in here."

You can also open those doors, author through author, by noting who the folks you are reading cite as well as quote within the text. Reading the references and bibliographies can turn up interesting new possibilities, especially when you see them repeated by more than one of the writers whose work you admire.

You can build your reading community in a similar way by listing some of the teachers you admire who are struggling with the same issues as you are. Like Sharon Frye in her interview with Maureen Barbieri, you can ask them which authors they are reading, both professionally and for pure enjoyment.

We often encourage teachers to imagine some of their favorite researchers and favorite people attending a dinner party to discuss the teacher's research question. We've had teacher-researchers envisioning conversations about community between Parker Palmer and Jerry Garcia, or discussions of mainstreaming between Helen Keller and Donna Shalala. When you imagine what people with different interests would consider in discussing your research question, you cut through accepted notions of what the critical issues are. These fanciful conversations can lead to all kinds of new possibilities for literature reviews.

In her "fantasy dinner," Suzanne Kaback (1997) took this concept to its playful extreme, inviting nine mentors (living and dead) "to sit at my table, eat fine food, and discuss my latest question about teaching reading" (112). She found that the imaginative dialogue she created as her mentors "talked" to each other about her research question helped her differentiate more clearly the shades of difference in their reading theory and brought her own theory and practice into sharper focus. The whimsical touches in her dialogue make it an enjoyable as well as informative read. For example, when Lev Vygotsky notes that her shrimp bisque is as good as his grandmother's borscht, Suzy modestly replies, "That's high praise, especially from a guy who's not actually alive" (122). The evening ends with her modern husband doing the dishes while she retreats to her office to write up what she has learned from the dinner party in her teaching journal. (For more information on this exercise, see the Research Workshop in this chapter.)

An equally enjoyable task—though one that is limited to the living!—is to write letters to teacher-researchers whom you admire, enlisting their ideas and book recommendations as a way to build your reading community. Teachers we know have been inspired by the work of Joanne Hindley, Joan Countryman, Jill Ostrow, Tom Romano, and others, and have picked up their pens to tell them so.

Emily Tso, when she read *My Trouble Is My English* (Fu 1995), wrote a letter to the author, Danling Fu, telling her about her own father's struggles learning English in the United States, and posing questions about ESOL (English for Speakers of Other Languages) instruction today. Danling wrote back, answering her questions, sharing her current research, and sending her e-mail address so they could continue to communicate about their mutual passion for working to improve ESOL instruction. (For more information, including Emily's and Danling's complete letters, see the Research Workshop in Chapter 8.)

Expand Your Horizons

We encourage you to wander through the library stacks, picking up journals in disciplines you wouldn't ordinarily connect to your research endeavor, perhaps in disciplines you never knew existed. We discovered the *Journal of Mental Imagery* on a library stroll like this. This journal makes for fascinating reading; it reports on the study of mental images—everything from daydreaming to drug hallucinations to the annual issue on the mental images we form when we read and write.

Another benefit of expanding your reading horizons in this way is your exposure to a field of new terminology and fresh metaphors. Look for those metaphors in your new reading, challenging yourself to ask not what it *is* but what it is *like.*

You may also find new terminology and metaphors in the writings of familiar authors you've never actually read before. That's right—we're talking about reading primary sources. Don't always rely on secondary interpretations of a well-known theorist's work. If you are studying social interactions around learning, for example, it's important to hear Vygotsky in his own words and make sense of what you believe he is exploring. You may be surprised to discover you see a different angle in his work that speaks especially to your research and that another reader might not notice.

The Internet is a growing medium and has resources that can help you in your research quest. Besides the obvious benefits of increasing your professional connections through virtual communities such as mailing lists and news groups, you have access to a wealth of information previously out of your reach. And much of this information is available at little or no cost. The following are some listservs, Web sites, and on-line journals for teacher-researchers:

Teacher Research Special Interest Group of the American Educational Research Association

http://www.ilstu.edu/depts/labschl/tar/

National Writing Project (Teacher Research Section)

http://www.gse.berkeley.edu/Research/NWP/tchrsrch.html

Action Research Collaborative, St. Louis

http://info.csd.org/WWW/resources/arc/arc.html

Networks: An Electronic Journal of Teacher Research

http://www.oise.utoronto.ca/~gwells/journal.html

Show Me Action Research Online Journal

http://info.csd.org/WWW/resources/arc/arcdata.html

XTAR Forum of Teacher Researchers

http://www.ced.appstate.edu/~cathy/xtar.html

To join XTAR, send an e-mail message to listserv@lester.appstate.edu, leaving the Subject line blank; in the body of the message, write Subscribe XTAR Your Name. You will receive e-mail confirmation.

A number of services mimic the library stroll that we recommend. If you don't have ready access to a large research library, you might want to subscribe to a service like Uncover Reveal. This search service and others will periodically send you the table of contents for all the journals you request. You only pay when you order a specific article—a good way to eliminate the clutter of too many professional subscriptions and a streamlined means of seeing how your topic connects with research done in other fields.

It's easy to become overwhelmed by how much is available through Internet sources when it comes to reviewing research. One of the biggest challenges, in fact, is learning how to handle the overload of information. Ron Owston writes,

> I would say that one of the hardest things for me in learning to use the Internet was to get out of the habit of following every link I came across. I tended to get carried away following all the interesting links, so that I often forgot what it was I had been searching for! I often got lost and had to find my way back and force myself to become more focused on my immediate task. Once I became more familiar with the Internet and got into the habit of keeping focused, this became less and less a problem. Another difficulty was that I could not really locate the information I wanted because there

HOW TO "Ask Eric"
Stan Karp

The Internet and the World Wide Web have dramatically expanded the information resources available to those with on-line access. But whether all this information seems like a gold mine or a wasteland often depends on finding the right guide. One of the most comprehensive and flexible on-line guides for educators is AskEric (http://ericir.syr.edu).

ERIC, the Educational Resources Information Center, is a federally funded information clearinghouse. Researchers and college students know it is an indispensable academic tool providing annotated listings and abstracts of education research, studies, and papers. The ERIC database, now available and searchable on-line, directs users to voluminous full-text documents, typically available on microfiche in about one thousand libraries across the country. (It is also now possible to have many ERIC documents sent to users in printed or electronic versions for relatively modest fees.) The main ERIC site is located at http://www.aspensys.com/eric/index.html.

AskEric is a more user-friendly spin-off of the ERIC system developed by the Department of Education and Syracuse University in 1992. It describes itself as "a personalized, Internet-based service providing education information to teachers, librarians, counselors, administrators, parents." The AskEric service has several parts, but the most valuable are the Question and Answer service and the Virtual Library.

The Q and A service allows you to submit a specific request for information and receive a personalized e-mail response within forty-eight hours. There are limits, of course. AskEric supplies information about educational practice, policy, and research; it does not answer content-specific questions. ("For example, we are not a good source of information for discovering the causes of World War II or the average life span of a kangaroo.") But if you're looking for information about reading programs, block scheduling, the effects of class size on student achievement, or almost any education issue, AskEric is an excellent starting point. When a friend recently wanted to know if there was any legal basis to challenge the tracking system at her local high school, AskEric responded quickly with a long list of relevant citations.

The Virtual Library section of AskEric has additional resources for specific content areas and classroom uses. A useful section on "television companion materials" helps teachers find and order guides or student materials to supplement programming from a variety of educational channels. Another section lists over seven hundred lesson plans organized by topic and grade level.

Finally, for those content-specific or open-ended questions AskEric might not be able to answer, you can try the "Virtual Reference Desk" (http://www.vrd.org), which is also linked to the AskEric site under "special projects." This site directs users to reference services that can answer almost anything, and includes ways to "Ask an Author," "Ask a Librarian," or "Ask a Scientist" as well as links customized for parent inquiries.

So while AskEric cautions, "We do not replace an individual's own research," there's no doubt that if you have questions, AskEric has answers.

was just so much available. It often became frustrating. So I learned to use keywords and connecting words and concentrated on these words only, without getting off track. (1998, 3)

We agree with Ron Owston: use the Internet for its tremendous resources but stay focused and don't get carried away. Two good books to get you up and running are Owston (1998) and Cummins and Sayers (1995).

While many book lovers decry the rise of large bookstore chains and Internet stores, there are benefits for teacher-researchers. Many of the big Internet stores like Amazon.com and barnesandnoble.com will send regular customers lists of new books they might enjoy, based upon previous purchases. Having a list of good recommended books sent to us, based upon our past preferences, takes us back to the days when bookstore clerks knew each customer and anticipated what books they would want to read. And with the databases available now, the lists can be much more detailed and personal than they ever were in the past.

Read, Read, Read . . . and Then Write

Perhaps the most important reason to read like a researcher is that it will make you want to write. You'll see ways to connect your work to others', possibilities for a new contribution from your own research. You'll quake at the thought of trying to write as well as your favorite poet, or of piecing together a narrative as beautiful as your favorite novelist's, or of presenting findings as elegantly as your favorite teacher-researcher. Yet you'll still have the urge to put pen to page, as Donald Murray (1990a) warns: "Watch out. As you live and read there will probably come a time—especially if you don't believe such a time could come for you—when you will be invited to write or commanded to write or when you will simply have the itch to write. Then write. When you are in terminal middle age or beyond you may not be able to dance as you once intended or twist and turn toward the goal line as you once believed you could, but it is never too late to write—and all that reading you have done is stored away, waiting to be called upon as your words move across the page" (435).

RESEARCH WORKSHOP

You're Invited

Kimberly Hill Campbell

What do Dr. Benjamin Spock, J. D. Salinger, Deanna Troi, Howard Gardner, Paolo Freire, and Kermit the Frog have in common? They are all "invitees" listed by my graduate students in a research methods class. As my students worked to bring different perspectives into framing their research questions, I wanted them to think about individuals and wider communities that might inform their research designs and plans in new ways. So, I asked them to create a dinner party guest list of folks who would be helpful to them in pursuing their research questions.

The instructions for the assignment were simple:

1. Invite a minimum of six guests.
2. The guests can be anyone: dead, alive, even fictional.
3. For each guest, state your reason for inclusion and what you think or hope each would contribute.
4. Be as creative as you like.

Wow! The invitations were marvelous. As each teacher described their invitees, I was struck by how rich and varied each teacher's experience was, as were their invitations. One woman commented, "I think I would be intimidated to attend my own dinner party—so many great minds in one room." Her guests included a respected deaf teacher; a college chum; a mentor; Lawrence Van Der Post, the author of "the two best books I've ever read"; Anne, a friend whose American Sign Language interpreting ability "listens past the words and signs and conveys the concepts—the spirit as opposed to the letter"; and Counselor Deanna Troi from *Star Trek: The Next Generation:* "Her primary reception (and expression) of communication does not deal in realms of cultural biases, standards, or linguistic parameters. Her communication lies at the very expression/definition of life. . . . " Also, she has agreed to bring a replicator, so that everyone may eat whatever they desire." The final guest on the list was Winnie the Pooh, for his "simple, straightforward nature." God was also a consideration, but rejected because "I've never been able to get him/her in on a group discussion. God is good for one-on-one." Meril's hope was that the invitees would convene to discuss how she, as a teacher of the deaf, could enable her students to communicate, to explore the "concept of communication" itself. What does it mean to communicate?

Others predicted there would be fireworks at their parties—lots of heated, emotional discussion, lots of intense personalities. One woman had even designed a party that included an invitation to her father, her big brother, J. D. Salinger, and an old boyfriend who she described as "the guy who broke my heart." Her research question focused on the question of disciplining children, and each of these guests would have something to contribute. Her father could talk about his "eager use of public discipline." Her brother is described as the "primary victim" who could shed some light on how he was affected. J. D. Salinger, it was hoped, would add "any tips he could spare." And he was also included because of her "admiration for his writing."

Another student requested that each of her invited guests bring "their biases" and "some artwork that you have done in the past, or create something new. You can draw, paint, sculpt, etc. Be creative and have fun with this." Her research question was, How does art reflect gender in grades K–

12? She included in her guest list Mary Cassat, an artist who went "against her father's wishes and became a professional artist in a time period when women's paintings were accepted as hobby only." It was hoped that Mary could "shed some light on the pressures society places on children and what they can do to break unhealthy norms while discovering themselves."

Several teachers included menus in their dinner party invitations; one even enclosed a seating chart. Kristin's "Acting Out Amphibians" party seemed to combine the best of all worlds in what she describes as "a dinner party experience that is mind opening and only for the open-minded. Be prepared to act." It was to be hosted at the Monterey Bay Aquarium. The menu consisted of Brie, cheddar, and Swiss cheeses with crackers, home-made clam chowder, crab legs, squash, Ben and Jerry's Chocolate Chip Cookie Dough ice cream, peach melba, wine, beer, and water. Each hand-drawn invitation listed the name of the invitee and a brief description of their qualifications. On the reverse side was a detailed explanation of why this person had been invited and "what he or she would add." For example,

Connie Mayer

- Author of "Action Researcher: The Story of a Partnership," which is Chapter 6 of *Changing Schools from Within*
- Teacher of the deaf
- Signer

On the reverse side of the card Kristin wrote:

Why? Because she is a teacher of the deaf, and obviously a good one. She is innovative and loves children. Also she studies language acquisition of deaf children, which is the topic of discussion.

Add? Connie would add a wealth of knowledge to the party. I think she could provide lots of support and advice regarding acquisition and under-standing of vocabulary for deaf children. Plus, I want to know her better and thank her for publishing teacher research about deaf kids.

Kristin's plan was that each guest would be given the name of an amphibian, which they would then act out. This reinforced her research question, which looked at how deaf kids best mastered vocabulary. It also reflected her strong science background and her delightful, fun-loving approach to learning. Her quest list also reflected a central objective for doing the assignment: to discover other researchers who can support and inform your work.

During our discussions of the invitations and dinner plans, we added to each other's knowledge bases and provided names of folks who might be future experts to consult in our teaching. This workshop brought a sense of playfulness, creativity, and imagination into their research plans. While we were sharing and laughing, we were building our community—as teachers, learners, and researchers—in powerful ways. I was truly awestruck by the power of the imagination, of a community of learners, of spirited and lively discussions, voiced and voiceless, that were stimulated by the wonderings of teacher-researchers and enhanced by good food. I think we're onto something here.

featured TEACHER RESEARCHER

Reading Like a Researcher

Betty Shockley Bisplinghoff

I have stories to share. They are short stories about little pieces of life that have come to make a difference for me as a teacher-researcher. What I find especially interesting is how hidden the influences were in the beginning compared to how obvious and necessary they have become.

I live a storied life. There are daily joys and sadnesses, tensions and resolutions, beginnings and endings. I participate in the construction of the tales of my existence in varied ways. Sometimes I attempt to recast myself through the expressed visions of those who think they know me best or think they know what is best for me. At other times, I act more independently and directly in the dramas of my own becomings. We acquire our identities through the stories we act out and tell of ourselves, the stories we read, and the stories others tell about us. Through these cumulative collections of our storied selves we author anthologized lives that sit on the shelves inside us awaiting new and revised editions.

Suzanne Langer (1976) describes fiction as "virtual experience" and explains that "as participants we have only one life to live; as spectators [through reading], an infinite number is open to us" (117). James Britton (1970), another reader response theorist, adds, "Our minds tend to dwell on what has been happening to us . . . " to the point of generating "preoccupations" (100). These preoccupations seem to overflow into all that we do. Such are the reasons, I believe, that I cannot separate reading, researching, and day-to-day living, for each preoccupies my mind and adds to my life story.

Recognizing, accepting, and celebrating my current preoccupations while more consciously trying to build connective story lines among and between them focuses my thoughts for this paper. As Alice Walker (1984) once wrote, "What is always needed in the appreciation of art, or life, is the larger perspective. Connections made, or at least attempted, where none existed before, the straining to encompass in one's glance at the varied world the common thread, the unifying theme through immense diversity, a fearlessness of growth, of search, of looking, that enlarges the private and the public world" (5). The premise that when we read we are collecting both information and developing sensitivities while under the influence of guiding preoccupations is the basis for what has come to be my personal reader response experiment. Walker again accents my effort with "so much of the satisfying work of life begins as an experiment, having learned this, no experiment is ever quite a failure" (8).

Frank Smith (1983) claimed that "the secret of learning to write" was "reading like a writer" (103). By reading fiction as a researcher, I don't propose that we can learn to be researchers, but I do submit that there is an opportunity in fiction reading to rethink the style, language, and sensitivities of human science research that too often are lost when we restrict ourselves to reading only research like researchers. Smith also highlights those moments when as readers we pause to notice a new word or a well-written phrase and essentially have a chance to "catch ourselves in the act of learning" (103). These are the moments I have come to notice as one who now reads like a researcher. I catch myself in the act of seeing research connections between the lines of fiction.

This new awareness as a reader finds me effortlessly connecting what I read for pleasure and my prevailing interest in teacher research. There is not a book on my shelf that I have read in the last few years that does not contain a TR (teacher research) notation somewhere in a margin. This has become my shorthand cuing system for blending reading and research. Whenever I sense even a possible association, I brand the page with a TR. As a friend once told me, "Some of my best quotes for presentations come from fiction." For me, too, some of my best insights about research and life come from fiction. In fact, when I decide to try to understand something different, another culture, for instance, I first try to immerse myself in fictional representations of that experience. I know that to really learn, I have to feel deeply about the subject. Narrative that reaches out and pulls me into its place and time teaches me more than dispassionate texts.

Randomly picking Zora Neale Hurston's *Their Eyes Were Watching God* (1937) from my shelf, I can relive more than a well-told tale. I also revive associations made with teacher research. Hurston wrote, "Several men collected at Tea Cake's house and sat around stuffing courage into each other's ears" (148). I know what that feels like. I know the teacher research community I work with, the School Research Consortium supported by the National Reading Research Center at the University of Georgia, does just that. When we meet to talk about our research experiences, we are essentially trying to "stuff courage into each other's ears" as we attempt to move beyond the expected roles of teaching into areas many of us never expected to be a part of our professional self-definitions.

I also marked TR next to the section that included, "Janie turned from the door without answering, and stood still in the middle of the floor without knowing it. She turned wrongside out just standing there and feeling" (30). Shouldn't we do that as researchers, just stand still sometimes and allow ourselves to come out of our prescribed and all too often predictable orientations to resensitize, refocus our views? Another good lesson for the teacher-researcher me. Also, there are the powerful lessons on living that can somehow be said best within the safety of fiction, such as, "Then you must tell 'em dat love ain't somethin' lak uh grindstone dat's de same thing everywhere and do de same thing tuh everything it touch. Love is lak de sea. It's uh movin' thing, but still and all, it takes its shape from de shore it meets, and it's different with every shore" (182). I only hope that when all is said and done with my reading, researching, and my living, I will be viewed as more than Zora was able to write about that Turner woman, "She ain't a fact and neither do she make a good story when you tell about her" (142).

My stories of becoming a reader at a very late age, of maintaining my stance as a learner through graduate work, and building my definition of teaching to include research are the primary plotlines that continue to lead my personal reader response journey.

My Reading Story

I was old before I thought of myself as a reader; older still before I considered "researcher" to be an acceptable descriptor. Now I see both as essential to who I am. I knew myself as a wife, mother, and teacher long before "reader" even felt comfortable and necessary. As a child, I lived a privileged life with books arranged in cases and regular summer pilgrimages to the public library. But I hated the library, and the books in my home were just there for appearance' sake, not as any serious invitation to read. They were arranged "just so" with just the proper *Better Homes and Gardens* visual appeal.

The public library of my childhood was no more supportive of my tentative bond with reading and literature. It was an old Victorian home donated to the city. It smelled old, looked old, and sounded old. The floorboards creaked with each step like the bones of my grandmother, and all the books were lined up one next to the other in leaning support of their gray withered spines and yellowing pages. Reading did not beckon.

Not until someone I looked up to as a reader, someone I knew was an eager and enthusiastic reader, offered me a new look at an old decision—not to read—did I begin to review a place for reading in my life. My friend and co-researcher JoBeth Allen gave me three books for my thirty-ninth birthday. The books she chose for me were obviously carefully selected. She decided on books by Lee Smith because she was one of her favorite authors and Smith was from North Carolina, just like me. As I read, I relived the language and many of the family associations of my youth. I revisited familiar settings and heard the voices of my past. I learned that it makes a difference when you get to read things that accurately represent your realities—there are people who write, who know what you know, who maybe saw things that you saw, felt what you felt. With this kind of personal and pleasing reintroduction, reading soon grew to be a passion, a want-to, a have-to experience, a "virtual experience" that has become my ultimate spectator sport.

Writers such as Lee Smith as well as many others have continued to hold my hand, enabling me to create more junctures of promise between and among my readings and living. These points of cohesion create positions of strength formed from the intense response that is possible when the emotional and the intellectual are encouraged to scaffold one with the other. Suzanne Lipsett in her book *Surviving a Writer's Life* (1994) wrote, "I am not an intellectual and never have been; only, as both reader and writer, an intuitional, a responder from the deepest heart of the brain" (xviii). I worry and wonder at this rejection of companionship between intellectual and inspired understandings. Must one necessarily eliminate the other? Or, as I propose, could response from "the deepest heart of the brain" be the most intellectual challenge of all?

My Learning Story

Another reader response theorist, Judith Langer (1992) explains a view of reading in which "there are a series of stances or relationships the reader takes toward the text, each adding a somewhat different dimension to the reader's growing understanding of the piece. These stances are recursive rather than linear and are a function of varying reader/text relationships" (41). In her analysis of this process, she concludes that it is often the poorer readers who spend the most time "being out and stepping into an envisionment" (41). However, she also explains, "Even good readers face similar problems when they are confronted with more difficult texts. At any point where the language or ideas they are reading about are sufficiently discordant with their envisionments, readers might return to a 'being out and stepping in' stance in order to gather enough basic knowledge to permit them to continue their move through the piece" (41).

Recently, while trying to make sense of feminist theories, I found myself in just such a situation. Being confronted so intensely with such a wide variety of positions left me more than confused and anxious. I felt part of a desperate dance of "being out and stepping in," a dance that seemed to be getting me nowhere until I turned to story. In my women's studies class we were discussing radical feminism and at home I was reading *Sula* (Morrison 1973). Miraculously the "ahas" finally began to come. Characters in *Sula* helped make radical feminist issues gain a life. With this success, I began purposely to think about feminism through fiction and prose. This newfound handle on learning sustained me through a period of real discord, and with each new introduction to theory I looked for another authorial friend such as Morrison in *Sula* and Alice Walker in *In Search of Our Mothers' Gardens* to continue to guide me. Even Vivian Paley (1994) with her classroom story *You Can't Say You Can't Play* helped me reinterpret postmodern feminist theory as she struggled to rearrange the power structures within her kindergarten classroom, just as postmodern feminists challenge us to locate and redefine the structures that bind us. Having been a kindergarten teacher, this was a frame that made sense to me. I read fiction and stories of grounded experiences to support my new learnings. I read to keep my balance when walking that tense line between new and old learnings. It seems to me, our lives and learnings are storied as constant interplay between facts and fictions. Again Judith Langer (1992) contributes to my thinking: "Over time, understanding grows from meanings readers derive from the various stances they take along the way—getting acquainted, using meaning to build meaning, associating and reflecting, and distancing. Through these shifting relationships between self and text, readers structure [or restructure] their own understandings" (40–41).

My Researching Story

Judith Langer's stances differ from what another reader response theorist, Louise Rosenblatt, identifies as a reader's "predominant stance." Langer's stances are definitive of process, whereas Rosenblatt focuses on orientation. In other words, the process is the same but the orientation may differ per reading event. Essentially what I have come to understand from response theorists and from my own reading experiences, is that we read with selective attention, out of our own experiences and from our own questions.

When I read for pleasure, I find myself almost unconsciously making associations with issues of research. For instance, while reading *The House on Mango Street* (1989), by Sandra Cisneros, I longed for the skill and art to describe the scenes and scenarios of classroom experiences with such beauty and clarity. I think how remarkable it would be to read research that was so totally engaging and purposefully appealing to all the senses. Rosenblatt (1978) wrote of the process of "evoking the poem" (48) as a reader. I wonder why we cannot begin to evoke the idea of research writing that narrates the art as well as the method of human science research? Rosenblatt also recognized that any text may be read differently "under different conditions or by people with different urgencies" (36). The pretense that we can write research so cleanly that all who read it take from it the same interpretation is certainly unlikely.

Also from Rosenblatt, we understand that "the desire to see what happens next" is the most obvious version of the basic forward movement of the reading process" (54). Why, then, has it become such accepted practice in research writing to state your intentions within the first two paragraphs of a report or a conference presentation? "Developing anticipatory frameworks" (69) is also a recognized feature of the reading process based on Rosenblatt's analysis, but such anticipation has been all but lost to the academic reporter.

I also wonder what the research community could learn from the organizational structures of writers such as Ernest J. Gaines's *A Gathering of Old Men* (1983) or Randall Kenan's *Let the Dead Bury Their Dead* (1992)? In each of these works the author has succeeded in evoking an overall sense of a community through character studies of the citizens of each setting. Gaines ties his personalities together through a cohesive plotline, and Kenan identifies each of his characters through a series of short stories. Regardless of tack, both authors achieve a literate integration that is both engaging and inspiring. Could these creators of fictional realities also speak lessons for the presentation of case study research?

What could we learn from Amy Hill Hearth and her decisions about how to share the lives and wisdoms of the Delaney Sisters in *Having Our Say* (1993)? How much more important to our sensibilities as readers was her accounting of the interviews with the two sisters when she decided only to provide initial background/historical information and not to intervene or interpret the words of the sisters? Could this be an insight for the reportings of phenomenologists or other interview-based qualitative research?

And, what about Jamaica Kincaid's (1988) introduction to *At the Bottom of the River*? Could her example of writing with a stream-of-thought technique as if her mother's words could still be heard despite the passage of time be a model for researchers who are trying to establish their backgrounds and biases for the reader? Could they decide to talk to us in writing about the influences that still haunt their actions? I read. I wonder. I research. I hope for the "creative adventure" (Rosenblatt 1978, 52) in the work and pleasure of making meaning.

In learning about the meaning-making process of reading, many scholars have attempted distinctions between literary and scientific modes of thinking: "In this tradition, Suzanne Langer . . . speaks of subjective and objective realities, Louise Rosenblatt . . . speaks of aesthetic and efferent readings, James Britton . . . speaks of spectator and participant roles, and Jerome Bruner . . . speaks of narrative and paradigmatic thought" (Judith Langer 1992, 37). Bruner's (1987) stance that "full understanding is better achieved by using both the ordered thought of the scientist and the humanely inquisitive thought of the storyteller" (7) certainly seems most in tune with how I'm coming to see my reading like a researcher response.

The Teacher-Researcher Story

Louise Rosenblatt (1978) also views meaning as a "lived-through experience" (12). In what context could there possibly be more opportunities for lived-through experiences than the classroom? Teachers spend day after day in complex isolated worlds of meaning making that for the most part go unrecognized and unrewarded for their wealth of insight and knowledge about the learning process. As the Native American Wilma Mankiller (1993) knows so well, "An entire body of knowledge can be dismissed because it was not written" (20). The lives teachers lead are also very seldom textually embodied. Wallace Stegner in his novel *Crossing to Safety* (1987), wrote that "until it has had a poet, a place is not a place" (137). Teachers need to be poets for their profession and evoke through their reporting of their knowledges an intellectual history that can be claimed and exclaimed . . . this is our tradition! What the teacher-researcher should be able to write is a sense of her community. Again, Stegner supports the effort by counseling a good beginning, "to rub one word against another" (260). In such a way might we begin to construct pathways of both professional and personal empowerment. After all, according to Carolyn G. Heilbrun in *Writing a Woman's Life* (1988), "Power is the ability to take one's place in whatever discourse is essential to action and the right to have one's part matter" (18). Perhaps what each effort will produce in the end is something akin to Suzanne Lipsett's (1994) response to years of reading, "What this lifetime of reading, and reading fiction in particular, has yielded has been experience squared" (xviii).

What am I learning from my reader response experiment that can be put to practical use? First, I recall the voices of Don Graves, Nancie Atwell, and Lucy Calkins encouraging teachers to be avid readers. Linda Rief (1992), another teacher-researcher, wrote very directly about this issue when she said, "All teachers should be readers and writers, but teachers of language arts must be writers and readers" (10). I now add to this position the personal realization that it is important not only for me to be a teacher who reads but also a researcher who reads. By this I don't mean simply reading the peer-authored research of one's academic field but rather to continue to enrich our research activities and live our longings through fiction as well.

Fiction reading challenges me and maybe others to think like Alice Walker (1984) when she wrote, "In my own work I write not only what I want to read. . . . I write all the things *I should have been able to read*" (13). As a teacher, I feel I should have been able to read more research that more accurately reflected the complexities and realities of my classroom. As a teacher-researcher, I hope to add my part to a research effort that celebrates my community of teachers. Just as I try to teach to engage hearts as well as minds, so will I aim to write from the deepest heart of my brain.

Honest Labor: Writing up Research

7

All the good stories are out there waiting to be told in a fresh, wild way.

Anne Lamott

Teaching and writing are labor, and only those involved in birthing research projects in chaotic classrooms can understand fully what the experience is like. We remember some years ago talking to a man whose wife had just spent twenty-six hours in labor giving birth to their first child. We were clucking on about how hard that must have been for the woman. He brushed aside our concerns, saying, "Hey, it's not that bad. It's not like she was in labor all the time. I mean, you have a pain, but then you get a break for five or ten minutes. Heck, you can practically take a nap or read a magazine during those breaks."

When we read the expectations many university folks like us place on teacher-researchers, we sometimes feel like we are labor coaches with the sensitivity of that husband. This is especially true when we look at the advice and exhortations given to teachers about writing up their research.

The view from the outside doesn't acknowledge what the teaching process is like for those on the inside in the midst of busy classrooms. University folks tend to cheerlead too much and our rah rahs include the rant that teachers *do* have time to sit and write in the midst of their busy classrooms. Teachers are often told the weekend is the perfect time to revise the drafts they've been working on in the classroom. We might just as easily tell them to read a magazine or grab a nap in the author's chair in class during those moments when they aren't actually *teaching* their students throughout the day.

We do know a couple of teachers who write beautiful essays and books in the midst of their teaching day; they grab moments here and there between lessons and workshops. But this certainly isn't the norm. Writing, like labor, is a slow, hard process for most teacher-researchers. It requires a fair amount of time outside the classroom—quiet, unstructured time to let your thoughts percolate.

Teacher-researchers have a response for the experts who say writing can easily be integrated into the teaching day: It's much harder than you think. Teachers are in labor all day long, and no matter how nice the person is who holds your hand, the experience can only be understood and described by those who go through it. The rhythm of any good teaching day includes rapid and steady bursts of insight, delight, and unease about the learning of students and our role in it.

Writing and teaching take such different energies that many argue it isn't necessary for teachers to write up their research. Just the process of collecting the data and trying to analyze it will bring new learning and understanding to teachers. Adding the layer of writing up the findings and bringing them to a larger audience is a step many teacher-researchers don't want or need. And yet . . .

We've had our own professional lives transformed by a few great teacher research studies. We bet you, too, can identify books that marked your own emergence as a confident teacher—books like *In the Middle* by Nancie Atwell (1987), *Teacher* by Sylvia Ashton-Warner (1963), *36 Children* by Herbert Kohl (1967), and *Sounds from the Heart* by Maureen Barbieri (1995). We see quiet, persistent changes in our teaching over the years, changes that would not have happened without our reading the detailed accounts by other teachers about the learning in their classrooms. Even more transformative for us are the bits and pieces of writing done by teachers in the midst of research, like the snippets included in this book. This text is peppered with the writing of teacher-researchers, writing we wouldn't have had access to if those teachers hadn't done the labor of writing about their research.

If we're honest enough to acknowledge that writing up research is difficult, we hope you trust us enough to consider the possibilities anyway. We need more voices from teachers in journals and books, more accounts of how complicated and exciting learning can be when teachers look closely and aren't afraid to write about what they are seeing. The practical advice that follows is culled from the experiences of teacher-researchers who have managed to write and publish their work; they tell us that no other experience has brought them more professional growth.

Getting Organized

If you've reached the point where you're ready to write up your findings, the first thing you'll need to do is organize what you have to work with— the raw materials you've collected over the past months or years. Gather all this stuff, lay it out, and look it over. Your materials might include writing and reading logs by the kids, your notes or teaching journal, kids' projects, data analysis code sheets or charts, or photographs.

As you go through everything you've saved, look for the breakthrough moments, the instances when you discovered something about your kids and yourself. Begin to compile lists of those key incidents or events. Flag them in your notes, pull them off the transcripts. You need gallons and gallons of sap to make a cup of maple sugar—you need to look over all the raw stuff you have before you can distill it into the story of your classroom. We've often commandeered the living room from family members to lay out reams of notes, photos, and video clips with teachers who are starting to draft conference proposals, books, or articles. Writer Annie Dillard (1989) explains this process well, in *The Writing Life:* "How appalled I was to discover that, in order to write so much as a sonnet, you need a warehouse. You can easily get so confused writing a thirty-page chapter that in order to make an outline for the second draft, you have to rent a hall. I have often 'written' with the mechanical aid of a twenty-foot conference table. You lay your pages along the table's edge and pace out the work. You walk along the rows; you weed bits, move bits, and dig out bits, bent over the rows with full hands like a gardener" (46).

Once you pull out some of those breakthrough moments, you need to start writing. When you're drafting, it's probably not going to be a linear movement from page one to page two, from section one to section two. It's usually best to write about some of those moments of insight from your classroom in small chunks and as vividly as possible. What were students wearing? saying? The smallest details will be critical for making those moments come to life. If you get stumped in trying to re-create a scene, give yourself prompts: "I saw . . . ," "I heard . . . ," "I felt. . . . "

Many times it's the seemingly insignificant details that can make the scene come to life. Bonnie Friedman (1993) writes about the importance of details: "You may paint a soul only by painting a knuckle. You may convey terror or longing or regret or exhilaration only by giving us the color of someone's hair and exactly what she ate for lunch, and red high heels, and an attaché case's handle stained dark by the oils of a human hand, and a skinny buck-toothed girl singing 'Yes We Have No Bananas' on a black-and-white TV, and olives, and three o'clock, and the Scotch-taped hem of a Bergdorf Goodman dress, and venetian blinds, and a woman's eyes fixed for many minutes on a scarred tabletop, and a tin spoon ringing against the side of a mug. There are no shortcuts" (87).

Photos are a wonderful way to get ideas for free writing about the classroom. Use some of your photos as writing prompts, and you'll be surprised at the memories that are sparked because you've got a full-color reminder of an event right before your eyes. Once you've got some pieces of the story—strong, clear writing on critical incidents in your classroom—you can begin to see how these will fit together to tell a larger story.

The best writing coaches are often "distant teachers"—the authors of your favorite books on teaching and learning. Terri Austin, author of *Changing the View* (1995), credits her ability to write her classroom research to learning from a "distant teacher" whom she had never met:

In terms of style, I have to say that I learned to write by reading Nancie Atwell's *In the Middle.* I taught myself how to write like that, not that I'm anywhere near her ability, but that book probably is the most influential book for me because it came right at the time I became a teacher-researcher and when I was struggling not only to be a researcher, but to be a writer. It flowed like a story. I still have her original book in its original pink cover. . . . I have it marked out—this is how she introduced this, this is how she explained her record keeping, this is how she wove in the stories of her students. I taught myself how to write with this book. (personal communication, 1998)

We encourage you to reread your favorites—not as a teacher, but as a writer. Look at the leads to chapters—how do the authors draw you in? How do they lay out information on the page to make it inviting? How do they balance classroom incidents and anecdotes with practical advice? What kinds of materials do they put into their appendixes? Once you start reading like a writer, your favorite books will seem brand-new and full of practical tips to improve your own drafts.

Why Your Writing Matters

You won't be far into the process before you'll wonder if you really have something worth saying. As you lay out your raw materials, you're going to see big gaps in what you need. And as you begin to write up those moments of insight, you'll get discouraged about your writing ability. Know that all teachers who end up writing wonderful articles and books feel this way early in the process. Your first drafts, even if they look good to other readers, will seem pretty awful to you. Everyone writes terrible first drafts. That's the beginning step in writing up your research. Writer Anne Lamott describes why it's important to hold your nose and keep writing:

All good writers write [terrible first drafts]. This is how they end up with good second drafts and terrific third drafts. People tend to look at successful writers, writers who are getting their books published and maybe even doing well financially, and think that they sit down at their desks every morning feeling like a million dollars, feeling great about who they are and how much talent they have and what a great story they have to tell; that they take in a few deep breaths, push back their sleeves, roll their necks a few times to get all the cricks out, and dive in, typing fully formed passages as fast as a court reporter. But this is just the fantasy of the uninitiated. I know some very great writers, writers you love who write beautifully and have made a great deal of money, and not one of them sits down routinely feeling wildly enthusiastic and confident. Not one of them writes elegant first drafts. All right, one of them does, but we do not like her very much. (1994, 21–22)

And not all teachers do end up writing wonderful articles and books—it's important to be truthful here. There's a lot of writing already published from classroom teachers across the world; many topics have been covered beautifully by teachers in the past. But we wouldn't be encouraging you if we didn't know that most teachers do have something to contribute through writing and publishing.

Even if your work doesn't get published, we hope the process of writing it up brings you to a new understanding of your classroom. That's why teachers write—not to transform the field, or to be famous, or to get a book published. We write to understand our classrooms, our students, ourselves. Wrestling with words on the page, we finally understand why our research and teaching matters, and what we need to carry away from one year into the next. We see ourselves and our classrooms anew, in ways not possible without the intense reflection writing demands.

We also write to stay sane. We write to get some closure, however temporary, on the issues that plague us in our classrooms. As Susan Ohanian (1996) explains, "By turning pedagogy into narrative, a teacher can address the ambiguities and frustrations of teaching. More than that, narrative can contain these ambiguities and frustrations, at least for the moment, keeping them from running wild. *New York Times* book reviewer Anatole Broyard wrote, 'Always in emergencies we invent narratives.' What is teaching, if not day-to-day emergencies? . . . Every school would be a better place if teachers told their stories and those of the children" (13).

So abandon any pressure you feel to write something great or something that's just perfect for a certain journal or book publisher. Write first to learn more about your classroom through the writing. And if you have that as your goal, you're much more likely to write something many other teachers will want to read.

Getting Response to Your Writing

Once you do have some drafts of writing, even if they are just a few pages recounting incidents randomly, you'll need to get some response from others. Before you send what you've written off to a journal or book publisher, you should share it with at least a couple of close teaching friends and get their advice for what you should write next and what revisions are needed.

Here's the key question you'll want to ask yourself and those who respond to your work: What's the story here? Where is the narrative thread that can hold this all together? Finding that narrative thread will help you figure out what needs to stay in the writing and what needs to go.

When you get response from others, stifle the urge to accept or reject the advice of your reviewers immediately. As Robert Frost said, "Thinking isn't agreeing or disagreeing—that's voting." Mull over the responses, negative and positive, and see what you can use from them to make the writing better. We also like Peter Elbow's (1997) advice about conferring over

Tips for Writing and Getting Published

- The best way to start writing is to write as if you are writing a letter to a dear friend you've been out of touch with for a while. It's much easier to write a letter than it is to write an article. And before you know it, the imaginary letter will become the real article.
- There is never a "good" time to write. Now is as good a time as any.
- Write every day, even if it's only a few words or phrases. Writing to and with your students counts, too.
- Realize that many editors are not writers. Try to find someone to help you who is a writer and an editor.
- Get an outsider's view of the journal or publisher you want to work with: submission guidelines, upcoming themes.
- Get an insider's view of the journal or publisher you want to work with: tone of response, time for response, quality of response.
- Follow the rule of three—allow an article or proposal to be rejected at least three times before thinking seriously about revising it.
- A negative, hostile response from a journal says plenty about the insecurity of the editor and nothing about the quality of your writing.

writing: "When you get conflicting reactions, block your impulse to figure out which reactions are right. Eat like an owl: take in everything and trust your innards to digest what's useful and discard what's not. Try for readers with different tastes and temperaments—especially if you don't have many readers" (118).

If you're feeling courageous, ask someone outside of education to read something you've written. People with a little distance from the teaching culture can let you know immediately what jargon or phrasing gets in the way of the story you are trying to tell, and they can give you a sense of how wide an audience there is for your writing.

Many researchers we've worked with find the experience of presenting their work at a local in-service meeting, or a state or national conference, invaluable for drafting and improving their writing. Applying to present at a conference gives you a forced deadline for beginning to pull together a narrative.

Writing a proposal of one or two pages will get you organized for longer writing tasks. And presenting your work orally allows you to read cues from your audience. Their questions will push you forward in your thinking and help you go back to your classroom, writing, and thinking with an audience in mind. Noting when listeners seem engaged or bored can

Tips for Organizing a Writing Retreat

There is a long tradition of writers retreating from the busyness of their daily lives and carving out stretches of time where they can immerse themselves in their writing in a community of other writers. Many teacher-researchers are finding weekends devoted to writing with a trusted group—and even better, week-long summer writing retreats!—are a practical and enjoyable route for making sense of their data and writing it up for their intended audiences. Several of the teacher-researchers in this book—Terri Austin, Annie Keep-Barnes, Kimberly Campbell, Betty Bisplinghoff, Barbara Michalove, Kelly Chandler, and others—have found this a far more do-able alternative to rising at 4 A.M. to write, or trying to fit in time in the evening after responding to student work.

After taking part in several writing retreats ourselves, we're hooked. We encourage you to consider including at least a weekend with your teacher research group that's devoted to writing and sharing your work. These tips, culled from teacher-researchers from Maine to Alaska, can help get you off to a successful start. Happy writing!

- *Preplan and organize.* Choose your dates far enough in advance so that you can get dates that will work for the most members of your group and that give you enough lead time to be working toward the goal of having the necessary data and books on hand.
- *Choose a place away from school—an environment where you can be a writer.* The place is important, which is another reason to plan ahead. This gives you a chance to poll friends and colleagues about possible cabins, off-season rates for retreat centers, bed-and-breakfasts with reasonable rates, or even to write a small grant or request staff development funds. We've been at successful retreats at out-of-the-way bed-and-breakfasts, retreat centers, and the home of a group member who banned her family for a long weekend and scattered sleeping bags around the house.
- *Have meals catered or provided by someone else.* "Breaking bread together" is a central aspect of writing, talking, and thinking, but the preparation can really cut into your time. If your budget doesn't permit catered meals, you can enlist the support of a friend, family member, or even one member of the group who agrees to take on the responsibility on a rotating basis. It's an amazing gift to emerge from your writing cocoon to an already prepared meal, and colleagues ready to dig in and discuss your work in progress.
- *Try for at least three days.* It can take a while to get started and into the rhythm of daily writing.
- *Schedule long, unstructured blocks of writing time.* It's easy to get sidetracked with lots of discussion. We have found it helpful to get together the first evening of the retreat and negotiate a tentative daily schedule, with at least two inviolate hours of writing time in the morning and another two in the afternoon. Some members might want to plan on an early morning walk to get the day started, a special time for reading before or after lunch, or conference times. Create a schedule that works for your

group's needs. But keep the writing time central. It's surprising how much more writing you can accomplish when you are in the midst of a group of committed writers!

- *Have set goals.* Plan what will be accomplished before the retreat begins, and distribute these group and individual goals in advance.
- *Bring the writing supplies.* Make sure there's at least one printer that you can hook up to if you are using portable computers. Access to a copying machine is also a convenience, if possible. Bring pens, pads of paper, Post-its, highlighters, and whatever else your writing rituals depend on; don't assume you can just pick them up on site. And don't forget books—novels, poems, essays—whatever good reading you enjoy for that before-bed downtime and early morning preparation for writing. We have found the language of these novels and the good talk around texts found its way into our final writing results.

also help you decide what should remain in your writing and what should be cut.

You can often return to your research plan itself to give you a framework for your proposal. The origin of your research question is usually a good place to start. Another bonus of writing up a proposal is that the deadline forces you to consolidate your thinking and get it on paper and out the door.

You may want to present your work as part of a panel presentation (see Figure 7.1). This gives you a chance to plan together, talk through your ideas with others, and assemble a presentation that draws on the connections in your research. Some presentations are more suited to one person, with more time for in-depth explanations of the work or more audience participation (see Figure 7.2). Both of these accepted proposals can serve as models for you as you think about presenting at a local or national conference. Both presentations allowed these teachers to talk their way through what they had learned from their research projects and what would connect them with a larger audience. A publisher attended Jill Ostrow's presentation and encouraged her to expand it into a book-length explanation of her multiage math program. Her book, *Making Problems, Creating Solutions* (1999) was published two years later.

Giving Response to Writing

Writers depend upon other writers for response. If you want to receive helpful response to your writing, you'll need to learn how to give useful feedback to colleagues. The process of responding to others will give you clues about what kind of response can be most helpful to you.

We've learned that vague comments can often lead to worse second

Figure 7.1 Presentation Proposal

PROPOSAL TO NCTE NATIONAL CONFERENCE

Proposal Submitted by: Sharon Frye
Time Requested: A complete session of seventy-five minutes
Session Title: Listening to Girls: Opening Conversations—Making the Needs of Girls Visible in Our Schools
Annotation: A panel of teacher-researchers will share ways they have found to begin listening to girls and opening conversations about girls' issues in their classrooms.
Topic of Emphasis: Teacher research
Grade Level of Interest: Middle level (6–8) and high school (9–12)
Intended Audience: Classroom teachers
Format of Session: Presentation by panelists
Audiovisual Equipment: Overhead projector and screen, VCR
Sessions:
"Building Support for Girls: The Triumphs and Struggles of a Girls' Group"—Ellena Weldon (presenter and chair)
"Choosing Curriculum to Open Conversations"—Jennifer MacMillan
"Using Journals to Listen to Girls"—Sharon Frye

> Across the nation, often well-meaning teachers continue to deliver subtle but powerful messages reinforcing boys' dominance in the classroom. Curricula continue to reflect inequities, as materials by and about women remain peripheral and teaching approaches continue to favor predominantly male interactional styles.—*Girls in the Middle Working to Succeed in School*. AAUW Educational Foundation.

We, and the students we teach, live within a culture that continually sends messages about how women and girls should act and be. Growing up within this world, it is often difficult for us to step back and closely examine the ways in which classrooms (our own included) reinforce stereotypes, deny some girls a chance to speak, or facilitate the various ways in which our girl students *do* communicate. As teacher-researchers, we have a framework to step back, question what we do, and why we do it—and learn from our students how we can better meet their needs. As part of our research process, we explored the questions, What *are* the girl students teaching us about what it means to be a girl in the 1990s? How can we better hear what they are saying? What strategies do girls use to cope with environments that, if not intentionally, deliver messages that reinforce boys' dominance in the classroom? Can we provide the support structures within our heterogeneous classrooms to open up the conversations that need to take place for girls? In this presentation, we will share the ways in which we have asked these questions and have gained insight into our own teaching from the girls we teach.

Sharon Frye (Riverdale, Oregon) will begin the panel presentation by sharing from her year-long study on the diverse ways in which girls use journal writing and the writing process to express their voices. Using samples from her classroom and three case studies, Sharon will share the questions that shaped her research, the origins of these questions, and what she learned about what and how adolescent girls communicate through writing. (20 minutes)

Jennifer MacMillan (Beaverton, Oregon) presents methods for getting girls to discuss important topics that often go unspoken in the classroom. Using samples from workshops she gives for girls in Oregon and examples of girl-focused literature, she will explain the ways in which she facilitates conversations about fitting in, body image, trusting yourself, and creating a supportive environment. (20 minutes)

Ellena Weldon (Riverdale, Oregon) will conclude the panel discussion with what she has discovered about girls' experience by hearing what they say in girls' groups. She will share her experiences as a facilitator of girls' groups, and also the stories of three different case studies that demonstrate the varied ways in which girls respond to their environments. (20 minutes)

These presentations will take approximately one hour, leaving fifteen minutes for a discussion of the workshop participants' comments and questions.

drafts by researchers; and any initial response to writing needs to be tempered with a keen awareness of how much criticism the writer is ready and able to hear.

In the summer of 1997 the editorial team from *Teacher Research* (Kelly Chandler, Kimberly Campbell, and we ourselves) got together and compiled guidelines for reading and responding to writing by teacher-researchers. You can use these as a starting point for developing strategies for responding to writing within your own research community.

Reading the Manuscript

- Read the draft at least twice. We have often been surprised by what we discover during the second reading. The first time through, try to get a sense of the whole piece without thinking about how to fix it.

- Note the areas of the draft you want to know more about. Jot down what strikes you, and indicate questions you have.

- Ask yourself questions as you read:

  What am I learning? What's new here?

  Can someone on staff benefit from this piece? What would other teachers learn?

  Is this written in a teacher-to-teacher voice?

  Is there any tension in the piece (rather than a tone of "I have seen the light!")?

Figure 7.2 Presentation Proposal

MATHEMATICAL STORIES: BEYOND THE FACTS AND INTO THE REAL WORLD
JILL OSTROW

Children learn language by becoming immersed in language. Educators now know the importance of a holistic approach for young children to acquire written language. The connection between learning mathematical concepts and learning written language is now becoming widely understood through current teacher research. Young children not only need to be surrounded with mathematical concepts constantly, but they need to be challenged, given choice, and allowed to use a variety of problem-solving strategies.

I will talk about the importance of allowing, and encouraging, children to use a variety of strategies not only for solving problems, but when explaining problems they have solved. In order to internalize a concept, children need to explain in writing and orally how a problem was solved. Through these written stories of their thinking process, children not only begin to internalize concepts, they begin to transfer that knowledge to more complex thinking strategies. These strategies include drawing, pictures, manipulatives, and symbols.

As an adult, I am just now learning how to look at mathematical concepts visually. I was taught to memorize facts and algorithms. Now I solve the same problems my students do by using drawings, or explain my thinking by using pictures. I am a visual thinker, but because I was not allowed to learn this way, I assumed I was "bad" at math. Children need to learn to discover their own process for organizing and explaining their thinking and understanding concepts they need to learn.

In my presentation, I will talk about the importance of choice and challenge through problem solving. I will show many examples, slides as well as original work, of six- to nine-year-old children engaged in complex problem solving. I will explain and show children collaborating, discussing, writing about solutions, sharing, and creating mathematical presentations.

I will also show examples of how mathematical concepts can be integrated into language, science, geography, and history through problems that I and the children create.

I plan to present for forty-five minutes and allow thirty minutes for questions and discussion.

Is the research process described?

Are additional headings needed to improve the organization?

Are there any references I could recommend that might prove useful to the writer?

Responding

- As you write, try to picture the author reading your review. Think about the time and courage it took for this teacher to share the article.

We want these teachers to continue to research and share their discoveries. Frame your response so that the author will see what worked well in the draft and what worked less well. What would you say if you were going to have a writing conference with him or her? Try to keep in mind the kind of coaching that has been the most helpful to you as a writer.

- *Be specific* in your comments. Include direct quotes (with page numbers) in your examples of what worked and what didn't. Try to provide one or two concrete examples for every assertion you make, regardless of whether it's a strength or a weakness.
- Avoid educational jargon.
- Concentrate on the most important issues you'd like the author to address. You don't have to suggest ways to improve all aspects of the piece.
- If you wouldn't feel comfortable saying your comments to the author in person, don't write them.

We have found if you schedule a time to share drafts in a group, it's essential for the author to tell the group what type of advice will be most helpful. Some authors will be in the final stages of writing, ready for copyediting and response about word choice; others will wither if they hear anything but the most global responses to what works and what doesn't in their initial drafts. If you ask first, you're more likely to give the author advice that will really be used.

A Word About Rejection

We need to give a word of warning here about receiving response to your writing from journals and book publishers. We've received much helpful advice from caring editorial board members and reviewers from publishers. But we've also received pages of snotty insults from reviewers that drove us to tears. A vicious or just plain lousy response to your work isn't a reflection on your writing—it's a reflection on the pettiness and unprofessionalism of the reviewer. We urge you to write to the editorial board of a journal or publisher if you think a review of your work crosses the line from critique to attack. We all have a responsibility to make our profession more caring and responsive to teachers' writing.

Even a kind rejection of writing hurts. It's hard to separate our classrooms and our psyches as teachers from the writing we do about them. Nancy Mair writes about how hard it is to allow our writing to be judged by others:

Invariably, as I unfold the rejection letter, disappointment and shame explode in my gut and for days I can't draw a full breath. I feel spurned, degraded, hollowed out, tossed aside. . . . My imagination, given only a form letter to feed on, freely invents a judge—always a "real" writer of impeccable discernment, who, flicking his eyes over my pages, curls his lip in just the way my ninth-grade science teacher must have done on receiving my anonymous professions of passion, and perhaps even hoots once at my pretensions as he tosses them onto the rising refuse heap. Having been a judge myself, I know that these behaviors don't go on at every site of rejection, but we're not talking reason here. We're talking the death of the heart. (1994, 141)

Because we are all fragile as writers, it's helpful to know which journals have the most supportive editorial boards. Read journals you might submit your work to, and see if the tone of their published authors matches yours. We made the mistake early in our writing careers of submitting our work only to the largest journals in our field. We sometimes waited months for a response, only to get rejections with little or no editorial assistance for improving the draft. It was only after we began submitting to regional and state journals in our field that we began to receive quicker, more positive responses to our writing. Consider submitting your work to smaller forums at the start—local newspapers as op/eds, a district newsletter, a state interest group annual collection. As your confidence builds, progress to larger outlets for your writing.

But the most important advice of all is to carve out some time to write. Though it can be daunting to start, writing will take you to deeper layers of meaning in your research and will transform your identity as a teacher and as a researcher. Terri Austin now cannot imagine her teaching life without it: "Writing has become such a part of who I am. I started off thinking I was not a writer. And now that's one of the ways I identify myself: I truly think of myself as a writer. That doesn't mean it's easier, but it means I trust it will work. I've come to realize that you can't plan everything you write—sometimes it just happens. It pops up on the screen, and I'm just sort of surprised sometimes about things that I write. It doesn't occur to me until I get them down in print that, yeah, that's how I think" (personal communication, 1998).

Whether it's a memo to a teaching partner, a narrative for your research group, a proposal to share your work, or the beginnings of an article, we encourage you to start small—or big, if you wish—but do start! Surprises can't "pop up on the screen" if you aren't sitting in front of it, giving it a try. Take Terri's advice to heart: get started, trust, and enjoy the surprises that emerge from your writing.

RESEARCH WORKSHOP

Seeing What Is Not Seen: Another Reason for Writing up Teacher Research

Ruth Shagoury Hubbard

We sat together one evening in December, a group of teacher-researchers who had been conducting case studies in our classrooms. As we laughed and ate and prepared to share our final drafts with each other, we decided to reflect on what the process of writing up our research had been like. What emerged in our ten-minute free-writes was the discovery that what had helped most of us make sense of our data was the actual writing itself. We shouldn't have found this remarkable. As Donald Murray (1982) writes: "Your world is the universe you describe by using your own eyes, listening to your own voice—finding your own style. We write to explore the constellations and galaxies which lie unseen within us waiting to be mapped with our own words" (7).

During this process, some found surprises in the data, like Jean, who wrote, "What I thought had been the focus of my study became just one piece after I began writing." Or Ann, who stated, "As I was writing, I was surprised to hear myself writing that giving my students time to speak in class led to better writing."

Margie reflected on how writing had led her to see the pattern in her findings: "It wasn't until I laid out data, wrote and rewrote, that I could see a pattern—the real significance of the notes I had."

We decided that setting a deadline, having a date to bring our final (for now) published pieces to our group to share had helped us analyze and bring together in new and unforeseen ways the piles of data we had collected. Besides providing a way to *share* what we knew with other teachers, writing our case studies had helped us *discover* what we knew. Writing up our research is an important tool for researchers, guiding us to insights that otherwise might have eluded us.

The words of the poet Diane Glancy can encourage teacher-researchers to turn to their data with a new vision. In her published journal, *Claiming Breath* (1992), she writes: "In writing, life sinks/rises like the moon with new visibility. Another dimension. Seeing what is not seen in a different way than if we'd seen it" (54).

Teachers who have found avenues into writing share their suggestions in the following paragraphs. Perhaps their insights can help you and the teacher-researchers you work with bring your work onto the page.

1. *Use writing to help you brainstorm what you know and what you still need to find out.* After several weeks of collecting data on one student's learning, Monique Bissett found it helpful to give herself the goal of listing five things she knew about the student and five things she needed to find out. She wrote them in two columns in her teaching journal. When other

teachers in her support group tried this strategy, they found it helped to point out themes that were emerging as well as holes in the data.

2. *Make the time to write for ten minutes on what you are noticing and keep these anecdotal notes for later reflection.* In reflecting on what had helped her to conduct her case study, Tiffany Poulin noted, "The best thing I did was to take anecdotal notes early. Reviewing the narratives I had written at the end of one month helped me to remember in greater detail. In a sense, re-viewing what I had written helped me to see what I had *really* been see-ing." Lila Moffit agrees; she finds that setting time for herself at the end of a school day works best: "Having a computer and taking a few minutes each evening to 'revisit' Max gave me huge amounts of data with which to un-derstand his literacy journey. I couldn't write in class. I needed time and quiet to discover the meaning of his contribution to my day."

Some teachers, like Laura St. John, discover that in order to find that writing time they need to set aside a few minutes within their teaching day. "What works in conducting my case study," Laura writes, "is to specifically set ten minutes per day for writing. I remove myself from circulating and 'privately' do my work."

Find a way that fits your working style to write those brief anecdotal notes and reflections that can help to uncover what you are seeing in your classroom.

3. *Write brief memos or narratives about the themes that you see emerging.* "One surprising discovery I made in writing up my case study is that I as-sociated the term *risk taker* with Max," writes Lila Moffit. "I decided to cen-ter my write-up on that one literacy theme. Max was living it daily, ex-pressing it in everything he did and said in the classroom."

Memos might be two or three pages long, or as brief as a paragraph, like this memo Rick Osborn wrote that helped him bring together multiple data points to confirm a finding:

> I was surprised at how well my initial interview with my case study pre-pared me for examining her writing. After talking to Stephanie about some of the basic or elemental things that she does in her writing, I am able to see the same patterns in her writing itself. For example, Stephanie talked about how she would always write some quick notes down before she stopped writing so that she could remember where she had left off and what her thought pattern was. In her paper, I can see right where she has done this. Then, when I interviewed her again, I was able to confirm this. Stephanie has really opened up to me and allowed me to see quite a bit of what she is thinking.

4. *Write a letter to a teaching friend about what you are learning.* This can help put together what you are learning in new ways as you explain it to a new audience. Gina Brandt, a high school science teacher, complained that she was stuck when she tried to write up all that she knew about Mariah.

To help herself get over this obstacle, she thought about a teaching friend who would be genuinely interested in the issues she was grappling with in working to understand the way Mariah learns, and she wrote that friend a letter. In her letter, she was able to write in her own voice about her concerns, delights, and surprises, and wonder on paper about how she could best meet her student's needs. When she finished the letter, she had a working draft as well as a letter to a friend.

5. *With your support group, experiment with writing different kinds of leads.* The leads you find work to start your paper will help give you a frame and establish the tone of your paper. At one of our meetings, we brought in examples of anecdotal leads, "telling quotes," and setting-up contrasts—the kinds of leads that Nancie Atwell discusses in *In the Middle* (1987). In the ten-minute free-write that followed, social studies teacher Tom Ustach wrote the following anecdotal lead:

> I entered the rectangular room, sat at the rectangular table, and was introduced. The walls around me were as stale and white as the experts seated at the table. The psychologist opened the meeting by announcing, "Let's get this LDT going. Jim qualified LD, PS, handicapped in '83, '86, and '89. How'd he do last week, Academic Specialist?"
>
> "His current WISC-III is verbal—73, Performance—98, and FSIQ—83. His academic results were Reading—7.6/93, Math—5.4/81 and Written—3.2/68. I've never seen a high school student score so low. He has problems calculating simple addition and subtraction. He can't do basic counting."
>
> "Speech Pathologist," the psychologist called.
>
> "Well, I'm embarrassed to say," answered an elderly woman wearing milk-yellow 1970s mineral rock jewelry, "I inaccurately calculated his score. I used the wrong birth date. I can go up and re-do it real quick. Right now I got 74."
>
> "No, that's okay. If it's 74, then the new one will be even lower," said the psychologist. "Go on."
>
> "Well, his CELF-R was really low, too. I'll get it to you as well."
>
> "Where's his ERC case manager?" asked the psychologist.
>
> "Not here."
>
> "We'll get to him later, then, but I'll pass the B-5 around."
>
> Yes, these educational specialists are talking about my case study, who is not a lab rat or an astronaut, but a fifteen-year-old young man who is struggling with writing. He's really not just struggling with writing, but in surviving in a school system that structurally sets him up to fail. A working-class student, especially if he is a minority student, is rolling loaded dice each time he comes to class in today's public schools. My case study, Jim, has never hit a number in ten years of public schooling, and all the blame is placed on him.

When Tom shared his lead with our group, it was clear that he had found the way to frame his paper, drawing us all into his case study, which he went on to entitle "Playing the Numbers: Winning and Losing in Public High School."

Collect a range of examples of a variety of leads and experiment with them. Ralph Fletcher's *What a Writer Needs* (1993) has many different lead-writing suggestions and examples, such as the dramatic lead, the misleading lead, the leisurely lead, or beginning at the ending. As Fletcher writes, "The lead is more than the first step toward getting somewhere; the lead is an integral part of the somewhere itself. The lead gives the author his first real chance to grapple with the subject at hand. . . . The author writes for herself and she writes for her audience" (82).

Taking just ten or fifteen minutes to try a new lead and share it with your group or with a research partner can unearth new ways to frame your thinking, as it did for Tom. It's also a small enough task to put on a teacher research group agenda and still leave time for lots of feedback that can help keep your writing going.

6. *Set a deadline for a finished draft.* Perhaps this is the most important suggestion of all. Setting those deadlines forces us to *use* the writing to put out thoughts on paper for an audience. It gives us that all-important opportunity to think through our data, make choices, and find a focus.

RESEARCH WORKSHOP

Making Deadlines

Julie Housum-Stevens

I am an expert on deadlines. In fact, I am such an expert on them that I am writing this article on deadlines one week after missing my own. I couldn't find the turquoise notebook that had the notes I needed to write the article. That's a lie. I wasn't even sure in which of the twenty-five binders and two hundred notebooks and legal pads scattered (neatly) all over my house and my classroom the notes could be found, never mind what color the darn thing was.

If you never find yourself in this position, skip the rest of this article—you are way ahead of me. But if missed deadlines ever cause you to duck into the bathroom to avoid your principal, if you decide suddenly that you must clean your bureau and your closet instead of responding to that giant stack of journals, or if you can't even start doing your taxes because you've misplaced your W2s, I may be able to help.

At the very least, I can empathize. Setting and meeting deadlines are two of my biggest struggles, which means I am on a continuous quest for tips and tricks and tools that will both improve my organization and give me practice at meeting my goals—on time and in a reasonably sane state.

This past summer, I was with a group of teachers designing research studies to carry out in our classrooms this fall. As we were considering what kinds of support we would need to be successful, I said that I would need help setting and meeting deadlines to analyze my data and share my findings. Suddenly, everyone was recommending wonderful, simple, why-didn't-I-think-of-that ideas, which I frantically began scribbling down.

"These should be in an article!" I blurted, and just like that, I had a deadline to practice meeting. With thanks to my compatriots for sharing their good ideas, here they are:

1. Post a large calendar where you will see it frequently, and write down due dates, article, class, and grant deadlines.

2. Break long-term goals down; put several smaller due dates on the calendar instead of one final one.

3. Tell everyone you know about your deadline, especially nosy folks and your mom, all of whom will surely check up on you.

4. Use deadlines you already have—the end of the quarter, for example.

5. Tie as much of your work as possible to something you already do—a graduate class, a committee, etc. Make integration work for you like it works for kids.

6. Sign up to do a presentation as a part of a group—this will force you to prepare, because you won't want to let your peers down, but you won't be alone.

7. Do less regularly rather than more sporadically. Avoid setting yourself up for failure—start small and add.

8. Avoid giving yourself an out or an excuse (such as losing your notebook). Self-sabotage doubles your misery.

These ideas may not seem like much, but my hope is that you will find them useful and do-able, and that perhaps you will realize that no matter what you struggle with as a teacher-researcher, you are likely not alone. Write to me in care of Stenhouse if you have found tools around deadlines and organization that have been particularly helpful to you—I'm thinking of keeping this article going forever, or at least until I meet my deadline the first time around!

featured **TEACHER RESEARCHER**

An Ethnography of Change: Teacher Research as Dissertation

Jeanne Henry

In 1992 I completed my dissertation at the University of Cincinnati. The study was a teacher research project in which I examined the literary letters exchanged between me and my college students over the course of a semester-long developmental reading class, which I conducted following Nancie Atwell's (1987) reading workshop approach. Three years later, a thoroughly rewritten version of that study was published by Heinemann-Boynton/ Cook, and before I knew it, I began getting e-mail from doctoral students who had read the book and wanted to know how I had "gotten away with" my "controversial" study. I was a little taken aback that teacher research still was considered *so* controversial; however, my head came fully out of the sand when one student wrote, "My advisor told me that it's okay for teachers to write up their little stories, but it's not okay for doctoral students. She said we have to contribute 'meaningfully' if we want to join the professional community." I remember thinking, oh *that's* the problem: the idea of *doctoral students* doing teacher research. We are supposed to join the education establishment, not reinvent it.

Another student who wrote me cited the following passage from my book, *If Not Now:*

> Such a look. Mary Anne Pitman, the queen of qualitative research methods at the University of Cincinnati, has this look that suggests she must have heard you wrong because you surely would not have said anything so stupid in her presence. All I had said was that I wanted to do teacher research for my dissertation.
>
> "You can't study your own students and your own teaching objectively."
>
> We had been discussing whether or not she would serve on my dissertation committee. I was pretty sure the answer had been burned onto my retinas in the bare three seconds that I had been able to maintain eye contact with "the look." But we began debating, with Mary Anne mostly winning, and she apparently decided to see what I might do with my postsomething-or-other ideas about objectivity and subjectivity. Since Dr. Pitman is reputed to walk on water with the regularity other people eat lunch, I left her office knowing that her "take no prisoners" approach to sound research would mean that to convince her, I would really have to convince myself first. Otherwise, the odds were so in her favor that I would be packing my bags to go study literacy in some place that did not having working toilets and hot water, like the public schools. (Henry 1995, 109)

"What," my new e-mail correspondent demanded, "did you say to her? What were your 'post-something-or-other ideas'? I need to know!" Since it looks as if others are interested in pushing boundaries (and buttons) by comingling qualitative methods, dissertation writing, and teacher research, I thought I ought to elaborate on the arguments I presented that eventually won me approval to proceed with my study. Mind you, I did not "get away" with anything, except eighteen months of research and writing, but I did get to do research in a way that made sense to me. While I want this piece to remind all teacher-researchers that our work is political, transformative, essential, defensible, and *grounded*, my particular hope is that it will give doctoral students a springboard for challenging old assumptions about worthy research.

All I had wanted to do back in 1992 was ethnographically informed, qualitative teacher research, but this just happened to be nothing less than treachery to traditionalists. Conventional ethnographic wisdom denies the ability of cultural participants to maintain the detached objectivity considered a foundation for valid research. As an insider, immersed within the setting of my study, I would have to defamiliarize myself to the point of pathology to satisfy the norms of classical ethnography. Teachers are participants in classrooms, perhaps not as central to the activity as we often assume but quite present and highly motivated, nonetheless. The ethnographer, in the classic tradition, is to be a stranger in a strange land, out for the emic perspective, which can be obtained only by one who is in the process of familiarization, unfettered by taken-for-granted understandings and investments. Qualitative research, as I well knew, had had enough problems gaining legitimacy in education research, and there I was, wanting to use the method in a way that dispensed with its tenuous lease on respectability: distance, detachment, and "objectivity."

One way I could have designed my proposed study out of this seeming methodological malaise was to have stepped down the hall into someone else's classroom, thus dropping the "teacher-researcher" label. I would still be pushing boundaries, because of my familiarity with the campus and the community in which the research was being conducted, but I could have argued that I was not a stakeholder in this "strange" classroom and then limited my interest in ecological and ideational patterns to those within its four walls, thus pretending that what I had was hermetically sealed cultural space. Better yet, I could have traveled across town to conduct my research, in which case I could comfortably assert that I was a true stranger. But as Renata Rosaldo's (1989) wonderfully tongue-in-cheek saga of the Lone Ethnographer contends: "The guiding fiction of cultural compartments has crumbled. So-called natives do not 'inhabit' a world fully separate from the one ethnographers 'live in.' Few people remain simply in their place these days. When people say 'ethnographers and natives,' it is ever more difficult to predict who will put on the loincloth and who will pick up the pencil and paper" (45). Where is the strange land in which we can still be strangers? And should we find it, what are we to do with the growing number of uppity natives like me, who believe that we have the science to conduct useful studies and are beginning to prefer our own limitations—those both obvious and elusive—to those of some outsiders, who cannot reasonably be expected to lose sleep with us over the events that unfold?

Rosaldo's satirical story of the Lone Ethnographer studying the "Exotic Other" probably made more sense to me than any other methodological piece I read in graduate school. I suspect Rosaldo saw the same jungle movies I did as a child, such as Bob Hope's *Call Me Bwanna* or Abbott and Costello's *Africa Screams*. These are silly movies in which the White Devils get themselves out of the boiling pots into which the natives have thrown them for dinner, and we laugh, but the tension of the films is that the blundering outsiders did wind up in hot water. In some jungle films, friendly natives may cooperate, but they are always laughing behind their hands at the crazy ways of the White Devils who enter their midst full of their own notions, and end up misunderstanding everything. As a researcher, I no more wanted to be Bwanna than, as a teacher, I wanted him in my classroom. Theory can come from the most unexpected places.

I had come to the conclusion that in some education research the teacher is the equivalent of what Rosaldo refers to as the Lone Ethnographer's native sidekick. Teachers may fetch information, rather than paddle canoes, but it is clear that we are relegated to supporting rather than starring roles when it comes to knowledge making in education. We are under the lens, and not looking through it, which involves relations of power, as Roman and Apple (1990) point out. Generally, the researcher determines the research questions to pursue, which data will be collected in order to answer these queries, the analytic approach employed, and the significance of the findings. And unlike anthropology, the discipline from which we draw method, the findings of educational ethnography may come back to haunt the natives. No anthropologist will tell the Samoans how they *ought* to be going about their business, yet the studies conducted in our classrooms by education researchers, outsiders, are *intended* to shape our work as teachers. But are they *designed* to, when the teacher, object, enabler, and presumed beneficiary of the investigation, has little input in determining its subject or ultimate meaning?

Goswami and Stillman (1987) suggest that traditional research casts teachers in the role of "consumers rather than producers of knowledge about learning" (i). Actually, I have come to think of teachers as the consumed. In our compulsory research methods courses we are not taught to use these techniques to answer our own questions. In fact the "consumer" approach taken in many quantitative research courses designed for teachers at the master's level, while ostensibly intended to stifle our presumed terror at the sight of formulas by reassuring us that we do not have to actually conduct the studies we are asked to design, makes the message explicit: research is carried out by researchers. Practitioners are supposed to open up their classrooms, then wait and see the results. In keeping with my jungle metaphor, I have to wonder if classrooms are among the last colonies of an increasingly postcolonial world. Bwanna comes in with a plan, which he is vague but polite about—so the teacher does not mess things up by being too helpful, self-conscious, impressionable, or powerful—then he goes off to share his report with the other White Devils, and they develop theories and policies that will deliver us. In education research, the subject-object dichotomy is neither impartial nor objective; rather it is an increasingly controversial aspect of a rigid caste system in education that valorizes researchers but subordinates teachers, their questions, and their knowledge.

What is particularly insidious about the structure of knowledge making in education is that it sometimes serves to silence those who do the lion's share of work when it comes to educating the young: women. Traditional knowledge-making systems and hierarchies, whether empirical or eager-to-please positivist, evolved in the context of patriarchy. Neither of these bound systems, nor their consequences—silencing those who make meaning in "nonstandard" ways—have been questioned to the extent that (a) the foundations of knowledge making are crumbling, or (b) that the exclusions have been justified. These masculinist modes are seen as deductive, objective, detached, and authoritarian, whereas women's ways of knowing are being understood as intuitive, subjective, contextual, metaphorical, and relational (Belenky et al. 1986). Both modes of inquiry lead to meaning, but the former has been privileged and the latter has been marginalized. Teachers' concerns, as well as our ways of knowing, have taken a backseat to the pursuit of methodological virtuosity and the increasingly uncomfortable assertion of objectivity.

So, what are teachers' ways of knowing? Teachers gain their knowledge by spending more hours in the presence of students than researchers can ever hope to. Teachers, other than those who are trifling and should be doing telemarketing or selling cars instead, pay useful attention to their kids, and their ways of knowing are relational: grounded in the complexities of all that they may simultaneously represent to students, such as parent, adversary, love object, loser, caring adult, dispenser of approval, or authority figure. We also come to grips with what our various students represent to us: seekers, hard cases, like-thinkers, social causes, slackers, or anonymous names on a roster. Intuitively we know who is lying, who is trying to hide her abilities so boys will like her, or who is so busy "profiling" that instruction must be made to flatter if it is to ever matter.

While a researcher might not think it is a success story for a student to be able to sustain silent reading for a mere fifteen minutes, a teacher can recognize the very first time a student is able to read for fifteen consecutive minutes without scratching, belching, whistling, snorting, pinching, biting, or in any other way distracting the entire class for fifteen blessed minutes. And we understand our world not through the detached, visual, subject-object metaphors of the hard sciences (Keller and Grontkowski 1983) and all who emulate them, but through a multitude of sensory/experiential avenues. In a now famous metaphor, teacher-researcher Nancie Atwell (1987) described her reading workshop approach as an effort to re-create the rousing book discussions that went on at her dining room table. In my study, I compared my classroom to my stoop-sitting, trash-talking, gossipy, and vibrant urban neighborhood. Simply put, teachers' ways of knowing stem from a collaboration between consciousness and involvement, and not life experienced at a remove.

I am not arguing that conventional research has no value, or is always exploitative or offensive. Teachers need the works of researchers like Ray Rist (1970). We do terrible things sometimes, and we need others who are not knee-deep in our reality to point this out. Rist observed that ability group placement sometimes had more to do with students' socioeconomic background—including race, dialect, and cleanliness—than with their linguistic knowledge, which shook the field of literacy instruction to its very core. Since carcinogens, such as classism, racism, inertia, and indifference, can invade our teaching, we need outsiders who can point out what our perceptual limitations do not permit us to see.

Teachers also need the methodological brilliance of researchers like J. D. Marshall (1987) and G. E. Newell (1984; 1989), who study reading-writing relationships and have a gift for designing complex studies that separate signals from noise in recognizable classroom contexts. We teachers have radically variant strengths and weaknesses, and the illumination of outsiders, particularly those who have a real feel for method, can produce studies that stop us in our tracks and cause us to take a long hard look at what we call teaching.

But as anthropologist James Clifford (1986) argues, "Insiders studying their own cultures offer new angles of vision and depths of understanding. Their accounts are empowered and restricted in unique ways" (9). There is a need for the perspective of indigenous researchers. As a teacher-researcher, I cannot go home at the end of my investigation, write up the findings, and get on with my life. I have to return to my classroom with these new understandings in hand. What I learn is organismic and is rendered thusly, and not as a seemingly static slice of life told in the ethnographic present, "as if social activities were always repeated in the same manner by everyone in the group" (Rosaldo 1989, 42).

Teacher research is as informed by what we hope to be doing tomorrow as it is by what we are doing today. How we teach has to be analyzed against what we could be doing better as well as what we have done worse, and in this way, teacher research represents an ethnography of change. Whereas the goal of classical ethnography is to freeze "culture," teacher research cannot evade the possibility that bringing matters to consciousness may very well cause them to change. We laugh in classrooms, we mutter under our breath, we celebrate our accomplishments, and the beat goes on.

In classical ethnography and other qualitative research, researchers are taught to "bracket" or suspend their personal points of view, such as their senses of morality, justice, logic, and efficacy. This type of detachment provides only a partial story. Rosaldo (1989) asks why "ethnographers so often write as if a father losing a son or a bereaved person attempting suicide were doing little more than following convention?" (58). This detached point of view "persuades us to disregard, devalue, and even deny what we cannot measure, to act as though such things as love, life, optimism, wonder, and beauty do not matter much in an objective description of reality . . . and keeps us from an intimate participation in our world" (Jones 1982, 14). The researcher who expresses no passion about a failed teaching technique, or without advocating (or intervening) for the students he or she sees being denied, is operating in a virtual reality in which theoretical implications are more important than real-world consequences. This is what James Clifford (1986) calls a partial truth.

Those who have, hold, and declare an emotional stake, such as teacher-researchers, may produce a partisan telling, but the detached perspective is also positioned, and both face limitations. I wanted to study my own students precisely because I do care about them, and I wanted that perspective in my research. My lack of detachment, as a participant researcher, did not allow me to separate the knowledge of a failed technique from the pain of that failure. Nor did it allow me to sever a perceived inability to connect with a student from the feelings of rejection the experience entailed.

I did "bracket" my personal point of view during data collection by recording field notes that were as objective as a sentient being could make them. But my most important data source was the journal I kept in which I "bracketed" my experiences as a teacher conducting research. I wrote in it dreams I had about my charges, chance meetings with them outside the classroom, interesting conversations we had, and morbid thoughts about what kind of homes they must come from. My triumphs and doubts as well as biases, questions, and sarcastic asides filled these pages. I carped about the tedium of transcribing field notes and trying to organize and collect documents. I beat myself up for the shyness that kept me from being aggressive about pursuing some research questions, and I battled the constant demon of whether or not my research exploited my students. Conventional researchers look inside those "brackets" to see how their subjectivity might have contaminated their data. I did that, too, but I also reread my journal to see how my subjectivity might *inform* my data analysis and conclusions. I incorporated this knowledge into my narrative, and I owned it for the personal point of view that it was, both as a means of explaining why I had understood the events in my classroom as I did, and as a means of reminding my readers that my telling was consciously human and consequently fallible.

Peter Medway wrote that the primary difficulty of teacher research is in "making the familiar classroom strange" (Goswami and Stillman 1987, i). Yet to render the familiar strange, as does teacher research, requires no more distortion than does rendering the unknown into the known. Rosaldo (1989) puts this into perspective: "Social descriptions by, of, and for members of a particular culture require a relative emphasis on defamiliarization, so they will appear—as they in fact are—humanly made, and not given in nature. Alien cultures, however, can appear so exotic to outsiders that everyday life seems to be floating in a bizarre primitive mentality. Social descriptions about cultures distant from both the writer and the reader require a relative emphasis on familiarization, so they will appear—as they also in fact are—sharply distinct in their differences, yet recognizably human in their resemblances" (40). In all research, unfamiliarity is as much a struggle as is familiarity, for each requires a rhetorical sleight of hand that must redirect the reader's attention. That which is strange must begin to make sense, and that which is familiar must be made to seem distant. It is done with mirrors: the mirror the researcher holds up to him or herself, that which is poised in front of the natives, and the one aimed at readers. The accusation that a researcher has really "studied himself" is an unkind cut and an anthropological cliché meaning that the researcher has told his or her story of being in this exotic land rather than that of the natives. That this is an insult is mystifying, since it is in fact a simple statement of truth. Ethnography always is as much a study of the writer and the readers' cultures—in terms of how data are eventually rendered in a research report—as it is an examination of native rites. But as Clifford (1986) argues, "Acute political and epistemological self-consciousness need not lead to ethnographic self-absorption" (7). When subjectivity is deliberately used as a self-aware and purposeful resource, it can lead to pungent truths.

I was attracted to teacher research because it provided me with an opportunity to raise my own questions about practice and theory. By studying my own classroom, I could ask the questions I wanted to address without being silenced and without silencing another teacher. This latitude represents a long overdue democratization of knowledge making in education settings, a departure from the dichotomies of theory and practice, as well as subject and object, that inform other avenues of education research.

Along with other indigenous researchers, I am finding my way along shores I recognize as perilous, but I think this is terrain that must be explored—whether in Samoa or on Long Island—anywhere we seek to impose a narrative line upon experience in order to understand it, any place where the knowers and the known are treated as irrevocably discrete, and in any sphere where our Western tendency to see the world as disposable allows us to collect our data and to then scurry home without a backward glance. Representation from the outside is a foil to insider perspectives. The reverse can also be true, but fewer and fewer of us are content to let others do our talking.

As a teacher-researcher who very much hoped to produce a definitive study for public consumption, I did not function in an intellectual or analytical void. My subjectivity was tamed by the same theoretical frames, ethical considerations, previous research, and readerly critiques that operate within the work of conventional researchers. My competence as a doctoral student was measured by my ability to recite qualitative principles, chapter and verse, as well as my apprehension of appropriate reading, writing, and pedagogical theory. I was not winging it, as it were, but was trying to operate within the constraints I found valuable while I worked to reforge those I considered unsuited to my purpose and beliefs.

My dissertation represented an experiment in reflexivity. I hoped to avoid such an emphasis on the "self-absorbed Self" that I lost "sight altogether of the culturally different Other" (Rosaldo 1989, 7), but I knew that no one else could tell the story the way that I would. I trusted my teacher's knowledge, as well as my research expertise, and concluded that my telling would inform instruction and theory as valuably, although differently, as would that of a detached observer.

So, those were my "post-something-or-other ideas" or how I "got away with it." But the fact is that I had a doctoral committee, particularly a methodologist, willing to let me challenge conventional thinking, take my own professional risks, and find my own niche in the knowledge-making community. These professors instilled in me a belief in my own ethical standards, knowledge, professional instincts, and capabilities. They also offered me a climate in which professors are known to learn and learners are known to teach, and so it was no surprise that they were willing to let me forge my own path so that they too could see where it might lead. This, probably more than anything I had to say, was what allowed me to produce an unconventional study that, as things turned out, is reputed to be "a significant addition to the literature on revolutionizing reading" (Daane 1996). Great balls of fire! Who knew? But then this is exactly why doctoral students ought to be exploring new avenues of inquiry. As we novice researchers become members of doctoral committees, we need to remember that our cherished beliefs will be challenged by our best students. Not only should we support them, and their intellectual growing pains, we should learn with them as well.

Sustaining Research: Building and Extending Research Communities

8

Community means different things to different people. To some, it is a safe haven where survival is assured through mutual cooperation. To others, it is a place of emotional support, with deep sharing and bonding with close friends. Some see community as an intense crucible for personal growth. For others it is primarily a place to pioneer their dreams.

Corinne McLaughlin and Gordon Davidson

Not long ago, the space probe Voyager began transmitting pictures of Mars back to Earth. These images created a sensation around the world. The enthusiasm of the research team leading the mission from a command center in Texas was palpable. For a few weeks, the science sections of magazines and newspapers were dominated by this story. Journalists marveled over the genuineness of the researchers' "gee whiz" excitement, and photos appeared of the scientists wearing goofy 3-D glasses as they led press conference free-for-alls.

All that energy and ink devoted to . . . Mars. A big hot rock, with a history of silly lore about Martians. Space probes had been sent before, and when all was said and done, not too much new information was gained from the mission. But we all saw how much fun research could be for those who were truly engaged by their research topic and able to share their excitement in a community. It was contagious.

There is a special joy in our work when we see its connection to the work of others. For you, that might mean one special research friend at your school or across town. Regular phone calls, e-mail, and long walks a couple of times a month might be just the right formula that sustains your research or keeps it going between regular meetings with a well-established support group. Many teachers also find their community exists "out there" with people they haven't met yet but whose teacher research they read and immediately find connections in.

If you look at any teacher-researcher who has sustained her work over time, you quickly see another person, or people, standing in the shadows. Virtually all teacher-researchers depend on a partner or a group who shares their passions and provides reassurance when a project bogs down. Often we see only the findings of research in publications, or the images of researchers working with students as they collect and analyze data. The power of collaboration is much less visible; the process of working through issues of collaboration is almost never documented.

JoAnn Portalupi describes the subtle ways collaboration changes and extends the work of teacher-researchers. She compares the effects of collaboration to the flow of volcano lava:

> On a recent trip to Hawaii, my husband and I drove from the top of Kilhauea Volcano down to the ocean where a current lava flow was emptying into the ocean. I didn't know what to expect. As we descended the hill, the water came in sight and I could see the head of steam where the hot lava hit the cool ocean. The expanding fountain of steam was the only evidence of flowing lava. We arrived as the sun was setting. As the night sky grew dark, the red flowing lava became visible. Of course it had been there all along, but it needed the contrast of the night sky to bring it out. When we bring colleagues into the landscape of our classrooms, their presence provides the contrast that heightens our self-evaluative tendencies and makes visible that which is previously unseen. (1994, 98)

In the dark days of your research, it is your research community that will show you the value of all you are learning and doing, especially when it is hard for you to see the value of your work at that moment. It's heightened self-awareness but also a heightened awareness of the potential for your research to help others.

There is a wealth of research available that shows the positive benefits of social interactions—not just for teacher-researchers but for humans in general. Physical health is directly linked to how connected people are to other people. As Ornstein and Sobel (1987) write: "People need people—not only for the practical benefits which derive from group life, but for our very health and survival. Somehow, interactions with the larger social world of others draws our attention outside of ourselves, enlarges our focus, enhances our ability to cope, and seems to make brain reactions more stable and the person less vulnerable to disease" (18).

Most teachers already belong to different communities—within their schools, within their towns, within their families. We know how important these communities are to our health and survival. The challenge for teacher-researchers is to realize that some of these communities will change and shift as research becomes a part of our professional lives. Trusted colleagues can be threatened by changes in the way you talk about your teaching, your students, and your classroom. Teachers often need to form new communities to sustain their research.

This was true for Terri Austin, a teaching principal in Fairbanks, Alaska.

She found she had to distinguish between "school" colleagues and "research" colleagues as her research became more important to her:

> My school colleagues reminded me daily that I was just a teacher. I was told
> again and again that my job was only "to teach between 8 A.M. and 3 P.M.—
> anything else was unnecessary and made everyone else look bad." In look-
> ing back, I believe they felt I tried new ideas to show off or stand out. What
> they never realized is that I tried new ideas because I genuinely wanted my
> students to become better learners.
>
> Teacher research is often not easy. There are many obstacles that get in
> the way, but there are zesty events also. A community is essential. Your re-
> search colleagues will keep you going. Make the time to seriously plan your
> project, talk about assessment issues and plan your year. But do silly things
> too, like make pizza in a hubcap, giggle together. Those moments will hold
> you together when things get rough. John Wayne said, "Courage is when
> you're afraid, but you saddle up anyway." It takes courage to be a teacher-
> researcher. (1994a, 68)

Courage—and a community. One of the dark sides of teacher research
that is rarely written or talked about is how wrenching it can be for a teacher
to see her professional friendships change as she becomes more involved
and successful in her work. We devote a whole chapter of this book (Chapter 9) to this issue of shift in identity because this is a problem that surprises
many teachers when it emerges. The change is often felt more keenly by
women: "One of the most important prerequisites of the creative process for
a woman is the assurance that her work will not rupture the important connections of her life. Women are exquisitely sensitive to the possibility of
such losses. . . . [They] are often looked at askance or asked if they've managed to write, or paint, or compose without harming someone else. We have
to be quite tough to resist that sort of guilt" (Bolker 1997, 195).

Building a research community can be a way to increase that toughness
and keep your sensitivity at the same time. For example, Terri worked with
others to develop the Alaska Teacher Research Network (ATRN) almost a
decade ago. Four teachers in the Fairbanks area decided they needed to get
together with colleagues to talk about issues beyond bus schedules and
lunch duty rosters. From there, the group grew to include over one hundred
teacher-researchers throughout the state, linked through e-mail, phone, and
regular local and statewide meetings.

The group spends a week in August at a retreat, talking about their research from the previous year and their plans for the next. The goal at the
end of the week is that everyone will have a research question and some
sense of how data will be collected. The Fairbanks group continues to meet
monthly throughout the fall, with each meeting devoted to in-depth response to one member's research. In January, ATRN members meet again in
Fairbanks to exchange research progress and plans. Research is brought to

closure with a writing deadline of April 15—an easy deadline to remember because of taxes.

This group was able to continue its work because it had some clear goals and expectations. Other teacher research groups form much more loosely, with goals emerging over time. Because it can be so difficult to build schoolwide teacher research communities, we want to take an in-depth look at how teachers at one small school have managed to build a research community, without clear distinctions between "school" colleagues and "research" colleagues. Their process may help you find ways to create a research community that can energize your work.

The Evolution of One Teacher Research Group

Teacher research finds a place in individual schools and teachers' lives in many different ways. For some teachers, a graduate course or inquiry group is the beginning of the research process. For others, reading professional literature and seeing the value of research in other teachers' classrooms provides an impetus for getting started. But at Mapleton Elementary School in Mapleton, Maine, the teacher research group started in a more informal way—through jotted notes on the back of a restaurant napkin.

One evening in the fall of 1996, some Mapleton teachers and their teaching principal, Gail Gibson, went out for dinner after an in-service presentation on reading. "We're always trying to figure out how to help readers in our school who are struggling. Teachers were feeling frustrated—they felt like they needed more information than what they were receiving from books and workshops," explained Gail. On that napkin, the group sketched out first thoughts for what became a two-thousand-dollar mini-grant from a federal agency to learn more about teacher research. Kelly Chandler, a doctoral student at the University of Maine, was hired to assist the group in developing research skills over the next few months.

Gail found that involving an outside consultant in their case was critical for the success of the group: "We are always trying new things on our own, but we've found that we sustain a project or new initiative better when someone comes in first and helps us get started with it. This need not be more than a couple of visits, and assisting us in finding the best materials to read and discuss, but it was essential with this project."

We wondered why reading was chosen as the research topic, given that Mapleton has very high Maine Educational Assessment Scores in reading. An outsider viewing the scores alone might wonder how reading instruction could improve at the school. Gail laughed, and replied, "It doesn't matter how high the scores are. Every teacher has at least a couple of students in her class who aren't reading as well as they should, and this will always be something that concerns a good teacher." This is a clear example of the "careful gardener" metaphor for teacher research in action—until every student in every class thrives in reading, teachers will want to know more about how to best teach reading.

The group's evolution is chronicled by Kelly Chandler in the Featured Teacher-Researcher section of this chapter. She found the group had a few basic principles that sustained their work:

1. *Every teacher was free to choose how much she wanted to become involved.* "I have the same attitude toward teachers as I do toward students—I try to respect where they are, and help them move to whatever is the next phase of their development," explained Gail. The Mapleton teaching staff is typical of staff in any small rural community—there are veteran teachers with empty nests at home, eager to take extra time after school to discuss their research findings. Other teachers have young children who need more time and attention. Gail and Kelly worked with the teachers throughout the project to let them know this was not a short-term project, but a long-term commitment on the school's part to building inquiry into the school day. The teachers were trusted to decide what level of participation made sense for them.

"One teacher last year really struggled to attend meetings, and often she couldn't because she had a new baby and a lot on her plate. I respect that, because I've been there in my life, too. She came when she could, and did what she could. This year, she's found more time to take notes, and even used some of her research notes to make a point at a district curriculum meeting this fall. I was so happy to see that—to help her see last year that it's all right to have other priorities for her life, and to see this year that when she does have more time for research it's easy for her to integrate it into her professional life," said Gail. "When you tell teachers 'come in when you can, if you can,' there is a place for everyone, no matter what their personal situation is at the moment."

2. *As part of the research, teachers observed each other and compared their notes to develop their observation skills.* For Gail, consistent and frequent visits by teachers and herself to other classrooms have become an essential element for fostering an environment where teacher development remains central in staff planning: "You know, there is so much pressure on teachers. We always expect them to do better, and even great teachers are expected to maintain that high level of terrific work at all times. It's remarkable what a difference it makes to teachers when they have colleagues who recognize and note in concrete ways the skills evident in their teaching. It makes them very willing to listen to suggestions for improvement."

3. *The principal (Gail Gibson) was a full participant in workshops, reading discussions, and observational visits.* "Learning to take notes as a teacher-researcher was important in maintaining a rapport with the teachers—I was very nervous about this, being a new principal when this project began," said Gail. "When I went to do observations of teachers, I found myself naturally scripting notes and then going through and color-coding three different themes or patterns I saw in each observation. Once teachers

saw this was my process, and I was noticing so many positive things in their classrooms, they became very comfortable with my visits and looked forward to them."

4. *Money was budgeted to support the research throughout the year.* This dollar amount at Mapleton is small, but it's significant to Gail and the teachers. "I want to make the teachers feel cared for, and it's amazing what a boost it is to the staff when you surprise each of them with a small notebook of project planner paper [lined paper with a wide left margin] in their mailboxes," said Gail. "This week, I bought all twelve teachers a copy of a small new book on spelling they had expressed interest in—total cost with my professional membership discount was $112. When teachers know that a good article they read can be photocopied for their colleagues, or some money is available for Post-it flags for coding their notes, it sends a signal that research is valued here, and I value the extra work they are doing to learn research skills."

The focus of the research this year has shifted from reading instruction to spelling. "This was an obvious choice for us," explained Gail. "We have been yapping and yapping about spelling for years, so everyone was pretty eager to take a close look at the issues involved in teaching spelling." Teacher research at Mapleton involves individual teachers' taking extra time in their classrooms to gather data as well as time to meet together, visit other classrooms, and analyze the data. "Because it takes extra time, it's so important that it be something that the teachers really care about, that they can see as having an immediate effect on their practice and classroom needs," said Gail. "Spelling is also a topic that parents are concerned about, and they have many memories and experiences at home of standing at the sink washing the dishes at night, quizzing their kid on this week's words. It's something they want to understand and they see it as part of their 'job' as a concerned parent to help in some way with it."

The change this year in the research agenda includes more awareness on the part of students of their role as both research informants and co-researchers. "We just did report cards, and I have students write comments to their parents about what they've learned. I noticed 75 percent said something about their spelling development—they have become so aware of their strategies and the research going on in the school around this issue. There is so much more talk in the teachers' room, too—a palpable change in the intellectual climate as teachers get more and more comfortable with talking about their research and comparing their findings with those of colleagues," said Gail.

Lieberman and Miller (1995, 209) in a series of case studies of teacher-researchers, note that certain conditions must exist if teacher research is to lead to sustained schoolwide reform. The Mapleton teacher research group meets all these conditions. In the group, there are

- Norms of collegiality, openness, and trust
- Opportunities, time, and support for disciplined inquiry

- Teacher learning in context
- A reconstruction of leadership roles
- Participation in networks, collaborations, and coalitions

Gail doesn't know where or when the spelling research will end, or how the teacher research group will evolve, but integrating inquiry into Mapleton's daily agenda has already been a big success: "It's made every teacher aware of how much control they really have in their classrooms, and how much ability they have to make those classrooms better. It has increased every teacher's sense of autonomy and skill in this school, and the value of that to me is immeasurable."

The Mapleton teacher research group raises important questions for any teacher-researcher who is thinking about forming an inquiry group. Teachers need to think first about what they want their community to be. Some view communities as a safe place to be nurtured in their work, with few expectations and demands; others require a set schedule and firm guidelines, with a goal of having the group keep them on task in their work. If you have a mix of researchers who want to socialize around research projects as well as researchers who are very task-driven, you will quickly have conflicts emerge in your group. It's necessary to spend time at the beginning working through what group members expect from the group, and how much time will be required to participate.

The following are some key questions:

1. *Are members allowed to float in and out of the group, missing meetings?* The more flexible the community at the start, the more participation you will have. But it can be difficult to sustain a group if attendance is too intermittent. Much time can be spent at every meeting orienting new members or those who missed the last meeting.

2. *Is there an end point or goals for the group?* The goals for ATRN and the Mapleton group were very different, but there were goals and expectations in each group. The Alaska researchers end their individual projects with writing in April; the Mapleton researchers have a new collective project each year. You'll want to make sure to talk about how your group can balance individual and collective goals.

3. *Is there a leader for the group?* Who is responsible for organizing the group? Natural leaders can emerge, but there can also be tensions around who controls and sets the group agenda. Discussing the roles and responsibilities of group members at the start can bring unconscious issues of voice and ownership to the surface before they have a chance to fester and disrupt the community.

4. *Are you making time for "zest" in your group meetings?* The meetings should provide a chance to talk and laugh together as well as to focus on teaching and research. Because schools can be isolating places for teachers to work, there is often a tendency to spend meeting time on "teacher room talk." Though venting can be therapeutic, groups also need time to create a

different culture for themselves, which can begin with setting a new tone for the meetings. The Portland Area Teacher Research Network varies its meeting places, choosing new cafés, neighborhood restaurants, or microbreweries to treat themselves to different environments. The participants consider their work serious and thoughtful yet joyful. Their meetings feel like gifts to themselves, adding that "zest" that Terri Austin recommends.

District Support

A strong teacher research group can help you bring energy back to your school and to your district, creating a culture of inquiry within them. The Clayton Action Research Collaborative, in Clayton, Missouri, is a fine example of a grassroots effort that has helped promote the kind of support teacher-researchers need districtwide. This committed group of teachers from across grade levels meets monthly to share their own projects and support each other's work, inviting any interested teachers and administrators to join them on an occasional or regular basis.

Each summer, they sponsor a one- to two-day summer institute, and they collaborate with the Clayton school district's staff development program to offer workshops throughout the year focusing on strategies, techniques, and resources for conducting classroom-based research. As part of their 1998 summer institute, the Clayton researchers sponsored an evening with administrators, staff development professionals, and university educators to discuss possible collaboration strategies and the genuine needs of teacher-researchers. Much of the meeting was a celebration of the quality of the district response. Teacher-researchers spoke with enthusiasm about the recent establishment of small grants, support for teacher research as part of the professional development process, and district willingness to provide time and materials. They stressed that the most important support of all was the clear message from the administration that it recognizes that the time spent on classroom-based research is valuable and appreciated by the district.

In order to continue to aid teachers new to research methodologies, members of the Clayton Collaborative act as "teacher-researcher team leaders" in the buildings in which they work, and they are paid a small stipend for the support and leadership they provide.

Erich Jantsch (1980) applies chaos theory to organizations and sees organizations growing in efficiency when people in them act as "equilibrium busters." No longer caretakers of order, they are the individuals who "stir things up and roil the pot" until work is reorganized in new and innovative ways. The teachers in the Clayton Action Research Collaborative show what is possible districtwide when "equilibrium busters" help to redefine school structure from the inside out.

Resources to Build Research Communities

As the teacher research movement has grown in the last decade, so has the resource base to support school-based research. Teachers throughout the world have regional and national programs that can assist them as they work to develop research skills.

Regional Research Networks

Many research partnerships have sprung up throughout the country to support teacher research. We hesitate to mention too many of these partnerships because most are short-term alliances that evolve and change as the needs of teacher-researchers change. The best way to find out if there is a regional teacher research group near you is to call your local college or university and talk with the education professor who teaches research courses for teachers.

An example of an inquiry network that has been sustained for many years is the Western Maine Partnership, coordinated by the University of Maine at Farmington. This loose alliance coordinates inquiry groups throughout the western region of the state. Teachers meet regularly to discuss curricular and social issues, sharing data and strategies with others who grapple with the same concerns. The Western Maine Partnership also funds mini-sabbatical leaves for small teams of teacher-researchers.

In Maine administrators call and receive information about the groups and distribute it to teachers. They provide release time for teachers to participate in regional research programs. Most important, this work counts for teachers as professional development. It makes sense for teachers to be able to substitute participation in an inquiry group or a professional research meeting for an in-service event that might not be as valuable for them. Regional and statewide collaborations are more likely to be sustained if credit and support are granted for meetings by administrators. If you're not sure if your principal would support your participation in a research group, just ask. In our experience, it is rare that a principal or superintendent would not support a teacher's desire to learn more about research.

Many other states sponsor annual conferences in support of teacher research. Most state and regional conferences sponsored by curricular groups (e.g., the National Council of Teachers of English; the National Science Teachers Association) have sessions within their conferences devoted to presenting and fostering teacher research among participants. You can call the national office of any of these groups to find out if they have a special interest group for teacher-researchers. The International Reading Association and the American Association of Educational Researchers both have large, active special interest groups for teacher-researchers. They can provide members with the names of teacher researchers in the local area as well as with pamphlets that detail strategies for research.

Grant Opportunities

Many teacher research efforts begin with small grants to support development of research skills. More districts are making small grants available to their teachers, and it is wise to investigate what is available locally for support (see Figure 8.1) The Spencer Foundation funds large and small projects in teacher research. Currently, its Practitioner Mentoring and Communications grant program is the most helpful for teacher-researchers interested in forming research groups because it funds proposals that build teachers' research skills within inquiry communities.

Figure 8.1 Grant Application

SCHOOL DISTRICT OF CLAYTON GUIDELINES FOR ACTION RESEARCH GRANT PROPOSALS

As part of the District goals to support classroom-based and schoolwide inquiry, grants will be again be available next year to Clayton staff members who design an action research project. Grant money may be used for materials, stipends, consultants, transportation, and other relevant expenses. One or more grants will be awarded, not to exceed a total of $5000. The Grant Review Team will evaluate and will make recommendations for approval to the Assistant Superintendent. Grant applications are available through the office of Director of Professional Development and Planning. In the event we receive more proposals than funding will permit, priority will be given to grants that reflect building or District goals.

Grants will be awarded based on the following criteria:

- Clear questions, problems, or focus of inquiry for which data can be collected and analyzed
- Well-developed calendar of proposed activities related to grant
- Implementation during the 1998–1999 school year

There are two application deadlines for action research grant applications:

- June 15 for awarding the first $3000
- September 14 for awarding the remaining $2000

Applications are due in the Office of Director of Professional Development and Planning (Catherine Von Hatten) by the above deadlines.

Grant recipients will be expected to submit a project update to the Coordinator of Action Research (Lori Geismar-Ryan) by January 31. In May, project recipients will write a year-end summary report and make a presentation on the status of their project at the monthly meeting of Clayton's Action Research Collaborative. Following presentation to the Action Research Collaborative, grant recipients will be supported in sharing their findings with staff members through PDC sessions, *Curriculum Quarterly* articles, staff meetings, and local Action Research Conferences.

For more information or assistance in completing the proposal, please contact Lori Geismar-Ryan at the Family Center.

Action Research Grant Application

Name (s) _____

Position _____

School _____ Date _____

1. Classroom issue, topic, or question you will try to answer. Indicate the focus of your research, the issues you will investigate, or the question you will try to answer.
2. Rationale. Explain why you want to do this project. What is the need, what will be the benefit, and for whom?
3. Outline your proposal.

   - Who will be involved (include staff members, students, parents)?
   - What actions will be taken and where will the project occur?
   - What is the proposed time line? (Indicate the schedule for implementation, data collection, analysis, report writing, completion.)

The National Council of Teachers of English, the New England Reading Association, the International Reading Association, and their state and local affiliates all have grant programs to assist individual teachers and small research collectives initiating literacy-related studies.

Subscribing to professional journals and making copies from the journals available in the teachers' room can help teachers become aware of teacher research funding opportunities. In addition, administrators should seek out newsletters that highlight funding opportunities for teachers. For example, *Education Week* regularly lists grant opportunities for teacher-researchers.

Schools can also take advantage of the Internet in building teacher research awareness and skills. XTAR, the international listserv for teacher-researchers (see Chapter 6), regularly posts conference, grant, and writing opportunities for teachers.

What's amazing about the growth of teacher research in the last few years is the burgeoning sense of community in the movement. We think back to those scientists who led the Mars mission and imagine them as children looking at the stars and envisioning travel to distant planets. We're fortunate to live in an age when we don't have to travel far to realize our dreams as researchers in community with others. These days, we need only a few keystrokes and an Internet connection to get help with a data collection problem from colleagues across the world. We also have many successful models, from schools all over the country, for forging new connections with teachers just down the hall when we tackle research questions together. Teaching can be a lonely profession; we've learned research need not be.

RESEARCH WORKSHOP

Expanding Your Community: Letters to Teacher-Researchers

"How strange that we, as teachers, are asked to share our knowledge with students but are rarely asked to share our knowledge with each other," Cindy Quintanilla notes. "Having the opportunity to read what other teacher-researchers have written—and responding in a personal letter—was eye-opening for me. I was recently asked to write and publish some of the work my team and I are involved in, but my greatest concern was, Who will read this and what do they care? Yet now I know that someone out there will read it, and hopefully can find some useful thread to adapt to her classroom."

As we look for communities to help sustain our work, we can reach beyond our immediate local and regional networks and discover teacher-researchers who share our interests, research passions, and classroom tensions. And we can take it a step further and communicate with those distant colleagues, expanding our communities and supporting each other beyond geographic boundaries.

We have found that there are many benefits to taking the time to sit down and write to the teacher-researchers who have influenced our thinking or motivated us to make significant changes in our classrooms based on their research and classroom stories. The authors who receive the letters clearly benefit, too, of course: as Cindy notes, it is important for teachers who write up their research to realize that, yes, their work and words have reached an audience, their ideas have found a mark and made a difference.

When Annie Keep-Barnes (1994) first wrote the honest and wrenching story of her work with a seven-year-old boy (see Chapter 2), it was for her immediate research community, the Alaska Teacher Research Network. When they encouraged her to share it with a wider audience, she had no idea the impact it might have for other teachers. A letter like the following one, written to her by high school teacher Bret Freyer, demonstrates the power of her words for teachers across grade levels:

Dear Ms. Keep-Barnes,

Thank you for your 1994 article entitled "Real Teachers Don't Always Succeed." You have helped me remember or realize several things about teaching and literature about teaching.

I, too, have read too many "Teacher as Savior" books. Your fresh breath of reality in the beginning of your essay really rings true for me. In book after book, students are inspired, they make huge turnarounds, they even decide not to kill themselves after being in a dynamic English class. Should I be questioning my literature program? I don't think I've saved any lives. These models of English classrooms either make me say, "Oh, come on now," or "Geez, what am I doing wrong?"

Thank you for reminding me when I present "language arts" to students, I need to show the excellent and the mediocre. I learned much by watching your struggles. I am reminded that I also need to show the struggles of readers and writers to my students. How else can they see that what we do is real? Real readers and real writers struggle with reading and writing. Because you showed me your frustrations and your difficulties, I recognized the reality of my students and myself in your teaching life. Thank you for reminding me that each teacher's story has something for me.

I, too, have not always been successful with my students. Sometimes I feel, as you did with Robert, that everyone is making excuses for a student or looking for someone to blame, but no one is really doing anything. I, too, have felt that maybe I am not pushing a student hard enough, or getting to know the parents well enough, or otherwise not doing my part soon enough or thoroughly enough. While it seems teachers often beat themselves up after the fact, I don't think you did. You simply reflected on Robert's situation with a hope of learning about yourself. That is what a good teacher does. You did for yourself what you would expect your students to do—learn from the lesson.

Thank you for reminding me that often success comes in small ways, like your success with Robert. If his desire to buy you flowers isn't a success, nothing is. He saw in you something positive about school. Because of that he probably listened more closely to you as you explained his "auditory channel" strength to him. He probably learned something about himself, because of the kind of person you are, that he would never have learned from the "demanding" teacher. I cherish moments like the time Ursula Winter ran into my class with her social studies paper claiming that practicing in English class was what really made her write an "A" social studies paper. Thank you for reminding me that I need to hug those memories tight.

I, too, feel the urgent need for success, not only for my students, but for myself—maybe even more so for myself. Maybe that is why those memories are so important. I used to think this was selfish, but I don't anymore. We are so much like our students, aren't we? We are prideful beings who measure ourselves against the myriad yardsticks we conjure for ourselves. We can't help it. I've stopped fighting it. I want to be good at what I do. I want to be good at it for me, and I want to be good at it for the students I teach. These are inseparable realities. I see memories of your experience with and research on Robert that you can hold onto. Thank you for reminding me that these selfish urges are alive in me. As I read, I found myself saying, "That's okay, Annie, that just means you are human" and "That's the mark of an excellent teacher!" We immerse ourselves so much in our work, that we are susceptible to drowning in the water of the burdens and responsibilities which envelop us. Maybe we need to be submarines, willing and able to bang around on the coral reefs of education. Those reefs can be destructive . . . and beautiful.

Were you hard enough on Robert? Only you can answer that. I think, though, that you are just hard enough on yourself. That you had the courage to share that will help me to be hard enough on myself.

Thank you for reminding me that this is okay—as long as I keep searching for the learning in the lesson.

Sincerely,

Bret Freyer

Bret's moving letter to Annie is the kind of detailed, thoughtful response to writing any author would appreciate hearing. On a deeper level, it is also the kind of more personal response that a letter format can offer, showing that Bret is really taking this opportunity to "talk" to Annie, person-to-person, letting her know the thoughts that went through his mind as he read her honest reflections and self-criticisms.

Bret's letter also demonstrates the power of the act of writing itself. In composing these words to Annie, Bret crystallizes the main messages he takes from her work and brings back to his own teaching the further resolve to "be just hard enough" on himself.

Teachers we know have written letters to teacher-researchers for a variety of reasons, often to thank them for their work and respond to their research on a personal level. Other times, the letters are a chance to share ideas and insights with a distant colleague who might be able to act as a sounding board or offer further resources.

Emily Tso's letter to Danling Fu contains elements of both. Emily recognized a kindred spirit in Danling Fu when she read *My Trouble Is My English* (Fu 1995) and wrote to tell her so, also asking the questions that were on her mind:

Dear Danling Fu,

I am Emily Tso, an Asian American language arts teacher. My parents came to the U.S. from China; my father arrived at age 12 and my mother after college. My younger brother and I were born in the U.S. and have lived here all our lives. Several years ago my father's career as an electrical engineer turned into a professorship overseas; he has been teaching in Singapore almost eight years. I inherited my love for literature from my father. He, like so many Asians, made a difficult career choice long ago to pursue a practical and well-paying job over the books that he loved. I happened to marry a family medicine physician, which has given me freedom to pursue teaching, reading, and writing without the usual financial worries.

I am now finishing my Master of Arts in Teaching degree. I taught international students English as a Second Language for two years in Portland, plus one summer in China. I stopped teaching to raise a baby. My husband and I plan to live and work in China—we hope in five years—so I have pursued researching and teaching ESL as preparation for the future.

I am reading *My Trouble Is My English.* I have only read the first third of your book, which is fascinating. Yours is the first teacher-researcher book I have read specifically about ESL students and Asian students' experiences in particular. I appreciate your careful interviews of Tran, Paw, Cham, and Sy, especially their direct quotes. You did not have to create their characters; you let them speak their own personalities, questions, and ideas. I liked the extensive family background you gave because it obviously had great impact on these four students, as it does for each of us.

Reading about Tran, Paw, Cham, and Sy's various literacy experiences before entering an American classroom reminded me of my father's education. Growing up during the war and Japanese occupation in China, my father hardly attended any public school. When he fled to Hong Kong—I think he was eleven—he studied there for a year, then followed his father to the U.S. My father entered New York Public schools not knowing a word of English and now I realize he was probably not fully literate in Chinese either. I find it almost impossible to imagine the steep learning curve he faced day after day as he learned a new language. I find it almost as difficult to understand Tran, Paw, Cham, and Sy's motivation to pursue an endless trail of worksheets for three years. Difficult to understand, yet admirable.

What is going on inside ESL classrooms today? How are students learning and how is that learning being integrated with what happens in their mainstreamed classes? How can teachers work better to communicate student needs, outcomes, and learning methods? The last thing teachers need is more paperwork or another committee meeting, but some way must be found to help connect ESL students like Tran, Paw, Cham, and Sy to mainstream U.S. culture. Students like these should not be relegated to watching culture rush by from the sidelines. Who will help them? Who will make a difference?

Thank you for your writing and your research. Your book helps me think more clearly about real-life struggles for ESL students. I look forward to reading more and perhaps further communication with you in the future.

Sincerely,

Emily Tso

One of the most exciting aspects of writing to teacher-researchers is the continued correspondence this can generate. A few weeks after mailing her letter, Emily was delighted to receive a response from Danling, in which she offers to continue their correspondence so that they can discuss and explore the issues that are important to both of them.

Dear Emily,

So thrilled and touched by your letter. Thank you for writing to me expressing your thinking and response to my book. I am also pleased to find a colleague who is Asian, which always excites me. There are many reasons for so few Asians in education, reasons like practical, cultural, linguistically, so on. In my community, people admire me and at the same time pity me for majoring in education. I enjoy it!

Currently, in addition to being a professor in the university, I also work in a middle school in Chinatown in New York. I am seeing the worst situation for the new Chinese immigrant children, much worse than what I described in my book. Anyway, we are trying hard to improve the instruction and program for the children, but any change takes a long time. I wish we could have more teachers like you, understanding those children, and having a passion for them. Sometimes they made me want to give up my professorship to work in the schools in Chinatown. That may sound too naive.

Please write to me any time you want to. I am enclosing my e-mail address. "Get on line" is the most convenient way nowadays! I am catching up with the fad.

I left China thirteen years ago and haven't been back for a visit yet. I will go back to China next summer. At present, my parents are here, helping me with the housework. I have a fifteen-year-old son, at the moment going through his adolescent syndrome. I was divorced last summer, so being the single parent of a teenage son is hard enough for me. Anything else you want to know about me, besides being a researcher and author? It is hard to imagine an author being a real person, having real-life problems, isn't it?

Keep in touch. Thank you again.

Sincerely,

Danling

Danling offers not only to continue to discuss issues of ESL instruction but writes on a more personal level. She emphasizes that "authors are real people." Several teachers who have received letters back from teacher-researchers have commented on the fact that it helps them realize that the authors they read are teachers like themselves, not magical beings. The research any teacher-researcher does in her classroom has the potential to expand beyond the borders of her classroom and community.

As Cindy Quintanilla concludes in her reflections on the practice of writing letters to teacher-researchers, it can serve as a real invitation for continued growth: "I will continue to look for and read what other teacher-researchers are doing. I think it is vital to maintain a reciprocal relationship . . . in which we can share and offer feedback. This has truly been the most growing experience for me as a teacher yet in my short teaching career. I just hope I can continue to grow and keep my eyes open to new and changing opportunities."

Letter writing has a certain magic to it, and even if you ultimately decide not to mail your letter, you will benefit from the increased engagement with research that has had an impact on you. It's really quite easy to correspond with any author in print: simply write in care of the publisher or journal, and your letter will be forwarded to the author. We encourage you to follow the lead of teacher-researchers like Bret, Emily, and Cindy and make it a point to connect with your publishing colleagues—expanding your own thinking in the process as well as your teacher research community.

featured TEACHER RESEARCHER

Emergent Researchers: One Group's Beginnings

Kelly Chandler

What follows was written during the first few months I served as facilitator for a teacher research group in Mapleton, Maine. Most accounts of groups like this one (see Ernst 1994; Goatley et al. 1994; and Marsella et al. 1994) are written after the network has supported its members over a lengthy period of time. In contrast, the story I want to tell here is about the initial stages of the group's formation. It was written in the midst of the work, while both the pain and joy of growing were keen and immediate.

My understanding of this group and my role in it is emerging slowly, in fragments. So, instead of writing a narrative that smooths out the rough edges, I've decided to present a series of samples from the data I collected during those first few months. This will allow you to draw your own conclusions about what the data mean—which isn't so far from the process I engaged in myself.

10/30/96 Excerpt from grant, "Discovering Best Practices Through Action Research," written by Martha LaPointe, Lynne Brabant, and Lois Pangburn.

No one way of teaching reading serves all students. Yet those who are most confused are often the ones on whom we try "everything going" hoping that something will make sense for that child. Our students who are struggling with reading will benefit if we engage in staff development to familiarize us with the best research on reading and help us to assimilate that research into our daily practice.

Through professional reading and action research under the guidance of a trained facilitator, participating staff members will

- Familiarize ourselves with the most up-to-date research on reading
- Begin to assimilate that research into daily practice
- Explore what good readers do and don't do in the context of making meaning from text
- Evaluate our decision making in the context of daily reading instruction
- Improve our ability to differentiate instruction for diverse learners

As Cochran-Smith and Lytle (1993) explain, "When teachers conduct research as a regular part of their roles as teachers, they become critical, responsive readers and users of current research, less apt to accept uncritically others' theories, less vulnerable to fads, and more authoritative in their assessment of curricula, methods, and materials" (19).

12/28/96 Excerpt from my journal.

Tomorrow I begin my stint as "researcher in residence" at Mapleton Elementary School. Martha, Gail [the school's teaching principal], and I figured we'd have two meetings in two weeks while I'm here every day, then schedule them less frequently after the group gets off the ground. Eight of the 11 teachers in the school, including Gail, have decided to participate. I'm planning to do some observations and model some different kinds of notetaking. Bought a new project planner notebook today—those wide margins are great for cooking my notes—and I'm ready to go.

12/29/96 *Excerpt from my journal.*

Observed and took notes in Lois, Martha, and Gail's rooms today and made tentative appointments with Judy and Lynne. Lois met me at lunch with her hands on her hips: "OK, where are my notes?" so I scurried to the photocopy machine to make her a copy. When we went over them together in the teachers' room, our conversation drew in a number of other people and took most of the lunch period. Right before it ended, Martha showed up and said, "Hey, what about me?" but we had to meet after school.

I was surprised to see how much they wanted the feedback, and how interested they were in the data (especially the gender differences I noticed in the way the first graders were drawing their pictures). I need to remember how rare it is that teachers have anyone else in their rooms except for their obligatory evaluations. That makes what I'm doing—and what research partners will do for each other—all the more important, yet potentially very scary.

I'm a little nervous about tomorrow [our first official meeting], but more relaxed after spending the day in classrooms. I don't think I need to "lesson-plan" so much as be responsive, and a lot of the facilitation can be just what it was at lunch—sharing my notes, asking questions, etc. This isn't a class, and I'm not responsible for their learning—*they* are. And they want to be.

12/30/96 *Agenda from first meeting.*

Research is a high-hat word that scares a lot of people. It needn't. It's rather simple. Essentially research is nothing but a state of mind . . . a friendly, welcoming attitude towards change . . . going out to look for change instead of waiting for it to come. . . . It is the problem-solving mind as contrasted with the let-well-enough-alone mind. It is the tomorrow mind instead of the yesterday mind.—Charles Kettering

- Free-write about expectations: What do you hope to get out of this experience? What are you excited about? nervous about? wondering about?
- Brainstorm: What do we already know about teacher research?
- Nuts and bolts

  Notetaking basics

  Readings

  Research partners

Kelly's role

To do for next time

- Generating possible research questions

12/29/96 *Noted on chart paper at first meeting.*

Teacher research [Group brainstorm on what we associate with this term]

Support/help

Outside observer

What to do with our research/notetaking

Collecting data

Getting organized

Asking open-ended questions

Collaboration

No more isolation

Not the scientific method

12/30/96 *Excerpts from teachers' writing about their expectations for the group.*

I want to get under the surface of my classroom. I like the way it looks and feels most of the time, yet I know there is so much happening in the students' minds that I'm not aware of. . . . I ask them to write often about their thinking but I never get back to analyzing the data they've provided me. I want to get a handle on looking for patterns, making sense out of them, and making good decisions about where to go next.—Martha, Grade 3

I'm nervous! I always feel as though I'm not doing anything well enough, especially reading. I've used basals and hated it. However it did make me feel like I was on track. I'm hoping you'll be able to help us feel better about what we're doing, give us some guidance on guided reading, and help us look for answers.—Lynne, Grade 1

[When I first began] my notes seemed dumb—I wrote down things like "read well" or "good job." When I'd read it over at night I'd think, "Well, that's helpful!" But the more I kept at it, the more I noticed as they read. The more I wrote, the more helpful my notes were to me as I puzzled out what the reader was doing and what they needed me to be doing. Now I want to do this better—I know I'm not always seeing what I need to see. I want to be clearer on what each reader is doing or attempting to do, and I want to make more informed decisions about how to help that reader move forward.—Lois, Grade 1

12/30/96 *Assignments for next meeting (1/7/97).*

1. Find ten minutes a day, preferably at school rather than at home, when you can write in your teaching journal.

2. Document how you spend your school-related time for the next
   week. Try to keep track in fifteen-minute intervals.

12/30/96 *Excerpt from my journal after first meeting.*

In general, I feel pretty good about how tonight went. They're eager to talk,
to learn from each other—I think they need to learn to trust themselves and
each other more, though. It takes *time* to build trust and understanding, and
I'm not always patient. Sometimes I'm like the museum tour guide who
rushes you through the exhibit so you can "see everything" when all you
want to do is savor a few wonderful paintings. Part of the problem is that
this kind of work is so intellectually energizing to me that I get consumed
by it. It's fascinating and *real.* It can truly help to make change. It's not being
locked in the Ivory Tower—it's working with kids and teachers, rolling your
sleeves up and getting dirty.

12/31/96 *Excerpt from my field notes.*

[Lois asked me to take notes during her individual reading conferences. She
was also keeping notes as she worked with kids.]

9:25 A.M. Doug: *Rosie at the Zoo* [Cowley 1984]
Skips "and": "Let's go—- see." (Rdg for mng?) Stops at "she"—2nd line of
p. 4—this surprises me. For "looked," LP pts to pic cue, rereads what he's
done: "Take off the -ed. Do you know that word?" LP suggests finger point-
ing. D skips another -ed word, bothered by skip and doesn't get to end of
sentence b/c he's missing verb. They read chorally (good idea here). LP:
"What do you think that lion was thinking?" D: "He was mad." D attacks
"elephant" with emph. LP calls att. to " " to cue "said." "For"—good miscue
to skip and let him problem-solve. Now he's fgr-ptg on last pg. Gets "lifted"
w/ no pic cue. LP pts to pic cue to help him get "over." D rereads w/ exp.
Smiles @ end—gets the punchline. "Thank you, Doug."

12/31/96 *Lois's notes on the same conference.*

Doug: *Rosie at the Zoo.* (read before)

- Rereading
- Uses finger when needs to
- Uses his lesson on "she" and finally begins to see it

12/31/96 *Excerpt from my journal.*

Yesterday I borrowed an easel from Gail's room so we could chart our
brainstorms during the meeting, which we held in the teachers' room. I forgot to take it back after we finished, then decided I wasn't going to when I
noticed the teachers who hadn't been there, as well as itinerant folks like

Carol [the gifted-and-talented teacher], reading it as they wandered through. Maybe it ought to stay right there.

1/2/97 Posted by me on the easel in the teachers' room.

Tips for Your Teaching Journal

1. Find time to write (i.e., while your kids are in chorus or P.E., at the beginning of writing workshop, the last 10 min. of lunch).
2. Start with 5 min.—time it—then move to 10 later.
3. Write fast; don't censor.
4. Start with "I wonder why . . . ," "I was surprised when . . . ," or "I noticed . . . " when you get stuck.
5. Write a letter to your research partner (share it if you feel comfortable).
6. Make your writing time sacred. Don't allow interruptions.

1/2/97 Excerpt from my journal.

I've been wondering about how to support Athena. I know she has some reservations about participating in a project that might be time-consuming. With a small child and another on the way, she has more responsibilities at home than most of the others. And she's one of the few whose classrooms I haven't visited—on one hand, I don't want to invite myself in if she's not comfortable; on the other, I don't want her to think I'm not interested in what she's doing. I guess I'll wait and see what happens.

1/3/97 Excerpt from my journal.

Directly after school, I go to Athena's room to find Dory, a second grader who has promised to read aloud to me. I have to wait for Dory because Athena is busy teaching her and two other late-bus boys how to take the lunch count and record the names of students with free choice for tomorrow. They will train their successors. Later, Athena tells me that she got the idea from our reading this week—*Taking Note* (Power 1996)—which suggests delegating easy administrative tasks to students as often as possible. "This only takes me three minutes, but hey, that's three minutes I can use," she says. I guess people need to come on board in their own way, on their own timetable.

1/6/97 Excerpt from my field notes.

7:45 A.M. Lynne came into the library, where I was looking for a book—asked if I would visit her class this week during reading "if you have time." "I really enjoyed having you in there last week." Then she asked if I would help her figure out what to do with Marie—identified those kids with little sound/symbol correspondence as her persistent problem this year. I suggested she make that her research question: "That way you'll be working on it and not just feeling frustrated and guilty." She wondered if she'll get enough useful information from focusing on just a few struggling kids, but then seemed to reconsider: "I do have Maries every year."

1/7/97 Excerpts from discussion at second meeting.

Gail: I didn't write one word this week. This afternoon I started to "fake" it, to document my schedule for the week, but Kelly caught me and made me stop. I've got my research question, but it's hard for me to take notes.

Martha: What did you learn from that?

Gail: That I'm disorganized. I don't like to write and I run away from it. I also lost the form I made to document my schedule—and I need a form.

Enola: [to me] I did what you said and wrote down everything I did. I should take these home and show them to my husband when he wonders why I'm ready for bed at 9:00!

Athena: [When I reviewed my notes about my schedule] I found out I didn't say "Hurry up," and "Be quiet" as much as I thought I did. . . . I told Kelly my problem was management, but maybe it isn't such a problem.

Lynne: I keep wishing I had a notebook around my neck. I keep saying, "Wait, I want to hear what you're saying."

Martha: [agreeing] The first day I was saying, "Wait a minute, kids, I haven't got my clipboard." Today some of them were saying they'd like to take notes. By the end of the day *they* were taking notes with a clipboard.

[She reads an excerpt from a student's notes to the group.]

Diane: Could we schedule them [the third graders] to come to *my* room [and take notes]? [General laughter.]

Several people express feelings of inadequacy where reading instruction is concerned.

Gail [to the group]: You have absolutely no idea how good you are. I'm sick and tired of hearing you say you're not good reading teachers. Learning from one kid [in a case study] makes you a better practitioner for all of them. It's hard to learn from 25 at once.

Diane: Why can't you trust your own experience?

Gail: Why can't you trust your kids to show you what you need to know?

1/7/97 Excerpt from Lois's journal.

I just reread through all my entries in my journal and I have to laugh! Often the children's sentences will begin with a thought and before they finish they have something written twice or put a word in 3 times or something else that makes it a bit of a jumbled mess. . . . Well, I attributed that to fine motor and letters and sounds and that they just forget where they're going or what they were saying. Maybe, but I just reread my own sentence that said, "For some of the kids the growth is incredible *for some of the kids.*" What is that, Mrs. P? Are you struggling with fine motor or sound/symbol correspondence? Or are you just a writer, scooting along here with your thoughts and your pen, and your mind is thinking ahead of your pen? I think I just discovered here that they are writers and I'm a writer, and we do the same things.

We talked about notetaking and writing today with Kelly after school & the question came up . . . as to whether we need to be writing or not. Well, I think I need to be writing—through my own writing I'm learning about my students' writing. That's what I learned today.

1/8/97 Excerpt from my journal.

I observed in Athena's room today—she invited me to come in at yester-day's meeting. I figured out last week that it's more comfortable for the teacher if I focus my first observation on something other than *them.* In Lois and Lynne's rooms, I spent my first visit observing small groups of kids drawing at the independent center. The teachers got interesting data about students, but it didn't put them on the spot so much, and they could get used to having me around.

Anyway, I got to Athena's room expecting to do the same thing, but she had a parent volunteer working with the "independent" group. Decided it would be less intimidating for Maureen [the ed tech] to have me observing her with a group of readers than it would be for the parent. At least Maureen's seen what I do with Lois. So that's what I did. At lunch I brought Athena her copy of my notes, and we sat down in the teachers' room to go over them. Maureen asked if she could listen in—now, why didn't I think of that? She is, after all, the one whose teaching I observed! The three of us sat in a row on the couch and talked over the data. Athena is very interested in the idea of developing codes for discussion contributions (OT for "off-topic," StS for "student to student comment," and so on).

1/8/97 Excerpt from my letter to the group.

As I was thinking about yesterday's conversation about taking notes, it occurred to me that one of the toughest ways to start is with a blank page (i.e., the way I've been scribing for you in your classes). All that white space can be intimidating. . . .

The attached sheet [see Figure 8.2] is a copy of a form I used for notetaking while teaching Children's Literature last semester. . . . I kept the form on a clipboard and occasionally wrote down things students said in class while I was teaching. I tended to write a lot while students were working in groups (that's when I tried to pay attention to the students who

Figure 8.2 Notetaking Form

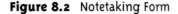

didn't speak much in whole-class discussions). I often used codes of some sort: * for "participated in discussion," L for group leader, or R for "did read-aloud today."

I hope this gives you another model to consider. Depending on what you're looking for, you may want to devise a form that allows you to use quick codes or check marks to keep track of data, rather than a lot of writing.

Your fellow wonderer,

Kelly

1/9/97 Excerpt from my notebook.

Today Martha read this free-write in the teachers' room at lunch. Each morning she walks four times around the school in a quarter-mile loop.

Comparing Footprints and Notes

While taking my early a. m. walk around the school I noticed my first footprints in the snow (from my first turn) were already being covered by the blowing snow as I made my second trip. . . . This day I had been thinking about keeping consistent, persistent notes and how it's easy for some but difficult for others. Observing my tracks made me think that they were a lot like notes.

Some tracks were already covered by my next trip around, just as observations can be forgotten in the very next minute if not recorded. Other steps landed side by side. Just as some observations will connect or piggy-back with the last and the next. Still others seemed to pile up, thus the first was obliterated by the subsequent three, and yet some tracks from yesterday were frozen in ice. An observation that won't be forgotten because it was written, recorded forever.

Everyone applauded. I think she's got a lead for an article, if and when she decides to write it.

1/9/97 Excerpt from my field notes.

[Martha was concerned that students' notes during group time have a "tattling" tone. We realized that kids probably need a model of the other kinds of things a notetaker might want to write about, so I took the following notes—complete with a few abbreviations and some direct quotations—to share with the students.]

12:57 P.M. Group on rug, sitting boy-girl. Mrs. L. tells me that the class has tried a new idea for penmanship. Then she talks about how writers need feedback, but it needs to be helpful, not hurtful. I show how Mrs. L gave me feedback on an article. Then Mrs. L. reads a poem about what to say to snowmen and asks gp to provide fdbk for the author. Jack noticed his cat's name. Mrs. L. writes notes on stickies as kids talk.

> Hal: likes poem—should rhyme more, though.
>
> Jenny: Use "Frosty" instead of snow.
>
> Mrs. L.: Was there anything you liked the sound of?
>
> Lisa: I liked how it goes "blizzard" and "blow"—sounds like you're in storm and it's blowing hard.
>
> Ricky: lkd. "Arctic" & "Antarctic."
>
> Jonathan: noticed that Antarctic has 2 wds in it: "ant" and "arc."

Mrs. L reviews imp. points. She explains that each group will give fdbk to writers—written on sticky papers for poet to use to write second draft.
1:17 Students go to meet in gps of 4.

1/9/97 Excerpt from my journal.

Today I posted a "quiz" [see Figure 8.3] with items for each member of the group; it was lighthearted and silly, but it did spur some conversation as people tried to complete it at lunch. It (I hope) also reminded them that everyone is contributing and growing.

Figure 8.3 Quiz for Teacher-Researchers

Teacher Researcher Quiz, or Who's Doing Good Things All Around You?

Fill in the initials of the person who said or did the following. No one is used more than once.

K, IB, IP, 2H, 2K, 3L, 3B, 4T, 5G, RR

1. _____ Her journal helped her to discover that her original wondering wasn't as pressing as she thought it was.

2. _____ "I wish I had a notebook around my neck. Wait! I want to hear what you're saying."*

3. _____ "By the end of the day [my students] were taking notes with a clipboard."

4. _____ She talked about the importance of mental notes: "I don't always write it down, but I think about it."

5. _____ She enlisted her ed tech partner as a notetaker during readaloud time.

6. _____ "Observe one kid at a time. Don't [do it] just once. Get everything down--you don't know what might be important."

7. _____ She has already figured out how to use address labels for notes on individual students.

8. _____ She devised a form--with some expert help at home :)—and took her first notes of the week yesterday.

9. _____ She expressed a sentiment shared by others: "It would be easier for me to strip and do a dance here in the teachers' room than to write."

10. _____ She talked about how beginning to "cook" her notes is helping her to make next-day decisions.

* This is a good idea. Why couldn't you have a little notebook around your neck for those unexpected gems of data?

The kids seem to have gotten used to the idea that someone—either their teacher or me—will be taking notes during class. I was observing reading conferences in Lois's room today: six kids and the two of us were at the kidney-shaped table, and Lois was working with them one at a time. While waiting for her turn, Michelle asked if she could read to me, so we moved our chairs a short distance away from the group. She couldn't have read more than a page of *Cookie's Week* [Ward 1988] when I felt a little tug on my sleeve. There's Cathy, with my notebook and pen in hand. (I'd left them on the table.) "Don't you need these?" Yeah, I guess I did.

Martha's making a new fashion statement this week—she covered the insignia on a baseball cap with a piece of paper that says "Taking Note" and told her kids that they're not supposed to disturb her when she's wearing it unless it's an emergency. Today she took notes while they worked for almost 20 minutes, and *not a single kid* interrupted her. They had a few minor problems—someone needed a pencil, someone didn't get the directions—but they solved everything themselves. I guess teachers aren't the only ones who learn to be more independent through teacher research.

1/10/97 *Excerpt from my journal.*

Experimented today in Athena, Enola, and Judy's rooms using lunch slips as a form for tallying contributions. It seemed to work well, although I sometimes got caught up in my desire to take running notes, rather than tallying, and there just wasn't enough room. Carole [Enola's ed tech] has been taking notes during read-aloud time, so I showed her the lunch-slip idea. I think it would work well for her, and maybe for Vicky and Maureen [the other ed techs], too.

1/10/97 *Posted on the message board before I returned to the university.*

Dear T/R's,

What a whirlwind 2 weeks! You're on your way. Here's another question to consider: How will you sustain the positive energy that's building? I know you can do it!

Teacher-researchers need lots of time and support. Have you enlisted a research partner (or two) yet? Have you figured out how to get another pair of eyes in your classroom? Do you have someone to share your notes with yet? You can do for each other everything (and more) that I've been doing this week. In fact, you need to. That's the point!

I'll be back for our next meeting on Thursday, 1/30.

1/13/97 *Notes from telephone call with Gail.*

Lynne showed up at school today with a 3" by 4" notebook as a necklace—she wasn't kidding about wanting one! Dismantled her gym whistle to use the cord and clip. Took several pages of notes and made one for Lois [her research partner], too.

1/13/97 *Excerpt from Gail's letter to Vicky, her ed tech.*

Dear Vicky,

Just a note to tell you how much I enjoy working with you and appreciate the extra things you do to make Mapleton a better school! It's nice to know I can count on you to support the students—and me. Your finding and buying the journal meant a lot to me. First, it showed me that you see the significance of the work we're trying to do in teacher research. But more important, it demonstrated your confidence in the importance of your contributions to our school. When I saw you sharing the journal with the other teachers, I thought, "It is possible to work in a school where all the adults recognize the importance of their role in student success."

I also want to thank you for sharing with the students how you write in your journal. It was the perfect example to set a good model of writing for real reasons. And it also showed them how much you care about their behavior.

I know we still have a lot of work to do with the fifth graders and these two examples may not seem that important to you. But believe me when I say they are examples of what good teaching is all about!

1/20/97 Excerpt from my weekly e-mail message to the group.

Here's a great quote from Carol Avery:

> Research does not bring answers but rather raises questions. It keeps opening doors. When I was a child I had a book and on the cover of that book was a little girl reading a book and so on. I think teacher researching is like that book cover. It offers the potential to keep going on and on. That's exciting to me. (Quoted in Bissex 1996, 173)

Before you can begin that spiraling process of raising one question after another, you have to start with your *first* question. What is it going to be?

I hope your reading is going well. Please feel free to write, e-mail, or call me with questions and responses, either to the readings or to work in your classrooms. I'm still here for you even though I'm far away.

Until next week,

Kelly

P.S. I'm not the only one who can use the message board in the teachers' room, you know. It seems to me like a good place to post quotes, notes, and requests for help—a teacher research graffiti board, so to speak. See how it works.

1/21/97 Posted on the message board by Gail.

Quotes to ponder:
"Through conversations, we started to realize that some of our previous decisions had been too hasty. . . . In the rush to be helpful, we may not have given the child the benefit that comes from reflection on observation. When we began to dig deeper, we were surprised to see how often we were mistaken about a behavior."

"Be patient toward all that is unsolved in your heart and try to love the questions themselves."—Rainer Maria Rilke

1/22/97 Quotation posted by Diane next to the light switch in her kindergarten room.

"Be patient toward all that is unsolved in your heart and try to love the questions themselves."

1/23/97 Posted on the message board by Lois (on gray paper!).

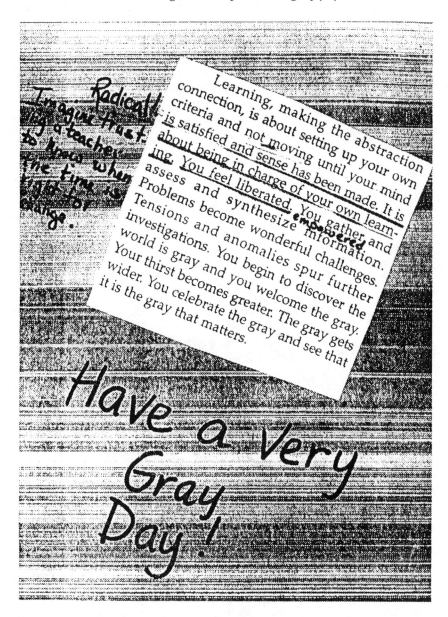

"Radical! Imagine trusting a teacher to know when the time is right for change," written by Diane.

1/25/97 Posted on the message board.

To: All Researchers
Re: Thursday's meeting with Kelly

Kelly says: Narrow your questions. Narrow, narrow, narrow. If you don't, you'll have too much to do, and you'll feel overwhelmed.

Martha wonders about planning to stay an extra hour or so on Thursday. If you know, and your family knows you'll be late, there won't be pressure to leave before you feel ready. We can bring some hearty snacks to keep us going.

What do you think?

1/26–1/28/97 *Some responses to the previous memo.*

Sounds fine to me—as long as I don't need to cook! Could we spend some time leveling the new books?—*Gail*

I hate to be a bah-humbug but I can't stay past 4:30. I have to make sure I'm fully prepared for a Friday sub, I have Christina [a picture of three-year-old Christina is pasted next to the note], etc., etc., excuses, excuses! [a growly face is drawn].—*Athena*

I'm in, but I have O. M. [Odyssey of the Mind] until 4.—*Lois.*

1/30/97 *Excerpts from free-writes at beginning of third meeting.*

I've been thinking and thinking and thinking!! I've thought about myself, my students, my classroom, my expectations, trying to figure out the dynamics of why the class functions like it does. I formed some opinions, then realized I was working from hunches, not data. I really was stuck in the old paradigm—not using the teacher-researcher model. Oops!

I talked too much, didn't write enough; thought too much, didn't document enough.—*Gail, Grade 5/Teaching Principal*

Am hearing real positive vibes from other schools from staff development. Lots of interest out there. Several have asked me to share professional books.—*Judy, Grade 2*

1/30/97 *Noted on chart paper at third meeting.*

Our evolving research questions:

[Grade levels are listed in parentheses after the researcher's name. More than one version was sometimes drafted with the help of the group.]

Athena (2): How can I manage reading conferences so I have a more accurate picture of individuals' needs? Version 2—What tools can I use to help manage reading instruction?

Gail (5): What records can I use to help manage reading instruction?

Lorna (4): What happens when fourth graders work in literature circles?

Martha (3): How can I help my students to become more independent learners?

Version 2—How can I help my students to assess their own work? Version 3—What happens to self-assessment when students write their own rubrics in [need to decide on subject]?

Lynne (1): How do I better meet the needs of my struggling readers?

Version 2—What can I learn about struggling readers from Marie and Lance?

Enola (3): What activities encourage students to become good spellers?

Judy (2): How can I form guided reading groups according to students' strengths and weaknesses?

Kim (5): How do reading journals help students become better readers?

Version 2—What is the effect of reading journals on students' reading?

Lois (1): How do read-alouds affect my students' reading and writing?

1/30/97 Group brainstorming to help Enola get started with her research question.

First, need to

- Define a good speller
- Do some professional reading/talking about spelling
- Try different activities and keep track of how they work
- Find out what spelling strategies students know and use

Data collection strategies:

- Interview or discussion with students about what it means to be a good speller
- Survey about spelling [school has one]
- Test them on high-frequency words [pre- and post-]
- Samples of writing; examine for spelling
- Observations/notetaking
- Have kids keep track of the spelling words they use in their writing

1/30/97 Excerpt from my journal after third meeting.

The group got off to a rocky start tonight. After a few minutes of free-writing, I asked everyone to say a little bit about how things had been for them since our last meeting. Writing narratives was evidently really stressful for many of them, Lorna's in the middle of Maine Assessment testing—it's been a tough two weeks. A litany of apologies about "not doing enough." They seem to have an idea in their heads (where did it come from?) of what "good" teacher-researchers should be, and they don't feel they're living up to it. This surprised me. Because I see these teachers as so capable, it's easy for me to underestimate their self-doubt. This work is a big risk for them; they're navigating in uncharted territory. I need to think some more about this.

1/31/97 Excerpt from my journal.

Copied Beth's [music teacher] schedule today. She has kids for 30-minute blocks on Thursday and Friday—perfect opportunity for me to meet individually with teachers or for them to observe in their research partners' rooms. Also talked to Lois, Lynne, and Gail about getting coverage for one teacher while the other's kids have music—research teams could meet that way.

2/1/97 *New research questions.*

[Gail, Lois, and Martha have lunch at a restaurant on Saturday, and two of their research questions get changed or refined. Gail makes a plan for data collection on the back of a placemat.]

Gail: What kinds of support do students need when they select texts for independent reading?

Martha: How does partner reading with kindergartners affect struggling third-grade readers?

2/3/97 *My message on board before returning to the university.*

It was great to be with you these last two days. You're doing good, important work. We'll meet again on Thursday, 2/13. Plan to bring your research question with any subquestions and your tentative plan for data collection. Also, bring some data (in any form) related to your question to share and discuss in small groups. We'll spend some time discussing the readings (I promise).

"Everyone needs a child to teach—it's the way adults learn." I hope you learn a lot from your kids over the next two weeks.

2/10/97 *A group brainstorm [without me] posted on the message board.*

Latest Research Question: How can a restaurant meet the needs of hungry, celebrating educators on Feb. 13? *Kelly's birthday is 13th.*

Subquestions:

- What restaurant? *Ruby's Winnie's Mai Tai [circled] Pat's*
  Let's meet over "coffee" and eat around 4:00. I need to leave at 5:00. LB
- Define "hungry" & "educators."
- When will be the best time to gather data? *Any time after school—Lynne and I are available for pie testing—we don't want to brag but . . . we do consider ourselves experts in this area. LP*
- Who meets the criteria for "celebrating educators"?

How will we gather data? In pairs so if a mistake is made you'll have someone to blame! or verify! :-)

Survey: Who's going?? Sign below, please

Lois	Vicky
Lynne	Gail
Enola	Lorna

Judy   Martha
Athena

2/10/97 Excerpt from Lois's journal.

Gail came in to observe me today. How did I feel about it? It was really interesting and different. I did not feel nervous or intimidated. She was really busy notetaking and that made me feel (because, I guess, of having had Kelly do all the notetaking and sharing it with me) like this was for *me*. Then, when Gail came down after school and we went over her notes—again, it felt like this helped me. I really do not ever recall feeling like that about an observation before.

2/11/97 Notes from telephone call with Gail.

Gail began her classroom observations yesterday with Lois. She scribed during reading time: "It worked pretty well, although sometimes I got so caught up in what the kids were doing that I forgot to take notes." After she left, she began to make some notations in the margins and to underline certain things that had to do with classroom management, references to read-aloud [which is Lois's research question], and the book language students were using. She said she began to look for patterns because of our recent conversations about "cooking" and coding data.

2/13/97 Excerpt from my journal after fourth meeting.

Because of my birthday party at the Mai Tai restaurant, our meeting was much less formal than usual. We didn't actually examine any data, as we had planned, nor did we discuss the reading, which was also on our agenda. Nonetheless, we were quite productive. Kim [a teacher from another school] joined us again.

We ended the meeting with everyone sharing a positive or interesting moment from the last two weeks. That worked well, and I think we should begin with it next time—probably focusing more on "interesting" than positive, since those led to more research-oriented conversations. Here's what everyone shared:

> *Athena:* Michael found a book independently by the same author and with the same main character as a read-aloud she'd done, and he's become totally inspired as a reader.
>
> *Enola:* Isabel read *Penny for a Hundred* (Pochocki 1996) in two sittings to the class, then David found the word *stollen* [used in *Penny*] in his biography of Boomer Esiason.
>
> *Vicky:* She read to Wally [new kid in Lynne's class] in the hall to make him feel more comfortable, then gave him her shoelaces so he could go to gym.

Lois: Her new approach with Eric [a struggling reader] has been working. They've been making sentence strips and sending them home. The next day, they paste them into a big book. Eric has been using a pattern: "I can make a cake, I can make a . . . " and his friend Jeremy has been reading the book and treating Eric like a real author.

Lynne: Marie [a first grader who has been using letter strings] wrote "VLNTIN" on the first page of her book.

Martha: Lately, several of her least independent students have been muttering, "Oh, not that hat again," when she puts on her notetaking cap. They know they're going to have to solve their own problems!

Gail: Jim [another struggling reader] has been listening to *The Secret Garden* (Burnett 1938) on tape. He's created a space for himself behind the door, where no one can disturb him, and he listens for hours at a time.

Judy: The second graders responded really positively to reading partners with the fourth graders, which started last week.

Lorna: Bob [a fourth grader] was so nervous about reading with his second-grade partner that he had to hide his shaking knees with a book.

2/14/97 Excerpt from my field notes.

I'm sitting in the teachers' room reading Lois's journal, and Vicky [ed tech working with Gail, Diane, and Lynne] just came by to ask me about teacher research: "I want to be a better notetaker." She's been taking notes during Gail's read-aloud and occasionally during reading workshop. "What exactly should be in these notes?" she asked. She talked about recording students' off-task behavior but knew that wasn't the kind of information she wanted. She also talked about how the special education evaluator came in the other day and saw Alison as "really out of it," but Vicky's notes told a different story: Alison was listening and contributing—"one of the few girls that do"—even as she fiddled with her glasses. I told her about *Taking Note* and encouraged her to borrow a copy [she got one from Lois].

We also talked about how she felt comfortable at last night's t/r group meeting but she "never would have come if Gail and Lynne hadn't asked me." I encouraged her to come again—need to do the same with Carol and Maureen [the other ed techs]. We're really missing the boat by not involving them more.

2/14/97 Excerpt from my journal.

I talked with Lorna about lit circles during the last 15 minutes of her music time today. She was trying to figure out what kind of discussion preparation would work best: giving each group a question to start with, having the kids generate questions on their own, or sharing their journal entries as Routman suggests in *Invitations* (1994). My first instinct was to try to help her choose, then I realized we had both slipped back into the paradigm of teacher as ultimate decision maker rather than researcher. So I suggested that she try all three methods and keep track of how they work for each group. We also discussed having the kids write to gather more data and generated a list of several questions she might ask them to tackle. I also suggested taping the discussions but not transcribing them unless they were really interesting. (Kim made me realize the pitfalls of that at last night's meeting.)

I also met with Judy to go over her running records. It was good to have them last night to look over and make some notes—I felt much more organized. She's going to study four kids she's concerned about, and she's focused her question on how to use the data she collects to choose appropriate texts for those students. Her question really dovetails with Gail's, Lynne's, and Martha's, so I'm looking forward to our next meeting, when we'll share data in small groups. Between now and then, Judy's going to use some of the leveled texts in the bookroom to establish some baseline data, then I'll help her to analyze the running records when I get back. I also suggested she borrow *Keeping It Together* [Morrison 1994] from Lois—good review of running record conventions, with some material on analysis.

2/16/97 Excerpt from my weekly e-mail message to the group.

Hope you had a fun, restful vacation.

For the next two weeks, let's focus on collecting data related to your research question. If you've gotten out of the habit of writing 10 minutes a day (preferably at school) in your teaching journal, try it again. At our next meeting (Tuesday, 3/11) we'll discuss the reading we agreed to do—really, we will—and do some preliminary analysis of data. I'll be here during that whole week (3/10–3/14), so be thinking about the best ways for me to help you.

Happy researching!

Kelly

2/20/97 Excerpt from Martha's letter to me after reading the first draft of this article.

From the point of view of one involved in the story, you seem to have captured some of the turmoil we all were feeling as we began this adventure. These are the patterns I felt emerging as I read your draft:

- *Notetaking:* Getting the feel for what is important to note. What to do with the notes once we have some. Getting used to having someone take notes on an activity vs. notes that are judgmental. Getting over the feeling of a critical/evaluative observation. You've shown that you are learning as we are learning as the students are learning.

- *Message board:* This emerges as an important element and emphasizes the importance of recording. This community space allows anyone who stops to have access to our thinking—it must raise questions for those itinerant people who cannot be with us every day. It allows those who haven't bought in officially to remain part of the club. It leaves a trail for you to discover what's been happening while you're away.

- *Group share of notes:* We all learn from those sessions even though they are informal. When they are held around the table, the feeling is one of more openness. It's easier to listen in; we can look over the shoulders of the primary participants. When they are held on the couch, the conferences feel more closed. I think these sessions are helping us overcome the feeling of being in the fishbowl. Because the notes focus on the students, it is easier to look at our own role as teacher.

- *When will we:* Throughout there runs a strand of unfinished business: this represents our status. There is the continued promise to discuss those readings. The plea to level books. When can we get into each other's rooms to observe? What do we want to observe when we are there?

- *Refining research questions:* Finding our question within the random notes we started with. Realizing that this isn't an assignment but a way of life used to inform our teaching, to do better for the students. Refining questions over Saturday luncheons. Loving your question.

I must admit that I'm resisting the urge to bring this piece to some sort of artificial closure. As a writer, it feels strange just to trail off. As a researcher, however, that's probably appropriate. After all, the work the piece describes is continuing. Ours is "unfinished business," as Martha puts it. I hope that you've seen patterns emerging across the pages, although they may not be the same patterns that Martha saw, that any other member of the group might see, or that I'm seeing even as I write.

Identity: Balancing Round Stones

9

Now I become myself. It's taken
Time, many years and places;
I have been dissolved and shaken,
Worn other people's faces . . .

May Sarton

Everything we do and experience shapes us into "becoming ourselves." For teachers, this means a combination of what drew us to
teaching in the first place, our own teacher lore accumulated from our
experiences in the classroom, our readings, our colleagues' insights, and the
memories of individual students that are always tucked into corners of our
minds.

The changes in our teaching lives as we shift toward a teacher-researcher
stance contribute to the process of "dissolving and shaking" our sense of
self. Our relationships with our students shift and cause us to rethink our
identity in the classroom and the different roles we play. Seeing connections
to the larger education community as teachers exchange their discoveries
and stories creates a different sense of purpose and, for many, a renewed
commitment to learning and teaching. The most positive change teachers report is a growth in professionalism, with more joy and commitment in the
call to teach.

Veteran teacher-researcher Terri Austin writes about the "hard fun" at
the heart of the role of teacher-researcher:

> I'm learning to play many roles. In the classroom, my students and I are col-
> laborators in research. Together we find our questions, gather data, and ex-
> amine the results. Professionally, I try to keep up with current literature and
> ideas. Politically, I've learned that I have to deal with higher powers such as
> the administration and the school board. Sandwiched somewhere in there is
> a personal life. I must admit there are days when I wake up and think of all
> the deadlines looming and I wonder, "Woman, why are you doing this?"

241

But I really know why. I love the challenge. I like puzzling out possible so-lutions to complex questions. I love struggling to find just the right word to say what I mean. I like to see if I can do it, and that means I need to be many different kinds of people, sometimes all at once. (1994a, 72)

Terri's teaching life is re-formed through the many roles she takes on. She is reclaiming her authority in her profession; her teaching and research are authored by her words and actions. She is in touch with the truths that inform her teaching, and she is acting from the integrity of those beliefs. We believe this is what makes the balancing act of teaching and researching not only possible but central.

There is a place in San Diego where you can learn to balance round stones. Literacy researcher Gerry Duffy heard about this place from a friend, who reported his amazement at seeing some people succeed at what seemed impossible: taking two round stones and getting one to sit on top of the other. Duffy (1998, 778) reports the conversation between him and his friend as going something like this:

Me: Some people could balance the stones and some couldn't?

Him: Yes.

Me: So what made the difference? How come some could and some couldn't?

Him: Well, it's hard to explain. The crucial difference didn't seem to be whether they knew a lot about stones or a lot of techniques for balancing stones.

Me: So what was it, then?

Him: Well, it seemed like those who could do it had everything lined up.

Me: What do you mean, lined up?

Him: They had everything in alignment. They seemed to know who they were and where they were going and had everything together; they were confident of their function in their world.

Me: Okay, but I don't see what that has to do with being able to balance round stones. So what if they had everything together?

Him: Because they knew who they were, they could keep their minds un-cluttered, stay centered, and focus their spirit on the task at hand. By know-ing what they stood for, they could transcend the inherent impossibility of the task and bring harmony and balance to the stones by channeling their energy in a focused way.

Me: Sounds spooky to me.

When Duffy thought about this conversation, he saw a connection be-tween successful teachers and the round stone balancers, and wondered "whether something similar might explain the success of inspired teach-ers. . . . Would teachers who know who they are and what they stand for be like my friend's successful stone balancers, who use their unique sense of self to focus their energies despite difficulties?" (778).

The stories we hear from teacher-researchers support Duffy's conjecture about the importance of a strong sense of identity in making daily teaching and research decisions. These teachers certainly don't know all the answers, but they are operating from a theoretical framework and vision based on evidence: evidence harvested from their own classrooms and viewed in the context of other researchers' work as well. Their habits of mindfulness have freed them up to pursue their work with confidence.

This doesn't mean a smug self-satisfaction with "the right way" but an openness to questions at the heart of our teaching. It also means having enough trust in ourselves to bring our questions to trusted colleagues with a willingness to listen and learn and to integrate new insights into our theoretical framework or see where the gaps between our theory and our practice lie.

Stacy Neary invited a colleague, Mike, to visit her classroom and offer some advice on working with Rose, a child who didn't seem very interested in her writing or in publishing any of her stories. Mike sat in on Stacy's conferences with Rose and was able to give Stacy advice on stepping back and taking more time to listen to students like Rose. His discussions helped her see that in her eagerness to help this reluctant writer, she was taking Rose to a place she had no intention of going. "Rose, being the obedient student, did answer my questions, but lacked any emotion in doing so." Based on Mike's feedback, Stacy changed the way she was working with Rose, and learned a lot about her own identity as a teacher-researcher in the process. In her 1998 essay about Rose, she concludes,

> I'm not sure who this case study is supposed to be about. I thought it was about Rose, but I've learned too much about myself to say that now. Rose and Mike have taught me the value of listening and what it truly means to "teach to the child."
>
> In closing, I believe there are two lessons I have learned from this experience. One is the acute lesson of listening. My listening in the past, I'm afraid, has been more with my ear than my heart. I can already tell that my new listening skills have made an effect on Rose. She is more interested in her writing and not only wants me to read her writing, but publish it, too. Her engagement shines in the colorfully drawn illustrations that she now shares with the class during literacy workshop.
>
> Rose has also validated a belief I have carried over the year—a belief that speaks to self-reflection as the first form of problem solving. I believe that most of what I find fault with in my classroom is a reflection of me, whether it be the student's failing grade, off-task behavior, or a lack of interest in writing. I believe that the teacher must first look at herself. It is surprisingly painful how often we come to find it is not the child who needs to adjust. As Rose showed me, you cannot look at another and not learn about yourself.

This new knowledge of self, especially in relation to others, can cause difficult shifts in relationships with colleagues. In any discussion of the change in identity for teacher-researchers, a "dark side" emerges that is seldom brought to light for frank and open talk. The old strategy many teachers have employed of "closing the door and teaching" doesn't work to reform education. But when you open the door and not only share what you're doing schoolwide but with a larger community, you show your own enthusiasm for your work in a place where others don't share that excitement. Many teachers have talked about the loneliness that comes when they begin to identify themselves as teacher-researchers.

One teacher-researcher who recently published a book on his classroom research was saddened by his growing isolation from colleagues at his school. In a recent interview, Rich Kent talked about the pain of that isolation: "I know I am doing important work for myself and my student colleagues," he told us. "My practice is changing, evolving, growing—it's got its struggles, and all that. But because of the research I do, I feel good about myself and my kids feel good about themselves. But, at the same time, I can't share any of that with my colleagues at school because they don't want to hear it. That aloneness, it just makes my stomach ache some days."

Like Rich, Terri Austin found that as her research agenda grew, she needed to depend on support from a wider research community than that of her own school and also draw strength from her work in the classroom. In her article "The Well-Dressed Alaska Teacher-Researcher," she concludes with how she brought seemingly incompatible forces into a kind of personal survival plan:

> To survive, I learned to be three people. In the classroom with my door shut, I was free to be creative, innovative, and excited with my students. The energy of my students and the confidence I saw in them gave me the added strength to continue. I kept seeing the benefits for them: I couldn't just stop and quit in the middle. In the peer community at school, I learned to suppress any kind of intellectual thought or enthusiasm about teaching, and I, too, talked about recess problems, student behavior, and duty schedules. I did this because I needed to survive. These were my peers, colleagues, and friends, and I learned it was best if I fit into their concept of school. At home and with my fellow teacher-researchers, I could be the kind of professional I really wanted to be. I could be excited about my project and my observations. I knew that I could discuss problems openly and others would seriously consider them. The teachers in this group would often send me articles to read or ideas to consider. They were my fence to lean against when parents or my staff pushed against me. I also have a close friend, Shirley, who is a teacher-researcher and even though we don't teach in the same school, we talk frequently. We act as critical friends for each other's projects. We'd spend hours on the phone or over tea after school working out possible solutions, suggesting articles or books to read and reread and then discussing them. We became walking resources for each

other. I worked through many types of problems as I talked with Shirley; just being able to talk to someone who believed in me helped tremendously. (1994a, 79)

University faculty also experience these changes in community and in the purpose for their work as they come to value and practice teacher research. University researcher Jerry Harste redefined his role with teachers as his own research agenda began to include teacher research:

The reason I really got interested eight years ago in teacher research was because I thought, I have got to stop speaking for teachers. What I tended to do was work with them in creating curriculum, and then I'd write it up and get all the credit! And it really bothered me. I said, "I'm going to have to stop this!" How is it that I can support teachers in writing up their own stuff? Researching their own stuff? I was trying to make sure their voice came through, but I'm not sure that works. That's what drove me to operate very differently. (personal communication, 1998)

Teacher-researchers challenge the identity of university researchers who work with them all the time. "Writing up the stuff" of teacher research usually means books and journal articles for university folks; teachers often have different audiences in mind. They don't necessarily identify with academic writing communities, and they often have to build new audiences for their work from scratch. In this way, they are slowly challenging and changing the values of the university professors who work with them.

Syracuse University Professor Kelly Chandler (in press), in her case study of Lorna, a fourth-grade teacher-researcher, found her own identity and role changing as she looked honestly at the way Lorna chose to present her research to others:

Lorna's work challenged my assumptions about the best way to present teacher research findings. Since writing is a regular and rewarding part of my life, it was sometimes difficult for me to see why anyone who had done the kind of research Lorna had—rich, generative, and useful—wouldn't want to write it up and share it with other teachers. For months, I harbored a secret hope that I would be able to convince her to do so, with the offer of coaching and editing if she needed it.

In retrospect, however, I see that it was Lorna, not I, who was heeding JoBeth Allen's recent call for teacher-researchers and those who collaborate with them to look beyond traditional print sources when considering outlets for disseminating their work:

[Writing for journals] is an artifact of many teacher research groups starting with or working in collaboration with the universities. . . . And we have to learn new things—new ways of reaching different audiences—or we're really sunk. . . . [Our research] needs to be presented to the school board, it needs to be in the local paper, it needs to be shown to civic groups, to Rotary—that's where the presentations need to be. (quoted in Chandler 1998, 65)

Lorna's presentations had been made to groups of people whose attitudes she could influence; she wasn't merely preaching to the converted. When she spoke to the students in my college reading course, she offered a spark of possibility to preservice teachers who will help to shape the culture in our schools in the very near future. When she and another introduced the idea of teacher research to the school board, they began a dialogue about honoring students' voices in curriculum development that may be continued at a later date. In a time when calls are loud for more standardization at the state and national levels and less decision-making power in individual classrooms, it is absolutely vital that teachers be opening up these conversations with local stakeholders whose support they may need very soon.

The solution for many teachers and university professors who find their roles and identities shifting is to form new, school-based research communities.

Many professors and teachers have also taken the dramatic step of starting schools, public and private, that have research at the center of their learning agendas. For these new school communities, balancing a May deadline for learning a new data analysis technique with completing the last of twelve state-mandated fire drills is surely the equivalent of balancing two very round stones! But there are a growing number of teachers, professors, and children who are thriving in sites where research is celebrated and mulled over every day.

Teacher-researcher Kimberly Campbell recently left her classroom to take on the job of leader of a group of teachers hired to create a new high school. Though Kim no longer has her own classroom, she is able to translate her teacher-researcher role to her new job description. She provides numerous professional resources for the faculty, including a section of the library devoted to teacher research publications. And she continues as a researcher in her own professional life, reporting findings to her staff through monthly letters as well as keeping a journal about her work and spending time cooking these data (see her Featured Teacher-Researcher piece in this chapter). She relies heavily on gathering information from students, staff, and parents through observations, surveys, and interviews to do her job.

Kim is not alone. Many of the veteran teacher-researchers cited in this book are finding that their identity as teacher-researchers is appreciated in new schools they have often founded with the help of colleagues. Nancie Atwell's Center for Teaching and Learning (Edgecomb, Maine) has been operating for nine years and opens its doors to teams of teachers nationwide. The Manhattan New School, with Principal Shelley Harwayne, has quickly become a national model for what is possible when a corps of dedicated educators teach, research, and write along with their students. Terri Austin at the Chinook Charter School, and Karen Gallas in California are part of a growing number of teacher-researchers who combine support for other teachers with classroom research in their roles as teaching principals.

University educators are changing their roles, too; professors like Jerome Harste, Heidi Mills, and Timothy O'Keefe have created "Centers for Inquiry" in Indiana and South Carolina, teaming up with teacher-researchers to help create new schools that have a broader vision of what inquiry can be, and that place the identity of teachers and students as researchers directly at center stage.

These examples are all of fledgling new efforts by teachers and professors to understand and honor the power of teacher research in school communities. Part of the drama and energy of teacher research come from being in the midst of change—we don't know how this story will turn out for the education community as a whole, how all of our identities will be redefined in the coming years as more teachers find a place for research in their lives. We hope we are at the sunset of the old ways of identifying teachers and professors narrowly, with separate agendas for learning and growth. We can hardly wait to see what's on the horizon for all of us as the sun rises on more new schools in the coming years, formed by teachers and professors who value knowing themselves and their students in new ways through research.

RESEARCH WORKSHOP

"A Secret Hidden in Plain Sight": Reflecting on Life Experiences

"Good teaching requires self-knowledge," writes Parker Palmer (1998). "It is a secret hidden in plain sight." As we rethink our identities in the classroom, we illuminate our sense of ourselves and our roles with our students, each other, and the larger education community. Without intentional attention, our evolution can go unexamined, and in the process, we can lose the opportunity for self-knowledge that can aid our teaching. Besides uncovering the hidden dimension in our changes in identity, it can be extremely helpful to dig back into our teaching roots: What drew us to teaching in the first place? What are the threads in our teaching lives and commitments that ground us and keep us teaching?

Karen Gallas, in a recent interview, reflected on the role her background in anthropology played in her teaching life, noting that in retrospect it is one of those threads that stands out clearly: "Now that I'm down the line a little bit, I see very clearly that it has [had an impact]. And it really has influenced the kind of work that I do. I find it interesting to look back on the choices that you make early in life. You know, you think you're doing them on instinct, and somehow or other, they seem to circle back and then begin to make sense in the larger picture. Those early interests come back" (quoted in MacKay 1999).

Like Karen, we can benefit from examining patterns in our lives and how they have shaped our identity—and how our identity continues to evolve. The following suggestions may help you begin a dialogue with colleagues about what has shaped, informed, and transformed your teaching life.

I Used to . . . But Now I . . .

Teachers in the Clayton Action Research Collaborative invite members to come to their first meeting with a reflection that focuses on their change. Using the simple format of parallel lists, these teacher-researchers share with each other brainstormed lists of what they used to do and what they now do.

Cathy Beck was surprised to note how many aspects of her teaching had changed over the years:

I used to . . .

1. Teach grammar in isolation
2. Be confrontational with students who were breaking class rules
3. Distance myself as a person to my students
4. Be content with the status quo in my classes
5. Never write with the students
6. Rarely give class time for writing
7. Pay little attention to the affective part of students
8. View myself as the "expert" on all things English
9. Make hard, fast rule ("No late papers!")
10. Never use my own writing as a model in class

Now I . . .

1. Teach grammar in mini-lessons or in individual conferences with students, using their papers as the "worksheets"
2. Remain calm and respectful throughout the discussion of the infraction
3. Reveal myself, warts and all, to students so they get to know me as a person
4. Make a vigorous effort to provide opportunities for students to be actively engaged
5. Write and share my writing with students on a regular basis

6. Always provide large amounts of class time for prewriting activities, drafting, revision, and sharing

7. Focus on the affective because I realize the importance of addressing that side of the students before I can make progress with the academic side

8. View myself as a learner who learns with and from the students

9. Recognize the importance of flexible deadlines, especially for those students who are having the most difficulty—they often take longer to produce less

10. Frequently use my own writing as a model in class

Cathy used her list to celebrate her growth and the changes in her language arts teaching stance. But other teachers find they remember things they used to do that were wonderful practices but that over the years they stopped doing. Virginia Shorey, an English as a second language teacher, remembered the home visits she used to make that had been central to her teaching and committed herself to once again make those visits with the families of her students.

Time Line of Professional Development

Kathryn Mitchell Pierce brought a different kind of teaching life reflection to her teacher research group—one that helped her look over her career, note patterns and evolving interests, and ultimately map out her future direction (see Figure 9.1). Kathryn's review of her teaching passions and interests came together as she forged her plans for continued work. And sharing her time line helped her colleagues think about their own. The time line needn't be a narrative. You could chart the highs and lows of your professional development on graph paper in a quick fifteen-minute session with teacher research colleagues. It can be fascinating to share these, note similarities and differences, and use each other's graphs to help add to your own.

Reviewing Work and Reflections

Your classroom is a veritable archive of historical information that can help you review your life as an educator. There are many data sources available to put you in touch with your experiences. You can:

- Reread teaching journals, class records, and notes
- Look back through the historical data in school newsletters, narrative assessments, and notes on planning, including lesson and unit plans

Figure 9.1 Teaching Life Review

TIME LINE OF PROFESSIONAL DEVELOPMENT

Early Career—Student Teaching/Early Teaching

- *Three-to-eight-year-old lab school, British infant school experiences.* Watching children move up through the program beginning as three-year-olds and continuing through sixth grade—longitudinal look at children; upward influence of early childhood curricular experiences on the ways I thought about organizing elementary curriculum; working with multiage/multiyear groups of children and planning learning experiences that were based on "discovery learning" techniques.
- *Concept webs for integrated curriculum planning.* Developing a method for planning integrated curriculum units based on conceptual webs that began with a book, topic, or concept and then branched out to touch each subject area or different ways of studying the central focus.

Mid-Career—University Teaching

- *Literature discussion groups, evaluation of literacy learning, collaborative curriculum inquiry.* Opportunity to work with classroom teachers in their classrooms and on questions that affected their daily work and moved all of us ahead in our understanding of how to support student learning.
- *Teacher study groups.* Participating in and initiating/supporting teacher study groups in a variety of contexts and on a variety of literacy-related issues; learning experiences for child and adult learners focused on the value of small-group inquiry projects.
- *Alternate sign systems.* Studying alternate sign systems—semiotics—to gain insight into the reading and meaning-making process; helped me to value art, music, movement, drama, math, and language all as systems for making and sharing meaning and to seek ways of incorporating these into my own and my students' learning experiences.

Current Career—Glenridge School

Year One

- *Reading teacher literature reviews.* Collaborative experience with other classroom teachers, using and reviewing children's literature.
- *Literacy committee.* Developing and refining the literacy curriculum documents.
- *Multiage.* Working with others to create, support, and document the multiage pilot program at Glenridge.
- *Curricular Issues.* Coming to terms with a mandated curriculum, re-creating professional understandings "from the inside out," from a classroom perspective.

Year Two

- *Literacy curriculum implementer.* Working with classroom teachers and creating support materials to strengthen the implementation of our new curriculum.
- *Curricular issues.* Multiage experiences within a grade level curriculum, supporting inquiry and highlighting art as a sign system in inquiry, developing efficient strategies for documenting student work and growth.

Year Three

- *Literacy committee.* Struggling reader document.
- *Clayton Action Research Collaborative.* Creating an ongoing group, developing strategies and structures to support others.
- *Multiage.* Focusing on multiyear plans for a mulitage classroom with specific emphasis on seeing math from an inquiry perspective and continuing to work against arbitrary grade-level divisions in the teaching and assessing of mathematical concepts.
- *Curricular issues.* Contained focus on art as a sign system; new focus on talking and learning in small groups in the math curriculum, particularly multiage math problem-solving groups.

Future Career—New Questions, New Directions

- *Math problem solving.* Taking a closer look at how children use small-group talk to explore and wrestle with complex math concepts; looking for ways to broaden consideration of math content beyond grade levels and to capitalize on vertical strands in development of mathematical thinking.
- *Action research collaborative.* Energized by the support of the collaborative, becoming more systematic in my own classroom inquiries and seeking ways of systematically documenting my work and sharing it with others.
- *Role of art in inquiry.* Using what I've learned about semiotics and the information available in the district on the "Reggio Approach" to early childhood curriculum that values art as one of the hundred languages of children; continue to refine the ways I support children in using art in their inquiry experiences.

- Review previous end-of-the-year reflections and goal statements
- Reacquaint yourself with student work that you have saved

Who Are the Teachers Who Have Shaped You?

Remembering a teacher who made a difference in your life can help you reconnect with those mentors from the past. Parker Palmer (1998) often asks the teachers to introduce themselves by telling a story about their mentors. "As these stories are told, we are reminded of many facts about good teaching: that it comes in many forms, that the imprint of good teachers remains long after the facts they gave us have faded" (21). He goes on to ask, "What is it about *you* that allowed great mentoring to happen?" In this way, you discover your qualities as a student that this teacher was able to draw out in you—a very revealing exercise.

When we discover the "secret hidden in plain sight"—our inner identities as teachers and learners—we are better able to work from a position of strength. In answer to Gerald Duffy's question, Would teachers who know who they are and what they stand for be like my friend's successful stone balancers, who use their unique sense of self to focus their energies despite difficulties?, we believe the answer is yes. We invite you to try these strategies as a start—and invent new ones—to help you reconnect with the teaching knowledge you already possess.

featured TEACHER RESEARCHER

From Teacher-Researcher to Administrator-Researcher

Kimberly Hill Campbell

In leaving my classroom and my teacher research to take on the job of high school principal, I was hopeful that I would become part of a community of teachers committed to teacher research. I was fortunate to take a job as leader of a group of teachers hired to create a new high school. We were giddy with the prospect of what our school could be and anxious to document how well all our dreams and theories played out in reality.

Our high school is based on the research done by the Coalition of Essential Schools. This framework provided us with a research base to support the design of our school. We could look to other Coalition schools and the Coalition publications for research findings. Although much of the Coalition research was conducted and written up by outside researchers, it provided us with an initial starting point for looking at our own school.

Within our building, our first step in developing a community of inquiry was to include teacher research as part of our evaluation goals. In addition to setting a personal goal and a teaching craft goal, I ask teachers the following questions (see Figure 9.2):

> What are you interested in researching this year related to your classroom?
>
> Consider what you wonder about. What might be a source of tension? List your goal.
>
> How will you conduct your research?
>
> How can I support you in your research?

Some staff in this new high school were experienced teacher-researchers. For the most part, however, this concept of teachers looking at their

Figure 9.2 Goal-Setting Conference Response

1. What is your personal goal for the 1997-98 school year? Think about what might support you in your classroom work or an interest or project that would support your lifelong learning.
Personal Goal:

Striking a good balance between work and personal life

How will you evaluate this goal? I will feel good, have energy, feel prepared for class & feel I am doing my best work.
Observation & what I reflect/say

How can I support you in this goal? Being open to conversations, Listening, helping me problem solve, sometimes telling me to go home, providing resources,

2. What is your classroom/teaching craft goal for the 1997-98 school year? Think about what you'd like to try or refine related to the craft of teaching.
Teaching Craft Goal:

Use student input to develop a curriculum for JR/SR world Studies

How will you evaluate this goal? Culminating assessment → symposium art ex.
Personal observations   show what they know
student comments
and response to the work

to opportunities

How can I support you in this goal? Say yes, help me plan backwards as I gather ideas, be a sounding board for ideas, problem-solve challenges, time to visit with/observe other teachers incl. Robert Rydell & maybe Bill Bigelow

3. What are you interested in "researching" this year related to your classroom? Think about what you wonder about—what might be a source of tension in your classroom.   & Tim Gillespe Linda too. Christensen
Teacher Research Goal: What roles do journals play in the development of students as writers.

How will you conduct your research? look at journals & how kids use them, involve student in evaluating how they use journals & whether or not they help them improve as writers, look at student writing

How can I support you in your research? examples for writing growth.

Sounding board
talk about what I'm finding
listen
brainstorm

- Do they pull anything from their writing to develop as finished pieces?
- How does it differ from in-class writing?

classrooms was new. I was encouraged by teachers' willingness to think about their classrooms and come up with questions that would help them make sense of what was happening there. Some of the questions or topics explored were the following:

What roles do journals play in the development of students as writers? (See Figure 9.2)

What types of assessment are most effective? How can I vary my assessment methods? How should I develop scoring guides?

How does the work we do and the conversations we have in a girls'
group translate into how girls perform in academic classes?

As a result, in addition to classroom observations based on the clinical
supervision model, I knew about teachers through their research. This most
often took the form of conversations. It was exciting to hear teachers enthusiastic about their discoveries. And to see how the research answered some
questions but also led to more questions. For example, the girls' group research changed midyear. Ellena Weldon, the teacher, discovered the girls
valued the group but were not willing to give up their lunch time to meet,
and before and after school meeting times were not practical. Rather than
give up on the idea, Ms. Weldon chose to conduct one-on-one interviews
with the girls. In the process, she discovered that these girls were quite self-
aware. They could articulate their strengths and their concerns. And they
identified some group dynamics issues that we needed to look at as a staff
to ensure that all girls were comfortable sharing their ideas in a classroom—
given that our girls represented only one-third of our total population, it
was not surprising that they felt overwhelmed and underappreciated at
times. The research helped this teacher see the girls in a new light. Several of
the girls commented to me that they really appreciated this time spent with
Ms. Weldon—they now saw *her* in a new light.

A second support method for creating our teacher research community
was resources. I provided copies of articles to staff. Sometimes the article
went to the whole staff; other times I selected an article based on the
teacher's area of research. Wherever possible, I worked to select articles
written by teacher-researchers. In addition to the journal *Teacher Research*, I
looked to the Coalition publication *Horace*; the *English Journal*; *Educational
Leadership*; and *Bulletin*, published by the National Association of Secondary Principals. On occasion, I searched the Internet or perused periodicals
in college libraries. A professional library exists in my office with a shelf devoted to teacher research. I add to it each year and circulate teacher publication catalogues to the staff for their suggestions for shelf selections.

My final tool for supporting a community of teacher-researchers is to
continue to be a researcher in my own professional life. This includes reading other researchers' work and sharing my discoveries with staff; I try to
write a letter to them once a month. Keeping a journal about my work and
spending time cooking these data remains part of my toolbox, too. I also
teach research methods. This year, I did a presentation to the district staff on
teacher research. Teachers were then able to join one of three groups to pursue in greater depth: case studies, notetaking, or framing a research question. I provided the resources for each of these groups, and they were facilitated by district teacher-researchers with whom I had worked in previous
classes or workshops. At staff meetings, I cite observations I have made before making suggestions for changes in practice or process. I ask staff to
share their observations as well. We also utilize surveys to gather

information from students, staff, and parents. These survey results are then compiled and shared.

At the end of the last school year, we conducted focus groups for the first time. Staff members suggested possible topics for these groups, and were generous and flexible in allowing us to meet with groups of five to seven students. We thought these meetings would take about thirty minutes. In reality, they took at least an hour and could have gone on for much longer. Students were asked to describe a celebration—something that went well—and share a suggestion for how we might better meet their learning needs. We talked about the tension between confidentiality about student matters and students' need to know what's happening (particularly when students ended up leaving our school). Finally, we shared our schedule for the upcoming school year and highlighted how it reflected students' comments and concerns regarding the current schedule. I conducted these focus groups with the help of our high school counselor. It really took both of us to facilitate, hear, and respond to all the comments. These comments have now been compiled and will be shared with staff at our fall in-service meeting.

My hope is to continue with the research support tools I have listed, and to continue to develop more tools. I would like to create more time for teachers to be in frequent conversation with each other about their work. Our new block schedule provides for some common prep time. I also hope to make staff meeting time more about the work of teaching than about the procedures of school. Much of this procedural stuff can be handled in a memo. Granted, it takes a lot more of my time to write the memo, but the few times I did it last year provided all of us with time to talk about the craft of teaching. So it is well worth the effort.

If we want to create schools where kids are passionate about learning, we will need passionate-about-learning teachers. I submit that the kind of reflective wondering that is teacher research fuels this passion in teachers.

featured TEACHER RESEARCHER

One Moment in Two Times

Karen Hankins

It was 6:30 in the morning, and I was already at school. I never sleep the night before the first day of school and always arrive early. It doesn't happen that way again all year long!

We were opening a new school, and that smell of newness added to the odd feeling of teaching in a different place with new carpet, new dolls, new books, and new crayons. I carried in boxes and bundles from previous teaching years: evidence of past children. Opening the boxes filled with bulletin board decorations, booklets, drawings, and "i luv u mz hanknz" notes reminded me that the preplanning week is really focused on preparing for the children. Soon they would arrive and I felt ready.

But I wasn't ready for Cedric. He was delivered to the door between two older brothers, each holding (dragging) him by the collar. Except for size, they could have been clones of each other. Cedric smiled and took off like the proverbial bat out of hell. He was truly out of control. He said nothing that I could understand. He would not sit in a group, nor did he play with anyone.

Eventually, I found a way to keep him with us. Instead of insisting that he sit in the group, I drew a huge circle on the floor with tape . . . yes, on the brand-new carpet. While we had group time, he was to stay seated within the circle. He rolled back and forth within the circle, but he didn't run.

Cedric liked to paste things, so he would sit at a work station—as long as no one was there to distract him—and paste for long periods of time. He didn't want to follow instructions for a project; he just wanted to paste and be left alone.

On the playground he ran with no seeming interest in games or focus on where he was headed. He had a sense of boundary, though; he only ran so far and then back again.

At lunch he finished everything on his plate before the child beside him even sat down, which prompted us to arrange for extra food for him.

That was his second year of kindergarten, I learned, and talks with last year's teacher from a different school were full of heartbreaking stories. No one would listen when she suggested that Cedric needed more than she could give him.

To cut a long saga of several months into a sentence, Cedric began to take Ritalin. I saw a different child, then, one who sat during group time, contributed a bit, and began to be able to tolerate other children next to him. He began to give me indications that he wanted his work to look like the other children's, and he would patiently chew on his shirt while I helped him to make corrections. He was in control of his behavior for the first time, and proud of it, but he was definitely still walking way outside the norm in a classroom community. He was different, and it didn't take even the most casual of observers long to ask me about him.

Corsaro and Eder's (1994) conclusions about children constructing and negotiating friends doesn't seem to apply to a child who takes little notice of those around him except to run away. At first, Cedric didn't seem to fit their assertion that children make "persistent attempts to gain control of their lives and to share that control with others" (114). If one of those themes did begin to emerge for Cedric, it was a growing sense of the need for control on his part. At first he sought to establish that control away from others, rather than trying to establish friendships. The medication helped him to tolerate other children at closer range and for increasing amounts of time.

In February, I took candid photographs of the children for Valentine's Day cards and realized happily that Cedric would now stay in one spot long enough to be photographed. When the pictures came back, I looked with warm teacher eyes at the children I had given my heart to that year. I came to Cedric's picture and felt a sense of agony, a gnawing uneasiness just looking at it. I found that, as so often happens to me, I wasn't seeing that picture. I was really seeing a picture of my own sister in kindergarten.

What if the teacher doesn't know she needs help? What if she gets lost? I'm so scared for my sister. She's so little and so different.

It was an experiment Laura Fortson wanted to try in our college town. She wanted to have a kindergarten when there was no public kindergarten. She wanted it to be integrated and filled with art, music, dance, and the joy of literature. She wanted inclusion before people knew the word. The law of the land did not yet guarantee the right to public education for mentally challenged children.

My parents enrolled my sister Kathy. They didn't even ask if a child so limited would be accepted. What state of denial allowed my parents to take my baby sister and leave her in that room of people who might not have my watchfulness?

Kathy was blessed with beauty. When she was at rest, her countenance gave no hint of the tumult within her. But at nearly six years old, she still spoke in incomplete sentences and communicated with other children with aggressive two-year-old pushing, pulling hair, and pinching. I was eighteen years old that year, and like all eighteen-year-olds, I knew everything—certainly more than my parents. I worried.

After a couple of days, a phone call came from her teacher. Could my parents come in for a conference?

My mother went ready to prove to the teacher that Kathy belonged in the school. The evidence was clear for her in a Polaroid picture that we had made the first day of school. My sister was sitting at my brother's drum set with her blonde hair flying and her drumsticks held high. The photograph captured her playing and singing a song she had learned that day in kindergarten. It also captured the giftedness she had in music, the joy she felt in it, and the beauty of her face. For my mother, the picture represented Kathy's connection to school, and she hoped the teacher would be able to see it, too.

The conference went well. The teacher really just needed to know how best to facilitate Kathy's experience. She didn't ask my parents to remove her from the class. This teacher was one to emulate: I logged that in my mind, and it never left. I still wonder what that picture said to her.

The photograph may have captured the moment, but it didn't capture the reality of that child at home or at school. If a soundtrack had been available, a listener would have heard a steady, rhythmical beating on the drum and a melodious voice with a childlike yet mature timbre singing the melody of the song in perfect pitch. The words, "I am a young musician. I like to play a tune," were sung, "Ah wa wa wa beteshope, Ah na na ba da do."

Kathy sang the same syllables over and over again. I learned to sing the song with her, and we sang it the same way each and every time. Her sounds held both the giftedness and the challenge, the pleasure and the pain of her longing to communicate.

The omitted data would have told another story altogether. Without the sounds and smells surrounding the captured visual moment, we get incomplete knowledge.

From the photo, one is able to understand the giftedness of all children, even the outliers. If I had omitted that set of data from my assessment of Kathy, I wouldn't have seen the whole child. On the other hand, to believe that the picture of normalcy equipped her to walk unchallenged in the land of the predictable curve would have doomed her to negative comparisons. She wanted to belong, she wanted to have friends, but she didn't have the skills to gain access to her peers.

And so, I continue to stare at this handsome youngster's picture, which I intend to send home to his mother. What will it tell her about Cedric's days in school? Will she know how far he's come to be sitting fairly close to another child? Will she see the normalness of his activity or hear the child she knows so well at home?

Once again, the picture is incomplete. For me, it represents how far we've come and how far we still have to go. In the same dizzying moment, it reminds me of the calm before the storm before the rest of Kathy's school career. I find myself caught for one moment in two times. The past serves to inform the present moment with Cedric, as knowing Cedric helps me answer questions from the past about my sister.

I look behind Cedric's picture to the charts and papers and plastic bags of teaching material and think back on the day I met him. That room at 6:30 in the morning had no lived-in sounds or smells. Everything was so orderly, so clean. The room was so full and yet so empty. No evidence of work produced, no paint jars spilling over, no stacks of papers, no play dough ground into the carpet, no pieces of puzzles lying around. I liked how it felt, I liked how it looked, but I knew it held no child's story . . . not yet. It sat in readiness, but it wasn't school.

Even before the children showed up, I know now I was expecting Kathy. She continues to come. This year her name is Cedric.

featured **TEACHER RESEARCHER**

Why Worry? The Case for Self-Definition in Teacher Research

Suzanne Jacobs

I'm a university professor. You should know that before you read any further. Probably, if truth were told, the editors should have thought twice about letting me into this book. The whole point of this book, including its freshness, its urgency, and its authentic voice, is to conduct a conversation between teachers about teacher–initiated questions. I'm a teacher, but I'm also part of an institution whose members have historically set the agenda of questions *for* teachers. Admitting me to this book admits a discourse tradition not always friendly to teaching but one of which I am necessarily a part: the university tradition of research.

Watch out. Be aware that the university's long history of ideas about research methodologies has a formidable impact on any endeavor describing itself as "research." Research with a capital R, the university's knowledge-making activity that so often is funded by government and corporate grants, has been a marker of difference between the university and the school. So strong has this difference been, and so marked the borderline between the two institutions, that traffic between them has traditionally been all one way: teachers have come to the university for knowledge, but until recently no one has thought of traveling across the border in the other direction. But now that traffic has begun to flow both ways—as university people such as myself increasingly cross over to join a community of researchers who come from both countries—we find ourselves asking how to do this other style of research (with a small r), teacher research. The "how" question is one that university people have constantly asked: How are we doing this research? What is our methodology? On my part there is more than a little worry that those of us who have traveled here bring nothing in our suitcases except the research methodologies constructed by university researchers. My point is that worrying is a healthy state of mind. It does no harm to wonder whether research with a capital R has such an energy and momentum that it will come to dominate the crossover culture recently built up by university-school partnerships. A little worry might be a good thing.

In this essay I make two suggestions. One is to worry and the other is to work. The expertise argument is always powerful: who, after all, is better equipped to run a large and important research enterprise than experts in research? Why shouldn't people experienced with the big R show us how to do the little r? Worry, I say, about such arguments. As for work, the teacher research community must work in order to establish a credible sense of its own areas of expertise. To do that, this book and other forums need to encourage conversation about its goals and methods, in order to establish its research identity.

First, let us consider worry. Why should we worry? When? And how should worrying be done?

We should worry when good teacher research seems to be happening, but no one remembers to recognize its procedures, to name them, or to discuss and evaluate them. Fortunately, there are people taking notice—people I will return to in a moment—but they seem to be few in number. What worries me most are those cases in which the people who discuss and evaluate the procedures are not the same as those who *do* the research. This is the same old split we've always worried about, the division of teaching communities into bosses and workers, or those who say "do" and those who say, "all right, I will." The crossover spirit, or crossing back and forth between the role of researcher and the role of saying how-to-do-research, is really the defining spirit of the teacher research movement. Goals, methods, and procedures for projects within this movement have been worked out collaboratively. First one and then another of the community has taken on the role of saying, "Now, how are we going about this?" Worry, I say, if you find yourself part of a research community whose procedures are never talked about or if the time spent talking about them has decreased.

In addition, I advise careful scrutiny of all advice about procedures in printed form coming from absent experts (such as this article). I advise making a crucial distinction regarding the source. Is the procedural advice the product of teacher research experience? Or is it advice emanating from outside the teacher research community, authored by someone whose expertise is in a different sphere, say physics or literary criticism? Take a careful look. Expertise from another sphere might well be useful, but take care to adapt it.

Worry, for example, if the how-to advice you read contains no descriptions of actual research projects, if it reads like a generalized guide to every teacher research situation, rather like the Ten Commandments.

Worry about guidelines that assume a lack of intelligence on the part of teachers, advising them, for instance, to make sure their research questions are "important, not trivial." (Both of these worries refer to an article [Chamot 1995] in a recent ERIC *News Bulletin*, purportedly put together to help teachers with teacher research.)

Worry about guidelines with mixed messages. For example, the Chamot article suggests that teachers should read representative recent research because they don't have the time to conduct an exhaustive literature review. The mixed message is that you'll be doing fine, but it's really not good enough.

Worry, in general, when the tools for descriptive research are shown by the guidelines to be a necessary evil. Here is an example: "Introspective techniques such as diaries, think-aloud protocols, or self-ratings can provide rich descriptions and insights into individual learners, but they are subjective and depend for accuracy on how well learners are able to report on their own thoughts and feelings. The fact is, the purported measurement of human mental and affective processes is at best an extraordinarily inexact science" (Chamot 1995, 6).

If you find yourself reading procedural advice of this kind, realize that you're listening to an argument between qualitative and quantitative traditions. The writer in this case uses language that has developed out of the quantitative tradition: "exact science," "subjective vs. objective," and "measurement." Ask yourself if that's a tradition appropriate to your project.

In this book, readers are not likely to find the rhetoric of objectivity that has just been illustrated. But elsewhere the rhetoric is powerful. Why would a writer such as the one just quoted, who clearly wants to validate the efforts of teachers, end up being as condescending as she is if she didn't feel an obligation to "exact science"? Many large education organizations still buy the philosophy that certainty is possible, and that one travels toward certainty by replicable experimentation, piecing together an increasingly accurate picture until eventually a truth emerges that will apply across the board. In brief, as Cochran-Smith and Lytle (1990) point out, the university tradition of research typically values generalizability. What this means in practical terms is that funding agencies and sometimes even district administrators of school systems are apt to respond to applications to fund teacher research with the question, How is such research going to produce findings that can be widely disseminated? How will your findings work from the top down?

Indeed, worry is necessary. In answer to the question, How should worrying be done? I suggest that readers pull together a list of words such as "exact science" that form the vocabulary of evaluation within the university research community. Isolate language that characterizes the standards of research in this community and shows the type of research that people do. One might begin with *generalizable,* as shown on this list:

generalizable

rigorous

systematic

theoretical

Add in the nouns that are typically part of this vocabulary:

methods

documentation

forms of documentation

theory (in contrast to "practice")

theorist (in contrast to "practitioner")

analysis

framework

standard

And then notice the possibilities for combination:

theoretical framework

practitioner methods

rigorous methods

methodological rigor

systematic documentation

standards for generalizability

And so on. Now select the terms that help you with your work. Worry about the ones that appear to set up an opposition between university research and classroom research, for example, by ranking the two kinds of research.

All this speculation about the university research idiom came home to me with force when I came to a consideration of my own situation. I recently co-authored a book, *Mindful of Others: Teaching Children to Teach* (1994), with a fifth-grade teacher, Suzanne Brady, which is very much a teacher research endeavor. In raising the issue of how to define ourselves as teacher-researchers, we explain that we are both interpreters, both of us document and analyze, and both of us initiate questions, usually stimulated by the contributions of the other.

But others find it easy to pigeonhole my co-author, Suzanne Brady, differently. She tells the story of how she went to a National Council of Teachers of English conference one year, walked into a "Roundtable on Research" with the intention of sharing her experience in teacher research, only to realize when she got there that *teacher-researcher* was not part of the accepted language. In fact, even the term *teacher* had been given a twist. When she introduced herself as a teacher of grade 5, someone at the table exclaimed, "Oh, a practitioner!" They made her welcome, she said, but they were surprised she had come. The others, apparently, were "theorists" or "researchers." They were university people. The term *teacher* would have showed their commonality; the term *practitioner* showed their difference. In the book, Brady asserts her determination not to be excluded. "I was a researcher *and* a teacher," she says. "And I really did belong at that table."

Words make a difference. Words are the conceptual building blocks of any education research and specifically research on teaching. Productive worriers will ask themselves whether teacher-researchers, having set themselves out as different from other researchers, now have an obligation to say who they are, and whether that self-definition must be set against traditional research and incorporate some of the vocabulary mentioned so far in this essay. What kinds of confusion and misunderstandings will result, they ask themselves, if teacher-researchers don't do this? How might they be seen as second-rate imitations of real researchers? as wannabees and failures?

Turning now to work, that business of defining the methods and goals of the teacher research community, let us continue with this question of how the type of words listed previously are part of the problem of self-definition. How can the community define itself as research and yet show its important differences from the research traditions of the university?

Who we are, it seems to me, is a borderland community. We are situated between two dominant cultures, the school culture and the university culture. Gloria Anzaldua in her book *Borderlands/La Frontera* (1987) has described the borderland between the United States and Mexico as a crossover territory where people mix Tex and Mex, speaking as many as five varieties of English, each of the varieties showing a slightly different impact of the two cultures and two languages on each other. Rather remarkably, these mixed varieties have become a means for the borderland to create its own cultural identity—its own way of standing up to both dominant cultures. My point is that teacher-researchers can likewise create a cohesive community culture of their own, even when they borrow vocabulary from the dominant languages, so long as they creatively construct meanings for that vocabulary that apply to their own brand of work.

The university is not the only dominant culture; school administration has its own lingo, which might be branded (after Giroux 1984) the "efficiency language." Student learning is seen as depersonalized product, output measured against input by means of standardized tests; materials are seen as teacher-proof. This language unfortunately requires that knowledge be simple enough to quantify. As a member of the borderland community, I much prefer to borrow the university's ample vocabulary for problematizing knowledge—for asking questions about its permanence and certainty. Can I borrow the university's more problem-centered idea rather than the efficiency idea? Can I borrow part of the university culture without bringing in the aspects of its Research apparatus that in some instances have dominated and controlled research about teaching?

A small but growing number of people have begun to discuss these matters in print, no doubt spurred by the size and number of teacher research efforts: by the activity spawned by the sites of the National Writing Project, by the sites of the Bread Loaf Institute, by other institutes, and by self-initiated teacher research groups (see Bissex and Bullock, Branscombe et al., Cochran-Smith and Lytle, Gillespie, Goswami and Stillman, Mohr and Maclean, and Myers). Most of these people have borrowed the university idiom of research, including many of the words in the previous list, but have given the meanings of these words a twist in order to make them useful.

Take, for example, Marilyn Cochran-Smith and Susan Lytle. In several publications (e.g., 1990, 1992, 1993) they have set out alternatives to traditional modes of research, showing how teacher research is no less theoretical than other research; its "theoretical frameworks" are merely different and possibly more complex. Likewise, modes of documentation are no less "systematic," though they are different. These authors reject "generalizability" as a criterion of excellence, but they accept the assumption that there must be standards and criteria in order for evaluation to take place. Standards, they say, will be developed over time by the people who do the research—by teachers.

For further illustration of the way language is borrowed and adapted by the borderland community, look at the words of Dixie Goswami, another vigorous definer of this community's style. Like Cochran-Smith and Lytle, she frequently redefines university idiom to shape a vision of what we do and how we can do it better. In her phone interview with Tim Gillespie (1994), she makes a case for teachers as "methodologists" and as "theorists." In an interesting exchange with Gillespie, she works out a definition of *replicability* that she claims applies to teacher research: "It's not going to be replicable in the sense that I've controlled variables . . . ," she explains, "but I have a deep obligation to tell you what we did, how we did it, and why, so that we can keep on doing it" (Gillespie 1994, 99).

Likewise the word *validity:* "'Is it valid?' That's the same question my husband asks when he's doing physics," points out Goswami, "and I want to rephrase it to say, Is it meaningful for us? Does it make sense to participants?" (98). Goswami is clearly rewriting the language of university research to give definition and purpose to what she does at Bread Loaf.

This is the work of self-definition. This is necessary work. And it will be furthered as the community members talk to one another about their goals and methods, then talk again, repeating this process until they hear an echo: the words that were originally uttered coming back but enriched by their contact with diverse activities within the teacher research community, the borderland community. That diversity is crucial.

My question is this: Why is it that the voices belong almost exclusively to those who are employed by universities? When teachers speak—as in, for example, the collections of Cochran-Smith and Lytle or Branscombe et al.— they report what they discovered and how they came to discover it, but I do not hear them saying much about why it was a good idea to follow the course of discovery that they followed rather than a different course. I hear university people on the topic of alternative methodologies, but in the increasing number of works by teachers coming from Stenhouse, Heinemann, and Teachers College Press, I do not yet hear such discussion.

One of the few teachers' voices that I hear on this topic is that of Patricia Carini. (Carini's work is hard to obtain in print. I found it in Margaret Himley's book *Shared Territory* (1991).) Carini is quite explicit and detailed about how teachers create knowledge related to the classroom. She employs a case study methodology combined with detailed responses from other teachers in a discussion format. Yet it's quite clear from her description that she sees little need to define her method—which she calls "deep talk"—with reference to the research vocabulary. Perhaps that's understandable. She is not employed by a university. Here, then, is someone living in the borderland contributing to its evolving language by drawing on the sources of the lay vocabulary, then giving these ordinary words a specialized meaning.

What I do not see in my own work, nor do I see in other publications either, is much attempt to use research concepts (such as those listed earlier) in order to describe our methods and goals. In our book, when we addressed this topic of methods and goals, we did not call what we were doing *teacher research*; we called it something else. What I now realize is that we used the terms *teacher collaboration, social action in the school,* and so forth—as though our concern with the teacher as professional maker of knowledge was a concern cut off from teacher research. The vocabulary we used at this point was not contradictory to, or at cross-purposes with, the research-style vocabulary listed earlier in this article. But in our consciousness at the point of writing the book the two vocabularies did not overlap. It was as though early in writing the book we decided we were no longer in the territory of research. We were in a different place. Looking back, and looking at our state of mind, I see a distinct ambivalence about our relationship to research and its language.

Perhaps it's not always necessary to avoid so completely the language of Research with a capital R. A healthy borderland community can adapt, as Goswami does, a term such as *validity* so long as community members embed the word in their own contexts rather than slavishly imitating the university's model. At the same time it is crucial to recognize words such as

Carini's "deep talk" as equally important to the task of describing what we do in the community and how best to do it. This is why teachers' voices in this matter of methodology are crucial; words reflecting their frames of reference are necessary to the discussion. Because such words are lay words— apparently ordinary—they are easy to dismiss.

Language from both bordering countries, the university and the school, as well as such lay vocabulary, will be useful in our developing Tex/Mex culture. Let us keep in mind the many examples through history in which people who settle a new territory develop a mixed sort of language that turns out to have great value for them, reflecting the richness of the two parent cultures as well as the spirit of working together across diversity. Such borrowing and adapting is the alternative I see to domination.

As far as I can tell, a borderland community of teacher-researchers is actually in place. There really is a spirit of cooperation rather than a split between those who say how and those who do. But a little worry is a good thing. I'll be happier when I see more attempts by teachers to articulate their research values. When I hear teachers describing how they do their research in words that clearly come from the teaching culture, then I'll stop worrying. Right now, I'm listening to the language and waiting to hear those words.

10 Students as Research Partners

You trusted me and in my own subtle way I discovered meaning that once wasn't there.

Lynn, a student in Richard Kent's *Room 109*

The Siletz Indians have a proverb about the importance of apprenticeship in learning: "One who learns from one who is learning drinks from a running stream." None of us would argue with the importance of students' seeing their teachers as learners, emulating their processes, and learning from their example. But the flip side is just as important—if we as teachers step back and allow ourselves to learn from our students, we too can taste the refreshing, invigorating water of that running stream.

A natural by-product of conducting research in our classrooms is the shift in dynamics that occurs as students see the research process unfolding around them. Because their work itself, their insights and their reflections, are integral parts of the inquiry, they are no longer separate from the curriculum and classroom decision making. They also can become partners in the research process.

Whether our students are investigating classroom dynamics, exploring ways to change the curriculum, or examining how they or their classmates make sense of the world, their insights and perceptions are a key element in our work as teacher-researchers. Not in the old model as subjects of the research, or even in a more enlightened view, as curricular informants. We need to really "come out from behind the desk" and invite them to be co-researchers, digging in and harvesting data with us.

For some beginning teacher-researchers, the process of collaborating with students over research topics evolves naturally. As Robin, a first-year teacher, writes, "I began asking students to become more a part of the process, asking for feedback, comments, suggestions. I had never done that before, and it was so exciting to hear thoughtful, helpful comments from the students" (Ernst 1994, 69). Like Robin, many teacher-researchers we've worked with speak of the transformation of their relationships with their students as the students have become interested in the project and have become collaborators in the research. Learning from the insights of these teachers can help us put their strategies to use more purposefully. Rather than waiting for the incidental side benefits, we can *intentionally* invite students to be our research partners.

Terri Austin's research into her sixth-grade students' ability to evaluate their own learning is clearly a student-centered query, one that requires students' active participation. In the second year of her research, when she expanded her work, she wanted to move beyond collecting their written self-evaluations and recording interview responses as data points to analyze. She decided to share her research plans and wonderings with them right from the start, making it clear that they were partners in the year-long research endeavor. In August she wrote the following letter to her students, sharing her research proposal draft in a unique format (1994b, 122–124):

Dear Students,

Welcome to sixth grade. I'm looking forward to working with all of you. This will be a year when you grow taller, change shoe sizes, and learn a great deal. Last year, my students learned to assess themselves as learners. They learned to critically examine their growth and set goals. It is important for you to know yourself as an intelligent responsible person, and student/parent conferences will assist you. I will help you through this process, but I will not assume responsibility for you. I will step back from the role of being the only evaluator and give this gift to you. I have faith that you can do this and we will travel together in trust.

Last year, I wondered if students could assess themselves; I found out that they could. This year, I wonder what would happen if you, your parents, and myself agreed on some major ideas concerning you and education? Could we put aside what school says you must learn, and agree on important issues of learning just for you? After deciding on the kind of educated person you wish to be, all of us would decide how to reach that goal. Do you think that we could then take these individual plans, combine them, and arrive at a common set of goals for the class? Just like last year, when I didn't know if students could assess themselves, I don't know if we can do this, but I would like to find out.

I would like to examine carefully this whole process to decide if this is something that would help other sixth graders. To do this, I need to record some information. I will probably ask some of you and your parents if I could tape-record your discussions. I would like to know how you reach your decisions. I would also like to set up the video camera and record the evening with everyone here. After that first meeting, I will probably ask you and your parents to do some reflective writing about what we did together. This will help me understand your thinking. I'm unsure where we will go next, but together we will figure this out. I do know that we will have to look at these goals during our assessment time, but I am not sure exactly how we will do this. Again, together we will come up with a plan.

Beginning with our first quarter together, I will be keeping a log to record my thoughts. If you stay after school for the homework time, you will probably see me writing in my journal. This is a time for me to think about the events of the day. I will also do some reflective thinking about our working together on this new process. If there is anything you think I should particularly consider, please let me know. I will also listen to the audiotapes and videotapes. I'd like to know how you and your parents reach your decisions.

I've looked around and found a few books and articles that might help us while we are doing this together. I'll list them here so I won't forget them:

Language, the Learner, and the School by J. Britton.

Teaching and Learning Language Collaboratively by J. Collins.

Freire for the Classroom by Ira Shor.

What Works: Research about Teaching and Learning by the U.S. Department of Education.

Teamwork by C. Larson.

Literacy in Three Metaphors by S. Scribner.

Language and Thought by L. Vygotsky

Working Together to Get Things Done by D. Tjosvold.

In Search of Excellence by T. Peters and R. Waterman, Jr.

The Presentation of Self in Everyday Life by E. Goffman.

There is something about school that is so exciting; there's so much to learn and try. I can't wait to begin. I want to hear your ideas, I want us to know about each other, I want us to share laughter, I want us to create a community. I want to see if we can figure out this new project. Join me, and together, let's see what we can discover.

Love,

Mrs. A.

Notice how Terri opens the seams of her research process, explaining the notetaking, reflecting, and use of outside resources she will be relying on. Her students get a taste of her enthusiasm for understanding what is possible in their classroom and beyond. Out of this research grew a new structure for creating negotiated learning plans, self-evaluative learning, and reporting growth through student-led parent conferences (Austin 1995). The work that Terri and her students did together helped create a model that is being adapted by other students and teachers nationally.

When we invite students to help us understand and learn about the world from their point of view, it enlarges the range of possibilities for our understanding. And if we are open to these new possibilities, we may find unexpected new understanding. This was the case for math teacher Mike

Muir. In a year-long research study, he and his students explored the learning of algebraic concepts as well as their views on math, problem solving, and group work.

Rather than following a predetermined "scope and sequence" from a textbook, Mike and his students established objectives and followed the students' interests and questions toward those objectives. In terms of the curriculum, Mike was delighted with his ability to respond to the students at their points of learning and found he was in better touch with their mathematical understandings. But a darker side was uncovered as well. Mike was saddened to discover that in their eight years of schooling, his students had learned such things as "Math is irrelevant and comes out of a textbook"; "Success in school is measured by correct answers"; and "Kids don't know much and have many weaknesses as students." As Mike reflects in his article "What They Know,"

> I now know what [my students'] questions, curiosities, interests, concerns, and needs are because of the conversations, surveys, letters, and portfolios. These tools have also provided interesting insights into what my students know about learning, school, and mathematics, and I find these insights disturbing. But when we take the perspective of learning from our students about what they know, we need to take into account that they may have learned some things that we wish they had not. It is disturbing, but in the end we can learn from these insights about the realities of school and our instruction, and use them to shape our schools more as we would like them. (1994, 90)

Mike could have reported on half of his story: His students are now more engaged with math and see more connections to their everyday lives. They are more comfortable sharing their understandings and misunderstandings, allowing Mike to be a far more responsive teacher. But the other side is equally important, Mike concludes:

> As much as my students' questions about algebra compelled me to respond by teaching differently than I had in the past, their views on learning and school demand a response. Improved perceptions will come only as we listen to students and change how we teach, what we teach, and how we assess. I need to find ways to insure that our curriculum is well-connected to the students' world. I also need to get learning closer to the kinds of learning students see taking place outside of school. (96)

Like Mike, many teacher-researchers uncover aspects of a "hidden curriculum" with their students. Not only does it open *teachers'* eyes to negative views of learning and schools, but it is equally important for the *students themselves* to name these perceptions, bring them out in the open, and discover ways to make meaningful and lasting changes. When kids have teachers who invite honest responses, and thoughtful ideas and suggestions, they begin to see themselves as genuine partners in the research process, sometimes following and sometimes leading the way.

Jennifer Tendaro (1998) and her eighth-grade girls are a model for the kind of collaborative inquiry that makes a difference in the students' lives and learning and in the larger educational community as well. In a "Write for Your Life" literacy project in the Bronx, New York City, a group of fourteen eighth-grade girls launched a topic of inquiry where they read and conducted complex research on teenage pregnancy, and published a booklet to educate their community. "The forty-page booklet of stories and poems of waiting, warning, survival, and growing up, peppered with facts the girls had learned in their research and even a quiz entitled, 'Are you ready to have sex?' was titled *Our So-Called Teen Years*. It was distributed to students in our school, community health clinics, and local and state politicians, and Write for Your Life classrooms around the country," Jennifer reports. "I marveled at the poise of the girls sitting around me. Through research and reading, they had become knowledgeable not only about teen pregnancy but also about the process of forming a group to study a problem and working toward making it better" (90).

The students learned from their research that there were choices they hadn't imagined—and so did Jennifer. As she read her students' papers and reflections, and looked for patterns in her girls' learning, she discovered further evidence for students conducting self-generated research. She writes, "Every girl in the group, except two, chose to answer a question about her career. Julia asked, What kind of writer do I want to become? Felice's question was, What is the best medical school for me to attend? Yolanda wanted to know what kind of artist she should be, and Zarah's research helped her decide what type of law she might practice someday. One after another, they had discovered possibilities they thought were unattainable, and in the process of gathering reasons for not becoming teenage mothers, their earlier wariness that their futures careened in that direction fell away" (87).

The learning flows into ever-expanding circles. Jennifer and her students learned that they could be powerful forces for change in their own school and community. They published the results of their research, both in *Our So-Called Teen Years* and in Jennifer's (1998) article on their work together, "Worth Waiting For." They also passed the torch to next year's sixth-grade girls with a continued mentorship on the project.

Teacher-researchers like Jennifer and Mike are tackling the toughest questions their students raise and working with their students as genuine collaborators. Rich Kent talks about the benefits he has experienced as he conducts more research with his high school students, inviting an atmosphere of close inquiry: "I want the critical questions asked. I want to think about it and I want to have answers. And I want to be able to say, 'Huh, I don't know. I need to figure that out. I need to look more closely at that.' Now, it all seems so woven together—seamless. It's like my teaching is my research, my research is my teaching, my students are my colleagues. This is the way it is! I can learn so much from this collaboration" (personal communication, 1998).

Besides conducting long-term research projects and investigating the learning in the classroom itself, Rich also enlists his student in assessing broader district curriculum goals. At the end of the year, as a way to look back on the how he and his students had met particular literacy objectives, he made copies of all the written responses to their work, and distributed them to his students for them to analyze: "I had my students do it, and what they did was, in the margins of all my letters they wrote the instructive points from reading and writing. Then I took that information and aligned it with our state learning results, and then put up a sheet that the kids could go through and make check marks about how we matched what our state says we should be doing. It was a riot." The documentation showed that they had surpassed many of the curricular areas expected for that grade level.

When students are our co-researchers, we learn the ways they construct knowledge from their point of view. We also learn how our worlds intersect and how they differ. Working together as co-researchers can enlarge the range of possibilities for our understanding. Children and adolescents can teach us to be less adult-centric. And when they engage in this work with us, it can validate the creative strategies that children have for collecting data and reflecting on its meaning.

The research skills that the children practice as a regular part of their curriculum become part of their repertoire—part of their way of observing the world, interacting with the world, and significantly affecting it. This is true even for very young children. Jill Ostrow, a multiage classroom elementary school teacher, routinely invites her students to conduct research in the classroom (see her Featured Teacher-Researcher article in this chapter). Toward the end of one school year, the school counselor approached Jill about choosing a "child of the month" from her multiage 1–3 classroom. Jill was uncomfortable with the idea of setting one child apart in this way and told the counselor that *all* her children were worthy of being honored for their work that year, but that she'd think about it. As she often does, she brought the issue to the class, and Graham, one of the older children, said, "Oh, I think it should be Maria, 'cause she has improved so much this year." Jill asked Graham to write up a nomination for Maria to send to the counselor, and this is what he wrote:

About Maria

At the starting of the year, Maria was very shy and she couldn't write or read and she wasn't a very good group worker. After a while, we couldn't keep Maria quiet!

And not keep Maria from laughing neither! She's the best first-grade writer that I know and reader that I know. She's a very good group worker, too.

Good-bye.

Graham

This short piece shows Graham's skills as a social researcher. When he writes about Maria, he explains her progress both academically and socially.

He looks at her as a whole person, as someone who is part of the community. You can tell that he values her growth and improvement. This happened near the end of the school year, and over the summer Jill decided to continue to build on the children's abilities to be researchers, incorporating their strengths as observers of the learning that is occurring around them.

In the fall, the returning third graders began their most ambitious project yet—they conducted year-long case study research, with each one observing the growth and learning of one first-grade student over the course of the year. They all had case study notebooks that were stored in one corner of the room, and they kept their data and drawings, their surveys and interviews, in this notebook. This wasn't something that they did every day, or even every week, but there were periodic checkpoints and aspects of the research that they all conducted.

The way they began was very much like many teacher-researchers begin: The eight third graders were asked to take about ten minutes at some time during writing workshop to observe their case studies and write down as much as they could about what they saw, including what people say and do. As the year progressed, they chose other times in the day and areas of the curriculum in which to observe and work with their case study students. The kids became very skilled at taking these notes. Here are Lisa's notes on her case study, Katie, taken in February:

> Today Katie is doing her research. She is on her bibliography! Katie is thinking of what to draw. Katie said, "I want to draw a bunny, but I don't know how to draw one." Then she ate a bit of her apple and picked up her pencil and started to draw. When she was finished, she exclaimed, "I should write what it is so that people who read this will know what it is!" Then she wrote bunny. She sort of likes research, but she likes writing workshop better. Katie gave me a short explanation of why she likes writing workshop better than research, but before she could answer, Dave said, "Because you get to write whatever you want." "True! and you get to name it!" Then I asked, "Katie, is there any other way why you like writing workshop better than research?" And she replied, "Um, that's pretty hard." Now Katie is moving on to her project. Then I asked her, "What are you going to make for your project?" and she said, "I have to think!" Katie thinks she has improved a lot since the beginning of the year. Katie thinks that she's improved in reading more than anything this year.

The third graders who conducted year-long case studies examined all their data in June in order to write their findings for a real audience: their case studies' parents. While they found it a challenging task to condense their findings to the format of an informative letter to parents, they rose to the challenge. Lisa focused on Katie's improvement, sharing information about Katie's learning that gave her parents a picture of their daughter's active problem-solving skills:

Dear Mr. and Mrs. Molloy:

Katie has improved *a lot* since the beginning of the year!!! *Especially* in her writing. In the beginning of the year, her stories were just a picture and a tiny bit of writing! But now her stories are lots of writing and her pictures are good, too!

In the beginning of the year, she was reading just pictures. Now, she just finished a book called *All About Stacy*, which is a chapter book.

For problem solving, Katie doesn't just sit and twiddle her thumbs. She gets up and gets 10's strips and 1's squares to solve the problem. She also uses pictures.

The following are what you might want to do with Katie or have her do over the summer:

- Have her read for ten or fifteen minutes each night.
- Give her problems to solve (like problems that include math, art, and science, not just straight math facts!).
- Have her write for ten or fifteen minutes each night.

Sincerely,

Lisa

The researcher of Katie

Another third grader, Renee, wanted to show Carlin's growth, so she attached some samples from "the beginning" and "now." She was also honest about Carlin's needs as well as improvement:

Dear Mrs. Singer:

Here are some things that Carlin did in the beginning of the year . . . (see attached), and some stuff she has done recently (see attached).

As you can see, she has improved in writing. As I was writing this letter, I was showing TJ her work from the beginning of the year. He could barely read it. Then I showed him the other one and he read it perfectly.

In reading, the first thing she was reading was *Lulu's First Day of Witch School*. Now she's reading *Peanut Butter and Jelly*. I was reading that yesterday! Even at the beginning of the year, she was a really good reader.

In problems, sometimes she just sits around and does nothing (not to be mean or anything). But, on the other hand, she goes and gets 10's strips and solves the problem.

A thing you could do this summer is maybe give her some math problems or buy some books for her to read at night. And encourage her to write or do some observational drawings.

From Renee

Jill's case study research project with her students also enabled the researchers to think again about their own learning and work habits. There are multiple effects any time you enlist students as co-researchers. Teachers needn't begin with an elaborate year-long research project. There are ways to easily integrate data collection and analysis with students into the teaching and research you are doing now. Here are some simple strategies for getting started:

Invite your students into your research process right from the start, so they can help you frame your research question and define terms.   Just as Terri asked for her students' ideas at the onset of her research into student-led parent conferences, other teacher-researchers are finding ways to include their students' insights and perspectives even when their questions are at the "wondering" stage. When Maureen Miletta (1994) began her research into her interage 4–5–6 grades program, she found it essential to include the children's perspective. "We constantly questioned our practice, collected data, and modified the curriculum based on what we discovered" (166). Maureen writes that her views as a researcher became multidimensional when her students' perceptions were encouraged; they became true partners in research.

Kimberly Campbell, currently the teaching principal of Riverdale High School, enlisted middle and high school students as part of a team to create the vision for their new high school. These adolescents were involved in all stages of the planning, from creating a mission statement to meeting with the architects on building designs, to helping craft portfolio guidelines and interview questions for prospective teachers. It's little wonder that the resulting Riverdale High School is a school staffed by teacher-researchers and dedicated to continued schoolwide research.

Enlist students' help in keeping class records.   Daily class records can provide rich data, and our students can be an enormous resource in helping us collect it. In Ruth's graduate course "Language, Literacy, and Culture," students take turns recording the daily events that occur during class through the rotating chore of "Daily Class Historian," so that at the end of the term the class has a narrative class history reflecting the multiple perspectives of all the class members. Much younger students can also take regular minutes, as the students in Jill Ostrow's multiage 1–3 classroom do. During their Reading Workshop literature group discussions, they take turns recording the books each participant is reading and what she has talked about (see Figure 10.1).

Even five-year-olds can use visual representations to record their observations. In Jane Doan and Penny Chase's multiage K–2 classroom, the youngest students record their observations of classmates through sketches when it is their turn to be a class notetaker during whole-group activities.

When analyzing data, include kid-generated categories.   Student-generated categories give us new possibilities for viewing the data. Adolescents

Figure 10.1 Student's Summary of Book Talk

JESSICAS stoRey WAS
CAIID SARAhs UNICORN it's Abaut A
UNICORN WHY HAS A MAGIC
horn AND SARAH is the
uNiCCRNs ARAND

GEREK'S stcRY is CAIID AmY
Goes fishinG heR DAD is tAliM
heR A stoRY AbCut MUSSKiNS
AND they LiVD iN AbCMP
iN the WATeR.

AShleY stoRY iS CAIID
bRiGit the BAD AND Ashleys
CN the LAS GRAY CApteR AND
its CAIID MAGiC.
AND I!AM AT
the PArt where her DCA
DiSCPiRD.

from Noble High School in Berwick, Maine, spread their data on the floor and created categories from their written reflection (Appleby et al. 1996). These students are not unique in organizing their data in unusual ways. Seventh-grade teacher Carol Dennis enlisted her students' help in a home writing survey (see Figure 10.2). Her students displayed their findings on bar graphs, reflecting surprising patterns, such as one child's discovery that

Figure 10.2 Student's Data Collection Form

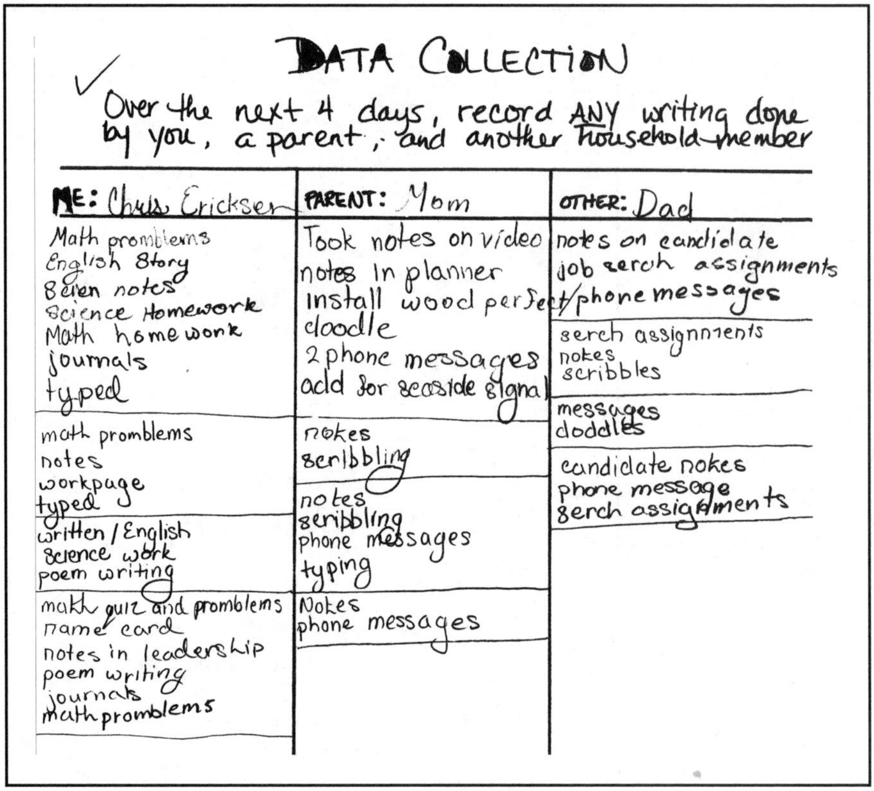
DATA COLLECTION

Over the next 4 days, record ANY writing done by you, a parent, and another household member

ME: Chris Ericksen	PARENT: Mom	OTHER: Dad
Math promblems English Story Seien notes Science Homework Math homework journals typed	Took notes on video notes in planner install wood perfect doodle 2 phone messages add for seaside signal	notes on candidate job serch assignments phone messages
math promblems notes workpage typed	nokes scribbling	serch assignments nokes scribbles
written / English Science work poem writing	notes scribbling phone messages typing	messages doddles
math quiz and promblems name card notes in leadership poem writing journals math promblems	Nokes phone messages	candidate nokes phone message serch assignments

her family's writing was seldom anything they "want to" engage in (see Figure 10.3).

Encourage students to reflect on their own teaching in the classroom. In many classrooms, the line between teacher and researcher often blurs as more and more children take on the roles of coaches and facilitators with other learners. In Jill Ostrow's multiage primary classroom, Stephanie and Lisa thought several of their classmates would be helped by learning what they called "the e lesson." They planned the lesson, carried it out, and shared their anecdotal records with Jill: "With the e lesson, it went pretty good. We had Fiona, Kelly, Tara, and Charles. With Fiona, she got three wrong, but she really tried hard and paid attention. With Kelly, she got them all right, and paid attention. With Tara, she got them all right and does not need to work it anymore, and knew them right away. With Charles, he got them all right, and he struggled a little." Their anecdotal field notes became part of the teaching record of the class—part of the fund of data that helped the entire class understand the learning that had occurred.

In Beverly Cleary's novel *Ramona the Brave* (1975), her seven-year-old

Figure 10.3 Student's Summary of Results

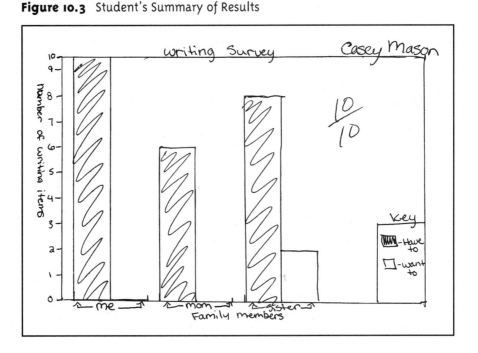

heroine asks, "Why don't grown-ups know that children think important thoughts?" Teacher-researchers know that our students think important thoughts, and that they have creative strategies for researching, imagining, collaborating, and theorizing. We all benefit when we encourage them to share their insights with us as co-researchers.

RESEARCH WORKSHOP

Making Meaning

Richard Kent

Near the end of our time together at Bread Loaf, Dixie Goswami introduced a simple yet revealing exercise to help us look more closely at our time together. I use this activity in my classes so that my students will see our purpose more clearly. Truly, this exercise gives form and order to what can be fuzzy or even chaotic thinking. It is a way to deepen and extend our analysis of what's been learned.

"Making Meaning" may focus on any aspect of one's class. Among other issues, I have had my young colleagues write about Room 109 English, portfolios, and themselves as students. Anything works.

Here's Dawn making meaning of "portfolios." I lead my students through each step, giving them about a minute for each of the first three.

The fourth step usually takes about five to eight minutes. [With younger students, teachers might try just steps 1 and 2, or have students work in pairs or teams to construct the brief paragraphs in step 4.]

Step One

Using single words, name some of what portfolios are to you:

frustrating

work

journal

nerve-wracking

balance

books

write

challenge

think

full

papers

edit

Step Two

Name the opposite of those terms to create a dialectic. This is important because reconciling opposites or reasoning contrary arguments help us arrive at the truth (there are always two sides to things). As always, teaching, learning, and living come back to balance, the year-long theme of our class.

frustrating	enjoyable
work	play
journal	empty page
nerve-wracking	relaxing
balance	unbalanced
books	television
write	illiterate
challenge	easy
think	stupid
full	empty

Step Three

Place some of the opposing words in a true sentence about portfolios:

"Putting together a portfolio can be nerve-wracking, but it is relaxing when we finish."

"You really have to think when making up a portfolio; it is not a job for stupid people."

"Although having portfolios instead of tests seems easy, it's really more of a challenge."

Step Four

In the final step, we use strict form to help us make meaning. Write one paragraph about portfolios consisting of five sentences using the following guidelines:

1. A five-word statement
2. A question
3. Two independent clauses combined by a semicolon
4. A sentence with an introductory phrase
5. A two-word statement

Portfolios are better than tests. Why are they better? We have control over what we learn; we're responsible for our education. Before I began my portfolio this year, I thought it would be easy. Ha ha.

Here are a few paragraphs I found particularly interesting about our class and portfolios:

"This class requires responsibility. Why can't I just relax for a while? I know that I can get good grades; I have to apply myself. When I figured out what to do, I improved. About time."—*Travis M.*

"In this class everybody is always working and I am always sleeping. How important is this class? Once I came in; I took a nap. Ever since, Kent's been on my back. I'm lost."—*Gene C.*

"This class learns about independence. Are you ready to work independently? I worked my hardest; I got credit for my effort. When I started this class, I was worried. Not anymore!"—*Lisa G.*

"Making Meaning" helps my students see the full picture. This activity reveals a certain truth about an issue or idea; what's more, this truth may not have been recognized by my students without the formula. From developing a balanced essay to working out life issues, this exercise helps my students think more completely.

The Trickle-Down Effect of Teacher Research: Students Adopting a Research Stance

JoAnn Portalupi

One early winter day, Faith and Vicki, two fourth-grade students, came bounding into class having just visited another classroom's writing share session. A colleague and I had swapped a small number of writers during this aspect of our workshops as a way to cross-pollinate the nature of talk and thinking in our individual classrooms. I was anxious to hear what these first two students thought, but they didn't stop to talk. Instead they ran straight to the writing center to grab paper and pencil. I watched as Faith huddled over Vicki while she jotted a list of suggestions for the third-grade classroom they had just visited. On the paper were four comments:

> Don't just say, "I liked the story." What about the story did you like?
>
> Make sure to tell what you want us to listen for before you read.
>
> Make sure to tell whether it's a finished piece of writing.
>
> When you say something, make sure you tell why you say it.
>
> Make yourself clear.

These two students had uncovered the underlying structure of our own writing share sessions, not to mention, some of my unspoken teaching intentions. Their observations became the topic of discussion the next time we shared writing together. On that day, we took a critical look at what was working well in our share time, and the ways in which we could make it better.

Teachers who research are highly engaged learners in their own classrooms. The same is true for students. The researcher's stance involves an attentiveness to the happenings around you and a curiosity to look beneath the obvious to understand what is really going on. Invite students to embody this stance and the classroom becomes a research community that focuses its camera on itself. We can wake students up to the questions they have about life in the classroom, teach them how to systematically gather information, and then collaboratively speculate on what the data reveal. As we do this, our teaching shifts to meet the intersecting needs of curriculum and students, and students become invested members in the larger community of the classroom.

Learning to Look and Listen

What happens when we teach our students to think like researchers? We give them tools to take responsibility for their own learning, since researching quickly takes on the persona of teaching. When Graves and his colleagues began asking students at Atkinson Elementary research questions about writing, the questions revealed themselves to be teaching questions. Ask, How did you choose that topic to write about? and students discover their own strategies for making choices. Ask, What did you do when you finished writing? and students attend to the ways in which they cycle back into a draft of writing.

True questions, questions worth pursuing, arise daily in classrooms. They rattle in the heads of teachers and students alike. One way to encourage students to pay attention to their questions is by sharing ours. I was curious about the self-identified problems fourth graders attend to in their writing. Students saw my interest in this question when I occasionally made it the "question of the day." On these days I began conferences by asking students to identify any problem they might be working on. I'd jot down their responses and later share the data with the class. Hearing the student-identified problems helped others read their own drafts more critically. This led us into discussion about the various ways writers solved their problems. In this simple manner I was modeling how to learn from a question.

Good research involves knowing where to find the answers to your questions. Donald Graves calls this "knowing where to place the bucket." When Brent, a small freckle-faced boy, wondered why his science group never finished tasks on time, I suggested a way to study the question. He took running time records of his group's activities over the next few days. The records showed how long the group took to negotiate tasks, keeping them from having ample time to devote to their projects. The written records helped them consider their actions, and they were able to improve their working habits.

Data Take the Shape of Their Container

There are many considerations about how to gather data. Which slice of the classroom falls under the eye? Are observations recorded with a video recorder or paper and pencil? Notetaking strategies may vary: some allow you to gather information quickly as well as facilitate the reading of the data. These strategies are also simple enough for young children to use.

When I wanted to study talk in whole-class share sessions, I used various methods of recording. Tape and video recording allowed me to make detailed transcripts. Other times I kept a log of just the teacher talk (questions and responses). One strategy was particularly helpful for student research later in the year. By making a diagram of the physical setting of our share session I could tally all comments and render an interesting picture of the pattern of talk in the group. This snapshot made it easy for us to review the data together.

When we looked at those diagrams, a cluster of questions emerged. Why was so much talk directed toward the teacher (T in Figure 10.4)? What did it mean that most talk came from students sitting close to the writer (see Figure 10.5)? If children sat in different places, would the pattern of talk change? What was missing in the lack of cross-talk between students?

Later, when our classroom became chaotic during writing workshop a child offered to map the traffic in the room. Using the same strategy, she made a visual representation of our class in motion. As we looked at the map together, we talked about the texture of the classroom during workshop: Where were the quiet corners? Which areas attracted movement and consequently more noise? We saw ways in which the newly changed layout of our room contributed to noise and were guided as we redesigned the classroom to work more effectively.

Often our research tools unknowingly promote learning agendas. When Lisa Lenz, a primary teacher from Caldwell, New Jersey, videotaped her students' oral performances of poems, she did not intend it to be a teaching tool. She wanted to record her students' performances. But when her first and second graders reviewed the tapes, they saw them as a way to critique and improve their performances. Using the videotape as one tool, they honed their readings for an audience. Eventually her students came to describe three stages of learning to read a poem well. Stage one is the time during which a child is getting to know the words. Stage two is when the child begins to consider the audience and works to put feelings into the

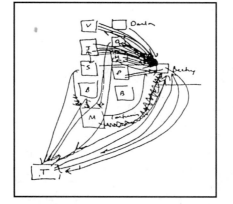

Figure 10.4 Diagram of Classroom Data

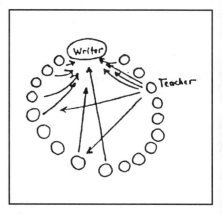

Figure 10.5 Diagram of Classroom Data

reading. Videotaping helps move the student to the final stage three reading, where now she can speak it well enough to go public. Lenz's first and second graders learned to pay attention from living with a teacher who paid attention.

As Lenz's first and second graders critiqued each other's performances, they were collectively reading the "data" of their classroom. In a similar spirit, sending Vicki and Faith across the hall to participate in another share session invited conversations leading to new practices. In each of these instances, students and teachers together form a community that raises questions, gathers information, and creates new understandings about teaching and learning.

featured **TEACHER RESEARCHER**

Partners in Research

Jill Ostrow

I was nearing the completion of my book when I experienced writer's block as I contemplated the lead to my introduction. Instead of shutting down the computer in utter frustration, I decided to consult the expert on leads: David. David is a third grader in my class of six-to-nine-year-olds. He is an exceptional writer who not only writes outstanding leads to his pieces of writing but also teaches small mini-classes to other children on the art of writing a good lead. I called David and explained my dilemma, and he immediately thought of a perfect story I could use to start the introduction to my book.

I never feel like I need find time to "conduct" my research, because my research is based upon observations I make of the children I teach. Yet they are more than just the subjects of the research I do, they are my partners. I call upon the children I learn with constantly as experts for my research. My kids know that I observe, question, and apply what I have learned from them. They are quick to jump in and share their insights as well. Recently, our classroom community experienced a tremendous loss when Danny, a very special member of our class, moved away. Danny acquired oral language at age six and many of his social skills were that of a typical three-year-old. We had, as a class, been observing Danny's growth over the last three years. He was very important to us and his move was traumatic. I was wanting to explain to Danny's new teachers just why his absence was so difficult for us. I was having trouble putting everything I wanted to say into words. I wanted to get across the amount of respect and love the children in my class felt for him. I decided to ask the kids to write the letters. I invited them to write a letter describing Danny to his new teachers. The kids were able not only to write what I was wanting to get across but to contribute many aspects I would have left out.

Besides asking the kids directly to help me with my research, they are always present in my thinking. Every time I "test" my philosophy of how children learn, I am using their responses and observing their behaviors. I was observing their responses during our study of the Civil War. Some educators disagree with our choice to study the Civil War with first, second, and third graders. Some argue the point that young children aren't yet ready to transfer historical information to their daily lives, thus making this type of study irrelevant to their curriculum. Yet, months after our study, we were looking at a calendar and saw that April 4 was the anniversary of the assassination of Martin Luther King, Jr. The discussion that followed was not only informative; it proved to me just how much learning they had gained because of that historical study. They had transferred not only specific information about the war and that time period but also the whole idea of racism and empathy. Now, we are studying the future, and the kids want to "fix" the mistakes of the past and present, and create a violence-free and racism-free future. They are also thinking about ways in which the people of this peaceful future will remember important civil rights leaders.

I include my children not only in the research process but in the actual presentation of the research as well. During the spring of 1994, six children presented with me at a National Council of Teachers of English (NCTE) regional conference. During our school open house, the children explain the philosophy of the classroom by showing slides of the classroom and answering questions from parents. I often ask them to write about topics I am researching in order to have their written perspectives.

When my book was complete, I asked Tessia to read through it before I sent it to the publisher. Tessia has been in my class for the last three years; not only is she aware of my research but she is quite interested in it. She proofread much of the book and offered her comments. *Research* is an everyday word in our room; it is also an everyday occurrence. I don't need to make time for my research because it happens naturally all day. The children see themselves as researchers as much as I consider myself one. Without the closeness, trust, and willingness of the kids, I would have *no* research.

Epilogue
Why Not Teacher Research?

The problem is the solution. Everything is a positive resource; it is up to us to work out how we may use it as such.

Bill Mollison

Some years ago, a friend of ours who is a kindergarten teacher told us the story of setting up a dramatic play area in her classroom. She decided the theme of the area for the first month would be a shoe store. The teacher threw herself into preparing the area for the children—she borrowed real foot-measuring tools from a local shoe store, got shelves from another outlet, and even had twenty boxes of old shoes, in a variety of sizes, neatly displayed.

During the first play period, the teacher told students they could do whatever they wanted in the play area. A large group eagerly congregated around the shelves and decided they would throw a pretend birthday party for a friend. They upended the foot-measuring device to use it as a cake stand and began to make greeting cards out of the shoe order forms laid out for their use. Their teacher gently, and then not so gently, began to nudge them toward other possibilities for the play area, with prompts like, "Gee, look at all these shoes! What else could you do here besides have a birthday party?" The kids blithely ignored her. After the birthday girl blew out the candles on the imaginary cake, each child one by one gave her a present to open. Not surprisingly, every present turned out to be a box of old shoes.

We think of this story when we think of the learning we've experienced in the past few years through working with teacher-researchers. We continue to have our notions of what teacher research is, or should be, upended by the actual work of teacher-researchers.

When we look at the history of our work with teacher-researchers, it's easy to see it being something like that play area shoe store. For years, we have presented research strategies with what we thought were open-ended purposes, encouraging teachers to develop and use research strategies for their own needs, but teacher-researchers haven't really given us what we expected. This text is full of the surprises we've experienced in learning from teacher-researchers. What we thought was a pretty open-ended conception of research in our early days was actually more constrained then we realized, or outside the realm of interest or need for many teacher-researchers. For example, we find that for many teachers writing up research in any kind of traditional or nontraditional way is still a struggle. Teachers tend to concentrate on immediate, local needs for their research, even as we urge them to seek larger audiences so that teacher research can have more of an impact on our academic world.

The flip-side image is also true. Teacher-researchers come to university folks with grown-up needs, concerns, and expectations for their research and how we might help them. And in our eagerness to help them, we might still be staying within a pretty narrow conception of what it means to go public with research. In other words, teachers might come to us with quite sophisticated and unique purposes for going public that demand diverse and creative approaches to going public—and university educators seem to be handing them box after box of old shoes.

After the preschool teacher got over her initial disappointment in the choices of the children, she was amazed at the creativity and learning going on in her classroom. We, too, have had to get over disappointment as we've seen some of our hard work and assumptions about research challenged by teachers. More than anything, it's made us shift our thinking—from what university researchers can teach teachers, to what we might learn in the future from teachers as the teacher research movement continues to grow. In the end, what endures is our wonder and respect at the ways teachers integrate research into their lives.

At the heart of good teaching—and good teacher research—is the learning and growth of our students themselves. As state legislatures one by one take on the task of challenging all of us—public school and university teachers alike—to account for the uses of our time and to teach to mandated, highly specific, and standardized curricula, there is a new sense of urgency about finding ways to show what happens when teachers search out new materials and tinker with their curriculum, design new challenges and base their teaching decisions on the data they collect from and with their students. Teacher-researchers can show that our inquiries matter at all levels.

In her recent book, *The Right to Learn: A Blueprint for Creating Schools That Work,* Linda Darling-Hammond sounds an eloquent call for students to engage in a variety of kinds of thinking through inquiry. She argues that the best way to achieve this is to have teachers who engage in the same kind of systematic inquiry themselves provide the learning that apprenticeships foster. We need to create these "new schools," she contends, because

traditional schools provide few incentives to support the efforts of teachers who are willing to look for the answers to the knottiest problems of teaching and learning, and who want to work with the students for whom attainment in education is especially risky and labor-intensive. Instead, bureaucratic schools' incentives encourage teachers to depersonalize and standardize instruction so as to comfortably handle large numbers of students in short blocks of time; to use pedagogical strategies that are as simple, self-contained, and routine as possible; and to avoid teaching the neediest students by moving to higher tracks or transferring out to more attractive schools as they gain seniority. (1998, 169)

Darling-Hammond urges us to work to create schools that provide genuine incentives for teachers—incentives that support the intrinsic rewards that come from increased success with their students and excitement in the possibilities that exist in creating their school environments and curriculum. Many of the teacher-researchers you have met through the pages of this book are working to create restructured schools with the kind of supports that will energize their work and their students' learning. These teachers' advice points us to what is possible in schools.

High on their list of priorities is time. When asked what she would use funding for if there were no constraints placed on it, Terri Austin immediately responded: "I'd buy time! Time to visit other teachers' classrooms, time to write, time to buy a colleague some sub time so we could meet and discuss our data, time to plan together with my teaching team." Other teacher-researchers echo the need for more—or at least different—uses of time.

And they have proposals for how we might accomplish this. Terri, Rich Kent, and Linda Christensen suggest that professional organizations—and school districts, too—widen the parameters of what can be requested in grant budgets to include buying time for substitute teachers, for extended writing, and for visiting other classrooms. The Clayton Action Research Collaborative advocates block scheduling and creative student programming to create several-hour blocks for joint teacher planning, staff development, and faculty governance. The International High School provides a "clubs" period for students for a full afternoon once a week. This time is used for faculty development—staff-guided learning, not training determined by someone else (Darling-Hammond 1998).

Karen Gallas suggests a strengthened partnership between schools and the university:

Teacher-researchers should be part of the university structure, and university teachers should be part of the classroom teaching structure, so that you have this rotating door, in which people go in and out of the classroom. You go in for a couple of years, come out ready to write and teach. I also think there are some structures that could be developed so that teacher research is seen as a different sort of endeavor and the school week may allow a teacher to have a day out of the classroom specifically to work on writing. (MacKay 1999)

Indiana University Professor Jerry Harste echoes Karen Gallas's call for new strategies for supporting teacher-researchers, working together so that we are all "connected to the profession differently," as he puts it. "One of the things researchers have to do is position themselves—and understand that position. I encourage teachers to make presentations, share their in-process thinking long before they ever think they're ready. It's important support to help them go to conferences, make sure they are on programs, and also to alter power positions, showing through my own process and behavior that I'm vulnerable" (personal communication).

If there is one thing K–12 teachers and university professors will always share, it is that need to show that our work is relevant and to bring it to a larger audience. One of our biggest struggles as university professors assisting teachers is to respect the different agendas teachers have for presenting their research to wider audiences, especially when that presentation doesn't involve any writing. But whether through conference presentations, discussions with colleagues, or the written word in op-ed articles or reports of inquiry, we need to get our work out to other teachers. Teachers respond well to teacher research studies because they are peppered with anecdotes from the classroom that connect with their own experience.

Teacher research challenges the notion that research reporting needs to be dry, distant, and filled with jargon. Those of us who choose to write our research can learn a lot about writing quality by examining classic studies by teacher-researchers. Best-selling teacher research studies like Jeanne Henry's *If Not Now* (1995), Vivian Paley's *Wally's Stories* (1981), and Jeffrey Wilhelm's *You Gotta BE the Book* (1997) are great reads—they are as well-crafted as fine novels in the way teachers, students, and events are portrayed.

Teacher research challenges the writing conventions in much education research, but we also believe that it has the potential to be the needed bridge between practitioners and university researchers. Teachers are demanding, in large part through their wallets, a research writing style and tone different than the scholarship that has dominated the research literature for decades.

At the same time, as teachers begin to complete their own research studies, they often need a new language to describe what they are seeing. What teachers scoffed at as "jargon" before they began their research sometimes becomes useful new terms to describe learning events. They see their classrooms in a new light, and the language of research in a new way, after trying to accurately describe their own findings.

Part of the future work of developing research strategies and resources for teacher-researchers involves understanding the needs of teacher researchers better, like those you have come to know through this book. We are also thinking hard about how to channel our energies away from helping teachers write up their work for academic journals, and toward more political, proactive vehicles. Teacher-researchers are coming to us sometimes with desperate needs, as they see the good work of curriculum reform undone by district and statewide mandates. We feel like we are in the midst of a shift right now, and teacher-researchers are helping us pivot toward a broader view of audiences for research at all levels.

Anne Lamott (1994), in considering writing, could just as easily be admonishing us about research when she says, "Writing is about learning to pay attention and to communicate what is going on. Now, if you ask me, what's going on is that we're all up to *here* in it, and probably the most important thing is that we not yell at one another" (97).

We are always "up to *here* in it" when we're talking about research, no matter what the educational setting. The battles between different researchers can be acrimonious and not always respectful. We are still often immersed in what Deborah Tannen (1998) calls "the argument culture," setting up one method against another, and not acknowledging that teachers and university researchers might have wholly different purposes for their work. This was evident to Glenda Bissex, one of the pioneers in teacher research, when she applied for her first college teaching position. She recounts this experience:

> "And what does that prove?" one faculty member challenged me during an interview for my first full-time college teaching job. I had just finished telling him about my dissertation, a longitudinal study of my young son's writing and reading development. Nobody on my dissertation committee had asked me that question, nor had I asked it myself in all the years I collected and pored through data, searching for patterns. I was confronted with an alien view from which—I too keenly grasped—my research appeared worthless. . . .
>
> What had I proven? I hadn't set out with a hypothesis to test in order to prove something to somebody. I'd started out with a curiosity whetted by transcripts of children's talk. . . . I was fascinated by what I was seeing. I guess I was so busy learning that I didn't worry about proving anything. Here was this wonderful growth unfolding in front of my eyes, and I wanted to truly see it. I wanted to probe it in places so I could know more than was on the surface. I was constantly looking for patterns as I reviewed piles of writings, tape recordings, and notes. Again and again, I asked, "What does this mean?" . . . As I look at it now, the question of what I proved appears thin and pale and irrelevant beside the richness of all the meanings I discovered, of all that I learned. I wouldn't have had any trouble answering the question, "And what did you learn?" (1996, 142)

Bissex goes on to explain the fundamental differences in aims of teacher-researchers that lead to miscommunication in research discussions:

> The word *research* suggests the researcher is "proving" something, frequently to someone else. . . . While *research* has the right literal meaning—to look again—its connotations may be wrong for what teachers are doing. We are not researchers in other people's classrooms, looking for proofs and generalizable truths, but reflective practitioners in our own classrooms,

searching for insights that will help us understand and improve our practice. That does not exclude us from finding generalizable truths, although we may not know when we have found them. (1996, 143)

We want to close with the idea that our work with teacher-researchers hasn't proved anything. Like Glenda Bissex, we are always brought up short when we're asked for concrete proofs of why this work matters. We still haven't found those generalizable truths about what teacher research is or will become, but we continue to learn so much.

What we've always seen in our work with teacher-researchers is a fundamental kindness—teachers care about listening to students, their colleagues, and their gut instincts about how their research agendas need to change. And it is this kindness and concern that will continue to be an antidote to the hostility and tension sometimes present as researchers with widely different values and beliefs tackle many tough issues of learning, diversity, and change in classrooms. As teachers take on the role of researchers, we hope their guidance can help us all write better, stronger, and wider about how schools need to change. We all need a voice in making these changes, and teacher research often brings the freshest perspective to old problems.

Most of all, teacher research is a gift. To the profession, helping us change the way we see old problems and bringing us new solutions. To research communities, showing us new research strategies and how to take risks in writing up research. To ourselves, reminding us of the energy and passion in learning that made us teachers in the first place. It is a gift that we're all working hard for, like the unmerited grace Annie Dillard (1989) writes of: "At its best, the sensation of writing is that of any unmerited grace. It is handed to you, but only if you look for it. You search, you break your heart, your back, your brain, and then—and only then—it is handed to you" (54).

No one in these pages has lied to you and told you mixing teaching and research would be easy. The words of teachers in this book include many images of broken hearts and sore brains, but all in the larger context of gratitude for how research is transforming their professional lives.

No matter what questions you may be asking about your teaching and students, we challenge you to answer with a question: Why not teacher research? Why not learn, as the teachers throughout these pages have, to find a place for research in your life? Research may never give you all the answers you crave, but it may help you find joy in living the questions.

Bibliography

Professional Literature

Alinsky, Saul. 1971. *Rules for Radicals: A Pragmatic Primer for Realistic Radicals.* New York: Random House.

Allen, Janet. 1995. *It's Never Too Late: Leading Adolescents to Lifelong Literacy.* Portsmouth, NH: Heinemann.

Ansay, A. Manette. 1996. *Sister.* New York: Morrow.

Anzaldua, Gloria. 1987. *Borderlands/La Frontera: The New Mestiza.* San Francisco: Spinsters/Aunt Lute.

Anzul, Margaret. 1993. "Exploring Literature with Children Within a Transactional Framework." In *Journeying: Children Responding to Literature,* ed. K. Holland, R. Hungerford, and S. Ernst, 187–203. Portsmouth, NH: Heinemann.

Appleby, Jon, Joanne Delaney, and Students from Noble High School. 1996. "Learning on the Way to the Imp." *Teacher Research* 4, 1: 69–84.

Arbus, Diane. 1972. *Diane Arbus.* Millerton, NY: Aperture.

Ashton-Warner, Sylvia. 1963. *Teacher.* New York: Simon and Schuster.

Atwell, Nancie. 1987. *In the Middle: Writing, Reading, and Learning with Adolescents.* Portsmouth, NH: Boynton/Cook.

———. 1991. *Coming to Know: Writing to Learn in the Intermediate Grades.* Portsmouth, NH: Heinemann.

———. 1996. "Wonderings to Pursue: The Writing Teacher as Researcher." Keynote address, fall writing conference, New Hampshire (October).

Austin, Terri. 1994a. "The Well-Dressed Alaska Teacher-Researcher." *Teacher Research* 2, 1: 66–80.

———. 1994b. "Travel Together in Trust." ` 1, 2: 122–127.

———. 1995. *Changing the View: Student-Led Parent Conferences.* Portsmouth, NH: Heinemann.

Barbieri, Maureen. 1995. *Sounds from the Heart.* Portsmouth, NH: Heinemann.

Bateson, Mary Catherine. 1994. *Peripheral Visions: Learning Along the Way.* New York: HarperCollins.

Belenky, Mary, B. Clinchy, N. Goldberger, and Jill Tarule. 1986. *Women's Ways of Knowing: The Development of Self, Voice, and Mind.* New York: Basic Books.

Bellack, A. 1966. *The Language of the Classroom.* New York: Teachers College Press.

Berg, Elizabeth. 1993. *Durable Goods.* New York: Random House.

———. 1994. *Talk Before Sleep.* New York: Random House.

———. 1995. *Range of Motion.* New York: Random House.

———. 1997. *The Pull of the Moon.* New York: Random House.

Bernstein, Leonard. 1981. *The Unanswered Question: Six Talks at Harvard.* Cambridge, MA: Harvard University Press.

Berthoff, Ann. 1987. "The Teacher as Researcher." In *Reclaiming the Classroom: Teacher Research as an Agency for Change,* ed. D. Goswami and P. Stillman. Upper Montclair, NJ: Boynton/Cook.

Best, J. W. 1977. *Research in Education.* Englewood Cliffs, NJ: Prentice-Hall.

Bintz, William. 1997. "Seeing Through Different Eyes: Using Photography as a Research Tool." *Teacher Research* 5, 1: 29–46.

Birnbaum, J., and Janet Emig. 1991. "Case Study." In *Handbook of Research on Teaching the English Language Arts,* ed. J. Flood, J. Jensen, D. Lapp, and J. R. Squire. New York: Macmillan.

Bisplinghoff, Betty, and JoBeth Allen. 1998. *Engaging Teachers.* Portsmouth, NH: Heinemann.

Bissex, Glenda. 1980. *GNYS AT WRK: A Child Learns to Write and Read.* Cambridge, MA: Harvard University Press.

———. 1987. "Why Case Studies?" In *Seeing for Ourselves: Case Study Research by Teachers of Writing,* ed. G. Bissex and R. Bullock. Portsmouth, NH: Heinemann.

———. 1996. *Partial Truths: A Memoir and Essays on Reading, Writing, and Researching.* Portsmouth, NH: Heinemann.

Bissex, Glenda, and Richard Bullock. 1987. *Seeing for Ourselves: Case Study Research by Teachers of Writing.* Portsmouth, NH: Heinemann.

Bolker, Joan. 1997. "A Room of One's Own Is Not Enough" In *The Writers' Home Companion,* ed. J. Bolker, 183–199. New York: Owl Books.

Bolster, A. S., Jr. 1983. "Toward a More Effective Model of Research on Teaching." *Harvard Educational Review* 53, 3: 294–308.

Bomer, Randy. 1995. *Time for Meaning: Crafting Literate Lives in Middle and High School.* Portsmouth, NH: Heinemann.

Brady, Suzanne, and Suzanne Jacobs. 1994. *Mindful of Others: Teaching Children to Teach.* Portsmouth, NH: Heinemann.

Branscombe, Amanda, Dixie Goswami, and Jeffrey Schwartz. 1992. *Students Teaching, Teachers Learning.* Upper Montclair, NJ: Boynton/Cook.

Britton, James. 1970. *Language and Learning.* London: Penguin Books.

Brown, Lynn, Carol Gilligan, and Amy Sullivan. 1992. *Meeting at the Crossroads: Women's Psychology and Girls' Development.* Cambridge, MA: Harvard University Press.

Bruner, Jerome. 1987. *Actual Minds, Possible Worlds.* Cambridge, MA: Harvard University Press.

Burton, F. R. 1991. "Teacher-Researcher Projects: An Elementary Schoolteacher's Perspective." In *Handbook of Research on Teaching the English Language Arts,* ed. J. Flood, J. Jensen, D. Lapp, and J. R. Squire. New York: Macmillan.

Calfee, Richard, and M. J. Chambliss. 1991. "The Design of Empirical Research." In *Handbook of Research on Teaching the English Language Arts,* ed. J. Flood, J. Jensen, D. Lapp, and J. R. Squire. New York: Macmillan.

Calkins, Lucy M. 1983. *Lessons from a Child: On Teaching and Learning Writing.* Portsmouth, NH: Heinemann.

Campbell, Kimberly. 1997a. "Celebrating 'Conscious Deliberate Thoughtfulness': An Interview with Deborah Meier." *Teacher Research* 5, 1: 11–25.

———. 1997b. "Survival, Sustenance, and Making Sense: Journals as Tools of the Trade." *Teacher Research* 5, 1: 146–149.

———. 1997c. "You're Invited." *Teacher Research* 1, 2: 57–62.

———. In press. "From Teacher Researcher to Administrator Researcher." *Teacher Research.*

Cazden, Courtney. 1988. *Classroom Discourse: The Language of Teaching and Learning.* Portsmouth, NH: Heinemann.

Chamot, A. 1995. The Teacher's Voice: Action Research in Your Classroom. *Eric/Cll News Bulletin* 18, 2: 1–8.

Chandler, Kelly. 1997. "Emergent Researchers: One Group's Beginnings." *Teacher Research* 4, 2: 73–100.

———. 1998. "Saying 'Y'All Come' to Teacher Researchers: An Interview with JoBeth Allen." *Teacher Research* 5, 2: 47–67.

———. In press. "No One Right Way: Lessons from a Teacher-Researcher." *Language Arts.*

Chase, Pennelle, and Jane Doan. 1996. *Choosing to Learn.* Portsmouth, NH: Heinemann.

Cisneros, Sandra. 1989. *The House on Mango Street.* New York: Vintage Books.

Clark, Kelli. 1997. "Harvesting Data." *Teacher Research* 4, 2: 182–183.

Clifford, J. C. 1986. "Introduction: Partial Truth." In *Writing Culture: The Poetics and Politics of Ethnography,* ed. J. C. Clifford and G. E. Marcus. Berkeley, CA: University of California Press.

Cochran-Smith, Marilyn, and Susan Lytle. 1990. "Research on Teaching and Teacher Research: The Issues That Divide." *Educational Researcher* 19, 2: 2–10.

———. 1992. "Student Teachers and Their Teacher: Talking Our Way into New Understandings." In *Students Teaching, Teachers Learning,* ed. A. Branscrombe, D. Goswami, and J. Schwartz. Upper Montclair, NJ: Boynton/Cook.

———. 1993. *Inside/Outside: Teacher Research and Knowledge.* New York: Teachers College Press.

Corey, S. M. 1953. *Action Research to Improve School Practices.* New York: Teachers College Bureau of Publications, Columbia University.

Corsaro, William. 1981. "Entering the Child's World: Research Strategies for Field Entry and Data Collection in a Pre-school Setting." In *Ethnography and Language in Educational Settings,* ed. J. Green and C. Wallach. Norwood, NJ: Ablex.

Corsaro, William, and D. Eder. 1994. "Children's Peer Cultures." *Annual Review of Sociology* 16: 197–220.

Cox, Dana. 1998. Interview. *Math by the Numbers: Seeing Is Believing.* WQED, Public Broadcasting System, Pittsburgh, PA, May 27.

Cummins, Jim, and Dennis Sayers. 1995. *Brave New Schools: Challenging Cultural Illiteracy Through Global Learning Networks.* New York: St. Martin's Press.

Cunningham, Andie. 1997."You Talk Too Much." *Teacher Research* 5, 1: 137–138.

Daane, M. C. 1986. "Review of 'If Not Now: Developmental Readers in the College Classroom.'" *Journal of Adolescent and Adult Literacy* 40, 3: 235–237.

Daniels, Harvey. 1994. *Literature Circles: Voice and Choice in the Student-Centered Classroom.* York, ME: Stenhouse.

Darling-Hammond, Linda. 1998. *The Right to Learn: A Blueprint for Creating Schools That Work.* San Francisco: Jossey-Bass.

Dewey, John. 1938. *Experience and Education.* New York: Macmillan, 1997.

Dickinson, Peter. 1992. *A Bone from a Dry Sea.* New York: Bantam Doubleday Dell.

Dillard, Annie. 1989. *The Writing Life.* New York: Harper and Row.

Dove, Rita. 1997. "To Make a Prairie." In *The Writer's Home Companion,* ed. J. Bolker, 151–163. New York: Owl Books.

Duffy, Gerald. 1998. "Teaching and the Balancing of Round Stones." *The Kappan* 79, 10: 777–780.

Early, M. 1991. "Early Research Programs." In *Handbook of Research on Teaching the*

English Language Arts, ed. J. Flood, J. Jensen, D. Lapp, and J. R. Squire. New York: Macmillan.

Eisner, Ellot. 1993. "The Emergence of New Paradigms for Educational Research." *Art Education* 46, 6: 50–55.

Eisner, Elliot, and Alan Peshkin. 1990. "Introduction." In *Qualitative Inquiry in Education: The Continuing Debate,* ed. E. Eisner and A. Peshkin. New York: Teachers College Press.

Elbow, Peter. 1997. "Options For Getting Feedback." In *The Writer's Home Companion,* ed. J. Bolker. New York: Owl Books.

Emig, Janet. 1971. *The Composing Processes of Twelfth Graders.* Urbana, IL: National Council of Teachers of English.

Erickson, Frederick. 1986. "Qualitative Methods in Research on Teaching." In *Handbook of Research on Teaching,* ed. M. C. Wittrock. New York: Macmillan.

Erickson, Frederick, and Jeffrey Shultz. 1992. "Students' Experience of the Curriculum." In *Handbook of Research on Teaching,* ed. P. Jackson. New York: Macmillan.

Ernst, Karen. 1994. "A Community of Teachers Learning." *Teacher Research* 1, 2: 63–74.

Fisher, Bobbi. 1991. *Joyful Learning: A Whole Language Kindergarten.* Portsmouth, NH: Heinemann.

Fletcher, Ralph. 1993. *What a Writer Needs.* Portsmouth, NH: Heinemann.

———. 1996. *Breathing In, Breathing Out: Keeping a Writer's Notebook.* Portsmouth, NH: Heinemann.

Florio-Ruane, Susan, and J. B. Dohanich. 1984. "Research Currents: Communicating Findings by Teacher/Researcher Deliberation." *Language Arts* 61, 7: 724–730.

Frazier, Charles. 1997. *Cold Mountain.* New York: Vintage Books.

Friedman, Bonnie. 1993. *Writing Past Dark.* New York: HarperCollins.

Frye, Sharon. 1997. "The Power of Deliberately Listening: An Interview with Maureen Barbieri." *Teacher Research* 4, 2: 42–58.

———. In press. "Owning Words: Vocabulary Interviews as an Assessment Tool." *Teacher Research.*

Fu, Danling. 1995. *My Trouble Is My English.* Portsmouth, NH: Heinemann.

Gaines, Ernest J. 1983. *A Gathering of Old Men.* New York: Vintage Books.

Gallas, Karen. 1994. *The Languages of Learning: How Children Talk, Write, Dance, Draw, and Sing Their Understanding of the World.* New York: Teachers College Press.

———. 1998. *Sometimes I Can Be Anything: Power, Gender, and Identity in a Primary Classroom.* New York: Teachers College Press.

Gillespie, Tim. 1993. "On Learning from the Inside: A Conversation with Glenda Bissex." *Teacher Research* 1, 1: 64–83.

———. 1994. "Interview with Dixie Goswami." *Teacher Research:* 2, 1: 89–103.

Gilligan, Carol, and Lynn M. Brown. 1992. *Meeting at the Crossroads: Women's Psychology and Girls' Development.* Cambridge, MA: Harvard University Press.

Giroux, Henry. 1984. "Rethinking the Language of Schooling." *Language Arts* 61, 1: 33–40.

Glancy, Diane. 1992. *Claiming Breath.* Lincoln, NE: University of Nebraska Press.

Glaser, Barney, and Anselm Strauss. 1967. *Discovery of Grounded Theory: Strategies for Qualitative Research.* Hawthorne, NY: Aldine de Gruyter.

Goatley, Virginia, Kathy Highfield, Jessica Bentley, Laura Pardo, Julie Folkert, Pam Scherer, Taffy Raphael, and Kristin Grattan. 1994. "Empowering Teachers to Be Researchers: A Collaborative Approach." *Teacher Research* 1, 2: 128–144.

Goswami, Dixie, and Peter Stillman, eds. 1987. *Reclaiming the Classroom: Teacher Research as an Agency for Change.* Upper Montclair, NJ: Boynton/Cook.

Graves, Donald H. 1994. *A Fresh Look at Writing.* Portsmouth, NH: Heinemann.

Grumet, Madeline. 1990. "On Daffodils That Come Before the Swallows Dare." In *Qualitative Inquiry in Education: The Continuing Debate,* ed. E. Eisner and A. Peshkin. New York: Teachers College Press.

Guide to Ethical Issues in Teacher Research. n.d. Available from National Writing Project, 5511 Tolman Hall #1670, University of California, Berkeley, CA 94720 (e-mail nwp@socrates.berkeley.edu).

Harris, Alex. 1987. *A World Unsuspected.* Chapel Hill, NC: University of North Carolina Press.

Harste, Jerome. 1990. "Foreward." In *Opening the Door to Classroom Research,* ed. M. W. Olson. Newark, DE: International Reading Association.

———. 1994. "Literacy as Curricular Conversations About Knowledge, Inquiry, and Morality." In *Theoretical Models and Processes of Reading,* ed. R. B. Ruddell and H. Singer. Newark, DE: International Reading Association.

Harste, Jerome, Virginia Woodward, and Carolyn Burke. 1984. *Language Stories and Literacy Lessons.* Portsmouth, NH: Heinemann.

Heard, Georgia. 1989. *For the Good of the Earth and Sun: Teaching Poetry.* Portsmouth, NH: Heinemann.

Hearth, Amy. 1993. *Having Our Say: The Delaney Sisters' First 100 Years.* New York: Kodansha International.

Heilbrun, Carolyn. 1988. *Writing a Woman's Life.* New York: Norton.

Henry, Jeanne. 1995. *If Not Now: Developmental Readers in the College Classroom.* Portsmouth, NH: Heinemann-Boynton/Cook.

———. 1997. "An Ethnography of Change: Teacher Research as Dissertation." *Teacher Research* 4, 2: 1–12.

Himley, Margaret. 1991. *Shared Territory: Understanding Children's Writing.* New York: Oxford University Press.

Hitchcock, Graham, and David Hughes. 1989. *Research and the Teacher: A Qualitiative Introduction to School-Based Research.* New York: Routledge.

Hodgkinson, H. 1957. "Action Research: A Critique." *Journal of Educational Sociology* 31, 4: 137–153.

Holbrook, D. 1964. *English for the Rejected: Training Literacy for the Lower Streams of the Secondary School.* Cambridge, UK: Cambridge University Press.

Holt, John. 1967. *How Children Learn.* New York: Pitman.

Hubbard, Ruth, Maureen Barbieri, and Brenda Miller Power. 1998. *"We Want to Be Known": Learning from Adolescent Girls.* York, ME: Stenhouse.

Hubbard, Ruth S., and Brenda M. Power. 1993. *The Art of Classroom Inquiry: A Handbook for Teacher Researchers.* Portsmouth, NH: Heinemann.

Huberman, Miles. 1996. "Moving Mainstream: Taking a Closer Look at Teacher Research." *Language Arts* 73, 2: 124–140.

Hurston, Zora Neale. 1937. *Their Eyes Were Watching God.* New York: Harper and Row.

Ingram, J., and N. Worrall. 1993. *Teacher-Child Partnership: The Negotiating Classroom.* London: David Fulton.

Jackson, P. 1968. *Life in the Classroom.* New York: Holt, Rinehart, and Winston.

Jalongo, M., J. Isenberg, and G. Gerbracht. 1995. *Teachers' Stories: From Personal Narrative to Professional Insight.* San Francisco: Jossey-Bass.

Jantsch, Erich. 1980. *The Self-Organizing Universe.* New York: Pergamon Press.

Jones, R. S. 1982. *Physics as Metaphor.* Minneapolis, MN: University of Minnesota Press.

Kaback, Suzanne. 1997. "Digestion Not Digression: A Gourmand's Invitation to Teacher-Research Chat." *Teacher Research* 4, 2: 112–123.

Karp, Stan. 1998. "Got a Question? Ask Eric." *Rethinking Schools* 12, 4: 25.

Keep-Barnes, Annie. 1994. "Real Teachers Don't Always Succeed." *Teacher Research* 2, 1: 1–7.

Keffer, Ann, et al. 1998. "Ownership and the Well-Planned Study." In *Engaging Teachers,* ed. B. Bisplinghoff and J. Allen, 27–34. Portsmouth, NH: Heinemann.

Keller, E. F., and C. R. Grontkowski. 1983. "The Mind's Eye." In *Discovering Reality,* ed. S. Harding and M. Hintikka. Dordrecht, Holland: Reidel.

Kenan, Randall. 1992. *Let the Dead Bury Their Dead.* San Diego: Harcourt Brace.

Kent, Richard. 1997. *Room 109: The Promise of a Portfolio Classroom.* Portsmouth, NH: Heinemann.

Kincaid, Jamaica. 1988. *At the Bottom of the River.* New York: Plume.

Kirby, Dan, and Carol Kuykendall. 1991. *Mind Matters.* Portsmouth, NH: Boynton/Cook.

Kohl, Herbert. 1967. *36 Children.* New York: New American Library, 1988.

———. 1994. *"I Won't Learn From You" and Other Thoughts on Creative Maladjustment.* New York: New Press.

Krall, F. 1988. "From the Inside Out—Personal History as Educational Research." *Educational Theory* 38, 4: 467–479.

Lamott, Anne. 1994. *Bird by Bird.* New York: Anchor.

Langer, Judith. 1992. *Literature Instruction: A Focus on Student Response.* Urbana: IL: National Council of Teachers of English.

Langer, Suzanne. 1976. *Problems of Art.* New York: Scribner's.

Lensmire, Timothy. 1995. *When Children Write: Critical Re-visions of the Writing Workshop.* New York: Teachers College Press.

Lieberman, A., and L. Miller. 1995. "Problems and Possibilities of Institutionalizing Teacher Research." In *Teacher Research and Educational Reform: Ninety-third Yearbook of the National Society for the Study of Education,* ed. S. Hollingsworth and H. Sockett. Chicago: University of Chicago Press.

Limerick, Patricia. 1997. "Dancing with Professors: The Problem with Academic Prose" *New York Times Book Review.*

Lincoln, Yvonne, and E. Guba. 1985. *Naturalistic Inquiry.* Beverly Hills, CA: Sage.

Lipsett, Suzanne. 1994. *Surviving a Writer's Life.* New York: HarperCollins.

Lytle, Susan, and Marilyn Cochran-Smith. 1992. *Inside/Outside: Teacher Research and Knowledge.* New York: Teachers College Press.

MacKay, Susan. 1997. "Breaking in My Research Tools." *Teacher Research* 4, 2: 154–156.

———. In press. "The Research Mind Is Really the Teaching Mind at Its Best: An Interview with Karen Gallas." *Teacher Research.*

Mair, Nancy. 1994. *Voice Lessons: On Becoming a (Woman) Writer.* Boston: Beacon Press.

Mankiller, Wilma. 1993. *Mankiller: A Chief and Her People.* New York: St. Martin's Press.

Marsella, Joy, Edna Hussey, Carrolyn Emoto, Judy Kaupp, Gail Ann Lee, Colleen Soares, Faye Takushi, and Teri M. Ushijima. 1994. "Making Waves: Exploring the Consequences of Teacher Research." *Teacher Research* 1, 2: 33–56.

Marshall, James. 1987. "The Effects of Writing on Students' Understanding of Literary Texts." *Research in the Teaching of English* 21: 30-63.

McFarland, K., and J. Stansell. 1993. "Historical Perspectives." *Teachers Are Researchers: Reflection and Action,* ed. Patterson et al. Newark, DE: International Reading Association.

Merriam, S. B. 1988. *Case Study Research in Education: A Qualitative Approach.* San Fransisco: Jossey-Bass.

Michalove, Barbara. 1993. "Creating a Community of Learners in Second Grade. In *Engaging Children,* ed. B. Shockley, B. Michalove, and J. Allen. Portsmouth, NH: Heinemann.

Miletta, Maureen. 1994. "Democracy Takes Time." *Teacher Research* 1, 2: 161–168.

Miller, Janet. 1990. *Creating Spaces and Finding Voices: Teachers Collaborating for Empowerment.* Albany, NY: State University of New York Press.

Mitchard, Jacquelyn. 1997. *The Deep End of the Ocean.* New York: Signet.

Mohr, Marian, and Marion Maclean. 1987. *Working Together: A Guide for Teacher-Researchers.* Urbana, IL: National Council of Teachers of English.

Morrison, I. 1994. *Keeping It Together: Linking Reading Theory to Practice.* Bothell, WA: Wright Group.

Morrison, Toni. 1973. *Sula.* New York: Knopf.

Muir, Mike. 1994. "Looking at What Kids Know: A Few Surprises." *Teacher Research* 2, 1: 88–97.

Murray, Donald. 1982. *Learning by Teaching.* Montclair, NJ: Boynton/Cook

———. 1990a. *Read to Write.* Fort Worth, TX: Holt, Rinehart, and Winston.

———. 1990b. *Shoptalk: Learning to Write with Writers.* Portsmouth, NH: Heinemann.

———. 1996. *Crafting a Life in Essay, Story, and Poem.* Portsmouth, NH: Heinemann.

Myers, Miles. 1985. *The Teacher-Researcher: How to Study Writing in the Classroom.* Urbana, IL: National Council of Teachers of English.

Neary, Stacy. 1998. "And Who Did You Say This Case Study Was About?" Unpublished essay.

———. 1999. "The Clay Queen." Unpublished essay.

Newell, G. E. 1984. "Learning from Writing in Two Content Areas: A Case Study/Protocol Analysis." *Research in the Teaching of English* 18: 265–287.

Newell, G. E., K. Suszynski, and R. Weingart. 1989. "The Effects of Writing in a Reader-based and Text-based Mode on Students' Understanding of Two Short Stories." *Journal of Reading Behavior* 21: 37–57.

Newkirk, Thomas, and Patricia McLure. 1993. *Listening In: Children Talk About Books (and Other Things).* Portsmouth, NH: Heinemann.

Ohanian, Susan. 1992. "Who the Hell Are You?" In *Whole Language: The Debate,* ed. Carl Smith, 58–62. Bloomington, IN: EDINFO Press.

———. 1993. "Counting on Children." In *Teacher Research* 1, 1: 24–36.

———. 1996. *Ask Ms. Class.* York, ME: Stenhouse.

Olson, M. W. 1990. "The Teacher as Researcher: A Historical Perspective." In *Opening the Door to Classroom Research,* ed. M. W. Olson. Newark, DE: International Reading Association.

Ornstein, Robert, and David Sobel. 1987. *The Healing Brain.* New York: Random House.

Ostrow, Jill. 1999. *Making Problems, Creating Solutions: Challenging Young Mathematicians.* York, ME: Stenhouse.

Ottenburg, Simon. 1990. "Thirty Years of Fieldnotes: Changing Relationships to the

Text." In *Fieldnotes: The Makings of Anthropology*, ed. R. Sanjek. Ithaca, NY: Cornell University Press.

Owston, Ron. 1998. *Making the Link: Teacher Professional Development on the Internet.* Portsmouth, NH: Heinemann.

Paley, Vivian. 1981. *Wally's Stories.* Cambridge, MA: Harvard University Press.

———. 1994. *You Can't Say You Can't Play.* Cambridge, MA: Harvard University Press.

Palmer, Parker. 1998. *The Courage to Teach.* San Francisco: Jossey-Bass.

Pareles, Jon. 1993. *New York Times,* February 24.

Perl, Sondra, and Nancy Wilson. 1986. *Through Teachers' Eyes: Portraits of Writing Teachers at Work.* Portsmouth, NH: Heinemann.

Portalupi, JoAnn Curtis. 1994. "Three Conditions for Growth: Time, Talk and Texts." *Teacher Research* 2, 1: 98–103.

Power, Brenda. 1995. "Crawling on the Bones of What We Know: An Interview with Shirley Brice Heath." *Teacher Research* 3, 1: 23–35.

———. 1996. *Taking Note: Improving Your Observational Notetaking.* York, ME: Stenhouse.

Rawlings, M. K. 1942. *Cross Creek.* New York: Scribner's.

Rief, Linda. 1992. *Seeking Diversity.* Portsmouth, NH: Heinemann.

Rilke, Rainer Maria. 1934. "Starting on the Path." In *The Soul is Here for Its Own Joy: Sacred Poems from Many Cultures,* ed. R. Bly. Hopewell, NJ: Ecco Press, 1995.

Rist, Ray. 1970. "Student Social Class and Teacher Expectations: The Self-Fulfilling Prophecy in Ghetto Education." *Harvard Educational Review* 40, 3: 411–451.

Rogers, Carl. 1983. *Freedom to Learn for the '80s.* Columbus, OH: Charles E. Merrill.

Roman, L. G., and Michael Apple. 1990. "Is Naturalism a Move Away from Positivism? Materialist and Feminist Approaches to Subjectivity in Ethnographic Research." In *Qualitative Inquiry in Education: The Continuing Debate,* ed. E. Eisner and A. Peshkin. New York: Teachers College Press.

Rosaldo, Renato. 1989. *Culture and Truth: The Remaking of Social Analysis.* Boston: Beacon Press.

Rosenblatt, Louise. 1978. *The Reader, the Text, the Poem.* Carbondale, IL: Southern Illinois University Press.

———. 1983. *Literature as Exploration.* New York: Modern Language Association.

Routman, Regie. 1994. *Invitations: Changing as Teachers and Learners K–12.* Portsmouth, NH: Heinemann.

Rudduck, Jean, and D. Hopkins. 1985. *Research as a Basis for Teaching: Readings from the Work of Lawrence Stenhouse.* Portsmouth, NH: Heinemann.

Ryan, Kay. 1998. "Poetry Alive: Reading Before Breakfast." *Hungry Mind Review* 46: 36.

Sarton, May. 1993. *Collected Poems 1930–1993.* New York: Norton.

Schaef, Anne Wilson. 1985. *Women's Reality.* New York: Harper and Row.

Schaeffer, Carolyn, and Kristin Amundsen. 1993. *Creating Community Anywhere.* New York: Perigee.

Schwab, J. 1969. "The Practical: A Language for Curriculum." *School Review* 78, 5: 1–24.

Secor, L., and K. Lylis. 1990. *Developmental Guide to Early Literacy.* Available from Secor/Lylis, P.O. Box 98, St. Albans, ME 04971.

Sega, D. 1997a. "Really Important Stuff." *Teacher Research* 4, 2: 174–175.

———. 1997b. "Reading and Writing About Our Lives." Teacher Research 4, 2: 101–111.

Shaughnessy, Susan. 1993. *Walking On Alligators.* New York: HarperCollins.

Shockley, Betty, Barbara Michalove, and JoBeth Allen. 1993. *Engaging Children.* Portsmouth, NH: Heinemann.

———. 1995. *Engaging Families.* Portsmouth, NH: Heinemann.

Short, Kathy G. 1990. "Creating a Community of Learners." In *Talking About Books: Creating Literate Communities,* ed. K. Short and K. M. Pierce, 32–52. Portsmouth, NH: Heinemann.

Smith, B. O. 1962. *A Study of the Logic of Teaching.* Urbana, IL: University of Illinois Press.

Smith, Frank. 1983. *Essays into Literacy.* Portsmouth, NH: Heinemann.

———. 1986. *Insult to Intelligence: The Bureaucratic Invasion of Our Classrooms.* Portsmouth, NH: Heinemann.

Smith, N. B. 1936. *American Reading Instruction.* Newark, DE: International Reading Association, 1986.

Stafford, Kim. 1997. *Having Everything Right: Essays of Place.* Seattle, WA: Sasquatch Books.

Stafford, William. 1982. "Things I Learned Last Week." In *Glass Face in the Rain.* Portland, OR: Estate of William Stafford.

———. 1998. "You Reading This, Be Ready." In *The Way It Is: New and Selected Poems.* Saint Paul, MN: Graywolf Press.

Stegner, Wallace. 1987. *Crossing to Safety.* New York: Penguin.

Stein, Mary, and Brenda Power. 1996. "Putting Art on the Scientist's Palette." In *New Entries: Learning by Writing and Drawing,* ed. Ruth Shagoury Hubbard and Karen Ernst. Portsmouth, NH: Heinemann.

Stenhouse Publishers. 1994. *Catalogue: A New Voice for Classroom Teachers 1994–1995.* York, ME: Stenhouse.

Tannen, Deborah. 1998. *The Argument Culture.* New York: Morrow.

Taylor, Jill M., and Carol Gilligan. 1995. *Between Voice and Silence: Women and Girls, Race and Relationship.* Cambridge, MA: Harvard University Press.

Teets, Sharon. 1998. "Listening to Children's Stories: An Interview with Vivian Gussin Paley." *The Active Learner: A Foxfire Journal for Teachers,* (February): 12–16.

Tendaro, Jennifer. 1998. "Worth Waiting For." In *"We Want to Be Known": Learning from Adolescent Girls,* ed. R. Hubbard, M. Barbieri, and B. Power. York, ME: Stenhouse.

Walker, Alice. 1984. *In Search of Our Mothers' Gardens.* New York: Harcourt Brace Jovanovich.

Wallace, James. 1997. "A Note from John Dewey on Teacher Research." *Teacher Research* 5, 1: 26–28.

Weaver, Connie. 1994. *Reading Process and Practice.* 2d ed. Portsmouth, NH: Heinemann.

Whitman, Ruth. 1997. "Climbing the Jacob's Ladder" In *The Writer's Home Companion,* ed. J. Bolker, 130–140. New York: Owl Books.

Wilde, Sandra. 1992. *YOU KAN RED THIS! Spelling and Punctuation for Whole Language Classrooms, K–6.* Portsmouth, NH: Heinemann.

———. 1996. *Notes from a Kidwatcher: Selected Writings of Yetta Goodman.* Portsmouth, NH: Heinemann.

Wilhelm, Jeffrey. 1997. *You Gotta BE the Book: Teaching Engaged and Reflective Reading with Adolescents.* New York: Teachers College Press.

Williams, Martin. 1993. *The Jazz Tradition.* New York: Oxford Press.

Wooldridge, Susan. 1996. *Poemcrazy: Freeing Your Life with Words.* New York: Clarkson Potter.

Wolcott, Harry. 1995. *The Art of Fieldwork.* Walnut Creek, CA: Altamira Press.

Zaharlick, A., and Judith Green. 1991. "Ethnographic Research." In *Handbook of Research on Teaching the English Language Arts,* ed. J. Flood, J. Jensen, D. Lapp, and J. R. Squire. New York: Macmillan.

Children's Books

Burnett, Frances H. 1938. *The Secret Garden.* New York: Viking, 1988.

Cleary, Beverly. 1975. *Ramona the Brave.* New York: Morrow.

Cowley, J. 1984. *Rosie at the Zoo.* Katonah, NY: Richard C. Owen.

———. 1990. *The Ghost.* Bothell, WA: Wright Group.

Dorris, Michael. 1992. *Morning Girl.* New York: Hyperion.

Gag, Wanda. 1928. *Millions of Cats.* New York: Putnam.

Gannett, R. S. 1948. *My Father's Dragon.* New York: Random House.

Glaser, Isabel J. 1995. *Dreams of Glory: Poems Starring Girls.* New York: Atheneum.

Lobel, Arnold. 1972. *Frog and Toad Together.* New York: Harper and Row.

Mowat, Farley. 1961. *Owls in the Family.* Boston: Little, Brown.

Paterson, Katherine Ann. 1978. *The Great Gilly Hopkins.* New York: Crowell.

Pochocki, Ethel. 1996. *A Penny for a Hundred.* Camden, ME: Down East.

Raschka, Chris. 1992. *Charlie Parker Played Bebop.* New York: Dutton.

Scieszka, Jon. 1992. *The Stinky Cheese Man and Other Fairly Stupid Tales.* New York: Viking.

Shreve, Susan. 1984. *The Flunking of Joshua T. Bates.* New York: Knopf.

Ward, Cindy. 1988. *Cookie's Week.* New York: Putnam.

Contributors

Jennifer Allen has taught third grade in Waterville, Maine, for the last eight years. She continues to conduct teacher research in her classroom as a way to inform her teaching. Jennifer obtained her master's degree in literacy education from the University of Maine.

Betty Shockley Bisplinghoff has been teaching and learning with students and fellow teachers for sixteen years. She is concurrently teaching sixth-grade language arts in Barrow County, Georgia, and working on her dissertation in language arts education at the University of Georgia. She has co-authored three books with JoBeth Allen and Barbara Michalove: *Engaging Children, Engaging Families,* and *Engaging Teachers.* She hopes to engage her committee's approval of her dissertation before the millennium!

Judith Bradshaw Brown recently earned her doctorate from the University of Maine. She currently teaches undergraduate and graduate courses in literacy education for the University of Maine at Farmington and Orono, and in-service courses throughout Maine. Before that, she taught secondary English, reading, and English as a Second Language, and worked with readers and writers of all ages in many locations in and outside of Maine for twenty-five years.

Sandy Brown teaches middle school art in Longview, Washington. When she's not teaching or going to graduate school at Lewis and Clark College in Portland, Oregon, she enjoys working in her pottery studio and spending time in the out-of-doors.

Kimberly Hill Campbell, a former high school English teacher, is the principal at Riverdale High School in Portland, Oregon. She continues to be passionate about teacher research and works with her staff to create an environment where inquiry is valued. Kimberly also continues her own research. She keeps a journal and develops a yearly question related to the work of the high school. The teacher research group she has been in for nine years is ongoing, and she is hopeful that they will find more time to meet.

Kelly Chandler is an assistant professor of reading and language arts at

Syracuse University. She previously taught high school English in Maine. She is currently finishing a book entitled *Spelling Inquiry: How One Elementary School Caught the Mnemonic Plague* (Stenhouse, in press) that was co-authored with the members of the Mapleton Teacher Research Group.

Sharon Frye is an English and social sciences teacher at Riverdale High School in Portland, Oregon. She recently published a chapter in *"We Want to Be Known:" Learning from Adolescent Girls* (Hubbard, Barbieri, and Power 1998), a collection focused on learning to listen to girls. Sharon also continues to focus on research within her classroom. She prides herself on developing strong student-to-teacher relationships. She cherishes learning from her students as well as watching them grow as reflective learners.

Karen Hankins is a first-grade teacher in Athens, Georgia. For over twenty years she has taught in suburban, rural, and urban elementary schools. While working on a Ph.D. degree in language education at the University of Georgia, she taught teacher education courses as well. Her current research interest—narrative as data, method, and theory—grew out of years of journal keeping. Contributions to several edited books and publications in *Teacher Research* and *Harvard Educational Review* focus on the use of memoirs in research. When people ask her what she'll do when she finishes her doctorate, she answers without hesitation, "Keep teaching little children . . . and write about the magic!"

Jerome C. Harste is an adjunct professor at Mount Saint Vincent University in Halifax as well as a professor of language education at Indiana University, where he holds the Armstrong Chair in Teacher Education. At present he is involved with several teacher research study groups, including undergraduates and teachers at the Center for Inquiry in Indianapolis and teachers and administrators in the Education as Inquiry Mount Saint Vincent University Master's Degree in Mississagua, Ontario, Canada.

Jeanne Henry has spent the last eighteen years teaching college reading and writing. Her book *If Not Now: Developmental Readers in the College Classroom* is a teacher research study of her work with college reading students in Kentucky. At present, Jeanne coordinates the undergraduate college reading program at Hofstra University in New York, where she teaches graduate courses in literacy studies and teacher research.

Julia Housum-Stevens lives in rural Maine with her husband and her dog Katahdin, where she stays busy learning from middle level readers and writers. She has just obtained her master's degree in literacy from the University of Maine, Orono, and occasionally she still misses a deadline or loses a notebook just to stay in practice.

Suzanne Jacobs, professor of English at the University of Hawaii in Honolulu, is the co-author (with grade 5 teacher Suzanne Brady) of *Mindful of Others: Teaching Children to Teach,* a book in two voices about collaboration and social responsibility in classrooms. She now works with the Hawaii Writing Project.

Jane A. Kearns recently retired after thirty-five years in education, including the New Hampshire Writing Program. Her book *Where to Begin* (1997) has both practical and reflective stories about teaching and learning.

Annie Keep-Barnes has been teaching for seventeen years in rural Alaska. She currently teaches at Chinook Charter School in Fort Wainwright, Alaska.

Joseph Kelley is currently teaching fourth-grade science and English in South Florida. He obtained a master's degree in literacy from the University of Maine two years ago. In Joe's twenty years of teaching, he has taught special education and grades 3–5.

Richard Kent teaches English, directs The Writing Center, and coaches soccer at Mountain Valley High School in Rumford, Maine. His latest book is *Room 109: The Promise of a Portfolio Classroom* (1997).

Christine Leland is an associate professor of language education at Indiana University, Indianapolis. Her classes meet on site at the Center for Inquiry, a public magnet-option school in Indianapolis where teachers and university interns engage in shared teacher research projects.

Susan Harris MacKay teaches kindergarten and first grade at Willamette Primary School in West Linn, Oregon.

Andra Makler, a former high school social studies teacher, is associate professor of education and chair of the Department of Teacher Education at Lewis and Clark College in Portland, Oregon. She sees teaching and learning as forms of inquiry grounded in curiosity, joy, and hope. She prefers questions to answers.

Jill Ostrow has spent the last seventeen years trying to answer the bombardment of questions that consume her every day she teaches! *Making Problems, Creating Solutions: Challenging Young Mathematicians* (Stenhouse 1999) is a culmination of a teacher research project that revolves around the mathematical processes of children. The new questions that plague her these days are growing from what she is learning from the graduate interns she is currently working with at Lewis and Clark College.

Susan Pidhurney knew she wanted to be a teacher when she was in elementary school and never considered another career. She has been director of a nonprofit nursery school and has taught prekindergarten as well as kindergarten and Reading Recovery. Currently working on a certificate of advanced studies at the University of Maine, she continues to do research on early literacy, focusing on the impact of the family on students at risk.

JoAnn Portalupi has spent the last eighteen years learning about teaching writing by working alongside children and their teachers. She is co-author of *Craft Lessons: Teaching Writing K–8* (Stenhouse 1998), a book that explores the questions, What can we teach young students about the craft of writing? How do we go about it? She currently teaches a field-based children's literature/language arts methods course at the University of Alabama at Birmingham, where she also directs the Mid-South Institute on Teaching Writing.

Michelle Schardt teaches in Portland, Oregon, in a bilingual primary school. She is finishing her master of arts degree program in teaching at Lewis and Clark College and is an active teacher-researcher.

Sherry Young teaches in a multiyear classroom of grades 2 and 3 in Waterville, Maine. She recently obtained a master of science degree in literacy at the University of Maine.

Index

action research, 15, 19
  goal of, 65
  grant proposals guidelines, 215–16
Action Research Collaborative, St.
  Louis
  Web site, 167
ADHD students
  refining research questions about,
  28
administration
  support for teacher research by,
  212, 213
administrator-researchers, 252–55
"after the fact" notes, 107–109
  benefits of, 107
  experimenting with, 108–109
  limitations of, 107
Alaska Teacher Research Network
  (ATRN), 8, 207–208, 216
Albright, Peggy, 96
Alexander, Wally, 83
  research plan, 56–59
Alinsky, Saul, 82
Allen, Janet, 16–17
Allen, Jennifer, 94
  "Exploring Literature through
  Student-Led Discussions," 149–
  50
  "Letting Inventories Lead the Way,"
  112–13
Allen, JoBeth, 121, 122, 138, 174,
  245
Amazon.com, 169
American Association of Educational
  Researchers, 213
American Educational Research Asso-
  ciation, 6
  Teacher Research Special Interest
  Group, 64
anecdotal notes, 193
  sheet, 85
  by students, 276
  teacher frustration with, 106–107
anthropology, 18, 247

anxieties
  about data analysis, 120
  of teachers, 115
Anzaldua, Gloria, 262
Anzul, Margaret, 153, 158
Apple, Michael, 199
apprenticeships, 266, 286–87. *See also*
  mentors
Arbus, Diane, 100
"argument culture," 289
art critiques, 80
art portfolios, 79
artwork inspiration study
  research brief, 78–81
Ashton-Warner, Sylvia, 15, 180
AskEric Web site, 168
at-risk students
  cultural differences, 35–41
At the Bottom of the River (Kincaid),
  177
Atwell, Nancie, 6, 7, 20, 34, 178, 180,
  182, 194, 196, 200, 246
audiotapes, 95–98
  analyzing without full transcriptions, 130
  of classroom activities, 96
  for student-led literature discussions, 154
  transcriptions of, 95, 142
  using in research, 96
audit checks, 120
Austin, Terri, 181–82, 185, 191, 206–
  207, 241–42, 244–45, 246–47, 267–
  68, 287
author's chair
  notetaking during, 106
Avery, Carol, 232

Bank Street School of Education, 6,
  162
Barber of Seville (Beaumarchais), 17
Barbieri, Maureen, 4, 7, 163–64, 165,
  180
barnesandnoble.com, 169

Bateson, Mary Catherine, 65
Bay Area Writing Project, 20
Beaumarchais, Pierre-Augustin, 17
Beck, Cathy, 248–49
Bellack, A., 18
Berg, Elizabeth, 7, 163–64
Bernstein, Leonard, 14
Best, J. W., 15
*Between Voice and Silence: Women and
  Girls, Race and Relationship*
  (Gilligan), 163
bilingual education
  research design, 69–72
Birnbaum, J., 21
Bisplinghoff, Betty, 121, 122, 138, 185
Bissett, Monique, 192–93
Bissex, Glenda, 3, 19, 20, 23, 32, 289–
  90
Blintz, William, 99–100
Bolster, A. S., Jr., 16
Bomer, Randy, 163
Bone from a Dry Sea, A (Dickinson), 22
bookstores, online, 169
Boothe, William, 18
Borderlands/La Frontera (Anzaldua),
  262
Brabant, Lynn, 220
bracketing, of personal viewpoints,
  201–202
Brady, Suzanne, 261–62
brainstorming
  research questions, 236–37
  by teacher-research groups, 224,
  235
  writing for, 192–93
Brandt, Gina, 193–94
Branscombe, Amanda, 264
Bread Loaf Institute, 263
breakthrough moments
  for writing, 180–81
"breathing respect," 90
Britton, James, 172, 177
Brown, Judith Bradshaw, 15–16
Brown, Sandy, 78–81

305

Articles from *Teacher Research: The Journal of Classroom Inquiry*

Allen, Jennifer. 1997a. "Letting Inventories Lead the Way." *Teacher Research* 4, 2: 159–162.

———. 1997b. "Reflections as a Teacher-Researcher: Exploring Literature Through Student-Led Discussions." *Teacher Research:* 4, 2: 124–139.

Bisplinghoff, Betty Shockley. 1995. "Reading Like a Researcher." *Teacher Research* 3, 1: 105–113.

Bradshaw-Brown, Judith. 1995. "We Have Met the Audience and She Is Us: The Evolution of Teacher as Audience for Research." *Teacher Research* 2, 2: 18–31.

Campbell, Kimberly. 1997a. "Survival, Sustenance, and Making Sense: Journals as Tools of the Trade." *Teacher Research* 5, 1: 146–149.

———. 1997b. "You're Invited." *Teacher Research* 1, 2: 57–62.

———. In press. "From Teacher Researcher to Administrator Researcher." *Teacher Research.*

Chandler, Kelly. 1997. "Emergent Researchers: One Group's Beginnings." *Teacher Research* 4, 2: 73–100.

Frye, Sharon. 1997. "Research Design." *Teacher Research* 4, 2: 166–167.

Hankins, Karen. 1996. "One Moment in Two Times." *Teacher Research* 4, 1: 24–28.

Harste, Jerome and Christine Leland. In press. "Testing the Water with Mini-Inquiry Projects." *Teacher Research.*

Henry, Jeanne. 1997. "An Ethnography of Change: Teacher Research as Dissertation." *Teacher Research* 4, 2: 1–12.

Housum-Stevens, Julie. 1997. "Making Deadlines." *Teacher Research* 5, 1: 161–162.

Hubbard, Ruth Shagoury. 1993. "Seeing What Is Not Seen: Another Reason for Writing up Teacher Research." *Teacher Research* 1, 1: 143–147.

———. 1994. "'A Little Too Little and a Lot Too Much': The Data Collection and Analysis Blues." *Teacher Research* 2, 1: 132–140.

Jacobs, Suzanne. 1996. "Why Worry?: The Case for Self-Definition in Teacher Research." *Teacher Research* 3, 2: 27–36.

Kearns, Jane. 1996. "Teaching and Researching Riffs." *Teacher Research* 3, 2: 1–4.

Keep-Barnes, Annie. 1994 "Real Teachers Don't Always Succeed." *Teacher Research* 2, 1: 1–7.

Kent, Richard. In press. "Making Meaning." *Teacher Research* 6, 1.

MacKay, Susan. 1997. "Real Magic: Trusting the Voice of a Young Learner." *Teacher Research* 4, 2: 13–21.

Makler, Andra. 1997. "A Toolbox of Questions about Teaching." *Teacher Research* 5, 1: 143–145.

Ostrow, Jill. 1998. "Partners in Research." *Teacher Research* 5, 2: 176–178.

Pidhurney, Susan. 1996. "Home-School Literacy Connections: Research Brief." *Teacher Research* 4, 1: 117–119.

Portalupi, JoAnn. 1993. "Strategies for Working Toward a Research Question." *Teacher Research* 1, 1: 58–63.

———. 1994. "The Trickle-Down Effect of Teacher Research: Students Adopting a Research Stance." *Teacher Research* 1, 2: 145–148.

Young, Sherry. 1997. "Focusing on Student Talk."

Note: The following two teacher-researchers' essays are used in the text, but not as Featured Teacher-Researchers:

Clark, Kelli. 1997. " Harvesting Data." *Teacher Research* 4, 2: 182–183.

Cunningham, Andie. 1997. "You Talk Too Much." *Teacher Research* 5, 1: 137–138.